The Art of Editing

The Art of Editing

Raymond Carver and David Foster Wallace

Tim Groenland

BLOOMSBURY ACADEMIC
NEW YORK • LONDON • OXFORD • NEW DELHI • SYDNEY

BLOOMSBURY ACADEMIC
Bloomsbury Publishing Inc
1385 Broadway, New York, NY 10018, USA
50 Bedford Square, London, WC1B 3DP, UK

BLOOMSBURY, BLOOMSBURY ACADEMIC and the Diana
logo are trademarks of Bloomsbury Publishing Plc

First published in the United States of America 2019
Paperback edition first published 2020

Cover design by Daniel Benneworth-Gray
Cover image: Carlos Delgado

Library of Congress Cataloging-in-Publication Data
Names: Groenland, Tim, author.
Title: The art of editing: Raymond Carver and David Foster Wallace / Tim Groenland.
Description: New York: Bloomsbury Academic, 2019. | Includes index.
Identifiers: LCCN 2018059731 | ISBN 9781501338274 (hardback: alk.paper) |
ISBN 9781501338298 (epdf) | ISBN 9781501338304 (xml-platform)
Subjects: LCSH: Editing. | Authors and publishers–United
States–History–20th century. | Authors and publishers–United
States–History–21st century. | Fiction–Technique. | Authorship. |
Carver, Raymond, 1938-1988–Criticism and interpretation. | Wallace, David
Foster–Criticism and interpretation.
Classification: LCC PN162.G697 2019 | DDC 808.02/7–dc23
LC record available at https://lccn.loc.gov/2018059731

ISBN: HB: 978-1-5013-3827-4
PB: 978-1-5013-6760-1
ePDF: 978-1-5013-3829-8
eBook: 978-1-5013-3828-1

Typeset by Newgen KnowledgeWorks Pvt. Ltd., Chennai, India

To find out more about our authors and books visit
www.bloomsbury.com and sign up for our newsletters.

Contents

Preface

Editors rarely speak about their craft in detail. On the rare occasions that they do, it becomes apparent that their position within literary culture is a somewhat paradoxical one. In 1994, for example, Robert Gottlieb, former editor-in-chief at Simon & Schuster and Knopf and editor of *Catch-22* and *Beloved*, was interviewed about his life's work by the *Paris Review* in a feature that ran under the heading 'The Art of Editing'. Gottlieb's responses displayed a degree of ambivalence towards the position in which he found himself. On the one hand, he openly discussed his collaborations with writers like Toni Morrison, John Le Carré and Cynthia Ozick and went into detail on particular occasions – like his success in persuading Joseph Heller to cut a particular chapter from his debut novel – when he had made notable contributions to seminal works of twentieth-century literature. On the other hand, he asserted confidently that 'the editor's relationship to a book should be an invisible one' (Gottlieb 1994, 186).

This ambivalence about editing is also, we might suggest, reflected in the timing and form of the interview itself. This was the first time that the magazine had made an editor the subject of one of its celebrated interviews with major literary figures. Since the *Review*'s feature on E. M. Forster in its inaugural issue in 1953, these interviews have focused overwhelmingly on authors of fiction and poetry; it was not until the fifth decade of its existence that an editor was chosen as an interviewee.[1] At the time of writing, there have been 241 'Art of Fiction' features compared with only three interviews with editors of fiction. The very existence of the 'Art of Editing' series, therefore, illustrates the ambiguous status of the editor in literary culture: it is generally agreed that editing is integral to literary production and that its practice constitutes an 'art', and yet detailed studies of its practitioners are difficult to come by. American literary history, as Jack Stillinger shows in his *Multiple Authorship and the Myth of Solitary Genius* (1991), is notable for its many examples of strong editorial intervention, but the critical attention given to these examples has primarily focused on earlier

[1] The first time that 'Fiction' was replaced in the 'Art of . . .' format was in issue 21 (1959) when T. S. Eliot gave the first 'Art of Poetry' interview.

figures such as Max Perkins (Stillinger 1991, 139–62).[2] Book-length treatments of editorial figures, such as A. Scott Berg's biography of Perkins or Helen Smith's of Edward Garnett, are extremely rare (Berg 2013; Smith 2017).[3]

As the most celebrated editor in the history of US fiction, Perkins exemplifies some of the tensions and opposing demands central to an understanding of the editor's art. His legendary editing of Fitzgerald, Hemingway and Wolfe makes him an illustrious archetype for the role, and Berg's biography – ambiguously subtitled 'Editor of Genius' and recently adapted for cinema under the pithier title *Genius* (2016) – has contributed towards making him a touchstone for discussions of editing practice.[4] One agent and former editor, indeed, claims that every single writer she has met harbours what she terms 'the Maxwell Perkins fantasy': namely, the dream of 'the editor who will pluck you from obscurity' and, through a combination of editorial brilliance and empathetic support, ensure that the writer is read 'decades from now' (Lerner 2017, 70). Perkins's example, however (enshrined in the prestige economy of contemporary publishing in the form of the Center for Fiction's Maxwell E. Perkins Award for achievement as an editor, publisher or agent, awarded annually since 2005), illustrates the obvious tension between the power inherent in editorial practice – the potential to affect and determine crucial aspects of a literary work – and the way it places the editor in 'a position of subordination and even service' (MacDonald and Sherman 2002, 1). Stillinger, for example, describes what he terms Perkins's 'pathological' self-effacement, noting that the editor maintained a lifelong insistence on the primacy of the author's role and consistently minimized his own contribution,

2 Several of the essays collected in *Editors on Editing*, for example – a handbook aimed primarily at writers that appeared in three editions, the most recent of which was published in 1993 – focus on Perkins as an exemplar of the craft; one contributor notes that 'trying to define the role of the book editor in American without mentioning [Perkins] [...] can be likened to writing a short history of aviation without the Wright brothers' (Williams 1993, 8).

3 While studies of the work of particular literary editors do exist, these tend to appear within studies with a more general focus such as Stillinger's (1991), Daniel Robert King's *Cormac McCarthy's Literary Evolution* (2016), or Evan Brier's *A Novel Marketplace* (2009), or critical editions that focus on a single work (such as the 1971 facsimile edition of *The Waste Land* that illustrated Ezra Pound's editorial changes to the poem). Evidence of the details of editorial activity is often recoverable only through archival study, published editorial correspondence or testimonies such as those provided in the published recollections of major editors such as Jason Epstein, Diana Athill and, most recently, Gottlieb (Athill 2011; Epstein 2002; Gottlieb 2016; Maxwell and O'Connor 1996; Perkins 1991). The tradition of critical editing has, of course, furnished much self-reflective consideration of editorial practice: James L. West's reflections on his editing of Fitzgerald, Dreiser and others, to take one example, were collected in his *Making the Archives Talk* (2011). In Chapter 1, I consider the distinction between commercial and critical editing and examine the practical and conceptual history of contemporary editorial practice.

4 Michael Pietsch, in fact, references Berg's biography as a formative influence, describing it as 'the best book I've ever read about editing' (Pietsch 2017c).

even when his influence was manifestly crucial (as it was in the case of Wolfe's novels) to the success of the published work (Stillinger 1991, 154–5; Berg 2013, 130–3).[5] Even when a powerful editor has played a significant role in shaping a writer's work, this fact has tended to be revealed only in retrospect.

Perkins's example also demonstrates the importance of the human element in editing relationships, since the textual relationship is determined in part by the idiosyncratic meeting of different personality types. At one level, this simply involves an acknowledgement that the working methods of writers vary dramatically and that the editor's role will vary accordingly. Perkins's textual work with Fitzgerald, for example, primarily appears to have involved offering advice on aspects of plot and character.[6] With Wolfe, he selected material, wrote plot outlines and assembled sections of narrative, taking on functions more generally understood to be authorial ones (Berg 2013, 121–30). Perkins's example also shows the frequent inseparability of an editorial relationship from one of friendship. His role appears often to have been a holistic one involving practical assistance and elements of pastoral care: Berg notes that Fitzgerald referred to the editor as one of his 'closest friends', that Perkins often acted '*in loco parentis*' for the author, and reports that in 1927, when Fitzgerald was looking for a quiet place to write in seclusion, the editor 'house-hunted for him' (Berg 2013, 79–80, 106–7).[7] The interconnection of professional and personal relationships – an expected factor in long-term working relationships – cannot, therefore, be easily separated from the textual exchange, a problem that will become very clear in the subsequent chapters. I note at the outset of this study, then, the way that the specificity and particularity of each editorial exchange resists the critic's generalizing impulse.

We can see the inherent paradoxes that the role of fiction editor contains: it is necessary but invisible, powerful but subservient, professional and personal, inherently collaborative but embedded in a context in which any editorial agency, no matter how extensive, will tend to be subsumed at the point of presentation into a paradigm of solitary authorship. Former *New Yorker* editor William Maxwell suggests that a successful editorial performance makes a degree of

5 Berg quotes Perkins' colleague John Hall Wheelock on the editor's famed humility: 'although I'm aware of no book [Wolfe's *Look Homeward, Angel* (1929)] that had ever been edited so extensively up to that point, Max felt that what he had done was neither more nor less than duty required' (Berg 2013, 130).

6 Famously, he requested more details on Gatsby's character, to which an impressed Fitzgerald replied that he himself had not known 'what Gatsby looked like or was engaged in' (Berg 2013, 60–3).

7 An unusual contemporary example of such pastoral care came in Jonathan Franzen's recent revelation that his editor at the *New Yorker*, Henry Finder, had been responsible for dissuading him from his plan to adopt an Iraqi war orphan (Franzen 2015, n.p.).

cognitive dissonance on the part of all involved not only inevitable, but also desirable: 'what you hope is that if the writer reads the story ten years after it is published he will not be aware that anybody has ever touched it' (Maxwell 1982, n.p.). In most cases, it is in the interests of each of the main players in the literary field – author, agent, editor, publisher, reader and frequently critic – to keep the focus on the creative activities of the author rather than those of the editor, a fact which goes some way towards explaining the relative dearth of scholarly studies on editing. The scholar of contemporary fiction interested in the work of editors is dependent upon the availability of archival materials as well as the willingness of authors, editors and publishers to reveal the genesis of particular texts. It is worth noting, then, that the editing processes described in this book are available for study through a combination of exceptional circumstances.

The second *Paris Review* 'Art of Editing' feature appeared in the winter of 2015, with the subject this time being Gordon Lish.[8] Interviewer Christian Lorentzen introduced the feature by remarking that it is customary 'for editors to keep a low profile and to underplay any changes they may make to an author's manuscript' and that Lish (who, he noted, is more famous than any editor since Perkins) represents a rare exception to this – an observation borne out by the fact that the editor used the interview as another opportunity to stake his claim for the success of Raymond Carver's work (Lish 2015, 206–210). Lish's appearance in the journal – and, indeed, his presence in the collective literary consciousness – owes a great deal to the infamy bestowed upon him by the 'Carver Controversy' occasioned by the revelations of his severe editing of the stories in Carver's first two collections. In this case, we owe our knowledge of the editing process not only to Lish's willingness to breach the unwritten codes of literary etiquette by making his own work visible, but also to the act of critical detective work that led D. T. Max to study and describe Lish's manuscript papers for the *New York Times* in 1998 and so reveal the extent of the editor's actions to the literary public (Max 1998).

This book has its origins in my fascination at the extent of Lish's editorial interventions in Carver's work and my surprise at discovering that these stories, whose scrupulously constrained narrative style had enthralled me along with so many other readers, had been decisively altered on their way into print. The revelation opened a window onto contemporary literary production that is all

8 The third of the 'Art of Editing' interviews to appear so far was with Maxine Groffsky, who worked as editor in the *Paris Review* itself from 1965 to 1974. It was published in issue 222 in Fall 2017.

too seldom available to readers, and the prospect of tracing these texts through their development from manuscript to print represented a unique scholarly opportunity. Carver's fictions are not the first to have undergone an extensive editing process, of course: the drastic nature of the revisions, though, along with the breadth of Carver's influence as a stylistic touchstone of contemporary literature and the extent of Lish's mediating and gatekeeping activities during the years in question all offered insights into the way in which editors function as key players in the production of fiction.

The publication of *The Pale King*, the final unfinished novel by David Foster Wallace, represents a very different, yet equally exceptional, opportunity to examine the editor's art in detail. The importance of Michael Pietsch's role in Wallace's career, from his involvement in the creation of *Infinite Jest* during the mid-1990s up to his present-day status as custodian of the author's legacy, has been explored only glancingly in analyses of the author's work. The circumstances of *The Pale King*'s emergence – Wallace's early death, the subsequent publication of the Pulitzer-nominated unfinished novel and the relatively brief interval until the opening of the archive of manuscript material related to the work – allow for a rare study of the creation of a recently published work by an author whose influence during his own lifetime was arguably as profound as that of Carver's.[9] The stylistic contrast between the two, as I discuss in my first chapter, could not be starker: Carver's early stories were integral to the emergence of the Minimalist movement in the 1980s, while Wallace's novels marked a generational shift away from Minimalism towards a more expansive, maximal mode of narrative.

My subtitle, which places the two authors side by side, signals the changing context surrounding their editorial processes as well as the notable stylistic shifts occurring in US fiction during the final decades of the twentieth century. Examining the manuscripts of two authors often considered as polar opposites allows us not only to juxtapose Wallace and Carver, who are rarely considered together except in passing, but also to compare the social and material history of two profoundly influential stylistic strains of recent US fiction. In this I draw upon a tradition of scholarship that attends to the textual multiplicity provided by draft materials of canonical works – in particular, that stemming

[9] The archive of Wallace's papers opened for research in September 2010; the materials relating to *The Pale King* became available for study in September 2012. See Schwartzburg for a discussion of the context surrounding the acquisition as well as a description of the processing of the papers (Schwartzburg 2012, 241–59).

from French genetic criticism, but also Jerome McGann's influential work on the 'social' nature of textual production, and that more commonly deals with the works of nineteenth-century and modernist authors.[10] The book is also informed by the recent turn towards the study of the social networks behind literary production that has seen its most notable iteration in Mark McGurl's *The Program Era*, drawing on the growing body of literary sociology that focuses on what Amy Hungerford calls 'the institutions and relationships that organize and shape' writing and its reception (Hungerford 2016, 3).[11] The editor exists at a crucial point within the nexus of forces that constitute contemporary literary production, being responsible for the identification and acquisition of literary talent, the hands-on work involved in bringing a text to publishable form and many of the key decisions involved in marketing and positioning a work so as best to determine its intended reception. The editor, that is to say, is an institution, and one of the most indispensable players in the process of literary production.

This book is underpinned by the belief that by making the editor's role the object of critical inquiry we can better understand the layers of mediation and negotiation involved in the works they help to produce. I do not claim to offer a comprehensive overview of editorial practice in American fiction; the difficulties I have outlined should make it clear that a more comprehensive work of this nature will require the work of many future scholars.[12] The case studies here are limited by the gender and race of the participants, for example, and it will become clear that the distinctive nature of the working methods of each participant – writing and editing being inherently idiosyncratic and unstandardized activities – resist sweeping generalizations. We will, however, gain insights into the complex and often conflicting forms of agency involved

[10] In Chapter 1, I present an overview of key concepts from genetic criticism. For an introduction to this, see Deppman, Ferrer and Groden; for examples of genetically inflected criticism that attempts to better understand literary productions through close analysis of the material facts of their genesis, see Hannah Sullivan's *The Work of Revision* (2013), Finn Fordham's *I Do I Undo I Redo* (2010) and Dirk Van Hulle's *Modern Manuscripts* (2014).

[11] See, for example, James F. English's work on the economy of cultural prestige (2005) and William Marling's *Gatekeepers: The Emergence of World Literature and the 1960s* (2016), which focuses on the mediating figures (editors, translators and publishers) involved in the circulation of works by García Márquez, Bukowsi and others. A growing body of scholarship considers translation, in Rebecca L. Walkowitz's words, 'as medium and origin rather than as afterthought' (Doloughan 2016, Walkowitz 2017, 3–4). See English and Underwood's introduction to the September 2016 issue of *Modern Language Quarterly* for a discussion of the burgeoning 'methodological exchanges between the humanities and the social sciences' (284).

[12] Along with the problems of access mentioned earlier, we should note the amount of labour involved in extensive textual analysis of multiple works.

in the genesis of the texts in question. The editorial relationships that emerge are dramatically different in some respects: the differences in form between Wallace's maximalist novels and Carver's short fictions make for a divergence in editorial method at a detailed level, and the clearly apparent *agon* at play in the development of the fiction bearing Carver's name is balanced by the relatively collegial negotiations behind the work produced by Wallace and Pietsch during the former's lifetime. Along with obvious contrasts, we will see some clear and sometimes surprising parallels.

My opening chapter explores historical and theoretical conceptions of the editor's role, examining the factors bearing upon editorial activity and drawing on genetic and textual criticism in order to focus the book's emphasis on textual process rather than product. It goes on to consider the historical contexts in which Carver's and Wallace's texts were published, examining the way in which Carver's stories became the accepted template for Minimalist fiction and framing Wallace's literary identity as a reaction to the overwhelming success of this model in the 1980s. From here we go on to examine the two case studies, each presented across three chapters. In Chapters 2 to 7 a detailed excavation of the editorial processes behind each author's work is followed, in each case, by a reading that draws out the implications for a revised understanding of the works in question.

In Chapter 2, I examine the legacy of the 'Carver Controversy' before returning to present a study of Lish's role in the development of Carver's work from the late 1960s onwards, tracing the textual development of the stories in Carver's first collection, *Will You Please Be Quiet, Please?* Drawing on this previously unstudied archival material, I argue that Lish was a powerful influence on both the development of Carver's aesthetic and the positioning of the author within the literary marketplace throughout the 1970s. Chapter 3 provides an extended treatment of the editing of Carver's *What We Talk About When We Talk About Love*, considering the way in which Lish's methods and aesthetic approach influenced the development and reception of one of the touchstones of 1980s US fiction and arguing that the work's legacy remains highly contingent upon Lish's editing of the stories. Chapter 4 examines the theoretical and practical difficulties that emerge as Carver negotiates the ambiguous legacy of his 'Minimalist' success, arguing that Lish's involvement in Carver's work must be seen as part of a wider pattern of influence visible through the editor's activities over a number of years. I explore Carver's ambivalent response to Lish's editing and argue that his own public statements on writing (in one essay, e.g. he famously claims that style is 'the writer's particular and unmistakable signature on everything he writes') hide a complex hidden struggle with his editor carried on over many years. Lish's editorial presence complicates the reception of a literary genre – the Minimalist short story – that is shown to depend heavily upon the assumption of a controlling authorial figure.

Chapter 5 presents a close study of the editing processes behind some of Wallace's key texts and analyses Michael Pietsch's involvement in the author's career, beginning with his acquisition and editing of *Infinite Jest* during the mid-1990s and considering his contribution to Wallace's subsequent collections of stories and essays. The bulk of the chapter focuses on the editing of *Infinite Jest,* the pair's lengthiest and most detailed collaboration. I trace the three stages of revision involved in the novel's production and consider how the process altered Wallace's approach to editing. Chapter 6 focuses on Pietsch's posthumous assembly of Wallace's final novel after the author's death in 2008. I explore unpublished scenes and differences between existing drafts from the author's archive in order to illuminate the difficulties involved in the processes of assembly and editing. The analysis shows Pietsch's own struggles with the chronic fragmentation in the work's manuscripts and traces the choices made in terms of the selection, sequencing and presentation of material. In Chapter 7, I return to a consideration of Wallace's own compositional processes in order to highlight the increasing importance, in the author's late work, of the urge towards narrative compression. This urge, I argue, is informed by auto-editorial demands, as the author – who did not show his editor any of the drafts for *The Pale King* during the years in which he was working on the novel – began to focus repeatedly on the problems of arranging and condensing his material. I examine how, in the absence of editorial assistance, Wallace's difficulties in developing a coherent narrative form – and in editing and arranging his own work – cause him to turn his focus to canonical models of narrative Minimalism.

Finally, I consider Carver's and Wallace's late work as evidence of what I call an 'anxiety of editorial influence' generated by the authors' experiences of editing processes and informed by a heightened awareness of the social nature of textual development. In Carver's case, I argue that his later stories betray an anxiety about textual interference that manifest in displaced allegories of co-creation and textual change in which the process of textual mediation haunts the compositional process. In the case of Wallace, we begin to see what happens when an author's continuing struggles with his material lead him to attempt to become, in effect, his own editor; the analysis here considers how this kind of auto-editorial energy becomes a driving factor in his late fiction as he subsumes the editorial function into his authorial performance. The art of editing may often be invisible, but its effects, as we will see, are lasting ones.

Acknowledgements

It should go without saying that this book has benefited from multiple forms of editorial artistry, offered and gratefully accepted over the course of several years.

Philip Coleman's knowledge was essential in the shaping of this book, and his keen editorial eye was invaluable on several occasions. Nerys Williams offered expert help and encouragement in the project's early stages, as did Ron Callan; Alice Bennett and Sam Slote gave perceptive advice and astute suggestions on methodology and direction. Haaris Naqvi and the editorial team at Bloomsbury have offered essential guidance at every stage of this process, and I am grateful to the reviewers whose comments helped me to revise the material in constructive ways. Colleagues at Trinity College Dublin and University College Dublin and in the Irish Association for American Studies offered regular encouragement and advice.

The community of Wallace scholars and readers has been enormously helpful during the years in which I have been researching Wallace's works. It has been my excellent fortune to find several of the most accomplished and enthusiastic members of this community close to home; in addition to Philip, Adam Kelly read sections of the manuscript and offered judicious comments, while Clare Hayes-Brady and Tom Tracey offered thoughts and coffee at crucial junctures. I have also benefited greatly from the dialogues on Wallace and contemporary literature carried on at several international conferences on Wallace's work and in several venues online, with Matt Bucher, Dave Laird and many others deserving of mention.

Thanks to Tess Gallagher for encouraging this research and for her generous assistance throughout. Thanks, too, to Gordon Lish for his cooperation and continued support. Several of those whose work is discussed within these pages were kind enough to give me their time in the form of interviews, and I am grateful to Tess, to Gordon, to Michael Pietsch and to Gerald Howard for their generosity. Thanks to the David Foster Wallace Literary Trust, Gordon Lish, Hachette Book Group, the Hill Nadell Agency, Knopf, Little, Brown Book Group, Penguin Random House and the Wylie Agency for granting permission to reproduce the quotes contained herein.

This research – particularly its essential archival component – has been supported at various stages throughout its gestation by the Irish Research Council, the Graduate Office of Trinity College Dublin, and the School of English, Drama and Film at University College Dublin. A work such as this one could also not have been completed without the dedication of the archivists and librarians who create and maintain the manuscript materials from which it draws. I would like to express my gratitude to the staff of the libraries that hold the archival materials I quote from – the Harry Ransom Center at University of Texas, Austin, the Lilly Library at Indiana University, Bloomington, and the Rare Books and Manuscripts Library at Ohio State University – for their help in navigating and reproducing the relevant materials in what was sometimes a complex and time-consuming process.

Parts of Chapter 4 first appeared in the *Irish Journal of American Studies*, Issue 4 (2015), and parts of Chapter 8 first appeared in *Critique: Studies in Contemporary Fiction*, Volume 58, Issue 4 (2017). I am grateful to the editors of these journals for permission to reprint the relevant sections.

The support of friends and family (both intellectual and practical) has been crucial throughout the time I was working on this project, and in particular I'd like to thank my mother Jean Lynch.

Finally, my deep thanks to Asia for her love and support, without which these pages would not exist. This book is dedicated to her and Seán.

1

'Stuff that editors do'

'Why not just have the editor write the book?': Random House versus Joan Collins

In February of 1996, Joan Collins spent several days in a Manhattan courtroom defending a lawsuit brought by her publisher Random House. In 1990 the publishing house had agreed a $4 million, two-book deal with the actress and author, but their relationship had broken down in the intervening years, culminating in the rejection of the manuscripts of the two novels in question – *A Ruling Passion* and *Hell Hath No Fury* – on the basis that both were below the required standard. Random House sued for the return of the $1.3 million advance; Collins responded by countersuing on the basis that she was owed the balance of the $4 million.

The case centred on the question of whether the author had turned in a 'complete' manuscript, as per the terms of her contract. Collins's agent, the *New York Times* noted, had persuaded the publisher 'to delete from their contract the customary requirement that the author turn in a "satisfactory performance" ' (Goodman 1996, n.p.). In her later account of the trial, Collins would note that this clause was 'the publishing world's most powerful weapon', allowing them 'not to pay for work they don't like' (Collins 1997, 4). The legal arguments thus came to hinge on the question of whether the word 'complete' was to be understood in qualitative or quantitative terms. The prosecution argued that despite the fact that Collins had turned in a manuscript of some bulk, its disorganized and incoherent nature meant that it could not be considered 'complete'. Collins's editor Joni Evans took to the stand to describe her feelings of 'alarm' upon receiving one of the manuscripts, claiming that it had struck her as being 'primitive, very much off-base'. Asked to elaborate, she described a text that was 'not in any shape to edit. This was a manuscript that was setting out characters but all over the map, with many themes not quite gelling [. . .] it was jumbled and disjointed. It was alarming.'[1] It did not, she claimed, have 'a beginning, a middle and an end' and was not yet in an appropriate state for submission to the publication and editing process (Collins 1997, 7). The defence, on the other hand, argued that the manuscripts' faults were provisional and unexceptional: Collins's defence lawyer went so far as to imply that 'a talented, skilful editor, working on a close basis with an author, could have helped [to] find a resolution' to the problems they contained.

Despite the central issue of the quality of Collins's manuscripts ('my literary ability', she later recalled, 'was on trial' (Collins 1997, 7)), the focus of the dispute soon shifted to the question of what exactly the editor's role entailed. Was Evans justified in refusing to give Collins line-by-line criticism even though previous editors had provided this to the author? Was she correct in her claim that the manuscript needed to be fixed in 'basic' ways before such detailed criticism was even possible? The defence called Rosemary Cheetham, who had previously worked as Collins's editor in the UK: she described an early editorial group meeting, hinting that Evans's editorial advice to the author on the plot had been misguided. Asked whether she herself would, as editor, have been capable of turning the manuscript into a successful work of commercial fiction, she replied in the affirmative, noting that this would have required detailed suggestions and page-by-page notes: the manuscript was, she argued, 'complete but not ready for press'. The defence then heard from expert witness Lucianne Goldberg, who had previously worked as a ghostwriter and editor, to provide an unambiguous verdict: 'Is it fixable? Absolutely.' When the prosecuting lawyer selected examples from the manuscript to demonstrate the fragmented, chaotic nature of its plot (e.g. instances in which one character's drug problem disappears inexplicably from the narrative and another character's life-saving heart operation is apparently alluded to as an afterthought), Goldberg waved her hand and replied, 'all of this is stuff that editors do'. Upon being asked whether Collins's manuscripts were in fact publishable, she replied, 'Absolutely. All they needed was some cutting and moving things around. All the stuff editors get well paid for.' Collins later approvingly quoted Goldberg's statement to the

[1] These quotes are taken from a 1996 documentary made for the US network Court TV (since relaunched as Tru TV). All subsequent quotes, unless otherwise noted, are taken from this documentary, which is (at the time of writing) viewable on YouTube (Worden 1996: URL provided in Bibliography).

court that 'Putting raw material right is what editors are *supposed* to do. They just use their blue pencil' (Collins 1997, 8–9, emphasis in original). When called to the stand herself, the author offered a paean to the importance of the editor's input:

> You neglect editors at your peril. They are 50% of the partnership after you've done the best that you possibly can with your manuscript. You go up to a point and then you can no longer do it anymore [. . .] there are some authors who can self-edit, but I am not one of them. I need an editor, and I am the first to admit it.

One report on the case neatly summarized the defence's position: 'writers write; editors "fix"' (Sjoerdsma 1996, n.p.).

In summing up the prosecution's case, Random House's counsel Robert Callagy rejected the idea that editors should have to do all this 'stuff', appealing to the jury's intuition as he asked them to preserve a distinction between the functions of author and editor:

> What the defence amounts to is that Joan Collins wanted Joni Evans to do Miss Collins' job for her. But if it was the editor's job to execute the plots and subplots and to develop the characters, write the descriptive passages and structure the drama, why would you ever need a writer? Why would anyone who could do that, be an editor instead of a writer? Why not just have the editor write the book? That's not the way it works. You know that, and I know that.

The jury returned a split decision, meaning that Collins could keep the majority of her advance. The author was ebullient, promising reporters afterwards that this episode would be added to the autobiography she had just finished writing for her English publisher. In this later account she focused on the positive aspects of the judgement, claiming that 'justice had been served' and noting that after delivering their verdict, the jury had insisted on meeting her, their faith in her literary prowess seemingly undimmed: 'each juror', she claims, 'requested I sign their copies of the manuscripts' (Collins 1997, 16).

The Collins case represents a rare moment in which the contradictions and paradoxes of the editor's role as well as the mechanisms behind the production of commercial fiction were made painfully visible. Different editors of the same author were pitted against one another in an attempt to clarify the acceptable boundaries of the editor's role, with the result that, as the *New York Times* noted, 'the distinction between an aggressive, take-charge editor and an outright ghostwriter became increasingly blurred' (Hoffman 1996, n.p.). Those on both sides appeared to agree that editing was an indispensable element in the social and cultural processes involved in the production of writing; the case's inconclusive outcome, though, suggested that neither of the expensively assembled legal teams in action had been able to persuade the jurors towards a consensus on what, exactly, editing was. The jurors, for their part, even after long days of listening to revelations about the surprising amount of 'stuff' that Collins's editors were obliged to do, apparently retained an allegiance to the powerful author-figure and their singular signature.

'Imagining what a text can be': Understanding the editor's role

The legal battle described above concerns an editing and publication process that is, in some ways, very distant from the ones I will be examining. Collins was working within a paradigm of celebrity publishing in which the degree of authorial attribution is expected to be lower than in the case of the serious literary fiction produced by Carver and Wallace. In the case of celebrity fiction, as Donald Laming notes, 'the author's name functions not as a guarantee of literary quality, but as a link between the book and pre-existing publicity', and even Collins's defence attorney was quick to concede that his client 'is not, and has not claimed to be, Hemingway or James Joyce or Proust' (Laming 2003, 100). However, the example illustrates many of the tensions and ambiguities attendant upon the role of the literary editor and serves as a useful background to the cases I will be considering here, both of which involve editorial interventions that go beyond the boundaries of the expected. It is worth noting, too, that these two worlds – that of the celebrity airport novel on the one hand and prestigious literary fiction on the other – are not entirely discrete in the way they are brought to the market. They can overlap in the figure of the editor, who, if he or she works in a major publishing house, is likely to have a diverse portfolio of authors spanning a range of generic and commercial modes.[2] John B. Thompson, indeed, argues that celebrity publishing is simply an extension of the 'fundamental dynamic' of contemporary publishing, in which the author's

[2] Pietsch observes that Perkins's success had a 'broad base' and that he edited a range of books including 'romance, comedy, humor, cookery'; Gottlieb has edited authors as diverse as Toni Morrison, Denis Johnson, Katharine Hepburn and Bill Clinton (Pietsch 2017a; Gottlieb 2016). Lish served as ghostwriter on several works of commercial fiction in the 1970s, while Pietsch's list of authors includes Donna Tartt, James Patterson, Malcom Gladwell and Keith Richards.

'platform' becomes – rather than one factor – the 'overriding factor' to be taken into account in the book's publication (J. Thompson 2012, 204).

I begin, therefore, by considering the reasons for the ambiguous nature of the editor's role and examining the ideas and practices that have come to define it. As Claire MacDonald and William H. Sherman note, the editor 'is at once a key player in the creation and transmission of culture and an elusive – often invisible – figure' (MacDonald and Sherman 2002, 1). Perhaps the first general characteristic to be noted about editing – at least insofar as it takes place in a commercial context – is its liminal, and hence 'elusive', status: as MacDonald and Sherman point out, the designation is, of necessity, a 'mediating term' (1). In what he calls a 'fundamental definition', Paul Eggert (2009, 156) highlights this act of mediation and usefully points towards a point of future publication as an inescapable aspect of the editing transaction: 'an editor', in his formulation, 'mediates, according to defined or undefined standards or conventions, between the text or texts of documents made or orally transmitted by another and the audience of the anticipated publication' (Eggert 2009, 156). An editor mediates, therefore, both materially and temporally: Pietsch has noted that he worked 'at the professional interface between [Wallace] and his readers', an explanation that highlights the way in which the editor's position is one that necessarily involves functioning as an intermediary in the service of the creation of a future textual product (Pietsch 2010, 11). Susan Greenberg formulates the editor's goal in more abstract terms as 'imagining what a text can be' (Greenberg 2010, 19).

The variety of practical tasks involved in this act of mediation, though, can be significant. As the Collins case demonstrates, the term 'editing' can refer to a range of activities and can be understood differently within different spheres of publishing. Identifying principles and methods in modern commercial editing is difficult, since standardization has traditionally been lacking and practices vary between individuals and between publishing houses. Both Thomas McCormack and Leslie Sharpe, in their respective guides to editing practice, bemoan the lack of professionalization of the editing industry and the absence of any common statements of theory or systematic instruction (Sharpe 1994, 4; McCormack 2006, 84). Peter Ginna points out that 'almost no American publishing house has any formalized instruction program', observing that most publishing skills are acquired through what is in effect 'a classic apprenticeship system' (Ginna 2017a, 4). As Collins discovered, editors may share identical job titles while understanding their function very differently; Matthew Philpotts argues that the role in fact requires 'a diverse range of often conflicting dispositions' including 'intellectual and literary', 'economic and managerial', and 'social and personal' (Philpotts 2012, 61). Gerald Howard, vice president and executive editor of Doubleday (who has previously edited both Wallace, as we shall see, and Lish),[3] provides a disconcertingly vivid image of the editor's idiosyncratic art in his claim that 'nobody really knows how an editor works besides his or her authors and possibly his or her assistant' (Howard 2016, 195).[4] The English language itself is unhelpful in allowing for distinctions between different aspects of the practice: within the tradition of the commercial publication of fiction, 'editing', as Sharpe observes, generally connotes a number of activities including reviewing, revising, redacting, refining, emending and correcting (Sharpe 1994, 1). These activities, or 'patterns of revision' will, as John Bryant observes, tend to be grouped as part of a single design or 'set of strategies' (Bryant 2002, 108) serving to act in a manner similar to that outlined by Foucault's author function, namely as a principle of specificity upon the text. An editor will typically be expected to 'bring out the author's voice in the strongest way possible' (Marek 1994, viii) and to display 'empathy with the author's *vision*' (Sharpe 1994, 131).[5] In the preparation of a fictional text for publication, an editor will inevitably bring his or her own aesthetic preferences to the text (McCormack identifies 'sensibility' as the key to good editing) (McCormack 2006, 75). The work done will include an awareness of a variety of social factors, though, most notably of its potential audience as well as the sensibilities (and perhaps the 'house style') of the publishing house in question.[6] The attribution for a published work of fiction will in almost every case be singular, though, with the author's name usually appearing unaccompanied on the book's cover and the editor's work rarely foregrounded. Editing consequently implies an awareness of this requirement

[3] Recalling his experience of editing Lish's novel *My Romance* (1991), Howard has written that the author's 'control-freak obsessiveness' made him 'a living no-editing zone'. However, Andrew Latimer, the editor of Lish's 2017 collection *White Plains*, reports that Lish has become more receptive to editorial suggestion (Howard 2007, n.p.; Latimer 2017, n.p.).

[4] Gary Fisketjon, who helped Carver to make the selections for his career-spanning collection *Where I'm Calling From* (1988) and is current vice president at Knopf, also points out that 'editors don't share their work with other editors' (Barrodale 2007, n.p.).

[5] Foucault famously writes that the author 'is a certain functional principle by which, in our culture, one limits, excludes, and chooses; in short, by which one impedes the free circulation, the free manipulation, the free composition, decomposition, and recomposition of fiction [. . .] [he is] the ideological figure by which one marks the manner in which we fear the proliferation of meaning' (Foucault 2006, 290).

[6] Bryant's definition of an editor's work demonstrates the contingency of the various social imperatives brought to bear: the goal of an editor, he writes, is 'betterment, however that may be defined [. . .] the editor attempts to bring the text closer in line with his or her notion of the writer's goal with his/her own personal agenda as a reader, or the agenda of the publisher or of a readership the editor presumes to represent' (Bryant 2002, 104).

and a movement towards a certain unity and reduction of textual variation, whether stylistic or thematic. (McCormack notes that it is the editor's lot to be anonymous and to 'serve the author' (McCormack 2006, 74, 84)).

A paradigm of singular authorship has long been the norm in the commercial presentation of fiction.[7] Carver and Wallace both developed their writing practice in environments (namely, the MFA programme and magazine publishing) where a story or novel would, despite the possible presence of multiple contributors to a fictional text, invariably reach the public under a single author's name. The critical difficulty of apprehending and defining the editor's contribution, Stillinger argues, stems not just from the persistence of the concept of singular authorship within literary theory but also from the practicalities of the publishing industry: 'An editor who made much of a claim as collaborator', he suggests, 'would very quickly find the authors giving their manuscripts to rival publishers. The fact is that authors themselves are among the most ardent believers in the myth of single authorship' (Stillinger 1991, 155). Pietsch concurs, noting that it is 'essential to the ongoing commercial relationship' that the editor remain invisible and that it can 'hurt' the author if changes become known (Pietsch 2017c). We see a kind of wilful blindness on the part of authors (as well as, perhaps, publishers and editors themselves) to the editor's role, and one that goes some way towards describing what happened between Lish and Carver. Stillinger's claim remains relevant, since single authorship is arguably more integral to the contemporary commercial presentation of books than ever. Robert Eaglestone and Jonathan Beecher Field, for instance, present the importance of authorial identity in contemporary publishing as a counterweight to the well-worn 'death of the author' slogan; they consider the way in which contemporary authorship is often constructed as a 'brand', taking Tom Clancy as an example,[8] and argue

7 Multiple authorship has, historically, rarely been acknowledged in the commercial presentation of fiction and, as Lisa Ede and Andrea Lunsford note in their exploration of authorship in *Singular Texts/Plural Authors*, could be said to have an anomalous place in contemporary literature. Like Stillinger, they highlight what they term 'The Myth of the Solitary Author', following the development of the concept of individual authorship from its roots in Descartes' conception of individual subjectivity through to the Romantic conception of solitary genius proposed by writers like Wordsworth, whose writings on the subject define authorship in terms of 'individuals writing alone' (Ede and Lunsford 1992, 85).

8 James Patterson, who is edited by Pietsch, is an even clearer example of the modern author-as-entrepreneur. A 2010 *New York Times* profile of Patterson described a production meeting in which Pietsch and the author discussed possible marketing slogans. The profile's author points out that the publishing house's treatment of its highest-selling author has evolved as a matter of commercial necessity, noting that Patterson's enormous commercial success since the 1990s ('since 2006, Patterson has written one out of every 17 hardcover novels bought in the United States') 'encouraged Little, Brown to fully embrace mass-market fiction' and that Patterson's single-minded, market-driven approach to literary production has resulted in the development of an editing process that is unusual in the book world. Patterson uses co-authors for almost all of his books (he has five regular

that the increased visibility of contemporary authors suggests a desire on the part of readers for 'authoritative interpretation' (Eaglestone and Field 2015, n.p.). Theadora Hawlin argues that contemporary publishing and media practices mean that the writer is now 'a key character in the life-span of a text', making them 'more crucially inextricable from their works than ever' (Hawlin 2017, n.p.). The testimony of major editors makes it clear that in the contemporary publishing ecology, the author is not just alive but a figure whose visibility tends to be an essential element of a book's presentation. Numerous accounts make it clear that the author's personality and appearance are more critical factors than ever in the acquisition and subsequent marketing of a book: Gottlieb describes how 'author promotion' became 'an essential publishing tool' from the 1980s onwards, while Pietsch claims that in the 40 years he has been in the business, 'the stress on the writer to be a public figure has grown' and states the bald facts of publishing logic in his assertion that 'the author is the best way to sell a book' (Gottlieb 2016; Pietsch 2017c). These considerations are not limited to the blockbuster novels of Clancy and Patterson and the celebrity fiction of Collins and are manifested throughout the world of literary fiction in the form of the book tour, the festival appearance and the author Twitter account, among others.[9]

The editor's work, of course, is not limited to the page, and it is with this discussion of marketing that we can begin to apprehend the distance between the bygone world of Perkins and Wolfe and that of Joan Collins's multimillion-dollar courtroom battles. The textual dimension of an editor's job may have changed very little (leaving aside the introduction of digital media into the process), and the essential aspects of the editor's contribution to the publication process have in some respects remained broadly similar. Jordan Pavlin, for example (editor of Karen Russell, Nathan Englander and Jenny Offill, among others), suggests that, despite changes to the industry, 'the core of an editor's role' remains 'remarkably unaltered': in the past, 'as now, the editor's first job was to acquire and edit the best books and to talk about them with passion and purpose' (Harris 2015).[10] The

co-authors, whom he himself pays), writing detailed outlines on the basis of which chapters are then drafted and returned for him to read; a recent *Vanity Fair* profile described him as 'the Henry Ford of Books' (Mahler 2010, n.p.; Purdum 2015, n.p.).

9 To give just one more of the many examples of how the publishing industry strengthens the link between the contemporary author and their work, we might think of *the New Yorker*'s recently established podcast, 'The Author's Voice', in which newly published stories are read by their authors.

10 Gerald Howard concurs, defining these perennial qualities as 'the exercise of informed taste and judgement', 'expert guidance' and 'infectious enthusiasm' (Howard 2016, 200).

commercial environment in which this job is carried out, however, has changed enormously, with the scale of production and investment expanding rapidly in the past half century. Thompson's sociological account of the publishing business presents the most thorough picture of this environment;[11] he describes how the 'wave of mergers and acquisitions' that 'swept through the industry, beginning in the early 1960s and continuing through to the present day' have 'transformed profoundly the landscape of trade publishing' (J. Thompson 2012, 102–3). Travis Kurowski et al. note that the introduction of Nielsen's BookScan in 2000 turned 'each author, no matter how big or small, into a data set of his/her book sales', while Thompson claims that authors now 'carry their sales histories around with them like a noose around their neck' (Kurowski, Miller, and Prufer 2016, vii; J. Thompson 2012, 199). The job of editing literary fiction during this historical period – roughly, the period covered by the case studies in this book – has taken place in an environment that is increasingly corporatized and data driven, and in which the figure of the author is central to each stage of the publishing process. Acquiring 'the best books' is a task that will, for an editor with a major publisher, now involve acquisition meetings, liaisons with sales teams and complex, Nielsen-informed calculations of risk and reward; 'talking about' the books, meanwhile, is a continuous process of accounting, strategizing and selling that Pietsch describes as 'managing processes on the author's behalf' (Pietsch 2017c). The book itself will, with very few exceptions, be presented as a single, unified entity, with little or no reference to these manifold forms of editorial labour.

'The workings of the work': Behind the stable text

This situation sits in marked contrast to the trajectory of critical editing methodologies in recent times. In an overview of trends in Anglo-American critical editing methods during the late twentieth century, Paul Eggert describes a 'gradual loss of belief among editors in the ideal text of a work' (Eggert 2009, 200). A combination of factors including the poststructuralist erosion of traditional notions of authorship, reader-response theory's emphasis on the role of readers

[11] André Schiffrin and Jason Epstein are among the publishers and editors who have reflected on the complex and relentless process of corporate consolidation of the publishing industry (Schiffrin 2000, 2010; Epstein 2002).

in constructing the meaning of a work and the influence of German editorial theory – which involves a far more self-consciously historical and 'archival dimension' than the Anglo-American tradition of critical editing – contributed to a growing resistance both to the 'author-centricity' (in Hans Walter Gabler's words) of much scholarly activity and the accompanying 'cultural assumption of a stable and finalised text' (Eggert 2009, 185–213; Gabler 2018, 176). The result of this has been, in Eggert's words, 'the welcome broadening of attention to the workings of the work' (Eggert 2009, 228).

Textual and genetic scholarship has increasingly emphasized textual process over product as well as encouraging a reflexive attention to the editorial assumptions and methods operating in critical editing projects. This reflexive attitude is exemplified by Jerome McGann's claim that 'editing, including critical editing, is more an act of translation than of reproduction' and his assertion that 'even good editing [. . .] necessarily involves fundamental departures from "authorial intention", however that term is interpreted' (McGann 1991, 53–8).[12] Genetic criticism has also developed a set of ideas and a critical vocabulary aimed at breaking away from the assumption of the primacy of the 'ideal' text (Groden 2007, x). At the level of critical vocabulary, the notion of '*avant-texte*' was introduced by French genetic critics as opposed to 'variant'; this category of textual material refers to 'the result of the critical analysis, reconstitution, and organization of all the extant documents related to the writing process one intends to examine' (Crispi and Slote 2007, 37).[13] Louis Hay emphasizes the way in which genetic criticism thrives on multiplicity as opposed to singularity, aiming to apprehend 'a plurality of virtual texts behind the surface of the constituted text' and attempting to make visible 'what Julien Gracq called the "phantoms of successive books" [. . .] that have disappeared along the way and forever haunt the finished compositions' (Hay 2004, 22). The possibilities implied by textual variety, here, are given precedence over the search for unity: the published work, in this approach, is 'only *one* among its multiple possibilities' (Contat et al. 1996, 2) and the static iteration of the 'final' text is viewed as one dimension of a 'text in movement' (Hay 2004, 23). The 'avant-texte' thus becomes 'a sort of text laboratory' (De Biasi and Wassenaar 1996, 29), and the

[12] Bryant's related notion of the 'fluid text' – the proposition that all texts are 'fluid' due to the different production pressures bearing upon each version – develops this emphasis on social influences on textual transmission and highlights the ongoing nature of cultural processes of interpretation (Bryant 2002, 4–6).

[13] The *avant-texte* is thus, as Wim Van Mierlo notes, not an archival source as such but a 'construct' (Van Mierlo 2013, 16).

rough draft becomes 'a protocol for making a text' (Ferrer 1998, 261): the study of these can enable the construction of a narrative of creation and the opening up of an otherwise inaccessible temporal context for interpretation.

Florence Callu has claimed that the twentieth century was the 'golden age of the contemporary manuscript';[14] Allan Friedman, in 2010, referred to 'the manuscript preservation craze' as 'a twentieth-century phenomenon that shows no sign of abating thanks largely to the continuing interest of research libraries and universities' (Van Hulle 2014, 4; Friedman 2010, 94). This 'craze' has, in conjunction with the contemporary success of both Carver and Wallace, led to the cataloguing and display of their work within a relatively short time frame. In Carver's case, the disagreement over the attribution of 'his' stories has arguably led to the availability of the manuscripts: Lish's maintenance and presentation of his archive, and his unwillingness (as a far less self-effacing and deliberately 'invisible' character than Perkins) to subsume his work under Carver's authorship have made the relevant documentation accessible. Both Carver and Wallace were working, for the most part, towards what might be considered as the end of the manuscript age, prior to the twenty-first-century move into digital methods of composition and transmission.[15] Genetic criticism has, of necessity, tended to focus on canonical authors whose 'avant-texte' is extensive enough to allow the application of its methods (examples include Raymond Debray Genette's work on Flaubert, or Catherine Viollet's on Proust) (Genette 2004; Viollet 2004). Much recent work in English-language criticism has focused on modernist authors such as Beckett, Woolf and Joyce, whose extensive (and often chaotic) manuscripts and notebooks provide a rich basis for genetic explorations.[16] The trend among repositories to collect and acquire the papers of living writers, however (which, as Sara S. Hodson notes, has 'grown dramatically' in the past 40 years), has begun to generate a rise in attention to manuscripts of more recent provenance (Hodson 2013, 166).[17] This book continues the extension of a genetic focus

[14] Callu made this claim in an essay written in French in 1993; the phrase used here is Van Hulle's translation.

[15] See Kirschenbaum (2016) for a history of how computers and word processing became incorporated into literary production.

[16] Sam Slote's examination of the creation of Chapter II.I of *Finnegans Wake*, for example, uses 'avant-textual' evidence such as notebooks and letters to trace the development of the writing and to explore the author's changing conceptualization of the work (Slote 2007, 181–213). Fordham, too, is concerned with 'reconstructing the events of writing' in order to examine the compositional process as a textual influence in its own right and illuminate 'the process encoded in the product' in order to illustrate his thesis that 'formation shapes content' (Fordham 2010, 28–31).

[17] See Eggert (2007); Herman and Krafft (2007) for examples.

to a more recent literary field than it has traditionally tended to encompass. With the opening of the Wallace archive, for example, Wallace scholars are beginning to confront questions about the status and relevance of manuscript material that have already become key ones in the study of several canonical high modernist authors, and to reckon with the existence of a shadow corpus perhaps comparable to the 'gray canon' of Samuel Beckett's archive (Gontarski 2006, 143). Toon Staes, for example, invokes genetic methods in his early reading of *The Pale King*'s drafts, while David Hering suggests that a genetic view can enable a 'dialogic and developmental' sense of Wallace's compositional strategies (Staes 2014b, 70–84; Hering 2016a, 8–13). John Roache reads Wallace's marginalia alongside his fiction while questioning the tendency to read this for evidence of origins or 'unambiguous truth' (Roache 2017, 11).

I draw upon genetic approaches throughout this study, particularly in my examination of *The Pale King*'s protracted composition, while also seeking to shift the traditional focus of genetic critics on solitary authorial production. Van Hulle's recent work, for example, integrates concepts from the field of cognitive science – in particular, the notion of the 'extended mind' – with the study of manuscripts in order to argue that 'writers' interaction with their manuscripts as part of the "extended mind" may inform their methods of evoking fictional minds' (Van Hulle 2014, 13–16, 244). While approaches like these can generate important insights for any study of literary drafts,[18] they largely take manuscripts as the occasion for the study of the activities of a singular mind as it moves through the process of creation. Genetic critics, as Van Mierlo has noted, tend to approach manuscripts as 'largely private and wholly idiosyncratic productions'; my focus, instead, is on the crucial pre-publication moment when the text is shared and, in McGann's words, 'socialized' (Van Mierlo 2013, 17; McGann 1991). Texts, I suggest – particularly texts whose attribution and/or composition is contested – may be more productively viewed as the result of competing and sometimes antagonistic agents.

Van Hulle's invocation of an extended authorial mind points to the way in which the genetic method is, perhaps, inescapably author-centred in nature. The idea of the work, after all, is still reliant on that of the author: a boundary has to be drawn around the work somewhere, and the author-figure is still needed

[18] I draw, for example, on Van Hulle's notion of the dialectical process of literary creation in my analysis of the composition of *The Pale King* (Van Hulle 2014, 246).

to connect the canonical text with its ephemera, its 'pre-text'. De Biasi defines genetic documentation as 'the whole body of known, classified, and transcribed manuscripts and documents connected with a text whose form has reached, in the opinion of its author, a state of completion or near completion' (De Biasi and Wassenaar 1996, 31). It is instantly apparent how essential the author-figure is to this definition: the author provides not only the entry point but also the warrant for the entire investigation. While the terms of the inquiry attempt to open the text to multiple readings, this is effected only by using the author-figure to delimit the space in which this is possible; in the attempt to dissolve the stable text, the genetic critic invariably invokes a stable author. This recourse to authorial documents and the attendant reconstruction of authorial intention has led critics such as Jenny and Watts to argue that genetic criticism is in danger of surrendering the critic's 'hermeneutical relationship' to literature and to question, in Crispi and Slote's paraphrasing, whether it is in fact 'a new discipline at all or merely a research tool' (Crispi and Slote 2007, 36). While genetic criticism may have derived energy from (and perhaps be animated by similar impulses to) Barthes's push to banish the author from critical consideration – the drive towards fluidity and indeterminacy of meaning, the opening of the text to a 'polysemic, free, and fecund Other' (Jenny and Watts 1996, 20) – its methods clearly place it elsewhere on the authorial spectrum. Fordham notes the attacks of those who suggest that genetic criticism, in its focus on canonical authors, 'feeds the romantic cult of the single autonomous author' (Fordham 2010, 21); Hay admits the importance of the author-figure, stating that the methods of genetic criticism invite fresh consideration of the place of 'the writing subject in the study of the literary object' and arguing that in studying literary production, we must be aware of the simple but problematic fact that 'the writer is present at the very heart of this process' (Hay 2004, 24).

This observation accords with the insights of a number of scholars who have, in recent decades, critiqued the tendency to take the 'death of the author' as an unquestioned *fait accompli*. Seán Burke emphasizes the 'biographical imperative', contending that any study of a text in relation to its contexts, whether historical or cultural, must acknowledge that 'an authorial life and its work allow such a passage to be made': 'the author', in his words, 'is that one category which clearly overlaps – one might even say conjoins – text and context' and forms an essential part of any attempts to 'break up the ideal unity of the work' (Burke 2008, 195–200). A recurring thread in my analysis is the way the editorial presence illuminates the persistence of this paradigm of single authorship in the reception and criticism of contemporary fiction in the face of the poststructuralist truism of the author's disappearance.[19] Additionally, the ubiquity of the model of single authorship in the world of commercial publishing means that critics have often viewed it as an inevitable paradigm for textual production. In this model, any extra-authorial contribution to the production of a text can be accepted as an extension of the author's intention, with the concept of 'passive authorization' implying that the author, in effect, 'signs off' on the assistance given by the editor (Crispi and Slote 2007, 37; Bucci 2003, 31). So, for instance, Günter Leypoldt, in defending his previous reading of Carver's story 'So Much Water So Close to Home' against new interpretations based on the revelations about the story's textual development, was able to dismiss the new textual evidence as an example of 'the type of influences to which authors tend to be exposed' (Leypoldt 2002, 318). In the light of the evidence of Lish's intensive editing, though, which clearly exists at some remove from an assumed model of harmonious editorial cooperation, this view seems untenable. Similarly, any discussion of a posthumous work such as *The Pale King* requires close attention to the high degree of mediation necessarily involved in publishing the work of an absent author.

In the examples I consider in this book, an examination of the editor's role demonstrates, paradoxically, the strength of the author-figure in the reception of these works. Marjorie Stone and Judith Thompson note that the idea of the solitary author 'remains remarkably persistent in literary criticism, the classroom, mass culture, the marketplace, and the law' (Stone and Thompson 2006, 11–12), and their reference to the first two of these spheres is, I believe, accurate: for the most part, critics, teachers and readers have continued to assume a default model of singular authorship. In addition to the theoretical paradox that Burke identifies – expressed succinctly in the declaration that 'the concept of the author is never more alive than when pronounced dead' – and the influence of the market, with its clear commercial benefits to publishers of developing an author's literary brand, we can identify obvious practical and methodological reasons for this tendency (Burke 2008, 7). An author's rise in stature within the academy will be reflected in the growth of a sub-field focused on their work and signified by their name (e.g. 'Wallace Studies'); both Carver and Wallace have

19 Jane Gallop reads the 'death of the author' concept alongside writings on literal authorial deaths in order to demonstrate its tensions and contradictions; Benjamin Widiss and Judith Ryan are among those who have explored the ways in which late twentieth-century novelists responded to poststructuralist ideas within their fiction (Gallop 2011; Widiss 2011; Ryan 2014).

been the subject of biographies, critical monographs (and, indeed, in the case of the latter, a Bloomsbury book series), conferences and societies.

The tendency is, I will argue, exacerbated in both cases by the repeated identification of both authors with the genres in which they worked; in the Minimalist short story and the maximalist novel, the author-figure looms over the work, either as a ruthless sculptor (or, yes, 'carver') of terse prose or as a prodigious creator of the encyclopaedic literary masterpiece. Carver's stories were celebrated precisely because of their starkness of authorial vision and their distinctive style, and the heated critical reaction to the editing revelations highlights the extent to which his reception relied on the presence of a particular kind of implied author informed by details of his biography. Wallace, meanwhile, has become a figure iconic enough since his death that scholars have repeatedly felt it necessary to attempt to reinsert some daylight between the life and the work: Roache is one of the most recent critics to issue a caution against succumbing to the temptations of the author's 'remarkably identificatory artistic persona' (Roache 2017, 27).[20] The continuing importance of the author's own persona and critical statements to the reception of his work, along with his increasing presence as a touchstone for cultural debates on sincerity, identity and gender, all conspire to place the authorial subject in a central position. It has rapidly become standard practice for critics to read – or, in Amy Hungerford's remarkable example, not-read – Wallace's work with close reference to his interviews, public persona and biographical record (Hungerford 2016, 141–68).

I concur, therefore, with Burke's insistence on the indispensability of the author in bridging 'text and context', and the impossibility of entirely setting aside authorial intention in literary analysis. I suggest, however, adding the category of the editor to his formulation, since the relationship between text and context is one in which the editor, as the primary mediating force, is also clearly imbricated. By focusing on the editor, we widen the object of genetic study to include not only the author's decisions, hesitations and progressions but also those of the other agents involved in the production of literature, and we begin to apprehend the dynamic interplay of the writing as it is contested and negotiated by multiple collaborating (and sometimes competing) agents. Conversely, by closely examining the interaction of the different forces that contributed to the development of a text, we can gain a more accurate picture of the author's

[20] Jeffrey Severs provides several examples of such cautions, noting that Stephen J. Burn was, in 2011, among the first to warn scholars not to 'hang on the master's words' (Severs 2017, 5; Burn 2011, 467).

distinct role in its production. Attending to the editor's role note only enlarges our sense of the 'social and institutional event' of literature (McGann 1983, 100), but can also clarify the author's – and our own – part in that event.

Posthumous editing and the question of audience

It is in the publication of the work of an absent author that we most clearly see the tensions between the various commercial and critical imperatives outlined above. Posthumous publications both highlight the problem of the author's intention – since the lack of an author to provide interpretation heightens the need for accuracy on the part of the critic – and ensure that a critical editor is obliged to display conflicting evidence clearly.[21] It is here that the differences between critical and commercial editing become more apparent, since the tradition of critical editing almost invariably presupposes editing the works of a dead author.[22] These differences hinge on the question of audience. In the case of editions intended for scholars, the need for an authoritative textual apparatus is the requirement of logic as well as tradition; in the case of mass-market publications intended for a non-specialist readership, on the other hand, the textual authority of the work will often be considered less as a requirement than as one factor among a number of others (namely, accessibility and marketability).

When the work to be edited is a posthumous one by an already canonical author, these paradigms collide with unusual clarity. An editor of a posthumous work by a major author may consider critical concerns as well as commercial ones, since the published book will likely be judged in an unusually immediate way by critical as well as commercial standards. There is no uniformity in the presentation of posthumous works of major authors, and since these books are frequently edited according to commercial practices, a critical apparatus is often lacking.

[21] This evidence will ideally be accompanied (in the words of the MLA's 'Guidelines for Editors of Scholarly Editions') by the 'appropriate textual apparatus or notes documenting alterations and variant readings of the text, including alterations by the author, intervening editors, or the editor of this edition' ('Guidelines for Editors of Scholarly Editions' 2011, 1.1).

[22] Examples can be seen throughout the history of literature, as some of the central texts of the Western canon are problematically incomplete in a way that compels continual editorial attention. Virgil's *Aeneid*, for example, demonstrates the way in which an unfinished text will require the editor(s) of each edition to repeat or repeal previous decisions on key textual features, and shows that even critical editors of the same era may disagree in these matters (Knox 2007, 11–12). The inconclusive textual status of *King Lear*, too, continues to generate fierce debate among Shakespearean scholars (Syme 2016a, 2016b; Vickers 2016).

Sarah Churchwell laments the fact that 'the degree to which they [posthumously published books] are edited is often disguised, even misrepresented, by people with a vested interest in the final product', and that this is often due to the legal circumstances of the manuscripts in question: 'literary executors tend to be relatives, and thus have an emotional investment, as well as a financial one, in the public image of the artist' (Churchwell 2009, n.p.). Several critics, for example, faulted Dmitri Nabokov's decision to publish his father's final work, *The Original of Laura*, in a 2009 edition which printed facsimile reproductions of the index cards on which notes for the planned novel were written and bore the subtitle 'A Novel in Fragments' (Walsh 2009; Theroux 2009). The book displays a mix of critical and commercial impulses: the state of the surviving textual fragments is scrupulously displayed in anticipation of a readership that includes Nabokovian critics, while the subtitle ('A Novel in Fragments') seems a purely commercial addition designed to suggest to the reader that the fragmentary character of the work is intentional and definitive rather than contingent upon its author's inability to see it through to publication. David Gates, though, suggested that *The Original of Laura* should, minor faults aside, 'serve as a model of how to publish a posthumous and unfinished manuscript', noting that the 'countermodel is the published version of Hemingway's *Garden of Eden* [edited by Tom Jenks for Scribner's and published in 1986], not a serious edition of a great writer's epic mess, but a market-driven remix, with no information about the extent of the high-handed cutting and splicing' (Gates 2009).[23]

Much of Hemingway's work has been posthumously edited, often by different editors, and sometimes to controversial effect: in 2009, for example, writer A. E. Hotchner protested against the appearance of the re-edited memoir *A Moveable Feast*, invoking Hemingway's 'right to have these words protected against frivolous incursion' (Hotchner 2009). Churchwell notes Hemingway's own protests against the posthumous edit of Fitzgerald's *Tender Is the Night*, whose structure was changed by Malcolm Cowley in 1951 in accordance with the author's expressed wishes (which appear to have been driven by commercial considerations) (Churchwell 2009, n.p.).[24] The fact that authorial wishes may be

[23] Several editors at Scribner's, including Pietsch, tried unsuccessfully to edit *The Garden of Eden* before it made its way into Jenks's hands. The manuscript was subsequently reduced from 200,000 words to approximately 70,000 (Peters 1991, 17–29).

[24] Similar issues surround the structure of Roberto Bolaño's final novel (albeit thus far without the same attendant controversy): the editors of *2666* argue that 'it seems preferable to keep the novel whole' rather than to publish it in five sections as the author requested, on the basis that this request was based on short-term monetary concerns rather than artistic vision (Echevarría 2009, 895).

posthumously interpreted in various ways (and that every unfinished manuscript is likely to be unfinished in a different way) mitigates against any uniformity of presentation.

Pietsch turned a lengthy Hemingway manuscript into *The Dangerous Summer* for Scribner's in 1985 (in his one prior experience of posthumously editing the drafts of a successful author), an example that merits mention for the way in which it highlights some of the difficulties involved in presenting Wallace's unfinished work. Pietsch was, at this point, 'not yet 30 years old' and was described as 'a tyro editor' by Charles Scribner Jr (Gessen 2011, 458). The textual situation surrounding the manuscript given to Pietsch was complex enough that his work upon it was, of necessity, an act of lasting creative mediation. Miriam B. Mandel's study of the work, *Hemingway's The Dangerous Summer: The Complete Annotations* (2008), highlights the enduring nature of many posthumous editorial contributions with its observation that 'today, when we speak of *The Dangerous Summer*, we generally mean this 1985 book, edited by Pietsch' (2008, 67). The work, a description of Hemingway's travels in Spain intended as an assignment for *Life* magazine, had grown far beyond the length requested for the story and, while excerpted and published over three issues, was never published in book form during the author's lifetime. The text that Hemingway left behind was, in the words of William Kennedy's review, 'a manuscript with elephantiasis' (Kennedy 1985, n.p.); Mandel writes that the text as published by Scribner's is 'a very complicated hybrid', since 'its words were written by Hemingway, but its content and shape were largely determined by other hands' (Mandel 2008, 68). Pietsch was given the manuscript by Charles A. Scribner Jr and subsequently edited the manuscript into a novella-length publication, removing many of the more detailed descriptions of bullfighting. Mandel ventures some criticism on the result, noting that 'Scribner's was not necessarily bound to the *Life* publication, and it is difficult to understand why they omitted so much material from the 1985 book version'; she also argues that 'the structure of the book' is 'affected by editorial intervention' (Mandel 2008, 75). The publisher's note to *The Dangerous Summer* admits that 'around 20,000 words have been cut, and it may come as a disappointment to Hemingway admirers that these cuts have been made', but expresses the hope that 'respect has been paid to his intentions': it does not, however, indicate where these cuts and changes have been made and is clearly a reader's edition rather than a scholarly one (Hemingway 1985, ix–x).

Pietsch, according to Charles A. Scribner Jr, did 'a wonderful job': Kennedy, reviewing the book in 1985, concurred, but mused: 'whose wonderfulness is it?' (Kennedy 1985, n.p.). Pietsch reports that the primary lesson of this experience was an understanding of 'the importance of an introduction that clarifies what the editor did and what licence has been taken' in the text's presentation, a reflection on the need for a critical apparatus borne out in the presentation of *The Pale King* (Pietsch 2017c).

That book's introduction forthrightly sets out the unfinished nature of the work and its progress to publication. As we will see in Chapter 6, though, the absence of a scholarly apparatus gives a veneer of completion to the text that has led critics to read it as a more complete and unified expression of its author's intention than is the case. The textual status of a posthumous work is always in danger of being misunderstood, since the clarity of the published text, which has often been emended and polished to provide a smoother reading experience, implies the presence of a corresponding clarity and finality in the drafts from which it is drawn. The editor's involvement in such works can result in enduring contributions to their transmission.

Raymond Carver and David Foster Wallace: From Minimalism to maximalism

In *The Program Era*, Mark McGurl argues that 'postwar American fiction has been driven by a strong polarity of minimalist and maximalist compositional impulses', representing these impulses diagrammatically as poles between which particular works (and writers) swing (McGurl 2009, 377). Carver and Wallace have long been taken to exemplify the extremes of both poles and their most celebrated works as high water marks of particular literary-historical movements. Wallace began writing at a time when Carver's stature within the US literary scene was immense: in 1983, a year before Wallace published his first story in the *Amherst Review*, Carver's third major press collection *Cathedral* was nominated for a Pulitzer Prize and the author received a Mildred and Harold Strauss Living Award that allowed him to resign from his teaching post at Syracuse University. By the time of Carver's untimely death from cancer in August 1988, obituaries were carried in the *New York Times* as well as hundreds of other newspapers in the United States and beyond; in the *Sunday Times*, Peter

Kemp famously declared him to be 'The American Chekhov' (Sklenicka 2009b, 481; Kemp 1988, 1).

During the early 1980s, Carver's fiction found overwhelmingly rapid critical and commercial success as well as a well-documented critical backlash. While the success of *What We Talk About When We Talk About Love* (hereafter *WWTA*) upon its publication in April 1981 was immediate and its importance immediately recognized by its author's contemporaries (Jayne Anne Phillips termed the stories 'fables for the decade' in the 20 April 1981 issue of *New York* magazine), dissenting voices were immediately raised (Sklenicka 2009b, 370). Judith Chettle, for example, reviewing the collection in the *National Review*, complained that 'Carver's litany of the ills of Middle America is so unremitting that the reader becomes increasingly incredulous. His spare style, where what is omitted is as significant as what remains, only heightens this impression of a human wasteland' (Chettle 1981, 1503). James Atlas, meanwhile, writing in the *Atlantic Monthly*, complained that Carver's 'lacklustre manner and eschewal of feeling become tiresome' (Atlas 1981, 91). Atlas, whose review ran under the title 'Less Is Less', was among the many critics who identified the stylistic economy and 'minimality' of the author's methods as, for better or worse, the crucial element in the collection (Robert Houston approvingly noted the 'relentlessly minimal' description), and he suggested that the resulting stories felt 'thin' and 'diminished' (Atlas 1981, 96; Houston 1981, 23). Anatole Broyard's review foreshadowed another soon-to-be-common critical move as he saw the collection as representative of much of what was wrong with 'current fiction', accusing the stories of 'a sententious ambiguity that leaves the reader holding the bag' (Broyard 1981, n.p.). The term 'Minimalism' was on its way into the currency of US literary critical discourse, and many were already using it pejoratively to denote a style deliberately limited not only in stylistic range but also in emotional and philosophical scope.

Carver's widow Tess Gallagher would later lament the impact of these early reviews and their influence upon Carver's critical legacy: 'The term [Minimalist] was invented to describe [*WWTA*], and it was not a compliment [. . .] it was as though the clock stopped in April 1981.' She notes the regularity with which Carver 'adamantly' rejected the label in his public appearances[25] and

[25] In the Winter 1988 issue of the *Michigan Quarterly Review*, for example, he declared: '"Minimalism" vs. "Maximalism". Who cares finally what they want to call the stories we write? (And who isn't tired to death now of that stale debate?)' (Carver 1988, 711). Similar protests can be found throughout his 1980s interviews (Carver 1990, 80, 126, 153, 184–5).

how the 'Minimalist' label has 'shaped the expectations of students, teachers, and general readers around the world' (Kelley 2009, 5). Despite the regularity with which Carver and others such as Amy Hempel would refute the label,[26] the association would be a lasting one: Cynthia Hallett notes that 'Carver has become the quintessential referent for minimalism' (Hallett 1999, 9). James Dishon McDermott notes that while the word 'minimalism' had been used in a 'scattered' fashion in literary criticism from the 1960s onwards (following its prominent appearance in critical discourses around music, painting and sculpture in the same period), 'the term came into widespread use only with the advent of Carver's fiction' (McDermott 2006, 13).[27] The problem for Carver was not just the critical reception of his own stories, but their importance as models for others. The stories would, in William Stull and Maureen P. Carroll's words, 'cut the pattern for minimalist fiction' (Stull and Carroll 2006). The author's enormous and rapid influence on contemporary writers was soon noted (Houston's review contains the claim that Carver's approach was being imitated by student writers even before *WWTA*), and from then on critics would rarely discuss Carver's career without emphasizing his importance for younger writers. The word 'Carveresque', used as a synonym for 'Minimalist', soon became a critical commonplace: in 1986, for example, John Barth wrote an essay entitled 'A Few Words About Minimalism' in which he mentioned Carver by name several times (coining, in the process, the playful label 'post-Vietnam, post-literary, postmodernist blue-collar neo-early-Hemingwayism' (n.p.)). Nick Hornby claims that 'in the few years before he died, Carver's influence was quite extraordinary' (Hornby 1992, 30); in 1987, an interviewer told Carver that 'some literary editors claim that nearly half of the short fiction they receive seems imitative of your style' (Carver 1990, 208).

Carver's work was at the centre of the national literary conversation during the 1980s and was the subject of frequently passionate debate by critics and fellow fiction writers. One of these writers, a young Wallace, weighed in on the debate

[26] Charles May notes that the word is 'one of those disreputable literary terms that one dare not use without placing it within quotation marks or prefacing it with "so-called". Everyone who was ever accused of being it has denied; everyone who ever applied it has apologized' (May and Hallett 1999, ix).

[27] McDermott distinguishes between 'an upper-cased "Minimalism"' used to describe the particular school of 1980s fiction and a more broadly applicable, lower-cased 'literary minimalism' that can be understood as, among other things, 'a shared stylistic practice centering upon absence' (McDermott 2006, 2). I follow McDermott in using the upper-cased word to indicate the school of writing associated with the Carveresque short story: in quotations, however, I have preserved the original letter case.

in his first published critical essay, 'Fictional Futures and the Conspicuously Young', which appeared in the *Review of Contemporary Fiction* in 1988.[28] The essay, which appeared shortly after Carver's death, mentions the elder writer's name three times and, while not explicitly criticizing his work, makes clear Wallace's disdain for the literary lineage it has engendered. Wallace identifies Carver as a central figure behind one of what he calls the 'three dreary camps' of contemporary literary production:

> Catatonic Realism, a.k.a. Ultraminimalism, a.k.a. Bad Carver, in which suburbs are wastelands, adults automata, and narrators blank perceptual engines, intoning in run-on monosyllables the artificial ingredients of breakfast cereal and the new human non-soul. (Wallace 2012a, 40)

'Ultraminimalism', Wallace goes on to argue (in a thesis later to be refined in 'E Unibus Pluram'), is defined by a simplistic opposition to 'the aesthetic norms of mass entertainment', and its 'deliberately flat' surfaces place it at 'an emotional remove of light-years' from its subject (Wallace 2012a, 47–8). Like metafiction, he writes, the form is a closed and doomed system: both are 'simple engines of self-reference'. Wallace suggests that the limits within which Minimalism operates are too suffocating to allow for continuing artistic achievement: both of the aforementioned forms are 'primitive, crude, and seem already to have reached the Clang-Bird-esque horizon of their own possibility' (Wallace 2012a, 65).[29]

Wallace's criticisms here are not unique, since Minimalist writing was repeatedly attacked for the narrowness of its vision and the political and moral apathy implied in its stylistic method.[30] Nor is his terminology original: in a 1985 essay entitled 'Shooting for Smallness: Limits and Values in Some Recent American Fiction' (later collected in his 1987 book *Middle Grounds: Studies in*

[28] Wallace's first novel *The Broom of the System* (hereafter *Broom*) had been published the year before; his debut collection *Girl With Curious Hair* would, after legal delays, appear the following September.

[29] Harold Bloom pronounced a similar judgement in the introduction to the Carver instalment of his series *Bloom's Major Short Story Writers* (2002), suggesting 'that Carver was a master within the limits he imposed upon himself' (Bloom 2002, 10) while professing an 'imperfect sympathy' for the author's stories.

[30] Ayala Amir usefully enumerates these criticisms in a review of Lish's 2010 *Collected Fictions*, noting that the Minimalist narrative voice has been 'accused of [. . .] emotional bareness, narcissism, lack of commitment to the society he/she lives in, and of duplicating and maintaining the alienation and reification of the individual in the capitalist way of life' (Amir 2012, 5). John Biguenet's (1985) essay 'Notes of a Disaffected Reader: The Origins of Minimalism' encapsulates several such charges, arguing that the 'impossibly constricted' worlds presented in Minimalist fiction denote a fundamentally 'asocial self' (Biguenet 1985, 40–5).

Contemporary American Fiction) critic Alan Wilde had described Carver, Ann Beattie and others as 'catatonic realists' and suggested that their mode of writing is limited by the way in which it 'assume[s] the pointlessness of any action whatever' (Wilde 1985, 351–3).[31] Wallace's comments, though, coming as they did in a lengthy polemical essay in which he articulated his critical ideas publicly for the first time, indicate both the omnipresence of the Minimalist model during the years in which he was first publishing and the fact that he saw Minimalism as the dominant literary form against which he would assert his writerly identity.[32] Wallace's draft of *Broom*, in fact, contained a pun on Carver's name which he cut on the advice of his then-editor Gerald Howard (Max 2012a, 68; Howard 1986).[33] Wallace appears to have felt this influence even after Carver's death. In his 1990 review of David Markson's *Wittgenstein's Mistress* he was moved 'to deplore its [the novel's] relative neglect & its consignment by journals like the *NYTBR* to smarmy review by an ignorant Carverian' (Wallace 2012a, 79);[34] and in 'E Unibus Pluram' (published in the summer of 1993, again in the *RCF*) he again decried 'the self-conscious catatonia of a platoon of Raymond Carver wannabes' (Wallace 2010, 64).

Wallace devoted much of his early career energy to the attempt to define and move beyond the limits of the models, variously defined as 'Minimalism', 'New Realism', and 'Neorealism', that took Carver as a reference point. Wallace's descriptions of his years in Arizona ('a highly, incredibly hard-assed realist school') tend to emphasize his alienation from these models, and a moment of self-analysis in his much-cited interview with Larry McCaffery ('I seem to like to put myself in positions where I get to be the rebel [. . .] I *chose* to go there') suggests that he deliberately attended a writing program in which his

31 In the aforementioned 1987 issue of *Michigan Quarterly Review*, incidentally, T. C. Boyle claimed the term for himself, in a clear reference to Carver's story 'Feathers' (which was first published in *The Atlantic* in September 1982 and included in *Cathedral* in 1983):

> Actually, contemporary North American fiction is too much of one thing – the safe, minimalist/realist story purveyed by a group I like to call the 'Catatonic Realists.' (You know the story, you've read it a thousand times: Three characters are sitting around the kitchen of a trailer, saying folksy things to one another. Finally one of them gets up to go to the bathroom and the author steps in to end it with a line like 'It was all feathers'). (Boyle 1988, 707)

32 Nick Levey notes that one of the earliest mentions of the word 'maximalism' in literary criticism comes in 1984, closely following the ascendance of Minimalism (Levey 2016, 3).

33 The pun involved the names of Carver and Max Apple (whose 1986 novel *The Propheteers* Wallace mentions in 'E Unibus Pluram' as one of several examples of fiction that treats 'the pop as its own reservoir of mythopeia' (Wallace 1993, 168–9)). Howard advised him that this pun was '"too cute and you'll be picked on for it. Drop it"' (Max 2012a, 68; Howard 1986).

34 A footnote here dismissively identified said Carverian as 'Amy Hempel, minimalist ordinaire' (Wallace 2012a, 79).

own sympathies with a more linguistically effusive tradition of postmodern fiction would place him in a continually oppositional stance (Lipsky 2010, 47; Wallace 2012d, 47, italics in original).[35] A short story collection was clearly the ideal venue in which to mount a critique of Minimalism, and *Girl with Curious Hair* is frequently analysed in terms of its engagement with Minimalist stylistics. Both Marshall Boswell and Kasia Boddy suggest, by way of example, that the 2-page 'Everything Is Green' is a clear 'critique of the minimalist mode' (Boswell 2003, 100), mimicking both the form and content of the Carveresque story in its trailer-park setting and use of sentences that 'read like a parody of monosyllabic minimalism'.[36] The clearest references to Minimalism come in 'Westward the Course of Empire Takes its Way', which unites fictional practice and theoretical polemics in a complicated critical engagement. The word 'minimal' echoes ambiguously through the story's dialogue, as D. L. uses it to criticize Mark's unresponsiveness and later declares 'I detest any and all kinds of minimalism' (Wallace 1997a, 251, 305).[37] 'Westward' goes on to provide a critique that closely resembles the description of 'Ultraminimalism' in Wallace's (1987) essay:

> It diverges, in its slowness, from the really real only in its extreme economy, its Prussian contempt for leisure, its obsession with the confining limitations of its own space, its grim proximity to its own horizon. It's some of the most heartbreaking stuff available at any fine bookseller's anywhere. I'd check it out. (Wallace 1997a, 267)

Wallace's assessment of the mode is highly ambiguous, mixing approval with scorn and highlighting once again the limitations and stultifying horizon of the Minimalist project. Implicit in the story is the promise as well as the attempt to move beyond these limits.

35 Boswell notes the 'prevailing ethos of Raymond-Carver realism' in Wallace's Arizona classrooms, while Max describes the resistance that his experimental stories met as a result (Boswell 2012a, 264; Max 2012a, 60–2).

36 Boddy argues that 'Everything Is Green' represents an attempt to both inhabit and parody the world of 'Carver's men', critiquing the world of the Minimal story while simultaneously exploring the problem of solipsistic failure of connection that is 'one of Wallace's most enduring and deeply felt preoccupations' (Boddy 2010, 33). A number of critics have found evidence of this stance within Wallace's early work. David Coughlan and Dan Tysdal find deliberate rewritings of Carver's stories in 'Church Not Made With Hands' and 'A Radically Condensed History of Postindustrial Life', respectively (Coughlan 2015, 164–5; Tysdal 2003, 66–83).

37 In addition, the lengthy 'Really Blatant and Intrusive Interruption' that disrupts the narrative refers to 'the Resurrection of Realism, the pained product of inglorious minimalist labour in countless obscure graduate writing workshops across the U.S. of A' (Wallace 1997a, 265).

Beyond the Minimal Mambo: The return of maximalism

Infinite Jest, of course, identifies and critiques the limits of the Minimalist method in both its form and content. As early as 1996, Tom LeClair remarked on the way the novel could be read as an allegory of its generation's 'aesthetic orphanhood' and as a continuation of its author's public critique of contemporary fiction (LeClair 1996, 33). Boddy and others have pointed out the novel's clearest moments of critique, such as the 'Minimal Mambo' performed by the dancers at Molly Notkin's party (Wallace 2006, 229; Boddy 2010, 31; Jacobs 2003, 25–6). The recurrence of the word 'catatonic' in various settings in the novel also suggests the evasive blankness Wallace perceived in the Minimalists' prose.[38] Formally, the novel represents – if by its size alone – the most enduring riposte to the ideal of the well-made Minimalist story. Andrew Hoberek argues that the novel's copious endnotes, in their relentless drive towards inclusion and their 'explicit awkwardness', constitute the clearest possible counterweight to the 'Hemingwayesque exclusion', plain-voiced inarticulacy and self-contained craft of Minimalist prose (Hoberek 2013, 213). Hoberek argues convincingly that Wallace's development was inextricably linked with Minimalism, suggesting that the overwhelming reach of the mode within the American literary world acted as a set of boundaries that the writer could usefully transgress and that Wallace 'takes a kind of pure joy in the violation of the proprieties laid down by minimalist practice and pedagogy' (Hoberek 2013, 214). Noting Stephen Burn's complaint that critics often situate Wallace's work in relation to 'a strawman postmodernism' (Burn 2011, 467) and that the writer's much-discussed engagement with the work of the metafictionalists of the 1960s demands a more complex assessment,[39] Hoberek writes that the many elements that Wallace ostentatiously adopts from 'encyclopedic postmodernism' strongly suggest 'that he turns *to* postmodernism in reaction *against* minimalism' (Hoberek 2013, 215, emphasis in original).

[38] James Incandenza is described as 'so blankly and irretrievably hidden that Orin said he'd come to see him as like autistic, almost catatonic' – while the summary of Incandenza's film 'Low-Temperature Civics', with its reference to an 'irreversibly catatonic' father-figure, hints at a link between the death-in-life state caused by the novel's Entertainment and the self-effacing, apathetic posture of the Minimalist narrator (Wallace 2006, 737, 991).

[39] Tore Rye Anderson and Mark Sheridan have examined the ways in which Wallace's work contains significant and often-overlooked continuities with writers like Nabokov, Pynchon and Barth (Andersen 2014a, 7–24; Sheridan 2015, 78–93).

Hoberek takes Wallace's 'renewed maximalism' to be emblematic of a larger literary-historical transition in which the pendulum of American narrative style swung decisively away from Minimalism:

> Wallace's work, and *Infinite Jest* in particular, reside at the tipping point of a major shift not in experimental fiction but in realism: from the small-scale domestic dramas of Carveresque minimalism to a revival of the large-scale, sprawling, multicharacter novel. (Hoberek 2013, 212, 224)

Wallace's work is taken here not just as catalyst but exemplar, a magnetic force pulling an entire generation of writers towards a more expansive and ambitious mode of literary expression as well as an ur-maximalist text representing the most noteworthy iteration of that mode. Wallace's contemporaries have testified to just such an influence, with several noting that his work represented a permission slip to transgress the boundaries drawn by Minimalism.[40] Writing about *Infinite Jest* as the novel's twentieth anniversary approached, Christian Lorentzen recalled that 'writers took to it like Marines sprung from a sort of literary boot camp, hunting for something beyond the minimalist vogue of the 1980s' (Lorentzen 2015, n.p.).

The return of Pynchonian maximalism would generate its own critical backlash, the most famous expression of which came in the form of James Wood's pair of critical broadsides after the turn of the millennium.[41] In the years since Wood made these arguments, though, the maximalist novel has flourished in both commercial and critical terms: examples are too numerous to list, but two award-winning novels from 2013, Eleanor Catton's *The Luminaries* and Donna Tartt's *The Goldfinch*, serve as notable iterations of the mode. In 2010 (the year in which Joshua Cohen's *Witz* and Adam Levin's *The Instructions* were both published), Garth Risk Hallberg asked, in an essay published in *The Millions*, 'Is Big Back?'; in May 2015, a *Vulture* article dubbed 2015 'The Year of the Very Long Novel' (citing Hallberg's 944-page *City on Fire* as one of its examples) and again returned to *Infinite Jest* as a precursor, claiming that 'Wallace's magnum opus was both the bellwether of VLNs [Very Long Novels] and a case study in how to

40 Among those who have done so are Dana Spiotta (Max 2012b) and Rick Moody, who claims that he was 'somewhat reviled in writing workshops for not being able to write blunt little sentences about working-class life in the pacific Northwest' and found in Wallace's work an alternative model (Silverblatt 2011).

41 Wood did not use the word 'maximal' in his essays for the *New Republic* and the *Guardian* – famously coining, instead, the phrase 'hysterical realism' – but his criticism of the relentless urge towards abundance and 'profusion' in the contemporary novel centred on the way its hyperabundant narratives and 'perpetual motion' supposedly masked a 'fear of silence' (Wood 2001, n.p.).

sell them' (Hallberg 2010, n.p.). The piece contained quotes from several editors, including Hachette Book Group CEO Michael Pietsch, who suggested that 'the promise of a book remains a unique pleasure in contrast to thumbing through 800,000 Instagrams. The idea that one mind has created this world for you is a unique and perhaps even more compelling experience to us now' (Kachka 2015, n.p.). The author noted the fact that Pietsch had edited *The Goldfinch* as well as *Infinite Jest*: the editor's attribution of books such as these to a singular creator ('one mind'), in deflecting attention from his own contribution, represents a characteristically self-effacing editorial stance.

'An artist, not a minimalist': Wallace on Carver

The critical and commercial developments of the previous decades have often served to situate Carver and Wallace at opposite ends of the literary spectrum, and there are several obvious ways in which the two writers differ. At a biographical level, the backgrounds of the two men present stark contrasts, with class and generation being the most notable markers of difference. Carver's background, as is well known, was decidedly blue collar: in his essay 'My Father's Life', Carver describes his parents' sometimes precarious existence, mentions the fact that his father worked as a labourer on the Grand Coulee Dam in Washington during the 1930s and refers to the shame of having a toilet that was 'the last outdoor one in the neighbourhood' (Carver 2009, 721). He was the first member of his family to go to college and even then, as McGurl notes, his 'social ascent through education was a protracted patching together of college credits over the course of several years while he worked and raised two children' (McGurl 2009, 299). Wallace, by contrast, as the precociously talented son of two university professors, had an educational ascent that not only was steady (being broken only by his periods of illness) but also had the auxiliary benefit of helping him to produce a published novel before his 25th birthday. His family was an intellectually active one in which grammatical mistakes would be discussed over dinner and memos would be exchanged to detail parental injustices (Max 2012a, 2–6). Carver's father sometimes mispronounced the words he knew (Sklenicka 2009b, 16); Wallace claimed to remember his father reading the 'unexpurgated' *Moby-Dick* to him and his sister when Wallace was five (Lipsky 2010, 49). While there is surely some retrospective self-mythologizing involved here – Carver's brother emphasizes that the family were not 'deprived' as children and Max suspects the

Moby-Dick story of being apocryphal (Sklenicka 2009b, 13; Max 2012a, 3) – the contrast between the writers' upbringing is beyond doubt. These backgrounds also help to explain the differences in their literary personae. Carver was, as Stull and Carroll note, 'no literary theorist' (Kelley 2009, 8) and his interviews and essays show him discussing literature in language of deliberate (albeit nuanced) simplicity. Wallace, on the other hand, was 'nothing if not extremely well versed in the dominant critical debates of his era', showing a remarkable degree of explicit engagement with theoretical and intellectual discourse in both his fiction and non-fiction writings (Cohen and Konstantinou 2012, xv).

The critical placement of Carver and Wallace as opposites, therefore, is understandable. It arguably obscures important affinities between the two writers, though. There is biographical evidence to suggest Wallace's admiration for Carver. When in Syracuse in 1992, according to Max, Wallace – accompanied by Jonathan Franzen and Mark Costello – drove to visit the street on which Carver had lived while teaching at the university there in the 1980s (Max 2012a, 166). Wallace, as Max notes, 'admired Raymond Carver, whom he distinguished from his minimalist acolytes. He was a man who had outrun alcohol in moving from a deflected style to a more sincere one, and Wallace doubtless saw the relevance to his own story' (Max 2012a, 317 note 27). Two books from Wallace's library show the author's clear engagement with Carver's work. His copy of *WWTA* is heavily annotated in at least two different pens, and it is likely that he used this in his teaching. Wallace also annotated Carver's stories 'Cathedral' and 'A Small, Good Thing' in his copy of the X. J. Kennedy-edited anthology *Literature: An Introduction to Fiction, Poetry, and Drama* (5th edn), chapter 10 of which is partly devoted to Carver's work. I will discuss some of these annotations in detail later, during my analysis of specific Carver stories, in order to show Wallace's engagement with the Minimalist narrative method and examine how this method was affected by the editorial process behind the stories.

Max's linking of addiction and sincerity points to an important and rarely observed similarity between the writers: both men regarded their struggles with addiction as central to their literary achievements and wrote this struggle into their work as a structural and thematic principle. At a thematic level, Carver's multitude of alcoholic narrators has been widely remarked upon, and several stories explicitly depict the process of recovery from alcoholism (his story 'Where I'm Calling From', for example, published in *Cathedral* in 1983, is set in an alcohol rehabilitation centre). Long sections of *Infinite Jest* follow the fortunes of a group of characters living in a recovery and treatment centre and portray the workings of AA in detail. Apart from the explicit diegetic treatment of addiction, some structural and stylistic features – such as the lengthy monologues spoken by recovering addicts in Wallace's novel – also clearly owe a debt to the demands of the rehabilitative process. As Max suggests, the psychological struggles involved in overcoming addiction could be seen as an important factor in the attempt by both writers to evolve a more sincere and humane style. Explorations of spirituality and post-religious faith could, in both writers' work, be linked to the recovery process: the narrator of 'Where I'm Calling From' spends Christmas in a halfway house, for example, and the importance of envisioning a 'higher power' in *Infinite Jest* is explicitly framed in the context of recovery from addiction (Carver 2009, 461–6; Wallace 2006, 366).[42] This explicit engagement with spiritual traditions is more evident when we examine the unedited manuscripts of both writers, as I will argue later in relation to Carver's story 'If It Please You' and sections of Wallace's *The Pale King*. Stull and Carroll note that 'in contrast to the ironic, self-reflexive "post-realist" experimental writers of the 1960s with whom he came of age, Carver followed Tolstoy in prizing something that sounds naïve but is fundamental: sincerity' (Kelley 2009, 1). Wallace was, of course, reacting partly to the legacy of the very same experimental writers,[43] and sincerity has long been understood as a key concern of his writing (Kelly 2014b). I will return to these thematic affinities later; for now, though, it is enough to note that their shared experiences and concerns illustrate that Wallace's attitude towards Carver was never a straightforwardly oppositional one.

It is notable that Wallace, as Max mentions, frequently went out of his way to exempt Carver from his attacks on Minimalism, training his critical sights on 'Bad Carver' and 'Carver wannabes' rather than on the writer himself. In 1997, Wallace referred specifically to the ending of 'So Much Water So Close to Home' as one of the exceptions to the 'set of formal schticks' that Minimalism became (Wallace 2000b). In two separate interviews, Wallace used the word 'genius' to describe Carver. In a conversation with Michael Silverblatt in 2000, in the context of a discussion on the way the notion of 'genius' has changed over the decades, he stated: 'I would say that Carver's a genius, but his persona was

42 In recent years, critics have increasingly begun to pay attention to Wallace's engagement with religious themes. I refer to several of these in my discussion of unpublished scenes from *The Pale King* in Chapter 6.

43 Wallace also discussed Tolstoy in interviews (e.g. with Kennedy and Polk, McCaffery and Lipsky (Wallace 2012d, 18, 26, 50; Lipsky 2010, 37–8)) and his library contains two separate annotated copies of Tolstoy's 'The Death of Ivan Ilych'. For an analysis of Wallace's engagement with this story, and with Tolstoy and Russian literature more broadly, see L. Thompson (2016).

anti-genius' (Wallace 2000b). Wallace had also used the word earlier in the course of his interview with McCaffery during his most explicit recorded discussion of Carver and his legacy, one important enough to be worth reproducing at length here. At one point in the conversation, Wallace complains that in his writing he never seems 'to get the kind of clarity and concision I want'. McCaffery replies by noting that 'Ray Carver comes immediately to mind in terms of compression and clarity, and he's obviously someone who wound up having a huge influence on your generation.' Wallace responds by framing Minimalism – again – as the obverse of metafiction and as one of two contrasting (and failed) responses to the problem of the author's problematic position within the text:

> Minimalism's just the other side of metafictional recursion. The basic problem's still the one of the mediating narrative consciousness. Both minimalism and metafiction try to resolve the problem in radical ways. Opposed, but both so extreme they end up empty. Recursive metafiction worships the narrative consciousness, makes 'it' the subject of the text. Minimalism's even worse, emptier, because it's a fraud: it eschews not only self-reference but any narrative personality at all, tries to pretend there 'is' no narrative consciousness in its text.

When McCaffery objects that this fails to accurately characterize Carver's work, in which 'his narrative voice is nearly always insistently *there*, like Hemingway's' (emphasis in original), Wallace replies at length:

> I was talking about minimalists, not Carver. Carver was an artist, not a minimalist. Even though he's supposedly the inventor of modern U.S. minimalism. 'Schools' of fiction are for crank-turners. The founder of a movement is never part of a movement. Carver uses all the techniques and anti-styles that critics call 'minimalist', but his case is like Joyce, or Nabokov, or early Barth and Coover – he's using formal innovation in the service of an original vision. Carver invented – or resurrected, if you want to cite Hemingway – the techniques of minimalism in the services of rendering a world he saw that nobody'd seen before. It's a grim world, exhausted and empty and full of mute, beaten people, but the minimalist techniques Carver employed were perfect for it: they created it. And minimalism for Carver wasn't some rigid aesthetic program he adhered to for its own sake. Carver's commitment was to his stories, each of them. And when minimalism didn't serve them, he blew it off. If he realized a story would be best served by expansion, not ablation, he'd expand, like he did to 'The Bath', which he later turned into a vastly superior story. He just chased the click. But at some point his 'minimalist' style caught on. A movement was born, proclaimed, promulgated by the critics. Now here come the crank-turners. What's especially

> dangerous about Carver's techniques is that they seem so easy to imitate. It doesn't seem like every word and line and draft has been bled over. That's part of his genius. It looks like you can write a minimalist piece without much bleeding. And you can. But not a good one. (Wallace 2012d, 45–6)

This lengthy consideration of Carver's artistic importance and of the way in which literary influence operates is revealing and, in the light of subsequent evidence, highly problematic. The 'vastly superior story' Wallace alludes to here is 'A Small, Good Thing', published in 1983 as part of *Cathedral* (two years after the appearance of 'The Bath'). The explanation of the story's textual genesis that Wallace gives here is one that was accepted by contemporary scholars, based on explanations given by Carver himself. In 1984, for example, Carver claimed that:

> I went back to that one, as well as several others, because I felt there was unfinished business that needed attending to. The story hadn't been told originally; it had been messed about with, condensed and compressed in 'The Bath' to highlight the qualities of menace that I wanted to emphasize – you see this with the business about the baker, the phone call, with its menacing voice on the other line, the bath, and so on. But I still felt there was unfinished business, so in the midst of writing these other stories for Cathedral I went back to 'The Bath' and tried to see what aspects of it needed to be enhanced, redrawn, reimagined. When I was done, I was amazed because it seemed so much better. I've had people tell me that they much prefer 'The Bath', which is fine, but 'A Small, Good, Thing' seems to me to be a better story. (Carver 1990, 102)

For many years, critics accepted Carver's claims that the chronology of the story's publication reflected that of its composition, and that the alternate versions of some of the stories in *WWTA* published after 1981 were revisions of ones whose potential he himself had failed to realize. We now know that these claims were not only incorrect but were in fact deliberate fictions constructed in response to the extensive editorial activity of Lish, and that Lish's interventions were central in determining our understanding of what would come to be called a 'Carveresque' story.

Wallace's discussion in 1993 of Carver's technique reads in hindsight as significantly more complicated and layered than it appeared at the time. He discusses Carver's 'minimalist techniques' in the assumption that the author was always responsible for those techniques; he refers to Carver's 'expansion' of a story that the author had in actuality restored to its original length; and he distinguishes between Carver and the legion of subsequent 'crank-turners' unaware that in Carver's case, as well as others, Lish was the one turning the crank. Wallace's identification of the 'original vision' behind Carver's 'formal innovation' becomes problematic when seen in this light and suggests a need to return to critical evaluations of Carver as well as to our understanding of Minimalism. Wallace's words also point to a fundamental tension between the persistent notion of individual artistic vision and the opening up of the text that has been a central aim of much twentieth-century literary theory: the use of the terms 'original vision' and 'genius' sits uneasily alongside his nods to reader-response theory and 'Barthian and Derridean poststructuralism' elsewhere in the same interview (Wallace 2012d, 40). The deconstruction of traditional paradigms of literary authorship found in the work of Roland Barthes, Michel Foucault and others has, as several critics have noted, left an ambiguous legacy for literary criticism. Critical theory has, it seems, irrevocably opened textual criticism to an understanding of the reader's role in producing meaning and to the plurality of possible readings available in any given text. It has also, though, as I have noted, retained the figure of an author at a submerged theoretical level as well returning to it in practice, and the author's 'disappearance' has failed to translate into the kind of widespread paradigm shift in the circulation of meaning prophesied by Foucault (Burke 2008, 165–9).

Both Carver and Wallace were aware of the tensions between the supposed absence of the authorial subject and their own artistic practice, and both showed a suspicion of the notion of the 'death of the author' that paralleled the growing critical resistance to the idea during the 1980s. Carver, as I will show in my final chapter, expressed his hostility to poststructuralist thinking and famously argued in one of his essays for 'the writer's particular and unmistakable signature on everything he writes' (a statement whose context I return to in detail in Chapter 4) (Carver 1990, 160, 2009, 728). Wallace, for his part, was not just receptive to poststructuralist ideas, but was (as several critics have shown) deeply marked by them.[44] He also put on record his deep ambivalence to the 'death of the author' trope, though: in 'Greatly Exaggerated', his review of H.L. Hix's *Morte d'Author: An Autopsy*, he affirms the importance of Barthes and Derrida while siding cautiously with the pro-life camp.[45] Both writers ultimately

[44] Derrida, De Man and Deleuze are among the many philosophers and theorists whose influence has been detected in Wallace's work (Kelly 2015, 50–2).

[45] Marginal notes in Wallace's copy of *Morte d'Author* suggest that he was fascinated by arguments on both sides of the debate, writing an approving comment beside both Barthes's statement that 'the modern scriptor is born simultaneously with the text' ('*cool*') and underlining Milton's contradictory declaration that 'a good book is the precious lifeblood of a master spirit'.

embraced a communicative model of writing in which the author's presence is a structuring element in the reader's experience. Carver's longer stories – as we can see more clearly in many of the unedited manuscripts – consistently valorize the attempt at emotional connection, enacting this attempt in their movement towards affective exchange. According to Lee Konstantinou, Wallace 'constructs his fictions around a drama of unfulfilled communication' and employs a meticulously deployed array of formal strategies in order to pave the way for the return of the author; Clare Hayes-Brady suggests that 'communicative exchange with the reader is the cornerstone of Wallace's artistic progression beyond the limits of postmodernism'; and Hering suggests that Wallace' fiction is characterized by 'a fixation on the author's dialogic relationship with the reader' (Konstantinou 2016, 168–9, 193–8; Hayes-Brady 2016, 63; Hering 2016a, 17).

Despite Wallace's placement of Carver into the category of solitary 'genius', he was highly aware of the importance of the social networks behind the production of art. The description of Minimalism he provides in 'Westward' goes on to mention Carver's editor by name as he laments 'the Resurrection of Realism, the pained product of inglorious minimalist labour in countless obscure graduate writing workshops across the U.S. of A., and called by Field Marshal Lish (who ought to know) the *New* Realism' (Wallace 1997a, 265).[46] While Wallace wrote these words without knowing the extent of Lish's direct influence on Carver's work, he was clearly cognizant of the editor's central position in the U.S. literary landscape. As he makes clear both here and in the aforementioned essays, Wallace gave much thought to the institutions and forces helping to shape American fiction during the 1980s, and his extended discussion in 'Fictional Futures' of the effect of MFA programs on contemporary writing echoes the concerns of several prominent critics (some of which were gathered in a special issue of the *Mississippi Review* in Winter 1985). Wallace's barb here reflects the fact that Lish was increasingly coming to be understood as a force in his own right. David Bellamy, for example, suggested in his 1985 essay 'A Downpour of Literary Republicanism' that Lish had become as important a literary player as the *New Yorker*, a one-man institution who had managed to exert 'vast influence' on the 'literary climate' (Bellamy 1985, 37–9). Lish's position was graphically mapped out in the 'Guide to the Literary Universe' presented in *Esquire*'s August

[46] The name is a reference to the unofficial title of 'Captain Fiction' that Lish earned while working at *Esquire* (Polsgrove 2001, 248); Amy Hempel's article of the same title in *Vanity Fair* in 1984 on Lish's fiction workshop helped to popularize the soubriquet. I will discuss Lish's background at greater length in subsequent chapters.

1987 issue, in which he was placed (along with Carver and Gary Fisketjon, who by that point was acting as Carver's editor) in the 'Red Hot Center'; Wallace was depicted, presciently, as being 'on the horizon' (Hills 1987). Lish's placement on the map reflected his influence at Knopf, and Wallace's reference to 'Field Marshal Lish' here reinforces the criticisms of the 'School of Lish' that Sven Birkerts had recently identified in his October 1986 essay of the same name.

Wallace, therefore, was aware of – and found it necessary to identify and critique – what Jerome McGann has called the 'aesthetic and literary horizon[s]' determining the production of literary fiction during the years in which he began publishing (McGann 2006, 72) while also operating within these horizons himself. Notes from papers belonging to Bonnie Nadell show that he asked his agent to send a story to Lish for possible publication in *the Quarterly*, Lish's newly founded literary journal (Wallace 1987b). Lish replied politely in the negative, citing a clash of schedules; he would not, he said, be able to publish Wallace's story 'Luckily the Account Representative Knew CPR' before December 1988, by which time *Girl With Curious Hair* was already scheduled to have appeared in print (Lish 1987). A note in the Lish archives, moreover, shows Wallace thanking Lish for his attention in a playfully cordial and complimentary tone (this reply appears to refer to a separate note from Lish):

> Dear Mr. Lish: Thanks for your nice note, and the even nicer note that crossed mine in the mail. I've asked my agent's assistant's secretary's receptionist's client-relations aide to petition a person of consequence to send you a much shorter story. Congratulations, by the way, on a really good magazine. (Wallace 29 Aug. 1987)

We can see this, perhaps, as a case of literary *realpolitik* – Wallace was, during these years, a young writer urgently trying to publish in several venues – but the notes also suggest that a straightforward division between Minimalist and maximalist camps is insufficient to account for the complex network of literary connections linking these writers and that Wallace's criticisms of Minimalism were, at least in part, tactical ones that allowed him to define his own aesthetic aims in opposition to the prevailing aesthetic configuration of the time.

The figure of the editor, then, touches on enduring questions of authorship and literary influence, complicating notions of individual authorship and posing challenges for a critical tradition that has oscillated between intense focus on the author and an attempt to do away with the author-figure entirely. The role of the editor also demands attention from the various critical perspectives – from

McGann's emphasis on the textual horizons involved in editing, to genetic critics' focus on the movement of writing across tangible documents, to McGurl's influential arguments for the importance of understanding the institutional settings of post-war American fiction – that seek to enlarge literary criticism's horizons through close attention to social and material networks. Each of these approaches is attentive to what I refer to as textual process: namely, the whole range of observable procedures and processes, from initial authorial note-taking to collaborative revision to the creation of the printed book (and beyond), involved in bringing a text into being. My focus on editing processes seeks not just to recreate the historical moment of textual production, but to historicize the text itself by tracing the specifics of its material history and examining the way in which different – and sometimes competing – forces and agents have acted upon it. In the following chapters, I bring these critical methods to bear on the editing of Carver's and Wallace's fiction in the belief that these varied perspectives – theoretical and specific, individual and social, abstract and material – can illuminate one another. The mediating role of the editor – so often invisible and so easily ignored – is, I argue, inseparable from the development, form and reception of these works.

2

'My only fear is that it is too thin': The roots of the Carver controversy

In 2012, Colson Whitehead wrote a comic piece for the *New York Times* entitled 'How to Write'. Proposing that the 'the art of writing' could be reduced to 'a few simple rules', the piece presented a list of instructions for aspiring writers, one of which ordered them to 'be concise'. Referring to 'the famous author-editor interaction between Gordon Lish and Ray Carver', Whitehead describes how, 'with a few deft strokes', Lish pared down the ending of a (non-existent) story about a shark attack 'to create the now legendary ending: "Help – land shark!"', commenting dryly that this 'wasn't what Carver intended, but few could argue that it was not shorter' (Whitehead 2012).[1] Another short sketch published in *McSweeney's* later the same year imagined Raymond Carver's dating profile as edited by Lish, with predictably terse results (Chen 2012). And in a 2015 interview, Vivian Gornick reminisced about the process of working with *Paris Review* editor Lorin Stein, recalling Stein's extensive rearrangement of the material and her own frustration with the process: 'at one point I said to him, *We're not going to become Gordon Lish and Raymond Carver here*' (Gornick 2015, n.p., italics in original).

Gordon Lish's editing of Raymond Carver has, in the past two decades, gone from being an obscure literary rumour to a readily available archetype of editorial interference. Among admirers of both men's work, this has been a cause of frustration. David Winters laments the fact that Lish's association with Carver as well as a small number of former students such as Amy Hempel and David Leavitt 'still sets the terms, and the limits, of his reception'; Douglas Glover refers disparagingly to 'the Lish-Carver debate circus' and its tendency to preclude any

[1] The supposed 'original ending' parodies the way in which many of Carver's endings contain a note of sentiment: 'In the original last lines of the story, Nat, the salty old part-time insurance agent, reassures his young charge as they cling to the beer cooler: "We'll get help when we hit land. I'm sure of it. No more big waves, no more sharks. We'll be safe once again. We'll be home".'

broader assessment of Lish's work (Winters 2016, 144; Lucarelli 2013, n.p.). For the most part, however, Lish's advocates have accepted his by-now-inextricable link to Carver's stories. Don DeLillo's comment that Lish has written 'fascinating American fiction' while being 'famous for all the wrong reasons', which first appeared on the Jacket of Lish's 1993 novel *Zimzum*, commends his friend's authorial prowess while leading with an admission of his editorial infamy. The quote has been recycled by successive publishers, with both O/R Books and Little Island Press adopting it in their promotion of Lish's late-career burst of fiction. For the publication of Lish's collection *Goings* (2014), indeed, O/R created a Lish 'twitterbot', a (supposedly) algorithm-driven Twitter account dispensing merciless 140-character snippets of editorial advice: while it did not mention Carver by name, the marketing strategy clearly played upon Lish's reputation for ruthless editing. In the wider literary imagination, it is understood that the work produced by Carver and Lish's interaction is too significant to be dismissed: Lish represents, at the very least, a significant footnote to any assessment of Carver's career, while Carver threatens to dominate any conversation on Lish's achievements.

The work itself, though, is arguably obscured in this 'circus'. While Carver's *Beginners* (the unedited version of *What We Talk About When We Talk About Love* (*WWTA*)) occasioned a large amount of journalistic interest upon its publication in 2009 and allowed readers to examine the textual differences for themselves, there has been relatively little scholarly attention to the differences between the texts. In 2006, the editors of *Beginners* (and long-time Carver scholars) Stull and Carroll declared that the discovery of the extent of Lish's editing meant that the questions that must concern future Carver studies are epistemological in nature:

> Who was Raymond Carver and what did he write? To what degree do the stories attributed to him represent his original writing, his editor's alterations for publication purposes, or Carver's unconstrained intentions with respect to stories published in multiple versions? (Stull and Carroll 2006, 2–3)

The answers to these questions have been slow in coming. In the decade following Carver's death in 1988, his editing relationship with Lish was neither widely understood nor meaningfully debated. The public controversy would only begin with the publication of D. T. Max's *New York Times* exposé 'The Carver Chronicles' in August 1998, in which he concluded – following an examination of the Carver manuscripts in the Lish collection at the Lilly Library in Indiana – that Lish had 'changed some of the stories so much that they were more his than Carver's' (Max 1998, n.p.). Over the following years, critics and scholars began cautiously to integrate these findings into their appraisal of Carver's work, with A. O. Scott, for example, arguing that Lish's edits were 'entirely alien to Carver's sensibility' and Leypoldt maintaining that the differences between the versions of the author's stories were ones of degree rather than kind (Scott 1999, n.p.; Leypoldt 2002, 318). Over the subsequent decade, readers were provided with more empirical evidence for Lish's influence on Carver's early fiction; in December of 2007, the *New Yorker* published a transcript of the manuscript version of the volume's title story (originally titled 'Beginners') allowing readers to see the specific changes that Lish had made as well as excerpts from the correspondence between author and editor. This process culminated in 2009, when *Beginners* was published as part of the Library of America edition of Carver's *Collected Stories* in the United States and as a standalone volume by Jonathan Cape in the United Kingdom; these editions contain detailed information on the complicated textual history of the stories, many of which appeared multiple times – with minor textual variations and sometimes with different titles – in various magazines and literary journals both before and after the publication of *WWTA*.[2] The year 2009 also saw the publication of the first comprehensive biography of Carver, Carol Sklenicka's *Raymond Carver: A Writer's Life*.[3]

The almost simultaneous appearance of these publications occasioned a great deal of comment and analysis, much of it of a partisan nature. Critics were often divided on the ethics and value of Lish's edits; while some, like Stephen King, were scathing of his influence on Carver's work (he refers to the editor's 'baleful' influence on *WWTA* (King 2009, n.p.)), others argued that his interventions had improved the stories (Harvey 2010, n.p.; Martin 2009, n.p.). Critics were led inevitably to ask which of the textual versions (to borrow terms used by Paul Eggert in his discussion of Theodore Dreiser's *Sister Carrie*) 'had the higher authority', the 'authorized' text represented by *Beginners* or the 'socialized' one incarnated in *WWTA* (Eggert 2009, 192). However, the focus on *WWTA*, and the

[2] In September 2015, Vintage Books published the first standalone US print edition of *Beginners* along with a digital edition of the collection. This publication had been delayed by ongoing negotiations over the digital rights to Carver's work; following an agreement between Gallagher and Knopf, the bulk of the author's backlist was published digitally for the first time in May 2015. *Beginners* has, at the time of writing, been translated into 17 languages.

[3] Other less orthodox biographical projects published before this include Sam Halpert's *Raymond Carver: An Oral Biography* (1995), Stull and Carroll's *Remembering Ray: A Composite Biography of Raymond Carver* (1993, eds) and Maryann Burk Carver's *What It Used to Be Like: A Portrait of My Marriage to Raymond Carver* (2006).

emotive nature of response to the revelations, meant that key questions remained under-explored. The extent to which terms like 'Minimalism' and 'Dirty Realism' are intertwined with Carver's early work; the extent to which Lish's editing of Carver's early stories represented a departure from the author's own aesthetic; the way in which this editing reveals Lish's own aims and editing techniques and suggests a much wider pattern of literary influence traceable through him – all of these questions merit further investigation. These questions, I suggest, inevitably go beyond the stories in *WWTA* and have thus far come up against limitations on textual availability: the stories in Carver's first collection *Will You Please Be Quiet, Please?* (1976, hereafter referred to as *WYPBQP*) have not been published in unedited form, due to the greater complexity of their textual states and the less controversial circumstances of their publication, and little critical attention has been paid to them. In the following pages I trace the beginning of Lish and Carver's collaboration, showing that Lish's influence on Carver needs to be understood over a longer timescale than previously considered.

'Spare, austere, stately': The beginnings of Carver and Lish's collaboration

Carver and Lish's first meeting took place in the summer of 1968, shortly after the former's thirtieth birthday. He was introduced to Lish, who was four years older, by their mutual friend Curt Johnson who, as editor of *December* magazine, had just published Carver's 'WYPBQP' (Sklenicka 2009b, 147). Prior to their meeting, the men's names had already appeared in print, with the 1967 double issue of *December* carrying (as Sklenicka notes) 'two new lines on the masthead: Associate Editor Raymond Carver and Special Editor Gordon Lish' (Sklenicka 2009b, 145). They struck up an instant rapport, and according to Maryann Carver's recollection, the question of editing was immediately raised:

> Lish told Ray he had read 'Will You Please Be Quiet, Please?' He 'raved about the story. He was high on it', Maryann recounted. Then Lish told the others that if he had been editing the story, Ralph Wyman wouldn't have stayed with his wife. If he'd written it, Lish told them, the story would have had a different ending. 'And I just looked him right in the eye', Maryann said, 'and answered, "Well, that's just the point, Gordon. It isn't your story. You didn't write it"'. (Sklenicka 2009b, 147; Burk Carver 2006, 214)

This is a memory recalled at some distance, of course, and one that could be coloured by what came afterwards (as we shall see, Lish would later rewrite the ending of this very story). It is believable, though, when one takes into account Lish's well-known confidence and brashness of manner (he was by that stage already an experienced editor, having founded the journal *Genesis West* in 1962 and published fiction by Donald Barthelme, Grace Paley and Leonard Gardner, among others, within its pages), and it chimes with the urgent spirit of literary exchange visible in the men's correspondence during the subsequent years (Lish 2015, 202–3; Sklenicka 2009b, 149–50). Their friendship deepened the following year, after the Carver family's ill-fated trip to Israel had led to a period of restless travel. When Carver returned to his job at Science Research Associates in Palo Alto (where he had rented a room in order to write in isolation from his family on weeknights), the pair began to meet regularly and exchange ideas and plans, one of which was for a co-published magazine called *Journal of American Fiction* (Sklenicka 2009b, 147–78). They were united in their admiration for Leonard Gardner's boxing novel *Fat City*, and when Carver needed a photograph for a 1969 story anthology, Lish lent the writer a work-shirt like the one in Gardner's author picture and used his Polaroid to photograph him at Lish's dining table. When the anthology was published, Carver would refer in a letter to Lish to the photograph in which 'you immortalized me in your ole denim work shirt' (Sklenicka 2009b, 175; Lish 2015, 205). The photograph, reproduced in Sklenica's biography, serves as compelling evidence that Lish was, from the early days of their friendship, working as a kind of co-creator of Carver's literary image, in a very literal sense; the author not only poses for the editor here in a carefully staged image of masculine literary authority, but actually wears his editor's clothes.

A letter from the following year suggests Lish's developing conception of how the author could be presented to the world. In July 1971, Lish wrote an extravagant letter of recommendation to James Hall, the Provost at the University of California, Santa Cruz, where Carver was applying (ultimately without success) for a position teaching poetry. Lish wrote that 'the bulk of Ray's poems and stories are spare, austere, stately' and went on to say:

> But my guess is that Ray is by disposition a poet first and finally. He values the well-made thing, the ellipsis, and a shape of decisive beginning and end. He is indeed a carver, onomatologic notion intended. I therefore suppose Ray's more ambitious achievements will be in poetry – and since his concern for his art is

> so intense, there's every reason to suppose he'll make a most able and inspiring teacher for those who are similarly committed. (Lish 1971)[4]

Lish's valorization of Carver's poetry seems almost disingenuous here and is perhaps little more than a favour for a friend: the two rarely appear to have discussed poetry in their correspondence, and Lish seems to have had very little input into the author's poems. However, the letter provides an early example of the way in which Lish framed his advocacy of Carver, and there is a noteworthy correspondence between the language used here – 'spare', 'austere', 'ellipsis' – and the terms that would later become critical commonplaces in relation to Carver's work. It also suggests the way in which Carver's image would develop in subsequent years and shows how his name itself contributed conveniently to this image as a ruthless 'carver' of prose: we can surmise that when Wallace punned on Carver's name in the draft of his debut novel (as mentioned in Chapter 1), he was playing on the same 'onomatologic notion'.

Lish soon left California in frustration at his textbook-editing job and within months was installed as fiction editor at *Esquire* (Sklenicka 2009b, 175–7). He had been recommended to *Esquire*'s Rust Hills (by Hal Scharlatt, then editor-in-chief of E. P. Dutton) on the basis of his previous magazine editing (Lish 2015, 202–3). Based on a remarkable letter to editor Harold Hayes and an ensuing lunch with Hayes and Hills, Lish was employed with the nebulous but demanding mandate to find and publish what he describes as 'something hitherto unseen – the New Fiction' (Sklenicka 2009b, 176–7; Lish 2015, 205). Carver wrote to express his delight at the news and, apparently responding to Lish's request, added that he did have 'a few stories on hand, and I'm sending them along within the next day or two' (Carver 2007, 12 Nov. 1969). Correspondence from the following month shows that he was already accepting Lish's advice on his fiction as well as reassuring his friend that such advice was welcome. He declared that he would take some of Lish's suggestions and that: 'Everything considered, it's a better story now than when I first mailed it your way – which is the most important thing, I'm sure' (Max 1998, n.p.; Carver 1969c). It is not clear what story is referred to here, but another letter from the same month thanks Lish for 'the most careful look' he gave to 'Friendship', stating that Lish's 'intelligent observations' had made the piece 'a much better story' (Carver 1969b). This story would later be published in *WWTA* (following further edits by Lish) as 'Tell the Women We're

[4] Reprinted by permission of Gordon Lish.

Going'. It is clear, then, that the editing relationship between the pair had deep roots: Lish was, in December 1969, already helping to shape a story that would not appear within the covers of a book for another twelve years. Any account of Lish's influence on the stories in *WWTA*, therefore, needs to go beyond the edits he made in 1980 and acknowledge a longer and more complicated sequence of genetic development.

Lish's contributions to Carver's early stories show the development of both of their respective aesthetics during what were important years for both men. During these years Carver began to publish his stories regularly while Lish moved with rapid success into the world of literary publishing, with these two processes being at times closely interrelated. During the years between their early correspondence in 1969 and the publication of *WYPBQP* in March 1976 Lish not only gave advice on individual stories but began to act as a sort of unofficial agent for Carver. The interconnection of the men's professional and personal relationships cannot be easily separated from the textual exchange: in 1971, for example, Lish took the unusual step of asking Carver to gather information about Lish's ex-wife in San Francisco, and Sklenicka suggests that the editor's promise to try to sell Carver's writing in New York may have come in return for this favour (Sklenicka 2009b, 197, 520n68, 69; Lish 2015, 205). Lish submitted the writer's stories not only to his bosses but also to others within the publishing world, such as editorial staff at the magazines whose offices were located in the same building as his own. In one letter Carver referred to the possibility of showing 'Fat' to editors at *Cosmo* or *Mademoiselle*, while Burk Carver recalls that Lish helped to place stories in *Harper's* and *Playgirl* (Carver 1970a; Burk Carver 2006, 240–1). Throughout this time, Carver would regularly submit stories to Lish, and these would be returned with the editor's textual deletions, additions and rearrangements. Carver would often incorporate these changes into the next draft of the story. Only in some of these cases was Lish acting in an official capacity as editor: in practice, though, he fulfilled many of the same functions of the role, as the men's correspondence would subject the story to the processes of revision and rewriting.

'A milestone, a turning point': The development of 'Neighbors'

In August 1970, Carver sent Lish copies of two stories, one of which was called 'The Neighbors'. He expressed doubts about both the title and the content of the piece, asking Lish to let him know whether he saw any promise in it (Carver 1970b). Lish subsequently edited the piece twice, and it would later become the first story in *WYPBQP*. Drafts in the Lilly Library show two versions of the story addressed to Carver's different addresses in California; both contain changes that altered the story's tone and implications, and some of these changes represent clear indications of Lish's own ideas on fiction as well as foreshadowing ones he would later impose in a more coercive manner upon the stories in *WWTA*.

The first version of the story is 12 pages long and the second (not counting Lish's second round of edits) is 8. To begin with, we can see that the story's progression was, quantitatively speaking, towards reduction. Lengthy passages of dialogue and exposition are deleted, particularly in Lish's first revision. Many of the changes serve to highlight the sense of ambiguity and menace in the narrative, and illustrate the value Lish places on mystery; Lish is reported as telling his classes to 'always strive for the uncanny' and that 'the reader loves the enigmatic, because the enigmatic becomes numinous' (Callis n.d., 27 Nov. 1990). Lish's edits to the opening paragraph of the story heighten this sense of 'epistemological uncertainty' (Addington 2016, 19), as his first round of changes removed the narrator's explanation of the emotional difficulties that drive the character's actions. Bill and Arlene Miller are introduced as a couple who feel as if they have, in comparison to their acquaintances, been 'passed by somehow':

> They talked about it sometimes~~. They felt there was this void in their lives, and they didn't know how to fill it.~~, **mostly in connection with the**
>
> ~~When they compared their~~ lives ~~to those~~ of their neighbours, Harriet and Jim Stone~~., they experienced vague, almost resentful feelings of envy that they wisely never discussed. For it~~ **It** seemed to ~~them~~ **the Millers** that the Stones lived a ~~much~~ fuller and brighter life, one ~~very~~ different from their own. (Carver n.d.(a))[5]

Carver's first draft states the central problem of the story explicitly within the opening paragraphs – namely, the 'void' within the couple's life together and the consequent unspoken feelings driving their dissatisfaction. Critics would later take the deliberate withholding of these statements to be characteristic of Carver's narrators: Mark McGurl, for example, uses a passage of Joyce Carol Oates's prose to show, by contrast, how 'unthinkable' it would be to find the narrator explaining a character's emotional state in a Carver story (McGurl

[5] Reprinted by permission of Gordon Lish. All rights reserved.

2009, 300). Lish's changes make Carver's explanation less explicit, and his second revision introduces a clear note of dramatic irony into its opening line: 'Bill and Arlene Miller were ~~no more nor less than any of their friends~~ **a happy couple**' (Carver n.d.(b)).

Lish also eliminated details of the world being depicted and removed information tying the narrative to a particular time and place. In his second edit of the opening paragraphs, for example, he removed the details of the couple's respective workplaces; in his first round of edits, he suggested that rather than listening to 'a clamorous Jefferson Airplane record' they simply listen to 'records'; and in his first edit, he removed a line explaining that the 'pictures' that Arlene finds in their neighbours' apartment are 'of Harriet, and they're wild. Jim must have taken them with the Polaroid' (Carver n.d.(a)). In a passage following Bill's survey of the apartment, Lish's first edit deleted several details; he removed several references to the objects Bill discovers, such as a 'paperback copy of Portnoy's Complaint' and a 'plastic package of pills', and removed the adjectives from a description of a 'handsome Philippine mahogany chest of drawers' (Carver n.d.(a)). The narrative method is clearly altered here, and the removal of a literary reference is, as we shall see, a move that Lish would later repeat.[6] Indeed, Lish makes the world of the story more hermetic in general, removing references to the outside world and – importantly – filtering out the characters' attempts to place themselves within that world:

> He tried ~~hard~~ to concentrate on **the** news~~, of the world and his community~~. He read the paper ~~through from first to last page, skipping only the classifieds, but none of it really interested or concerned him~~ **and turned on the television**. Finally he went across the hall ~~to knock vigorously on the door~~. **The door was locked**. (Carver n.d.(a)).[7]

The deletion of the phrase 'his community' here demonstrates the way in which Lish highlighted the characters' isolation and, as we will see in Chapter 3, anticipates his later edits to 'Community Center' in *WWTA*. Verbal communication between characters is frequently minimized and/or altered in Lish's editing, and 'Neighbors' also illustrates this. In Carver's original, the couple's erotic life is introduced by the characters' own words. In answer to

6 He would tell Callis's class in 1990 to 'write in a self-reflexive, self-referential way. This extends from constantly turning your piece back on itself to never referring to other writers or their work' (Callis n.d., 18 Oct. 1990 – paraphrase by Callis).

7 Reprinted by permission of Gordon Lish. All rights reserved.

Arlene's curiosity about why she has discovered him at home earlier than usual, he replies:

> 'Nothing to do at work', **he said.** ~~And I kept thinking about last night. I've been horny all day'.~~
>
> ~~'You're just saying that', she answered, but her eyes brightened.~~ She let him use her key to open the door. (Carver n.d.(a))[8]

Bill verbalizes his desire here, and Arlene clearly reciprocates it. By contrast, the edited version makes the couple's sex life less affectionate and plays up the sense of tension and anxiety in their relationship – in Lish's second edit, the phrase 'He grabbed for her playfully' is changed into 'He grabbed for her awkwardly' and a line where Arlene addresses Bill as 'honey' is removed (Carver n.d.(b)). Elsewhere in lines deleted by Lish during his first edit, the couple verbalize their anxieties – Arlene tells Bill 'I've been worried' – and bond over the experience in a much more affectionate and intimate way than in the later version (Carver n.d.(a)). Bill admits to having entered the apartment on his own and to locking the cat in the bathroom, to which his partner replies:

> 'Is <u>that</u> why she was in there? So you could look around in peace?' She began shaking her head back and forth, eyes widening as she started to laugh. 'Well, I think I'm beginning to see the light. Okay, so you'll go back over with me then? It'd be kind of fun in that case. But do you really think we should? I mean, you know'. (Carver n.d.(a))

The tone of the dialogue is shifted by selective omission, and details such as Bill's drinking problem are not specified. Lish also tightened and altered the dialogue in the final paragraphs of the story: the explanation for the couple's being locked out of the apartment is condensed and communicated tersely, while the penultimate lines in which Bill reassures them both – '"No sweat, he said [. . .] 'Don't worry'" [. . .] it was early yet, he could always raise the manager' – are deleted, adding to the tension and sense of dread that are so notable in the final edited version's ending (Carver n.d.(a)).

These changes have a significant cumulative effect, given weight by the story's crucial importance to Carver's career. Carver himself appears to have regarded it as a landmark moment: in a 1977 letter written in the first months of his sobriety, he reminisced to Lish about the time the editor informed him of its impending

[8] Reprinted by permission of Gordon Lish.

publication in *Esquire*, writing that 'my life has never been the same since' (Carver 1977).[9] At the time, he pronounced himself 'overwhelmed' at the news, which he viewed as 'a milestone, a turning point' (Carver 1969a, 2009, 966). As the opening story in his first major press collection, it would also set the tone for the collection and serve as the wider literary world's first encounter with his work. Indeed, it was singled out for comment in 1978 by Ann Beattie, who wrote that the story's ending 'seems almost mythic' and 'too perfect to paraphrase [. . .] It is as clear and stark as a light shone in your eyes, and it causes something beyond sadness' (Beattie 1978, 179). Carver's correspondence, however, reveals an early ambivalence about the story's stylistic evolution – 'sending along the redone "Neighbors" tho it looks & feels a little thin now, but see what you think' (Carver 1970a) – that identifies the fault lines upon which his relationship with Lish would later fracture.

'Neighbors' was included in a 1973 anthology entitled *Cutting Edges: Young American Fiction for the '70s* (Ed. Jack Hicks), with a short accompanying essay by Carver in which he describes the genesis of the story in ambiguous terms. Claiming that the story 'came together very quickly', he notes that:

> The real work on the story, and perhaps the art of the story, came later. Originally the manuscript was about twice as long, but I kept paring it on subsequent revisions, and then pared it down some more, until it achieved its present length and dimensions. (Carver 2009, 1014)

He then goes on to note the story's 'essential mystery and strangeness' and to worry publicly about its stylistic achievement: while the story is 'more or less, an artistic success' he writes that 'my only fear is that it is too thin, too elliptical and subtle, too inhuman' (Carver 2009, 1013–14). Here we see an early example of a pattern that would recur on a much more extensive scale several years later: Carver publishes a story that has been heavily edited by Lish and takes credit for the story's stylistic economy ('the real work', or the 'art') while simultaneously questioning, in print, the virtue of such economy. The author engages in an oblique paratextual meditation on the minimalistic methods with which he is beginning to be identified, a continuation (and a more eloquent elaboration) of reservations already expressed to Lish in private.[10] He does so

[9] 'Neighbors' appeared in the June 1971 issue.

[10] Gérard Genette's notion of the paratext comprises a work's title, introduction, illustrations and annotations as well as extratextual (or, to use Genette's word, 'epitextual') material such as interviews, private correspondence and other elements located 'outside the book'. Genette describes this as 'a

in a form that, with the benefit of hindsight, is difficult not to read as a veiled challenge to the editor whose work he both questions and fails to acknowledge publicly.

'The instant you offer an explanation is the instant you have sentimentality': Lish's changes to *Will You Please Be Quiet, Please?*

The years following his move to New York were productive ones for Lish as he consolidated his editorial control of *Esquire*'s fiction pages, assuming the enduring nickname 'Captain Fiction'[11] and soliciting work from – and, in several cases, building friendships with – many of America's foremost writers. Lish had begun to teach at Yale in the early 1970s and was writing his own fiction and sending it to magazines (as well as ghostwriting books for McGraw-Hill), setting a pattern of concurrent writing, teaching and editing activity that he would follow for decades to come (Lish 2015, 212; Sklenicka 2009b, 283, 360).[12]

In November 1974, Lish, having steadily cultivated relationships with book editors who could offer him stories, was offered his own imprint to publish fiction by McGraw-Hill (Sklenicka 2009b, 272). When Carver learned that he had been selected as the first author in this series, he wrote an effusive letter to Lish:

> Well, listen, can't exactly tell you how pleased and so on about the prospects of having a collection out under your aegis [. . .] I'll tell you this, you've not backed a bad horse [. . .] About the editing necessary in some of the stories. Tell me which ones and I'll go after it, or them. Tell me which ones. Or I will leave it up to you & you tell me what you think needs done or doing. (Carver 2007, 11 Nov. 1974)

Lish proceeded to edit the stories for inclusion in the collection, selecting 'twenty-two stories (out of at least thirty-four Carver had published)' and

zone between text and off-text, a zone not only of transition but of transaction' whose effect on interpretation is profound: the paratext is a 'threshold' which, he states (quoting Philippe Lejeune) 'in reality controls one's whole reading of the text' (Genette 1997, 1–2).

11 The name was given to Lish by Barry Hannah, and Lish used it thereafter in signing his internal memos at *Esquire* (Sklenicka 2009b, 213).

12 Lish's first novel *Dear Mr Capote* would be published in June 1983, three months before the publication of Carver's *Cathedral.*

proposing title changes for several of these (Sklenicka 2009b, 281). Lish made two rounds of edits on the majority of these stories; it appears (although the drafts are rarely dated) that many of these took place during the summer of 1975, as Lish first edited on copies (or photocopies) of the magazine versions of the stories and then carried out a second round of edits on typescripts made from the first round.

These changes show a high degree of consistency. Again, Lish tended to remove detail, create a sense of mystery and menace, and alter the relationships between characters. He frequently made the characters' dialogue coarser, and in 'A Dog Story' (which Lish retitled 'Jerry and Molly and Sam'), he amplified the crudity in the opening section to emphasize the narrator's rage:

> She was always turning up with some ~~crap~~ **shit** or other [. . .] something the kids could ~~fight~~ **scream** over and ~~screech at~~ **fight over and beat the shit out of** each other about. [. . .] for God's sake, when he didn't even know if he was going to have a roof over his head – made him ~~open and close his hands in his pockets. When he took them out to light a cigarette, they were trembling~~ **want to kill the goddamn dog.**
>
> **¶ Sandy! Betty and Alex and Mary! Jill! And Suzy the goddamn dog!**
>
> **¶ This was Al.** (Carver n.d.(e))[13]

Lish inserted line breaks here as he frequently would elsewhere in Carver's stories, and the effect, at the close of this opening section of the narrative, is to sound a note of comedy at the expense of the character being introduced. The list of names here (which belong to the narrator's wife, children, sister and pet, respectively) heightens the sense of the narrator's resentment at his various dependants and, of course, suggests the distinctive new title of the published story. The story also provides a clear example of the kind of attribution of dialogue – 'he said, she said' – that would become a cliché of Minimalism.[14] Early in the story, we find the following exchange:

> **¶ She said,** 'I see'.
>
> **¶ He said,** 'You don't mind, do you?**!** Jesus!'
>
> **¶ She said,** 'Go ahead, I don't care'.

[13] Reprinted by permission of Gordon Lish. All rights reserved.

[14] Lish would later tell his students that this form of attribution was punchier and more powerful: 'Don't use "asked" – "said" will do – same for "told me", etc. "Said" is forceful, direct, almost a punctuation' (Callis n.d., 13 Dec. 1990 – direct quotation).

> ¶ **He said,** 'I won't be gone long, ~~don't~~**. Don't** worry'.
> ¶ **She said,** 'Go ahead, I said. I said I don't care, didn't I? Go on!' **she said.** (Carver n.d.(c))[15]

'A Dog Story' is one of many in which Lish cut lengthy paragraphs from Carver's original. Many of these deleted sections follow Al's thoughts as he reflects upon his troubles and on his disastrous decision to surreptitiously abandon the family dog; for example, the day after the act, we are told over the course of two paragraphs that he feels as if 'his number was up', that he has avoided thinking about the dog all day and that the incident is coming back to him 'in snatches' (Carver n.d.(c)). The narrator also reminisces elsewhere in the same story about his early days with his wife as well as about his childhood.[16] The removal of these revealing flashbacks makes the narrator less reflective and his motivations more obscure; these memories humanize the narrator, inviting the reader's sympathy – albeit at the risk of mawkishness – and provide a context for his current feelings of entrapment and frustration. As he did elsewhere, though, Lish removed this background detail, presumably to minimize the emotional appeal to the reader; Callis quotes the editor as saying 'the instant you offer an explanation is the instant you have sentimentality' (Callis n.d., Oct. 1991).

Indeed, explanations are notable by their absence in all of the stories Lish edited, and the reason for a character's disquiet is rarely made explicit. That this is a recurring feature of Lish's editing is demonstrated by a number of changes to another story, 'Sixty Acres', in which the narrator is unsettled by his confrontation with a group of boys who he finds illegally hunting on his land. The lines removed by Lish are crucial ones, as the character gains some insight into his alienation and feels his way, through introspection, towards an epiphany. He examines his own sense that 'something crucial had happened' that he 'could not find words to describe':

> But ~~nothing,~~ nothing had happened~~, that was just it. He thought for a while. One thing, he had not *been himself*, that was partly what bothered him now. He couldn't explain it, but somehow he had not been himself. He felt that very strongly. He had been like a play actor standing there in the snow, making~~

15 Reprinted by permission of Gordon Lish. All rights reserved.
16 He recalls, for example, fishing for 'bass and catfish' as a boy and evokes the memory of a local character called 'Old Hutchinson'.

> ~~sounds, raising his arms. But if he was somebody else, if he wasn't Lee Waite, then who was he, what was he?~~ (Carver n.d.(f))[17]

The narrator of Carver's original is, however tentatively, searching for a sense of understanding, a search deliberately obscured by these revisions. Edits such as these have surely determined the assessments of critics such as James Dishon McDermott, who suggests that 'the Carver character is incapable of hearing an inner voice, or of communicating the few moments of insight she does experience' (McDermott 2006, 94). 'Sixty Acres' also demonstrates that Lish frequently removed references to nature, which he saw as being linked to sentimentality; Carver's characters often recall pastoral scenes at moments of crisis, and the natural world seems to function as brief respite from personal pain. The protagonist here deals with his anxiety by attempting an imaginative communion with the natural world:

> He closed his eyes and tried to ~~bring the land into mind, saw vaguely a few scattered fields with clumps of trees at the edges, a slow stream that came in from someplace and which beavers had dammed. Then, for some reason, he thought of Day's cows wandering slowly across his fields, going slowly into one field and then another, snapping off the barley and tall grass, chewing it and working it in their cuds a long time before swallowing. He held it all of a moment, and then it began to fade – the land, trees, even the beavers he imagined living some place on the side stream, until there was nothing left, only a herd of cows he'd seen once, airily suspended in his mind~~ **think**. (Carver n.d.(f))[18]

An entire paragraph is reduced here to eight monosyllabic words, giving us a kind of Minimalism in microcosm. The character's interiority, as well as the evocative rural scene he manages to create and briefly hold on to, disappears behind a screen of terse prose, and the long moment of mental activity that in Carver's original version leaves a 'suspended' trace is foreshortened to almost nothing. A pastoral scene is hidden behind a layer of revision and, again, a genetic view of these early stories complicates assertions[19] that would characterize the author's method as a consistently elliptical one.

Another recurring technique of Lish's was to make the transitions between adjacent sections of a story more abrupt by marking a section's close with a non-sequitur or a diegetically opaque sentence. Returning to 'A Dog Story'/'Jerry and

[17] Reprinted by permission of Gordon Lish. All rights reserved.
[18] Reprinted by permission of Gordon Lish. All rights reserved.
[19] McDermott, for example, claims that 'one of the defining features of Carver's narrative style is the omission of contextualizing information about characters' environments' (McDermott 2006, 90–1).

Molly and Sam', we see several examples. At one point the narrator reflects, '"My dog had brains [. . .] It was an Irish setter!"' Lish deleted the subsequent five lines (which, in the relevant draft, are illegible underneath his pen marks) in order to end the section on a punchline of sorts. On the following page, he added a line that makes the narrator more unhinged:

> Then he lit a cigarette and tried to get hold of himself. **He picked up the rake and put it away where it belonged. He was muttering to himself, saying, 'Order, order', when** ~~T~~**t**he dog came up to the garage, sniffed around the door, and looked in. (Carver n.d.(d))[20]

The final paragraph of Carver's original not only makes clear the central dramatic problem of the story – the fact that the narrator feels 'captive' – but also makes it clear that he is aware of this problem:

> ~~Al~~ **He** sat there ~~a while, then~~**. Then he** got up with a sigh. He walked back to the car ~~with his hands in his pockets~~. He didn't feel so bad, all things considered. ~~He didn't feel free, particularly—but neither did he feel captive any longer. He felt – well, nothing. He'd have to make up a story to tell Betty and the kids. Anything would do. And see about getting them another dog.~~ The world was full of dogs. There were dogs and ~~then~~ there were dogs~~;~~**:** ~~some~~ **Some dogs** you just couldn't do anything with. ~~He'd have to make it up to Jill, too, his rudeness of last night. Betty as well. He did feel bad about Betty. But she would come around with a present and lots of attention. A present for Betty, and a present for Jill. He began thinking about what he would get them. Something not too expensive, but something nice, too~~. (Carver n.d.(c))[21]

This paragraph is a prime example of the way in which Lish would apply the abrupt-transition technique to the end of a story: in Max's words, the editor 'loved deadpan last lines' and sometimes 'cut away whole sections to leave a sentence from inside the story as the end' in order to achieve them (Max 1998). The narrator may be unredeemed in Carver's original version – the final lines here, showing his intention to continue his adultery, could be said to constitute an anti-epiphany of sorts – but he is unmistakably aware of the consequences of his actions and their effects on others, and the comedy at the story's close sits alongside a sense of pathos absent from Lish's version.

[20] Reprinted by permission of Gordon Lish.
[21] Reprinted by permission of Gordon Lish.

Lish also truncated the ending of 'The Student's Wife' dramatically: editing on a copy of the story previously published in *The Carolina Quarterly* in 1964, he removed the final page and a half. The ending of the version later published in *WYPBQP* presents a startling distillation of the wife's unhappiness as she cries out: ' "God" she said. "God, will you help us, God?" she said' (Carver 2009, 100). Leypoldt identifies this story as 'one of [the] most illustrative examples' of a type of ending he calls Carver's 'arrested epiphany', arguing that the wife's 'arrested epiphany prevents her from understanding any of the reasons for her sense of menace' and that ultimately 'not only the plot's essential contour and meaning, but even its central conflicts remain blurred' (Leypoldt 2001, 535–6).[22] In Carver's original, though, the story continues as the husband is woken by his wife's lament: he finds her crying, and their children[23] soon appear in the doorway looking concerned. The narrator tries to console her, asking her what the matter is:

> ~~'What's the matter, Nancy?' he asked quietly. 'Can you tell me, sweetheart? Haven't you been to sleep? My God. Can you tell me what's wrong, darling?'~~
>
> ~~'I'll be all right', she said.~~
>
> ~~'Listen to me, darling', wetting his lips. 'Things are going to get better for us this year. Wait and see. Everything's going to be all right. The ships will all come in, we'll get out of this rat race yet. . .some nice quiet place. . .Just, just for God's sake don't worry about anything', patting her back gently. 'Just try and get some sleep'.~~ (Carver n.d. (i))[24]

This story, which ends with the narrator's wife lying in bed as he still tries anxiously to connect with her, is one that was surely improved by the severity of the edits. The continuation of the narrative beyond daybreak, the narrator's repeated and plaintive reassurances, and his literal enunciation of the couple's problems – money difficulties, the economic 'rat race' in which they are trapped – all dissipate the dramatic tension and 'indeterminacy' of the central situation and render the ending less effective (Leypoldt 2001, 536). The focus of the story is noticeably altered, though, and the intimacy of Carver's original ending and its wider scope – which takes in the couple's children (absent from

[22] Saltzman points to the story (along with 'Neighbors', 'Fat' and others) as an example of the way the author's endings 'are often abrupt, truncated' (Saltzman 1988, 15).

[23] One of whom is called Gordon, incidentally – this was changed to 'Gary' in the published version (Carver 2009, 97).

[24] Reprinted by permission of Gordon Lish. All rights reserved.

the final paragraph of the published version) as well as hinting at a wider social context – are lost.

Lish was evidently teaching Carver's work in his writing classes during the years in which he was editing it, and his workshop materials from November 1976 show that the stylistic struggle extended beyond the page. An assignment sheet presents a list of prompts, one of which invites students to consider the presence of sentiment in Carver's stories (Lish 1976). The editor is, here, implying a particular stance towards compositional method as well as towards Carver's fiction, and one that fits into a pattern of long-running and frequently indirect paratextual struggle over the style and authorship of Carver's stories.

Compression and consecution: 'Will You Please Be Quiet, Please?'

Like 'The Student's Wife', 'WYPBQP' was already an old story by the time it was edited for book publication, having been published almost a decade beforehand (in *December* in 1966). It became the title story of the book at Carver's insistence, as Lish had wanted the collection to be called *Put Yourself in My Shoes* (Sklenicka 2009b, 281); as such, it took on renewed importance both as the collection's flagship piece and its atypically lengthy closing story. Lish made multiple changes, and despite the story's length it differs dramatically from the version selected as one of the *Best American Short Stories* in 1967. As Sklenicka notes of Lish's changes to the collection in general, while he 'did not substantially alter the arc of events or the characters [. . .] he substantially refabricated their feeling' (Sklenicka 2009b, 283).

The story follows Ralph Wyman's realization that his wife betrayed him some years earlier and is divided (unusually, for a Carver story) into three numbered parts. The first portrays the domestic argument during which this revelation surfaces, the second details Ralph's solitary night-time journey around his town as he attempts to come to terms with this new reality and the third (and shortest) shows him returning home to an emotionally fraught, ambiguous reconciliation with Marian. Some of Lish's most noticeable changes come, again, in the transitions between sections. At the end of the second section Ralph is mugged, a violent experience that puts an end to his wandering and prepares him to return home. In his first edit, Lish deleted a 184-word concluding paragraph in which bystanders come to Ralph's aid and the protagonist reflects on the central problem facing him. He climbs to his feet and weeps, attempting to confront his emotions, standing 'shaking' as a 'vast sense of wonderment flowed through him as he thought again of Marian, why she had betrayed him' (Carver n.d.(g)). On the following page, Lish deleted a full passage in which Ralph goes to the hospital to get X-rays and looks at police photographs in a failed attempt to identify his assailant. During his second edit Lish continued this process, removing two lines from the end of the second section and shortening the opening paragraph of the third section from 138 words to 33, ensuring a more abrupt transition and reducing the degree of reflection in the narrative consciousness.

The ending of the story also owes much to Lish's work. As Sklenicka notes, in his edits, 'a three-paragraph (189-word) conclusion' is condensed into '93 words' (Sklenicka 2009b, 282–3). Again, this took place in two rounds. In the first round, Lish removed some phrases, added his own and compressed Carver's three paragraphs into one. However, his second edit of the ending was much heavier and is worth reproducing in full in order to illustrate the extensive and detailed level of textual alteration at play:

> He tensed at her ~~cold~~ fingers, and then~~, gradually,~~ he ~~relaxed. He imagined himself floating on his back in the heavy, milky water of Juniper Lake, where he had spent a summer years and years ago, and someone was calling to him, come in, Ralph, come in. But he kept on floating and did not answer, and the soft rising waves laved his body.~~ **let go a little. It was easier to let go a little.** [*No ¶*] Her hand moved over his hip~~. Then it traced his groin before flattening itself against~~ **and over** his stomach~~. She~~ **and she** was ~~in bed now,~~ pressing ~~the length of~~ her body ~~against~~ **over** his **now** and moving ~~gently~~ **over him and** back and forth ~~with~~ **over** him. He ~~waited a minute, and~~ **held himself, he later considered, as long as he could. And** then he turned to her ~~and their eyes met~~. **He turned and turned in what might have been a stupendous sleep, and he was still turning,** ~~Her eyes were filled and seemed to him to reveal layer beneath layer of color and reflection. He gazed even deeper. He saw in first one pupil and then the other the cameo image of the face that must be his. He continued to stare,~~ marvelling at the **impossible** changes he felt moving over him. (Carver n.d.(h))[25]

Some of the changes here are thematic ones consistent with Lish's approach to Carver's work, such as the deletion of a moment where a character recalls a particular memory (again, this is connected to an experience of nature: 'the

25 Reprinted by permission of Gordon Lish. All rights reserved.

heavy, milky water of Juniper Lake'). He changed the structure of the prose, removing a paragraph break in order to condense the lines ('No ¶') and also removed the intense meeting of eyes that occurs between the couple. Ralph no longer gazes into his wife's eyes (which are entirely absent from the final text), and his experience becomes an interior one.

We also see techniques that are emblematic of Lish's narrative technique of 'consecution', however. This principle of composition, which Lish used repeatedly in his workshops, was one that could structure a composition at a thematic and formal level; it denotes the way in which repetition and recursion could be used to achieve both 'structural' and 'acoustical' consecution and to 'logically link each narrative unit to its precursor' (Lucarelli 2013, n.p.; Winters 2016, 121). We see multiple examples of this kind of repetition in this final paragraph, from the replication of clauses and sentence structures – 'He [. . .] let go a little. It was easier to let go a little' – to the recurrence of particular words such as 'over' (a word which does not appear at all in Carver's original). The intense concentration of alliteration and acoustical repetition in the passage – 'stupendous sleep', the final sentence's thrice-repeated 'turning' – also ensures that the revelation that takes place in what Bethea terms the story's 'epiphanic sexual encounter' (namely, the final act of lovemaking that implies Ralph's acceptance of his wife's infidelity) is communicated through poetic rather than diegetic means. Indeed, Amir, Bethea, Nesset and Saltzman all single out the poetic and symbolic effects of repetition in the story's final passage (Amir 2010, 119; Bethea 2001, 55–6; Nesset 1995, 25; Saltzman 1988, 72). Bethea, in fact, returns to the story's ending in a 2007 article on Carver's technical debts to Hemingway, again with particular reference to the poetic and intertextual effects caused by the repetitions of the prose (Bethea 2007, 93–4). The importance of Lish's contribution here is clear, as specific textual features added in his editing are still debated more than three decades after the story's publication.

'The dark of the American heart': Defining Carver's vision

The lack of critical acknowledgement of Lish's involvement in these stories could perhaps be justified by simple reference to the 'passive authorization' given by Carver to his editor. It seems clear that the author was comfortable with the edits, judging by the tone of the correspondence at the time. Examining the textual changes before publication, he writes 'I think, all in all, you did a superb job of cutting and fixing on the stories' and closes by saying 'Gordon, I think this is going to be a book and a half. Reading them through the cumulative effect is very powerful indeed' (Carver 1975). Carver seems never to have protested the changes, as he later would in the case of *WWTA*, and never attempted to republish the unedited versions of the stories in his later collections. In considering Lish's contribution to Carver's career as a whole, though, it is clear not only that the changes made here foreshadow those at the heart of the later controversy – many of the changes Lish made are similar in type, if not always in degree, to the ones he would make to *WWTA* – but that the editor was essential in determining the parameters of the author's literary 'brand' from an early stage. Lish's blurb for the inside flap of the collection was unabashed in its proclamation of the author's increasing national importance, a stature secured by the bleak precision of his accomplishment:

> Here is the short fiction of a literary artist of the first rank, a maker of stories that deliver the dark of the American heart. With twenty-two harsh illuminations of our dazed exertions to endure, Raymond Carver announces his uniquely resolute vision. It is a vision that is shrewd, unflinching, exact, grave. In the sunless, post-speech world Raymond Carver sees, apprehending the grossness of our fixed destinies amounts to a kind of triumph, a small but gorgeous prevailing against circumstance. Here is the work of the increasingly influential Raymond Carver [. . .] in whose precise rendering on the page readers in pursuit of excellence in the national literature may all exult. (Sklenicka 2009b, 296)[26]

These words, acting as an official introduction to readers, present Carver as a sort of gloomy national prophet apprehending the inevitable, ominous eclipse ('sunless', 'fixed') of contemporary American reality: the narrative achievement, murky and inarticulate ('post-speech'), provides solace only in the unrelenting unity of its portrayal of that reality. These sentences, in hindsight, evoke the 'small, good thing' that Carver would soon write about. While Carver's phrase would refer to the possibilities of human connection, however, Lish's formulation (a 'small but gorgeous prevailing against circumstance') suggests a more 'grave' and fatalistic vision.

Lish's work during these years needs to be understood, at least in part, within the context of magazine fiction editing, in which the author will often be

[26] Reprinted by permission of Gordon Lish.

expected to accept significant changes to their manuscript in order to comply with demands of space as well as the magazine's own aesthetic. Both Pietsch and Howard point out that in this context, the author's vision is subservient to editorial demands in a way that differs from book-length editing, with the former suggesting that in a sense, 'the magazine is its own author' (Pietsch 2017c; Howard 2017). Indeed, Matthew Philpotts observes that the structures underpinning magazine editing can lend themselves to a 'charismatic form of editorship', a concentrated and often short-lived application of energy in which the 'personalized intensity and dynamism' of the editor manifests in ways akin to popular conceptions of 'artistic activity' (Philpotts 2012, 48–49). Lish was, however, as Carol Polsgrove has noted, an aggressive editor even by the standards of *Esquire*'s practices (Polsgrove 2001, 241). He has spoken of his 'gift' for editing, conceived of as either an 'intuition' or an 'act of recognizing', claiming that when he approaches a piece of fiction, 'I must have my way with it', and this forceful and often radical reinterpretation of the texts he received can be seen throughout the manuscripts in his archive (Lish 2015, 210–11; Lish 2018, 162). Some writers refused Lish's interventions outright. Don DeLillo refused to let Lish excerpt a section from 'Great Jones Street' in 1972, citing his discomfort with the kind of textual alterations involved; Vladimir Nabokov withdrew from an arrangement to serialize excerpts of *Look at the Harlequins!* in 1974 after seeing the severity of Lish's edits. In the latter case, Lish had excised entire paragraphs and literally cut and pasted blocks of text into new arrangements (DeLillo 1972; Sklenicka 2009b, 283–4).[27] Many authors were receptive to the changes Lish made to their manuscripts, however. Richard Ford's 'In Desert Waters', for example, published in the August 1976 issue of *Esquire*, includes many of Lish's line edits, which often involved deleting several sentences or changing their rhythm; a number of these survived into the opening chapters of Ford's debut novel, *A Piece of My Heart* (1976). Similarly, drafts of James Purdy's 'Summer Tidings', published in December 1974, show an extensive pattern of deletion and addition, with Lish frequently replacing multiple words within a single sentence.

[27] The novel had been cut to make it look, in the words of Fred Hills, editor-in-chief of McGraw-Hill at the time, 'like a straight autobiographical memoir of Véra [Nabokov's wife]' and its title changed to reflect this (the excerpt was named 'Myself Incomplete: A True Autobiography'); after receiving the page proofs of the proposed excerpt in the mail, the author, reportedly asking 'Who is this fellow Gordon Lish and what is he doing?', withdrew from the arrangement (Sklenicka 2009b, 283–4; Nabokov, n.d.).

In 1977 Capra Press published Carver's *Furious Seasons*, a collection of stories that had been excluded from *WYPBQP*; five of these would later appear in *WWTA*. The book contained a list of several dedicatees, and Carver removed Lish's name as he feared the editor would be embarrassed by the book. However, Lish answered that the stories in the book were 'goddamn wonderful' and reproached Carver for omitting him from the list (Sklenicka 2009b, 313–15). Lish took up a position as editor at Knopf within months, but Carver's chaotic personal circumstances and his slow consolidation of his sobriety meant that it would be over two more years before that collection would come to fruition. When Lish moved from *Esquire* to Knopf in 1977, he not only brought with him many of the authors whose stories he had already published but also imported the same approach, rearranging sections and line-editing book-length manuscripts with the same precision and severity. Robert Gottlieb, editor-in-chief and (from 1973 onwards) president of Knopf during Lish's time at the firm until he left for the *New Yorker* in 1987, describes Lish as having had 'a profound need to put his own imprint on fiction'; Lish was granted a significant degree of freedom to do so, since Knopf had not yet moved towards the expanded management structure that would come to characterize major American publishers in the coming decades (Gottlieb 2016, n.p.). Lish recalls feeling no responsibility to generate sales in his pursuit of distinctive fiction, while Gottlieb describes the acquisitions process during his tenure as having been entirely devoid of the structured sales presentations, launch meetings and spreadsheeted profit and loss projections to which today's editors are accustomed: 'when an editor wanted to acquire a book, he or she just told me and I said yes or no, and decided how much money we could pay' (Winters 2015, 102; Gottlieb 2016, n.p.).

Lish's work on Barry Hannah's books in the late 1970s and early 1980s is perhaps the closest point of comparison to his work with Carver, with his work on the 1978 collection *Airships* and the 1980 novel *Ray* providing a clear parallel in both its severity and its bridging of magazine and book publication. As Michael Hemmingson shows, the similarities between the manuscript evidence of both writers' work are significant: he describes, for example, how Lish 'line-edited photocopies of the stories from the journals they had seen print in', as he had with Carver's work (Hemmingson 2011b, 490). In several cases the journal in question was *Esquire*, and as such Lish saw Hannah's work (as he did Carver's) through several iterations, often refining his vision of a story in different stages. Several of these stories, such as 'Coming Close to Donna', show a similar spatial fragmentation to ones such as Carver's 'Mr. Coffee and Mr. Fixit', with copious line-breaks imbuing the narrative with a jumpy, disconnected feel; a facsimile of a page of Lish's edits to the manuscripts of *Ray* published in the 2015 *Paris Review* interview with the editor illustrates the extent of his involvement. Like Carver, Hannah struggled repeatedly with alcohol addiction, a fact that cannot be ignored in considering the willingness of both authors to invite this degree of editorial intervention. It was only in 1977 that Carver finally reached long-term sobriety, and while this achievement seems clearly to have fostered an increased sense of assurance in his own work, the effect was not immediate: Gallagher suggests that it 'took a while for the confidence of his sobriety to mature into action' (Gallagher 2017).

In a reply written only a few months into his long 'second life' of sobriety, Carver wrote a letter full of praise and thanks for Lish's years of help and looked forward to their next collaboration:

> You were there to read what I wrote and print it if you could. I ain't forgot any of that, any of it. Won't. We been around the corner a few times together, you and I. We've had a friendship, by God [. . .] My life has never been the same since, boyo. We ran them a good race for the NBA [National Book Award] too, didn't we? Next time – and your name will be on the Dedication page of <u>that</u> book – we'll take it [. . .]. (Carver 1977)

Carver's ambition and confidence are clearly visible here, and his obvious devotion to his editor is offset by an elegiac past tense ('we've had a friendship') that suggests a subtle shift in his sense of himself as an artist. This developing set of attitudes, along with Lish's certainty in his editorial vision, were combining to produce a complex dynamic that would come to a head with their next collaboration.

3

Minimalism in action: Making *What We Talk About When We Talk About Love*

What We Talk About When We Talk About Love, Carver's second major press collection, is often taken to exemplify an individual and collective aesthetic, with an 'indexical function', in Marc Botha's words, that has made it 'come to stand for minimalism as a whole' (Botha 2017, 15–16). Sklenicka observes that the book is for many readers both 'the quintessential Carver text' and 'the ur-text of minimalism', linking Carver's name with a Minimalist aesthetic to such an extent that the two have been joined in a *Jeopardy!* question (Sklenicka 2009b, 366–9, 405–6).[1] It was described in 2009 by Tim Adams of the *Observer* as 'probably the most influential story collection of the past 30 years', and a *New York Times* article from the same year suggested that *WWTA* was still among the most widely shoplifted books in US bookstores (Adams 2009; Rabb 2009).

As we saw in Chapter 1, contemporary reviewers such as James Atlas focused on the stylistic austerity and 'minimality' of the stories and the critical conversation quickly began to coalesce around this term. Within four years of its publication, an entire issue of the *Mississippi Review* (Winter 1985) would be devoted to an attempt to evaluate the burgeoning Minimalist scene. In her introduction to the issue (subtitled 'On the New Fiction'), guest editor Kim Herzinger noted the 'perceptible movement' in the preceding years towards a new fictional mode, lamenting the absence of a more precise scholarly label than 'Minimalism' but admitting defeat in the attempt to find one. She ventured a list of the main attributes of the prevalent fictional mode of the preceding years, which included: 'equanimity of surface, "ordinary" subjects, recalcitrant narrators and deadpan narratives, slightness of story, and characters who don't think out loud' (Herzinger 1985, 11). McDermott's retrospective definition in

[1] The clue in question was: 'The stories of Raymond Carver typified this style whose name indicates it does the most with the "least".'

his 2006 monograph on literary Minimalism is forensic in its detail and length and repeats many of the same features, highlighting the relative stability of the term's usage:

> 'Minimalism' refers to a short or short-short story that is nearly plotless, treating isolated moments or random, insignificant events; begins in medias res; is depicted, dramatic and filmic rather than expository or novelistic; leads nowhere or to a minor vastation or anti-climax; and favours the present tense. Characters inhabit working-class environments typified by economic disenfranchisement and menial empty work; an overwhelming consumerist culture of ubiquitous brand names and loud televisions; dysfunctional and ad hoc families; violence, alcoholism and drug abuse; rootlessness, and a bleak, quasi-Naturalistic sense of entrapment. The language of 'Minimalism' features simple diction and syntax, colloquialisms, a blank tone, lyricism directed towards surfaces and mundane objects, and an elliptical quality. (McDermott 2006, 13)

These descriptions contain obvious similarities in the way they both emphasize Minimalism's deliberate refusal of several possibilities of literary presentation: its insistence on surface rather than depth, 'ordinary' or 'menial' subjects rather than grand ones, a deliberately limited amount of plot and an affectless ('blank', 'deadpan') tone. Summing up, McDermott highlights 'the glaring lack of information' in Carver's texts, suggesting that the author 'has pared down a standard of fullness, substituting absence in the place of the style features we might expect to find in a work of realism' (McDermott 2006, 108–9).

Theorists of the short story would also come to emphasize the deliberate absence of narrative information in Carver's texts, using this as the primary means by which to situate his work within the development of the genre. In the wake of *WWTA*, Carver's fiction was placed squarely in the tradition suggested by Hemingway's famous analogy of fictional omission and ellipsis: 'The dignity of movement of an ice-berg is due to only one-eighth of it being above water' (Hemingway 1932, 154). Susanne C. Ferguson noted the 'deletion of traditional plot elements' (Ferguson 1994, 227) as well as the opaque, elliptical endings, and Charles May suggested that the 'bare outlines' of plot and 'spare dialogue' made the characters 'so lacking in language that the theme is unsayable':

> Characters often have no names or only first names and are so briefly described that they seem to have no physical presence at all; certainly they have no distinct identity but rather seem to be shadowy presences trapped in their own inarticulateness. (May 1994, 213)

May placed the volume within a lineage of short fiction that, following Chekhov, 'has pursued its movement away from the linearity of prose towards the spatiality of poetry [. . .] by radically limiting its selection of the presented event', making particular reference to writers like Carver and Hemingway 'whose styles are thin to the point of disappearing' (May 1994, 214).

Any analysis of Lish's contribution to the book, then, clearly ramifies beyond Carver's own career, a realization that surely contributed to the controversy and comment generated before, during and after *Beginners* came into print in 2009. In this chapter, I examine the changes made by Lish during the book's production, focusing on four stories in particular, in order to better understand the editor's contribution and clarify the implications for our understanding of Carver, Lish and Minimalism. A genetic study of the Lish manuscripts allows us to follow the text as it approaches the vanishing point that May identifies and to see, essentially, Minimalism in action.

'My very sanity is on the line here': The textual history

In May 1980, Carver met Lish in New York to deliver the original manuscript of the collection, which bore the working title 'So Much Water So Close to Home', and in response Lish informed Carver that he would seek a contract from Knopf (Sklenicka 2009b, 355). Carver replied with another warm letter in which he encouraged Lish to 'open the throttle' on the stories:

> For Christ's sweet sake, not to worry about taking a pencil to the stories if you can make them better; and if anyone can you can. I want them to be the best possible stories, and I want them to be around for a while. (Carver 1980g)

In a separate letter written the same day,[2] Carver wrote to express his trust and asked, 'If you see ways to put more muscle in the stories, don't hesitate to do so' (Carver 1980h). Another letter written eight days later can only be read, with hindsight, in an ironic light. Carver wrote partly to offer compliments on the memoir of Victor Herman, a Jewish-American former Soviet political prisoner, which Lish had ghostwritten. He singled out the 'narrator's voice' for praise, declaring that:

[2] Carver had omitted a line from the envelope address of the first letter and worried that it may have gone astray (Sklenicka 2009b, 355).

> It's a bafflement to me, and sometimes you'll have to tell me, why you've put Victor Herman, his name, on this book. I'm reading this book like a novel, God, it is a novel, and I'm taking real pleasure in it, and I just wish your name were on it my friend. Someday fill me in on this. (Carver 1980i)

The manuscripts of Herman's memoir in Lish's collection show multiple changes across at least four drafts and confirm that Lish did indeed craft the narrative in his distinctive manner, deleting entire pages and introducing regular line breaks to create a fragmented, elliptical and voice-driven tone (Herman n.d.). Within months Carver would protest against these techniques, as applied to his own work, in the strongest terms.

Sklenicka refers to Carver's original manuscript as 'version A' of the sequence; Lish returned a version to Carver the following month (version B), which contained a first round of edits and the new title. Carver accepted the changes and signed and returned his publishing contract straight away, despite the fact that he had yet to receive the final typescript based on Lish's editing. As Sklenicka notes, the author entered 'a binding contract for his book' while having consulted 'neither an agent nor an attorney' (Sklenicka 2009b, 356). Shortly after this, typescript C – in large part, the version we know as *WWTA* – arrived on Carver's desk.[3] The differences between B and C were significant enough to cause Carver a level of emotional distress that is clear from the ensuing correspondence. After a day and night of close comparison, he wrote a lengthy letter to Lish in which he proclaimed himself to be on the verge of breakdown in an attempt to persuade his editor to reverse the changes. Worried by the fact that several of the stories had already been viewed in their unedited form by other writers and editors (including Gallagher, Ford, Tobias Wolff and others), Carver described himself as 'confused, tired, paranoid, and afraid, yes, of the consequences for me if the collection came out in its present form' and announced: 'I'll tell you the truth, my very sanity is on the line here' (Carver 2009, 996).

Carver repeatedly begged Lish to arrest the publication of the book, alternately pleading ('Please help me with this, Gordon'), apologizing ('Forgive me for this, please') and demanding ('Please do the necessary things to stop production of this book'). Still struggling to regain equilibrium in his newly sober existence, he claimed that some of the stories were so close to his 'sense of regaining my

[3] The qualifying phrase here refers to the fact that Lish made some changes to the galleys, and therefore some differences (of which, as we shall see, several could be considered significant) exist even between version C and the published text of *WWTA*; to a large extent, though, these two texts correspond to one another.

health and mental well-being' that he feared he might 'never write another story' if the book were published in 'its present edited form' (Carver 2007, 2009, 993–6). Carver's entreaties were unsuccessful, however; in 1998, Lish told Max: 'My sense of it was that there was a letter and that I just went ahead.' Gallagher has claimed that a phone conversation took place after Carver's first letter in which Lish insisted to the author that he would not reverse his edits (Sklenicka 2009, 359). The crucial fact may simply be that Lish, in Gallagher's words, held the 'power of publication access', and as Sklenicka notes, the final judgement on Carver's feelings about the matter may be discerned in the fact that he would subsequently republish several of the stories in their original forms (Sklenicka 2009b, 359–62).[4]

In his subsequent letters, Carver 'slipped back', in Stull's words, 'into the deferential posture he had assumed toward Lish during his drinking years' (Carver 2009, 997). A letter written two days later shows that Carver had accepted the edits: 'It's simply stunning, it is, and I'm honored and grateful for your attentions to it' (Sklenicka 2009b, 358). While Carver now accepted the majority of the changes, he did argue for the restoration of specific details such as the title 'Distance' for the story retitled 'Everything Stuck to Him'. He also requested that one of the stories cut by 78 per cent and retitled by Lish, 'Mr. Coffee and Mr. Fixit' (formerly titled 'Where is Everyone?'), be dropped from the collection entirely. The story was already in press at *Triquarterly* (whose editor, he understood, was submitting it for a possible O. Henry award), and he made it clear that his own proximity to the piece (which concerned an alcoholic facing his own past) also presented a problem, asking Lish to discard it and claiming that 'I can't get any distance at all from that story' (10 July 1980). In the case of certain stories such as 'The Bath', as we shall see, he specifically urged Lish to restore some of the material cut in the second edit. These requests, however, appear (almost without exception) to have been ignored.

Over the course of the editing process, Lish changed not only the title of the collection, but also the names of ten of its stories. He wrote in lines and passages absent from Carver's original manuscript, regularly renamed characters and made a range of textual changes at an often detailed level.[5] Critics have tended,

4 Meyer observes that Carver later opted to include only seven of the seventeen stories from *WWTA* in *Where I'm Calling From* (1988) and that four of these are reprinted in their longer, fuller versions (Meyer 1989, 245–6).

5 In one case, he even halved the number of a hotel room from 22 to 11, as if to reflect the shortening of 'Gazebo' by almost half (Carver 2009, 237, 776).

however, to focus on the difference between version A (*Beginners*) and version C (*WWTA*) without examining the intervening stage. This is understandable, since this stage is unclear in the published texts: apart from isolated details given in the 'Note on the Texts', Stull and Carroll do not give a detailed account of the differences between versions B and C. Sklenicka has written that 'the first revised manuscript is not identifiable among the Lilly holdings' and that 'little archival evidence of the differences between versions B and C has become available to scholars', rendering the development of the editing process 'obscure' (Sklenicka 2009b, 356, 534n11). However, the Carver papers for *WWTA* in the Lilly archive are now clearly divided into Lish's 'First Rewrite' and his 'Second Rewrite', which correspond to versions B and C received by Carver.[6] A study of this material (along with the changes visible in Lilly's 'Master Proofs' and 'Printer's Mss' folders for the collection) makes it possible to follow a story's genetic development with reference to each stage of editing. In the following sections of this chapter, I examine differences between the various drafts – including the 'version B' typescript – in order to trace the evolution of the writing in key stories and arrive at a clearer picture of Lish's involvement.

Staying inside the house: From 'Beginners' to 'What We Talk About When We Talk About Love'

To begin with, we can note the change of the collection's title. Lish took the phrase from a line of dialogue in the story 'Beginners', and a closer examination of both the story and the line itself reveals much about the contrasting visions in its different versions, as the title functions to emphasize the thematic and tonal shifts in the narrative. The story was cut by 50 per cent, with the most noticeable deletion being that of its final 5 pages (Carver 2009, 1003). The base text[7] is

[6] Sklenicka noted that the enormous collection of Lish manuscripts had, at the time of her writing, 'not been fully arranged and catalogued', while an archivist at the Lilly Library states that the collection was approximately 'half-processed' in 2010 (Sklenicka 2009b, 536; Simpson 2017, n.p.). Correspondence with archivists at the library have not yielded a precise explanation of the change, but it seems likely that the Carver papers were rearranged as the collection evolved, with the result that the folders containing Lish's first rewrite were only made available after Sklenicka's visit.

[7] Namely, Lish's copy of the 'version B' manuscript (displaying his edits to typescript A) in Box 44 of the Lilly holdings identified as '*What We Talk About When We Talk About Love* 1st Draft', which Stull and Carroll used as the basis of their edition of *Beginners* (the editors write that they 'restored the stories to their original forms by transcribing Carver's typewritten words that lie beneath Lish's alterations in ink on the typescripts' (Carver 2009, 990)).

riddled with changes, and a study of the different stages of Lish's editing reveals the liberal insertion of paragraph breaks, changes in syntax and the occasional replacement of sizeable chunks of prose with entirely new (and invariably shorter) paragraphs. The story revolves around an informal symposium on love, as two couples sit drinking and discussing their past relationships. In the central section of the story, one of the men, a cardiologist (named Herb by Carver, but renamed Mel by Lish), tells a story-within-a-story of an old couple he encountered in the wake of their car crash, which lasts several pages. The couple's mutual devotion during their convalescence has, we find, made a lasting impression on him. As he addresses the group, Herb describes the intensity of Henry's feelings for his wife and the tenderness of their reconnection after being separated in hospital, a moment that represents one of the clearest examples of human connection in all of Carver's work:

> I pushed Henry up to the left side of the bed and said, 'You have some company, Anna. Company, dear'. But I couldn't say any more than that. She gave a little smile and her face lit up. Out came her hand from under the sheet. It was bluish and bruised-looking. Henry took the hand in his hands. He held it and kissed it. Then he said, 'Hello, Anna. How's my babe? Remember me?' Tears started down her cheeks. She nodded. 'I've missed you', he said. She kept nodding [. . .] We arranged it so they could have lunch and dinner together in her room. In between times they'd just sit and hold hands and talk. They had no end of things to talk about. (Carver 2009, 942)

The reference to talking here serves as allusion and example, as Herb reminds the group that the story is meant to illustrate how we lack understanding 'when we talk about love': 'I just had a card from Henry a few days ago. I guess that's one of the reasons they're on my mind right now. That, and what we were saying about love earlier' (Carver 2009, 943). Herb then assures everyone that the story ends happily, as the couple have recovered – 'sure, they're all right' – and have reunited with their son. Herb's story ends with an explicit reference to the conversation on 'the subject of love' which opens 'Beginners' and acts as a counterbalance to the violent story of Terri's former relationship, a positive illustration of the possibilities of love. In Lish's revisions, though, the couple's story (including their names) is deleted, and Herb's reverent admiration for the strength of the old couple's attachment is replaced by Mel's baffled, darkly comic incredulity:

> 'I'd get up to his mouth-hole, you know, and he'd say no, it wasn't the accident exactly but it was because he couldn't see her through his eye-holes. He said that

> was what was making him feel so bad. Can you imagine? I'm telling you, the man's heart was breaking because he couldn't turn his goddamn head and see his goddamn wife'.
>
> Mel looked around the table and shook his head at what he was going to say. 'I mean, it was killing the old fart just because he couldn't look at the fucking woman'.
>
> We all looked at Mel.
>
> 'Do you see what I'm saying?' he said. (Carver 2009, 320)

In Wallace's copy of *WWTA*, the title story is annotated on almost every page. Wallace's annotations are attentive to the nastiness in Mel's character, but he also sees these lines – as did many critics – as part of a sustained narrative strategy of elision suited to the elusive subject matter: '*love can't be discussed – can only be done obliquely, thru examples*' (Carver 1989, 151).

Mel's story ends (as does 'The Bath') with hospitalization and failed connection, and we are shown the calamity rather than the human connection that comes in its wake. In Carver's original ending, the dialogue between the characters continues and reaches an 'unabashedly theatrical catharsis' (Tracey 2017). Herb leaves the room, and his girlfriend Terri makes the startling confession that she had been pregnant with her ex-lover's baby at the time of his attempted suicide – and that Herb consequently performed an abortion – before finally breaking down in tears. The narrator's lover Laura comforts her, while he goes outside:

> I turned back to the window. The blue layer of sky had given way now and was turning dark like the rest. But stars had appeared. I recognised Venus and farther off and to the side, not as bright but unmistakable there on the horizon, Mars. The wind had picked up [. . .] I wanted to imagine horses rushing through those fields in the near dark, or even just standing quietly with their heads in opposite directions near the fence. I stood at the window and waited. I knew I had to keep still a while longer, keep my eyes out there, outside the house as long as there was something left to see. (Carver 2009, 948)

The movement towards openness and escape in the final lines hints at the ending of the later 'Cathedral' – 'My eyes were still closed. I was in my house. I knew that. But I didn't feel like I was inside anything' (Carver 2009, 529) – and suggests a redemption of sorts in which the boundaries of the 'house' of identity are at least temporarily transcended.[8] The tone of the story is dramatically altered in Lish's edit, and the final lines read as follows:

[8] The ending also seems clearly to parallel Chekhov's story 'Concerning Love'. The structure of Chekhov's story – a dinner party discussion on the meaning of love – may (along with Plato's

'I'll put out some cheese and crackers', Terri said.

But Terri just sat there. She did not get up to get anything. Mel turned his glass over. He spilled it out on the table.

'Gin's gone', Mel said.

Terri said, 'Now what?'

I could hear my heart beating. I could hear everyone's heart. I could hear the human noise we sat there making, not one of us moving, not even when the room went dark. (Carver 2009, 322)

The ending here is austere and abrupt: the blunt, monosyllabic question 'Now what?' is lent a stark existential terror by the suddenness of the termination, and the final lines leave a stylized, theatrical impression, as if the lights have gone out on stage. Wallace marked the final three sentences here with the words 'Do end', presumably indicating that he planned to teach the story in class.[9] These were written almost entirely by Lish: only the first line of the paragraph quoted above is present in the original manuscript. Nesset's discussion of this story is representative of the way in which the effects introduced by Lish have largely determined its reception: he writes that the couples 'end up paralysed by inertia, sitting in silence' and compares the darkness of the room at the story's end to the state of psychological and spiritual unknowing of the characters, who are engaged with 'a subject so elusive and powerful that its discoursers can only talk around it, and are left literally in the dark in the end' (Nesset 1995, 77, 92). McDermott takes the ending of the story as an exemplary one, writing that Carver's characters 'are like the couples of ["WWTA"] as the party comes to a close and they feel themselves powerless to sustain the connections they had established over the course of one evening' (McDermott 2006, 99). Hallett notes the theatrical dimension of the story and makes an explicit comparison to

Symposium) have provided the model for 'Beginners', and its final movement towards nature and sympathetic exchange between characters is paralleled in Carver's story:

> While Alehin was telling his story, the rain left off and the sun came out. Burkin and Ivan Ivanovich went out on the balcony, from which there was a beautiful view over the garden and the mill-pond, which was shining now in the sunshine like a mirror. They admired it, and at the same time they were sorry that this man with the kind, clever eyes, who had told them this story with such genuine feeling, should be rushing round and round this huge estate like a squirrel on a wheel [. . .] and they thought what a sorrowful face Anna Alexyevna must have had when he said good-bye to her in the railway carriage and kissed her face and shoulders. (Chekhov 2011, 118)

[9] Wallace often wrote the word 'Do' next to passages in the books he annotated; researcher Eric Whiteside argues persuasively that these are texts the author intended to teach, pointing out that Wallace wrote 'Do in class' next to a passage in McCarthy's *Blood Meridian* (Pitchel 2011, n.p.).

Beckett's *Waiting for Godot*, noting that the four characters on the story's 'stage' 'talk of going somewhere but never go anywhere' (Hallett 1999, 58).

The more hopeful title 'Beginners' hints at the possibility of renewal (a possibility also suggested by the narrator's encounter with nature at the end of Carver's original). When read in concert with Lish's changes to the story as a whole, though, the repetition in the replacement title contains an undercurrent of bleakness and absurdity, directing the reader's attention to the idea of love as an unknowable and unapproachable mystery (a 'human noise' made in the dark rather than an ideal to be struggled for). The phrase could be seen, then, not only as a microcosm of Lish's editing techniques but as emblematic of his work on the collection as a whole. Lish adapted the phrase during his first edit, changing the title of the story and using it as the title of the collection: Carver accepted the change and introduced an enduringly influential and adaptable phrase into the language (Carver 1980j).[10] Lish's change makes the title noticeably longer, of course, which may sit oddly with the legacy of this supposed 'ur-minimalist' work. However, closer consideration of the title shows that it incorporates many of the qualities and techniques that Lish sought in fiction. Lucarelli describes the importance of 'acoustical consecution' to Lish's poetics, mentioning 'recursive techniques in which sounds repeat in the form of alliteration [. . .] assonance [. . .] and consonance' and referring to the injunction by Gary Lutz (a friend and former student of Lish's) that 'the words in the sentence must bear some physical and sonic resemblance to each other' (Lucarelli 2013, n.p.). Lish has told his students that 'the force of English lies in its vowels' and urged them to 'resonate the stressed assonances in your work, in a phrase, a clause, a paragraph, a sentence' (Callis n.d., 4 Dec. 1990). The vowel-heavy, alliterative phrase '*What We Talk About When We Talk About Love*' demonstrates these qualities of assonance and acoustic resonance as well as any in Lish's own work, with its structural (and almost exact) repetition of two four-word phrases; it also demonstrates a kind of ostentatious, almost unnecessary repetition that, as

[10] The phrase has been the subject of homage by at least two fiction writers. Knopf has published both *What I Talk About When I Talk About Running* by Carver's acquaintance and translator Haruki Murakami (2008) and *What We Talk About When We Talk About Anne Frank* by Nathan Englander (2012), a collection whose title story – a rewrite, as its author has noted, of Carver's – won the 2012 Frank O'Connor International Short Story Award. The phrase has also shown itself to be a useful device for non-fiction writers: recent books have replaced its concluding noun with 'Faith' (Stanford 2018), 'the Tube' (Lanchester 2013) and 'Food' (Ferguson 2014). The phrase's ubiquity as a template for titling journalistic think-pieces and academic articles has been noted and criticized by several bloggers, one of whom points out the absurd range of topics – such as 'Drones', 'The Olympics' and 'Cloud Network Performance' – brought into its orbit (Cliffe 2013, n.p.).

Botha remarks of Gertude Stein's use of 'circuitous and cyclical patterns', places 'an emphasis on the immanence of language in itself' (Botha 2017, 76). While the phrase is present in Carver's original in almost the same form, Lish isolated and repurposed it (as he would do with elements of other stories) to achieve sonic and tonal effects that subtly affect the reader's experience of the narrative.

Lucarelli examines the way in which 'thematic consecution' is achieved in Lish-influenced stories through the use of 'rhetorical questions [. . .] image or word patterning and aphorisms' (Lucarelli 2013, n.p.): Lish's title can also be seen as an instance of such techniques, with the phrase ending in a clear focus on the story's subject matter and the repeated clauses suggesting the characters' obsessive and repetitive attempts to plumb its mysterious depths.[11] By paraphrasing Herb's remark as he introduces the story – 'I was going to prove a point [. . .] it ought to make us all feel ashamed when we talk like we know what we were talking about, when we talk about love' – and making it the title of both the story and the collection, Lish amplifies, through thematic consecution, Herb's question 'What do any of us really know about love?'(Carver 2009, 932–4); by cutting out the most moving parts of Herb's story, however, he excises the answer. Lish has opined that 'the best ending, for example that of *Moby-Dick*, is the annihilation of its beginning' and the progression of '*WWTA*' embodies this destructive trajectory, moving from the conversation-in-progress depicted in its first sentence ('My friend Mel McGinnis was talking') to Mel's – and the group's – stunned silence at the story's close (Callis n.d., 4 Dec. 1990).

Little human connections: From 'A Small, Good Thing' to 'The Bath'

'A Small, Good Thing', which was retitled 'The Bath' by Lish and cut by 78 per cent, would prove to be one of the most enduringly contentious edits for Carver. In a 1987 interview with Kasia Boddy, Carver said:

> It won a prize when it appeared in a magazine, but I felt it was a minor league effort, and I'm not happy with it to this day. I'm going to be publishing a *Selected Stories* and I'm not going to include 'The Bath'. I am going to include 'A Small,

[11] Two pages after his comment that love, in this story, could only be discussed 'obliquely', Wallace underlined the story's title at the top of the page and used a similar phrase to reiterate the elliptical approach to subject matter: 'title – can't be addressed except <u>obliquely</u>' (Carver 1989, 153).

> Good Thing', of course. But I don't do that kind of rewriting any more [. . .] I do all the revision when I'm writing a story, and once it's published I'm just not interested in it any longer. I want to look ahead. I think that's healthy. (Carver 1990, 200)

Here, Carver again repeats the erroneous claim that he expanded the longer story from the shorter one, a claim first made on the title page of the story as it appeared in *Ploughshares* in 1982: 'This story is expanded and revised from *What We Talk About When We Talk About Love*' (Sklenicka 2009b, 392). Carver was true to his word in relation to future publication, though, and chose 'A Small, Good Thing' for inclusion in *Where I'm Calling From*, his career-spanning 1988 collection, having already published the story in its original form and under its original title in *Cathedral*.

As we saw in Chapter 1, Wallace considered this to be the correct choice, and in this he was not alone among critics. Irving Howe's verdict on 'The Bath' was withering: 'The first version, I would say, is a bit like second-rank Hemingway, and the second a bit like Sherwood Anderson at his best, especially in the speech rhythms of the baker' (Howe 1983). Stephen King sees 'The Bath' as the prime example of Lish's 'baleful' influence on the collection, arguing that Carver's original version 'has a satisfying symmetry that the stripped-down Lish version lacks, but it has something more important: it has *heart*' (King 2009, n.p.). Murakami agrees that the longer version is 'certainly the superior work', although he argues (using a similar anatomical metaphor to King) that the shorter version has 'its own special flavour' due to the impression that the story 'has had its head lopped off for no reason' (Murakami 2006, 131).[12]

'A Small, Good Thing' introduces a couple whose son gets hit by a car on his birthday, following them as they lose him after a lengthy and emotionally devastating hospital vigil by his bedside. Meanwhile, they begin to receive threatening, enigmatic phone calls, which turn out to be from the baker of the boy's birthday cake, ordered by the mother before the accident and never collected. After the boy's death, the grief-stricken parents drive at midnight to the bakery to confront the man. When they explain what has happened, he asks them to sit down and bakes cakes for them, telling them of his 'loneliness, and the sense of doubt and limitation that had come to him in his middle years' and apologizing for his behaviour:

[12] Indeed, he selected the shorter version for inclusion in a 2002 anthology entitled *Birthday Stories*.

> 'I'm sorry for your son, and I'm sorry for my part in this. Sweet, sweet Jesus [. . .] I don't have any children myself, so I can only imagine what you must be feeling. All I can say to you now is that I'm sorry. Forgive me, if you can'. (Carver 2009, 829–30)

Wallace's notes on 'A Small, Good Thing' – again, seemingly written with the aim of teaching the story in class – observe that the baker is 'isolated' and that the encounter is redemptive for the couple: 'they get to heal through forgiveness' (Kennedy 1991, 285).[13] The story ends with the couple eating the baker's bread and listening to him speak, an unlikely scene of reconciliation and human connection that offers a measure of comfort to the traumatized characters. In the final lines, the couple break bread with the baker, hearing his story and taking what comfort they can:

> They listened to him. They ate what they could. They swallowed the dark bread. It was like daylight under the fluorescent trays of light. They talked on into the early morning, the high pale cast of light in the window, and they did not think of leaving. (Carver 2009, 830)[14]

The contrast with 'The Bath' is remarkable. Here, the story ends as the threatening calls begin, and we are not told whether the child lives or dies.[15] The mother returns home from the hospital to take a bath, and the tale stops abruptly in an ending of overwhelming confusion and menace:

> The telephone rang.
> 'Yes!' She said. 'Hello!' she said.
> 'Mrs Weiss', a man's voice said.
> 'Yes', she said. 'This is Mrs Weiss. Is it about Scotty?' she said.
> 'Scotty', the voice said. 'It is about Scotty', the voice said. 'It has to do with Scotty, yes'. (Carver 2009, 257)

[13] Wallace annotated the story in his copy of *Literature: An Introduction to Fiction, Poetry, and Drama*, an anthology edited by X. J. Kennedy.

[14] In his biographical essay, Stull names Chekhov's 'In the Hollow' as one of the stories which particularly influenced Carver's later work, and this influence is more clearly visible in 'A Small, Good Thing'. Chekhov's story, which depicts the meeting of characters shattered by a child's death and familial destruction, closes with an image of food being exchanged as a small consolation against grief: 'The old man stopped, looked at them both wordlessly, lips shaking, eyes full of tears. Lipa got a piece of buckwheat pasty from her mother's bundle and gave it to him. He took it and started eating' (Chekhov 1975, 187).

[15] Hallett also notes the indeterminacy of the final words of the dialogue, which 'are not conclusively from the baker or the hospital' (Hallett 1999, 62).

Max suggests that 'the story's redemptive tone' is altered to 'one of Beckettian despair' (Max 1998, n.p.). Lish's edit ends with the principal characters indoors, alone: Carver's original ending, though, as we see, ends with all three eating and speaking under the light of the windows. As such it could be read almost as a literal riposte to John Biguenet's later criticisms of the solipsistic and 'impossibly constricted' worlds represented in Minimalist fiction: 'Minimalism reminds us that light cannot enter a room through a mirror. Only a window admits the world. For the moment, some of our finest writers have their backs to the window' (Biguenet 1985, 45).

Unlike most of the stories in *WWTA*, 'The Bath' has – as explained above – been available in both its original and its edited form for many years. However, critics have uniformly accepted Carver's claims that the chronology of its publication reflected that of its composition, and that the alternate versions of some of the stories in *WWTA* that he published after 1981 were revisions of ones whose potential he himself had failed to realize. Chief among these claims is perhaps the one in the 1984 interview quoted in Chapter 1, in which he spoke of the 'unfinished business' calling him back to the story and his amazement at the fact that his rewriting had made the story 'so much better' (Carver 1990, 102). The story has tended to be taken as the chief piece of evidence for its author's move from Minimalism to a more expansive mode of fiction, a move neatly paralleled by Carver's own recovery from alcoholism. Saltzman credited 'the increased stability and ease in Carver's personal life' for the 'ventilation of the claustrophobic method and attitude' prevalent in his work prior to *Cathedral* (Saltzman 1988, 124); Stull claimed that 'During the 1980s his once spare, skeptical fiction became increasingly expansive and affirmative [. . .] his fiction was growing longer and looser, novelistic in the manner of Chekhov's late works' (Stull 1989, n.p.). Murakami states that 'The overwhelming majority of Carver's early works deal with loss and despair, but later an element of redemption enters in', claiming that the contrast between the two stories provides 'a vivid demonstration of the drastic change' (Murakami 2006, 131). Adam Meyer summed up this view with his influential verdict that Carver's career has 'taken on the shape of an hourglass, beginning wide, then narrowing, and then widening out again' and that 'Carver has undergone an aesthetic evolution, at first moving toward minimalism but then turning sharply away from it' (Meyer 1989, 239, 249). The assumption of a strong authorial vision in these statements, the temptingly clear linear narrative of individual aesthetic development and the well-known arc of Carver's personal life, all contributed to the story's status as a marker of its author's turn away from Minimalism.

The longer version, critics concur, shifts its focus to warmth, light, sympathy, connection and redemption, and represents a dramatic shift in tone. Hallett encapsulates this critical consensus, suggesting that the two iterations of the narrative 'cannot be identified simply as separate versions [. . .] they are not the same story; nor is one merely an extension of the other' and takes this contrast to be 'the most profound example of [the] change in Carver's style and vision' (Hallett 1999, 63). May agrees, stating that the longer version 'moves towards a more conventionally moral ending – acceptance'. The ending of the story, he claims, presents 'a clear image of Carver's moral shift from the sceptical to the affirmative, from the sense of the unspeakable mystery of human life to the sense of how simple and moral life is after all' (May 1995, 97). McDermott concurs with this view of Carver's development and suggests that the 'tableau of light and conversation' at the end of 'A Small, Good Thing' 'stands in direct opposition to the scene that concludes ['WWTA'], in which the couples fall silent as the room becomes dark'; he suggests that 'what is new' in the stories from *Cathedral* onwards is 'that the community of outcasts the earlier stories gesture toward but fail to depict is finally shown' (McDermott 2006, 111).

The Lish papers in the Lilly library contain two separate revisions of 'The Bath'. While critics have noted the differences between the various published versions, no detailed comparison has yet been made between the first and the second revision and of the specific changes that Carver was willing to accept. On the 10th of July 1981 (two days after the famous 4-page letter attempting to cease publication) when Carver had apparently accepted Lish's edits, he was still urging his editor to reconsider some specific changes:

> Please look through the enclosed copy of [*WWTA*], the entire collection. You'll see that nearly all of the changes are small enough, but I think they're significant and they all can be found in the first edited ms version you sent me [. . .] it's a question of reinstating some of those things that were taken out in the second version [. . .] I feel strongly [that] some of those things taken out should be back in the finished stories. (Carver 2007, 10 July 1980)

In the margins of the typed letter, a little further down, he hand-wrote: '"The Bath" which was 15 pp in the 1st edited version, and now only 12. We might have lost too much in those 3 pages'. A few days later, he made it clear that this was a deeply felt request:

> But do give those things a hard third or fourth look. My greatest fear is, or was, having them too pared, and I'm thinking of 'Community Center' and 'The Bath' both of which lost several pages each in the second editing. I want that sense of beauty and mystery they have now, but I don't want to lose track, lose touch with the little human connections I saw in the first version you sent me. (Carver 2007, 14 July 1980)

A closer look at the second revision of 'The Bath' allows us to trace the changes Lish made to the first revised version, which Carver appears to have been more willing to accept. These changes generally take the form of compression and deletion within paragraphs rather than the removal of large blocks of text in their entirety, but the cumulative effect is such that Carver evidently felt the changes were excessive. Indeed, Lish edited out several examples of what we might call 'human connections', moments in which the couple at the story's centre are granted expressions of compassion by minor characters. At one point, for example, a staff member at the hospital, described in Carver's words as a 'young woman', enters the room to take blood from the boy; she asks the boy's mother what has happened and looks repeatedly at the child in sympathy. The woman was changed in Lish's second edit to a 'technician', and these lines of dialogue and description were removed (Carver 1980d). Similarly, the editor altered the moment when the mother meets another couple in the hospital who are waiting on their son:

> The man shifted in his chair. [. . .] ~~He looked down at the table, and then he looked back at the mother.~~ He said, 'Our Nelson, ~~somebody cut him. They say he was just standing and watching. We're~~ **we're** just hoping and praying'. ~~He gazed at the mother and tugged on the bill of his cap.~~ (Carver 1980d)[16]

The look or gaze, in Carver's story, functions as a muted expression of sentiment, and characters are shown seeking (and sometimes verbalizing their desire for) understanding and solace.[17] The mother's concern is shown elsewhere in the 'version B' manuscript, as she follows the son's trolley as he is taken for more tests and 'stood beside the rolling thing and gazed at the sleeping boy'. As he

[16] Reprinted by permission of Gordon Lish. All rights reserved.

[17] In her comparison of the two previously published versions of the story, Hallett presents the elliptical version of this passage as an example of the 'miscued actions and brief dialogue of non-sequiturs' that contribute to 'textual dysfunction' and pervasive sense of broken communication in 'The Bath' (Hallett 1999, 62). Botha, too, observes the importance of failed communication: 'what bars Carver's characters, and by extension the reader, from exercising substantial political agency is precisely the missed encounter, the encounter which is not recognized as such' (Botha 2017, 55).

tended to do elsewhere, Lish removed moments in which a character attempts to reassure their partner: 'When the woman could not wake the child, she hurried to the telephone and called her husband at work. The man said to remain calm' (Carver 1980d).

In his second edit of the story Lish also highlighted the sense of menace and ambient fear, removing a sentence from the account of the fatal accident describing the 'man in the driver's seat' looking back to ensure that the boy gets up after the collision (Carver 1980c). The driver thus disappears from the story and is changed from a character with identifiable motivations to an unseen, menacing (and, in May's words, 'shadowy' presence) (May 1994, 213). The same process can be seen with the character of the baker in the final lines of the story. In his second edit, Lish removed three mentions of the 'man' calling Mrs Weiss, making the character simply a 'voice', a malevolent presence on the telephone:

> 'Scotty', the ~~man's~~ voice said. 'It~~'s~~ **is** about Scotty'**, the voice said.** ~~It has to do with Scotty, yes.~~ [']Have you forgotten **all** about ~~Scotty?~~ **him?'** ~~the man said.~~
> ~~And then the man hung up.~~ (Carver 1980d)[18]

The sense of absent or failed connection is also evident in the relationship between the central characters, the comatose boy's parents. Lish removed several lines, for example, in which the husband looks at the child and then stands beside the woman as they look out the window. Another scene in which the couple watch their unconscious son in hospital shows the way in which Lish subtly downplayed the connection between them:

> The husband sat in the chair beside her. He wanted to say something else**.** ~~to reassure her. But he was afraid to~~ **But there was no saying what it should be.** He took her hand and put it in his lap~~, and this~~. **This** made him feel better~~, her hand being there. He picked up her hand and just held it~~. **It made him feel he was saying something.** They sat like that for a while, watching the boy**,** ~~and~~ not talking. From time to time he squeezed her hand~~. Finally, the woman~~ **until she** took **it** ~~her hand~~ away ~~and rubbed her temples~~.
>
> 'I've been praying', she said. ~~She said, 'Maybe if you prayed too', she said to him.~~
>
> ~~'I've already prayed',~~ **'Me too',** he said. 'I've been praying, **too**', he said.
>
> ~~'That's good', she said.~~ (Carver 1980d)[19]

[18] Reprinted by permission of Gordon Lish. All rights reserved.

[19] Reprinted by permission of Gordon Lish. All rights reserved.

This moment serves as a genetic illustration of Saltzman's (1988, 144) observation that 'every extension of detail' in 'A Small, Good Thing' enhances its affective dimension and constitutes a 'development of the spiritual cost of the crisis'. The edits here subtly change the nature of the characters' actions – Carver's version reveals the husband's desire to reassure his wife and the fact that he 'held' her hand rather than simply placing it in his lap. This moment, in the original manuscript, sets up a textual echo with the moment when the narrator of 'Beginners' holds his lover's hand; the removal of the final line here (which is followed by a paragraph break) also removes the internal echo of the word 'good' with Carver's original title for the story (Carver 2009, 928).

Lish's additions here also create an intertextual link: the line 'But there was no saying what it should be' is very similar to the final line of the collection ('But then he could not think what it could possibly be' (Carver 2009, 326)), creating an altogether different resonance suggesting a larger story of inarticulacy and verbal failure in the collection. Lish also wrote the final line of this concluding story, 'One More Thing'. In Carver's original, the truculent, alcoholic narrator faces his wife and daughter as he is about to leave them and attempts to utter words that will atone for his behaviour:

> 'I just want to say one more thing, Maxine. Listen to me. Remember this', he said. 'I love you. I love you both no matter what happens. I love you too, Bea. I love you both'. He stood there at the door and felt his lips begin to tingle as he looked at them for what, he believed, might be the last time. 'Good-bye', he said . . .
>
> 'Is this what love is, L.D.?' she said, fixing her eyes on him. Her eyes were terrible and deep, and he held them as long as he could. (Carver 2009, 953)

Lish removed everything after the first line here, removing the husband's farewell speech and replacing it with the dry narratorial comment 'But then he could not think what it could possibly be.'[20] Lish's version presents us with a protagonist who is – to borrow May's words – 'trapped in his own inarticulateness' and who does not – to return to Herzinger's definition of the Minimalist protagonist – 'think out loud' (May 1994, 213; Herzinger 1985, 11). Leypoldt takes this moment as a prime

[20] This ending bears some resemblance to the sense of speechless paralysis present in some of James Purdy's stories, such as that afflicting the husband in 'Don't Call Me By My Right Name': 'He did not know what to say. He felt anything he said might destroy his mind. He stood there with an insane emptiness on his eyes and lips' (55). Lish has recalled that he was influenced by Purdy and Grace Paley when editing Carver's stories and that he particularly admired Purdy's sense of 'the dark, the unexplained, the uncanny' (Sklenicka 2009b, 215).

example of the lack of self-knowledge and understanding to be found in *WWTA*'s characters and states that at the end of this story, 'the reader is far ahead of Carver's character' (Leypoldt 2001, 539). In his changes to individual stories, Lish was inserting patterns that would alter the reader's experience of the collection as a whole, an experience defined by a sense of distance from a set of characters who are unable to verbalize or meaningfully confront their predicaments.

'Too abrupt?': Rewriting 'Friendship'

'Tell the Women We're Going' was, as mentioned in Chapter 2, one of the first stories that Lish had advised Carver on in the early days of their relationship. This is apparent from a letter Carver wrote to Lish shortly after the latter had taken up his position at *Esquire,* in which he thanked him for his observations on 'Friendship', the story's original title (Carver 1969b). The story follows two childhood friends, Bill and Jerry, as they leave a family picnic to go drinking and pursue two young girls, with tragic consequences; while Bill is eager to return to his wife and children, Jerry's behaviour becomes increasingly more sinister until, in a gruesome finale, he rapes and kills one of the girls. 'What's noteworthy about the story', as Max observes of the version the author gave to Lish in 1980, 'is the way Carver makes a boring afternoon build to murder' (Max 1998, n.p.); the primary effect of the narrative is the mounting tension of the pursuit and its uncertain outcome. We are shown glimpses of Jerry's rising frustration as he tries to 'open it up' while driving on the highway and hints of the reasons behind this: 'His hair was beginning to recede, just like his father's, and he was getting heavy around the hips' (Carver 2009, 832–5). Bill and Jerry chase the two girls in a manner that begins as flirtatious and playful. When the girls run in different directions, the men become separated; the narrative focus then shifts to Jerry as he corners one girl and the implicit menace of the story's premise finally comes to the surface. Over several pages of scrupulous description and dialogue, Jerry struggles with the girl, attempting to subdue and rape her, and the violence here is described in unflinching detail.[21] A final section, lasting roughly a page,

[21] We are told, for example, that 'When she tried to get to her feet again, he picked up a rock and slammed it into her face. He actually heard her teeth and bones crack, and blood came out between her lips' (Carver 2009, 842). The story is unusually violent for Carver's work, and Capra Press's Noel Young deemed it 'too gruesome for my quavering senses' when Carver submitted it for publication in 1977 (Carver 2009, 1000).

depicts Bill's arrival on the scene. We see his reflections and anxieties about the situation – 'he just wanted to round up Jerry, get back before it got any later' – and follow his shock as the reality and magnitude of the crime sink in. The final lines recall the story's original title, with the destruction of the men's friendship represented in a dramatic embrace:

> Bill felt the awful closeness of their two bodies, less than an arm's length between. Then the head came down on Bill's shoulder. He raised his hand, and as if the distance now separating them deserved at least this, he began to pat, to stroke the other, while his own tears broke. (843–4)[22]

When Lish edited the story for *WWTA* he cut it by 55 per cent, leaving out many of the details that accumulate in the original and changing the final pages of the story entirely. Here, the violence is contained in a few short lines which (as well as turning a murder into a double murder) provide a shockingly blunt ending:

> Bill took out a cigarette. But he could not get it lit. Then Jerry showed up. It did not matter after that.
>
> Bill had just wanted to fuck. Or even to see them naked. On the other hand, it was okay with him if it didn't work out.
>
> He never knew what Jerry wanted. But it started and ended with a rock. Jerry used the same rock on both girls, first on the girl called Sharon and then on the one that was supposed to be Bill's. (Carver 2009, 264)[23]

As Max observes, 'The pursuit is eliminated: the violence now comes out of nowhere and is almost hallucinogenic.' The story's ending leaves the reader with a huge interpretive gap as the shocking plot development is advanced in a single final line: Max suggests that this story constitutes a 'wholesale rewrite' (Max 1998, n.p.).

The difference between the version Carver gave to Lish – version A – and the published version – version C – is clear, and the two can be read side by side in the *Collected Stories*. However, as with the other examples here, an examination of the way the story develops between Lish's first and second rewrites illuminates the way the editor progressively changed its characters and overall tone. For example, in his second rewrite, the editor removed some of Bill's doubts about Jerry's behaviour, which in Carver's original function partly in order for the

[22] Reprinted by permission of Gordon Lish. All rights reserved.
[23] Reprinted by permission of Gordon Lish. All rights reserved.

reader to recognize their own. In response to Jerry's statement 'Guy's got to get out [. . .] You know what I mean?', the narrative shifts to Bill's thoughts, which Lish edited as follows:

> Bill ~~wasn't sure~~ **understood.** He liked to get out with the guys from the plant for the Friday night bowling league~~, and he~~**. He** liked to stop off ~~once or~~ twice a week after work to have a few beers with Jack Broderick~~, but he liked being at home too~~. **He knew a guy's got to get out.** (Carver 1980d)[24]

The elimination of the coordinating conjunctions here ('and' and 'but') and the addition of the approving verbs ('understood' and 'knew') change the mood and sense of this passage entirely. Bill's hesitancy is changed to unquestioning agreement, and the tone is changed to stereotypical male interaction: in the margins beside this passage in his copy of *WWTA*, Wallace wrote 'vapid, regular' (Carver 1989, 60). The Lishian repetition of a particular phrase – 'a guy's got to get out' – suggests a sense of complicity on Bill's part (Max argues that in this edit, 'Bill becomes just a passive companion to Jerry'). When the men go for a drink, Jerry asks about the absence of girls from the bar, and Lish changed the barman's response to a more vulgar innuendo: 'Riley laughed. He said, "I guess ~~there just ain't enough to go around, boys."~~ **they're all in church praying for it"**' (Carver 1980b). Beside this, in his copy, Wallace wrote 'nasty, sexual' (61). Towards the end of the story, during the chase – which, in the final version, takes place obliquely in a couple of paragraphs – Lish added an expletive that shifts the tone suddenly: 'Jerry said, "You go right and I'll go straight. We'll cut ~~them~~ **the cockteasers** off". ~~Jerry said~~.'[25] Wallace, underlining the final two words here ('cockteasers off'), wrote 'scary' in the margin (Carver 1989, 65).

Several reviewers singled out the story's ending for comment, generally negative. Houston's review asserted that, 'Carver resorts to a violence he hasn't earned for an ending, and comes near to breaking his own primal rule: "No tricks"' (Houston 1981, 24). Tim O'Brien's review presents the sudden, shocking violence at the end of the story as an example of a moment which strains credibility: 'the crime seems merely spontaneous, merely brutal, merely stunning' (O'Brien 1981, 2). LeClair singled out the same story as a failure of style, claiming that the attempt at a 'dramatic ending' falls flat: 'For Carver, simplicity works best at the low end of the scale' (LeClair 1982, 87). Wallace also had reservations about the ending, it seems, as his comments in the margin have

[24] Reprinted by permission of Gordon Lish. All rights reserved.
[25] Reprinted by permission of Gordon Lish. All rights reserved.

a critical tone that occurs nowhere else in his annotations: he asks 'Too abrupt?' and wonders 'What in 1st section explains the end?' (66). All of these criticisms are reactions to the work of the story's editor rather than its author.

The ending also emphasizes another important aspect of Lish's editing, namely the fact that his edits of the stories were carried out in quick succession and add a unified feel to the collection. Lish's changes, as Sklenicka points out, applied Poe's notion of the short story's 'unity of effect' to the collection as a whole, with the sequencing of the pieces causing individual edits to interact with those in the surrounding stories. Specifically, she observes that:

> Comparing the way Lish honed the endings of four stories from the middle of the book – 'The Bath', 'Tell the Women We're Going', 'After the Denim', and 'So Much Water So Close to Home' – reveals that in each case Lish's version ends with a held breath and suggestion of imminent violence. (Sklenicka 2009b, 369)

While the phrasing of this is imprecise – in the story under discussion here, for example, the violence is sudden and irrevocable rather than 'imminent' – the point is a valid one. Indeed, the ending of 'Tell the Women We're Going' is one of a number of moments in the collection that prompt the close reader to detect an intratextual link.[26] The story is one of two that close on the image of a rock, a link that emerged late in the editing process. In his second edit of the story, Lish added the repetition of the word 'rock', making it the focus of both of the final sentences: 'He never knew what Jerry wanted. But it started with ~~the~~ **a** rock. ~~that Jerry picked up,~~ **Jerry used the same rock on both girls,** first Sharon and then the one that was ~~supposed~~ **going** to be Bill's' (Carver 1980d).[27] This echoes the ending of 'Viewfinder', the second story in the sequence. On the printer's manuscript of 'Viewfinder', Lish changed the final lines to repeat the name of the object that the narrator throws from his rooftop: '"Again!" I screamed, and I ~~grabbed hold of another.~~ **took up another rock**' (Carver 1980f).[28] Here, thematic and acoustical consecution is being introduced not only at the sentence and story level, but across the collection as a whole. The endings of each of these stories, in Carver's originals, suggest moments of communion and reconciliation rather than sudden violence, and the resonances between them in *WWTA* are very different from those in *Beginners*.

[26] Randolph Runyon traces links such as these in order to illuminate the internal 'echoes' within each of Carver's collections, noting Lish's agency in the case of *WWTA* (Runyon 2013, 159–71).

[27] In the margin, Lish wrote to his secretary: 'Carol, new sentence after "rock"' (Carver 1980b).

[28] Reprinted by permission of Gordon Lish. All rights reserved.

When Carver collected his stories in *Where I'm Calling From* in 1988, he decided to exclude 'Tell the Women We're Going' from the volume entirely. It is difficult not to observe a symbolic parallel between the drastic revision and subsequent omission of 'Friendship' and the disintegration of his and Lish's own friendship, as the story's iterations span almost the entirety of the growth and disintegration of their editorial and personal relationship.

'A total rewrite': Human connection in 'If It Please You'

Another story whose 'human connections' Carver missed after the second round of edits was called (at this stage) 'Community Center'. Lish cut the 26-page manuscript by 63 per cent, removing the final 6 pages in his first round of edits (Carver 2009, 1001). The story's protagonists, James and Edith Packer, attend a bingo game in their local community centre; James is frustrated at arriving late, already unsettled ('I don't feel lucky') and becomes increasingly agitated as he sees a young 'hippie' couple cheating during the game. During the evening, Edith reveals that her illness has returned and when they return home, she sleeps while James finds himself alone with his fears. He begins to knit (a hobby, we learn, that he took up when he gave up drinking) and to reflect on his life. His anger at the couple's cheating dissipates as he considers their shared humanity – 'He and the hippie were in the same boat, he thought, but the hippie just didn't know it yet' – and he recalls the importance of prayer during the time when he was trying 'to kick the drink' (Carver 2009, 845–63). In the final paragraphs, James receives a revelation of sorts – 'He suddenly felt he had lived nearly his whole life without having ever once really stopped to think about anything, and this came to him now as a terrible shock and increased his feeling of unworthiness' – that prompts him to pray for 'enlightenment' on his situation. His prayers lead to an expansion of his vision, as he feels 'something stir inside him again':

> He lay as if waiting. Then something left him and something else took its place. He found tears in his eyes. He began praying again, words and parts of speech piling up in a torrent in his mind. He went slower. He put the words together, one after the other, and prayed. This time he was able to include the girl and the hippie in his prayers [. . .] 'If it please you', he said in the new prayers for all of them, the living and the dead. (Carver 2009, 863)

The final lines here, of course, closely echo Joyce's 'The Dead' as the narrative focus shifts dramatically from the specific to the general and the narrative consciousness moves towards a moment of spiritual awareness. Speech and prayer lead to what seems like a moment of redemption, and James' urge to communicate leads to understanding and release; Lish's deletion of the final 5 pages removes this sense of release and leaves the character arrested and frustrated.[29]

As we have seen, Carver had singled out the story when reiterating his concerns to Lish immediately after the second round of editing. In November, Lish came (at Carver and Gallagher's invitation) to speak to Carver's class at Syracuse, and a letter written a few days after this suggests that the event had been a success: Carver writes that the visit was 'extraordinary' and tells his editor that 'I feel closer to you than to my own brother.' However, it is clear that he was still bothered by some of the changes and again mentioned this story in particular:

> I wish those few changes we looked at in the motel that afternoon could be incorporated in the bound pages. I'm thinking particularly of the last sentence, phrase, whatever, for 'Community Center'. That gives the story its resonance. (Carver 1980n)

Carver was presumably referring to the final sentence of Lish's first edit, as James prepares to begin knitting: 'Then he set to work exactly where he'd left off.' Lish had removed this sentence (which suggests the character's determination to re-engage in the redemptive 'work' of living) from the second edit, and he reinstated it in edits made on the galleys, acceding to Carver's request. However, he also added some additional phrases, suggesting that he did not feel himself to be closely bound by the author's wishes. Further changes to the second set of proofs show him again returning to the final lines:

> Holding the tiny needle to the light, James Packer stabbed at the eye with a length of blue silk thread. Then he set to work—stitch after stitch. **—making believe he was waving like the man on the keel.** (Carver 1980e)[30]

The 'man on the keel' appears early in the story. The narrator describes the foyer of the community centre, the walls of which contain maritime photographs; one

[29] Stephen King singled this edit out for criticism in his review of *Beginners*, arguing that 'In the Lish-edited version, there are no prayers and hence no epiphany – only a worried and resentful husband who wants to tell the irritating hippies what happens "after the denim", after the games. It's a total rewrite, and it's a cheat' (King 2009, n.p.).

[30] Reprinted by permission of Gordon Lish.

of these shows 'a boat that had turned over ~~on the rocks at low tide.~~, a man standing on the keel and waving ~~at the camera~~' (Carver 1980d). Carver's first draft identifies this as one of the boats that has been 'driven ashore onto the sandy beaches below the town' (Carver 2009, 848), and the man in Carver's original is, as is clear from the end of the sentence, waving at a companion. Lish's edit to the line early in the story removes the social dimension from the man's action, making it an isolated wave without any clear audience; his change to the final line of the story, with its return to the same image, adds a note of hopelessness and absurdity to James' knitting. In his final changes to 'Community Center', then, Lish reinstated Carver's last line while including a final clause that subverts the character's actions and adds a note of mockery to the narrative voice.

Lish also changed the title of the story, again apparently without Carver's knowledge. The original title, 'If it Please You', refers to the phrase uttered by James as he prays for all of humanity, 'the living and the dead' (Carver 2009, 863). The subsequent title, 'Community Center', retains this focus on the wider social vision available to the recovering protagonist (albeit while the deletion of the story's ending introduces a note of irony). The final title was only introduced after the manuscript left Carver's hands entirely. It referred to a line that Lish changed in the master proofs: 'He'd tell them what was waiting for you after the ~~rings~~ **denim** and the ~~bracelets~~ **earrings**, after ~~the~~ touching each other and cheating at games' (Carver 1980e).[31] On the master proofs of the manuscript, Lish completed this process, changing the title of the story to echo James' bitter observation on the futility of their pleasure and the certainty of death. The sense of community and 'human connection' lost in this process would set the terms of the collection's reception and do irreparable damage to the two men's working relationship.

'Low-rent tragedies': The critical legacy

The reception of *WWTA* offers a vivid demonstration of the way in which, in Eggert's words, early readers and reviewers may 'unfold' a work over time, laying down critical parameters and 'influencing subsequent readings' (Eggert 2009, 187). The impressions of the work's first readers were crucial in determining its

[31] In his second edit of the story, Lish had already removed the word 'community' several times, removing the phrase 'community center' in one case with the word 'building' (Carver 1980a). Reprinted by permission of Gordon Lish. All rights reserved.

continuing interpretation: to Gallagher, it was 'as though the clock stopped in April 1981' (Kelley 2009, 5).

The critical vocabulary around Carver's work made frequent use of the phrase 'Dirty Realism', a designation which, when examined alongside the drafts of these stories, vividly illustrates the way in which Lish's changes were taken up by critics as defining 'Carveresque' traits. The lean, elliptical style of *WWTA* was often framed as a narrative mode specifically adapted to portray the working-class world of Carver's characters, and its silences taken as mimetic of the verbal paralysis of blue-collar America: LeClair, for example, wrote that the prose 'obeys the linguistic limits of [Carver's] subjects' (LeClair 1982, 87). Sklenicka notes that many critics were 'at pains to define who the characters are' and quotes the *TIME* reviewer's observation that Carver's primary concern is with 'the rage that ordinary folks experience' (Sklenicka 2009b, 368).[32] This 'rage' is certainly more visible in Lish's version of *WWTA*'s title story, as the reflective, melancholy Herb becomes the cruder and more confrontational Mel, who utters terse declarations like 'Let's finish this fucking gin' (Carver 2009, 320). This process continued into the master proofs of the book, as Lish introduced additional expletives ('goddamn', 'fucking') and changed 'there is nothing to joke about' to the terser 'What's the joke?' during his final round of changes.[33] Lish also deleted lines that contained specific literary references (as he had from 'Neighbors' years before), making the characters appear less educated.[34] In a comparison of two passages from 'The Bath' and 'A Small, Good Thing', Hallett notes the way in which diegetic information in the latter subtly alters the story's representation of class, as details about the father's background identify him as upwardly mobile: 'With college, an MBA, and a junior partnership in an investment firm, this Howard resembles few, if any, characters in Carver's early "blue-collar" fiction' (Hallett 1999, 64).

32 Michael Wood's contemporary review had observed that Carver's writing presents a world of 'motels, Almond Roca, baseball caps [. . .] and children with names like Rae and Melody' (Wood 1981, n.p.), unaware that both of these names had been substituted into the text by Lish (Rea was named Bea in Carver's original draft, while Melody was named Kate (Carver 2009, 231, 323, 762, 949)).

33 Where Herb says 'I'm a heart surgeon, sure, but really I'm just a mechanic. I just go in and fix things that go wrong with the body. I'm just a mechanic', Mel declares 'I'm a heart surgeon, sure, but I'm just a mechanic. I go in and I fuck around and I fix things. Shit' (Carver 2009, 937, 318).

34 Lish deleted the following lines: '"I like *Ivanhoe*", Herb said. '*Ivanhoe*'s great. If I had it to do over again, I'd study literature. Right now I'm having an identity crisis. Right, Terri?' Herb said. He laughed' (Carver 2009, 936). Blake Morrison points out that Lish also removes a line in 'Where is Everyone?' in which the narrator makes reference to a scene in a novel by Italo Svevo and suggests that the deletion here is made 'on the grounds that the lowlife characters wouldn't be sufficiently educated to read' (Morrison 2009, n.p.).

Boddy points out, in relation to the 'minimalist' movement in general, that 'much of the discussion of the new fiction was couched in terms of the access it provided into "low-rent" lives', noting that 'the phrase "low-rent tragedies", ubiquitous in Carver reviews, comes from *WWTA*'s final story, "One More Thing"' (Boddy 2010, 85, 97 note 12). The phrase 'low-rent', in fact, was a last-minute (and presumably unauthorized) addition by Lish. The editor wrote in the modifying phrase on the master proofs of the story, adding a note of socio-economic specificity to Carver's original line – 'Maxine said it was another tragedy in a long line of **low-rent** tragedies' (Carver 2009, 949)[35] – and creating a phrase that would be taken by many critics as summative not only of the entire collection but of Carver's oeuvre as a whole.[36]

The phrase would echo through several influential assessments of Carver's work. In the *New York Review of Books*, Robert Tower wrote that Carver's stories are 'low-rent tragedies involving people who read popular mechanics and *Field and Stream*, people who play bingo, hunt deer, fish, and drink' (Towers 1981, n.p.). In the UK, *Granta* introduced Carver to British readers in a 1983 issue entitled *Dirty Realism*, coining a term which successfully (and persistently) defined Carver's work as part of 'punchy new movement which [. . .] drew attention to America's under-belly'; the phrase was soon customized into labels such as 'Kmart Realism' that were, in McGurl's words, more 'tellingly contemptuous' (Hornby 1992, 33; McGurl 2009, 280). Editor Bill Buford's introduction was similarly clear about the social status of the stories' characters, describing the issue as a collection of 'unadorned, unfurnished, low-rent tragedies about people who watch day-time television, read cheap romances or listen to country and western music'. Again, the style was framed as a comment upon the impoverished ('unfurnished') lives of these characters (Buford 1983, 4–5),[37] and the presentation of the work, while undeniably effective, also served in Hornby's words 'to create an image that Carver was never really able to shake off (in the UK) [. . .] as some kind of spokesman for the mid-west poor' (Hornby 1992, 34).

35 Reprinted by permission of Gordon Lish.

36 Robert Rebein, for example, uses the adjective to describe both 'Will You Please Be Quiet, Please?' and 'Cathedral' (Rebein 2009, 9, 22).

37 Buford identified these characters as:

> Waitresses in roadside cafes, cashiers in supermarkets, construction workers, secretaries and unemployed cowboys. They play bingo, eat cheeseburgers, hunt deer and stay in cheap hotels [. . .] They are from Kentucky or Alabama or Oregon, but, mainly, they could just about be from anywhere: drifters in a world cluttered with junk food and the oppressive details of modern consumerism. (Buford 1983, 4)

On both sides of the Atlantic, Carver was celebrated as a chronicler of working-class American life and was praised for not condescending to his psychologically damaged, financially vulnerable characters. Sklenicka comments that it was as if reviewers fully expected such characters to be condescended to (Sklenicka 2009b, 368), and the author's perceived attitude could be said to have licensed a degree of condescension on the part of critics. In the *Partisan Review* in 1991, Morris Dickstein recycled the phrase 'low-rent tragedies' and noted approvingly that while Carver's characters are 'not especially sensitive or introspective', he 'never condescends to them or directly judges them'. He described these 'blue-collar characters' as living 'far from the mainstream of upper middle-class life, with its chic urban irony and sophistication'; the telling word 'mainstream', here, would seem to betray a degree of complacency in the critical perspective (Dickstein 1991, 507–9). Indeed, when Lish was contacted in 1984 to contribute quotes to a profile of Carver, he encouraged this critical perspective, describing Carver as an 'important writer' while offering ambiguously backhanded praise:

> It's not that his people are impoverished, except that they might be impoverished in spirit. It's not that they aren't educated, because in some cases they are. They just seem squalid. In every manifestation of human activity, they seem squalid. They're like hillbillies of the shopping mall. And Carver celebrates that squalor, makes poetic that squalor in a way nobody else has tried to do. (Carver 1990, 87)

The profile, which ran in the *New York Times Magazine* in June 1984 under the title 'Raymond Carver: A Chronicler of Blue-Collar Despair', further encouraged the distance between the world depicted in Carver's fiction and the readers to whom it was marketed. Lish's ambiguous assessment, coming after the breakdown of the men's relationship in 1983, diverged notably from that of Carver – who insisted upon his affinity with his characters, pointing out in an interview in the same year that 'I come from people like that' – and his identification of 'squalid characters' who were 'impoverished in spirit' contains more than a hint of the 'barely disguised symbolic class warfare' that McGurl detects in much of Carver criticism (McGurl 2009, 287; Carver 1990, 112). Lish's calculatedly reductive interpretation of the work for which his former editee was then being lauded suggests the lingering animosity of their parting and, as we shall see, fits into a pattern of paratextual struggle that would characterize their relationship in the coming years.

4

'It is his world and no other': Gordon Lish, authorship and Minimalism

In October 1980, months after the editing of *WWTA*, a review by Carver of Richard Brautigan's novel *The Tokyo-Montana Express* (1980) appeared in *Chicago Tribune Book World*. Carver offered qualified praise, arguing that the work should more properly be considered an 'uneven collection of prose pieces' and bemoaning its lack of quality control. He lamented the presence of too many 'space filler-uppers', declaring:

> You want to ask, 'Is there an editor in the house?' Isn't there someone around who loves this author more than anything, someone he loves and trusts in return, who could sit down with him and tell him what's good, even wonderful, in this farrago of bits and pieces, and what is lightweight, plain silly stuff and better left unsaid, or in the notebooks? (Carver 2000, 258–9)

'One wishes', wrote Carver, 'that this imaginary editor-friend had been stern with the author now and again' (Carver 2000, 258–9). Given the processes we have just examined, and considering Carver's immediate experience of an editor who had been, to say the least, 'stern' with him, there would seem to be a degree of cognitive dissonance at play here. This conflicted attitude to editorial intervention is one that recurs frequently in Carver's writings from the time.

Carver and Lish's disagreements over the stories in *WWTA* have been widely discussed, but it is clear that this struggle continued in less direct ways through the paratextual materials surrounding the book. A variety of documents from the months surrounding the editing process suggest Carver's oscillating attitude towards the limits of the editor's role and betray an ongoing submerged conflict between the two.

During the same period, Carver was expressing some hesitations about the materials relating to the publication of his forthcoming book. Sklenicka, for example, describes 'the extreme hype of Lish's copy on the inside flaps of the book, much of it referencing the story Carver wished to omit, "Mr. Coffee and Mr. Fixit"' (a semi-autobiographical story that, as we have seen, Lish cut drastically) (Sklenicka 2009b, 366–7). This copy is what Carver referred to in a letter from January 1981. While he approved of most of the 'cover copy', he expressed reservations about the way in which the stories were framed, noting his particular doubts about Lish's choice of adjectives in the description of their characters:

> But I wonder about the words 'hysterical', 'impotent', 'deranged'. It seems to me 'unable' would be a better word than 'impotent'. '"Unable" to explain the past' seems a better, or more preferable phrasing, than '"impotent" to explain the past'. The husbands are not, of course, 'deranged'. Not really, anyway. That's all. Love the rest of it, naturally. It's really very good. (Carver 1981a)

An earlier letter (from October 1980) mentions 'that pre-conference poop sheet you sent up'; the subject here is unclear, but it is possible that Lish planned to read from Carver's work during his November visit to Syracuse. In any case, the concern expressed by Carver strongly suggests that one of his own stories was mentioned in the sheet and that he objected to the emphasis on its stylistic compression:

> The ONLY criticism of the poop sheet you sent up is that sentence 'To begin with, such a story can't get any more reduced than it already is and exists only in the peculiarly crippled speech of its composition'. I don't like that, but the rest is fine, as I said. (Carver 1980m)

Carver's well-known essay 'On Writing', written during this time, reads in hindsight as a much stranger and more highly charged document than it did when it appeared in the *Book Review* in February 1981 as 'A Storyteller's Shoptalk'. It appears from the surviving correspondence that Carver had sent this to Lish at the end of December 1980, and that Lish's response was unfavourable. Carver urged him to reconsider his judgement:

> I hope you don't have reservations about the matter. Don't. Believe me, it is a good thing and it is going to be fine […] When you see it, I know you'll be able to get behind it. Don't worry!' (Carver 1981b)

While we can only guess at Lish's criticisms, we can certainly observe the potential tension in the fact of a writer sending his editor – who had recently cut that writer's work by half – a draft of an essay about the writing process that not only fails to mention that editor but also pointedly espouses the primacy of the individual artistic vision. In the essay, Carver defines the most important aspect of fiction as:

> A unique and exact way of looking at things, and finding the right context for expressing that way of looking [. . .] It's akin to style, what I'm talking about, but it isn't style alone. It is the writer's particular and unmistakable signature on everything he writes. It is his world and no other. (Carver 2009, 728)

It is difficult not to conclude that Carver – who, as Sklenicka notes, had nowhere expressed anger or questioned Lish's methods in his lengthy letter of protest against the second round of changes to *WWTA* (Sklenicka 2009b, 358) – was engaging here in a kind of passive-aggressive resistance to his editor's influence. Carver was already, by this time, writing stories for his next collection and had told Gallagher of his intention to publish the unedited versions at a later date (Sklenicka 2009b, 33; Kelley 2009, 4); it seems clear that he was attempting, by indirect means, to assert his identity and push back against the editorial influence he had experienced in the preceding year.

Declaring literary independence: *Cathedral*

The breakdown of Carver and Lish's working relationship took place during the publishing process for *Cathedral*. In the correspondence from this time, the shift in the dynamic of their friendship in the wake of Carver's newfound success (and, we can surmise, his ongoing attempt to achieve a distance from his former life) is clear. In August 1982, in advance of a planned round of editing, Carver wrote a long letter in which he pre-emptively asserted his authorial prerogative, noting the differences between his and Lish's aesthetic approaches and making clear his anxiety at the possibility of a repeat of the editorial process of *WWTA*:

> I love your heart, you must know that. But I can't write these stories and have to feel inhibited – if I feel inhibited I'm not going to write them at all – and feel that if you, the reader I want to please more than any, don't like them, you're going to re-write them from top to bottom. Why, if I think that the pen will fall right out of my fingers, and I may not be able to pick it up.

Claiming that he was 'not the same writer I used to be', Carver suggested that some of the new stories 'may not fit smoothly or neatly, inevitably, alongside the rest' and signalled that he was unwilling to consent to an extensive editing process that he imagined as an invasive medical procedure: 'But, Gordon, God's truth, and I may as well say it out now, I can't undergo the kind of surgical amputation and transplant that might make them someway fit into the carton so the lid will close' (Carver 2007, 11 Aug. 1982). A letter from a month later consists largely of a litany of Carver's burgeoning professional and financial success: he mentioned, for example, that he had been elected to the Board of Directors at Yaddo, that he had just sold a story to a magazine (*Grand Street*) for a thousand dollars and that he had recently been in New York to meet film director Michael Cimino to discuss the script (based on Dostoevsky's life story) that he and Gallagher were in the process of writing.[1] Carver wrote that he would deliver the manuscript for *Cathedral* after his next meeting with Cimino and promised that he would find a role for Lish in the movie if he wanted (3 Sep. 1982). These letters alone demonstrate the rapid upsurge in Carver's reputation and illustrate how the circumstances of the production of *Cathedral* were utterly different from those of his previous collection. On the eve of the publication of *WWTA*, Carver had sent Lish a lengthy letter pleading for the cessation of publication of the edited version of his manuscript; now, a little over two years later, he was scheduling the delivery of his latest manuscript after a meeting with a celebrated Hollywood director and offering to find his editor a minor part in the movie.

The editing process was one to which Lish still contributed, although it is clear that Carver took more control than he had previously, accepting only the changes he was comfortable with; indeed, Carver had met with Gottlieb when turning in the manuscript in order to insist upon his authorial prerogative (Gallagher 2017). Lish contributed changes of varying degree to almost all of the stories in the book, but both the nature and volume of these edits were minor in comparison to the previous collections. The manuscripts for 'The Bridle', for example, contain several of Lish's cuts, the majority of which were not taken. The editing of 'Fever' also shows Carver's increased control. The story is lightly edited until the final pages, but Lish suggested that Carver entirely cut the final paragraphs containing the protagonist's epiphany; Carver incorporated some of the line edits in the final pages, but kept all of the original ending (Carver 1982c). In 'Vitamins', Carver refused several changes, but accepted some line edits affecting the interactions between the characters. Lish had deleted several lines of dialogue that took place in the bar, between the protagonist, his girlfriend and

[1] The film was never made; the script was later published as *Dostoevsky: A Screenplay* (Capra 1985).

the menacing character of Nelson, recently returned from Vietnam: the result was to make Nelson more threatening and to mute the reactions and displays of emotion of the protagonists (Carver 1982a).

The manuscripts for 'Cathedral' show that Lish made a number of suggestions in his edit of the final story, many of which Carver accepted. These tend to be line edits affecting the pacing and tone of individual sentences, suggestions that subtly shift the tone of the story to a more 'Minimal' register without effecting the kind of substantial revision we have seen in the previous collections.[2] He proposed a change, for example, that subtly made the narrator's expression of his own predicament less eloquent: 'I guess ~~I'm agnostic or something. No, the fact is,~~ I don't believe in it. ~~Anything.~~ **In anything**. Sometimes it's hard.' Indeed, the lines that close 'Cathedral' show that Lish's edits, while small, played a part in the rhythm and texture of the story's much-praised ending:

> ~~In a minute~~ **Then** he said, 'I think that's ~~enough~~ **it**. I think you got ~~the idea~~ **it**', he said. 'Take a look. What do you think?'
>
> But I had my eyes closed. I thought I'd keep them ~~closed~~ **that way for** a little longer. I thought it was something I ought ~~not to forget~~ **to do**.
>
> 'Well?' he said. 'Are you looking?'
>
> My eyes were still closed. I was in my house~~ and~~**.** I knew that. But I didn't feel **like I was** inside anything.
>
> 'It's really something', I said. (Carver 1982a)[3]

In November, Carver sent Lish the dedication for the book: this was not made out, as he had promised years earlier, to the editor, but to Gallagher and John Gardner (Carver 1982e). We may speculate on the contribution of moments such as these to Lish's later sense of Carver's 'ingratitude'; in any case, the textual record shows the perceptible decrease in personal warmth (Max 1998, n.p.). The tone of Carver's letters to Lish became tenser over the coming months, and the relationship broke down in the spring of 1983. Gallagher reports that the decisive break came in a phone conversation after the appearance of the 1983

[2] For example, Lish urged Carver to remove culturally specific references, suggesting that he change 'cannabis' to 'a smoke', 'Chartres Cathedral' to 'this one cathedral', 'Sainte Chapelle' to 'another one' and 'Notre Dame' to 'the famous one in Paris'. All but the first of these were accepted. Elsewhere, he removed the brand name 'Crisco', replacing it with the generic 'gas' in the phrase 'You're cooking with gas now' (Carver 1982a). Incidentally, Murakami translated the story in 1982 and wrote in an essay in the same year (in the Japanese literary magazine *Gunzo*) about the difficulties of translating the phrase 'cooking with Crisco'; Murakami had based his translation on an earlier version of the story (presumably the one published in the *Atlantic* in September 1981), a fact that highlights the complex transmission history of even Carver's supposedly 'post-Lish' work (Marling 2016, 124–5).

[3] Reprinted by permission of Gordon Lish.

issue of the *Paris Review*, which featured an interview with Carver as the 76th instalment of the 'Art of Fiction' series; Lish was unhappy at the lack of public acknowledgement of his work by Carver (Gallagher 2017). The interview – which, in keeping with the usual 'Art of Fiction' format, included a series of detailed questions on the author's writing habits – exemplifies the delicate position in which Carver now found himself and shows his growing willingness to distance himself from the 'Minimalist' label, if at the expense of factual accuracy. Asked whether his methods of composition have changed in recent years, Carver recalls that he 'pushed and pulled and worked with' the stories in *WWTA* 'to an extent I'd never done with any other stories', reflecting that his new stories were 'totally different' and suggesting that this reflected 'a change in my life as much as it does in my way of writing'. Meeting the 'Minimalist' charge head on, he stated that:

> I knew I'd gone as far the other way as I could or wanted to go, cutting everything down to the marrow, not just to the bone. Any farther in that direction and I'd be at a dead end – writing stuff and publishing stuff I wouldn't want to read myself, and that's the truth. In a review of the last book, someone called me a 'minimalist' writer. The reviewer meant it as a compliment. But I didn't like it. There's something about 'minimalist' that smacks of smallness of vision and execution that I don't like.

Despite these reservations, he nevertheless highlighted his habits of meticulous revision, noting that while his first drafts constituted the 'scaffolding' of a story, 'the real work comes later, after I've done three or four drafts'. The phrase 'the real work', which Carver had used a decade earlier to describe the compressed precision of 'Neighbors', again points to the painstaking process of self-revision as the essence of his writerly art – a suggestion reinforced by the reproduction within the interview of several manuscript pages of 'The Bridle' showing Carver's own revisions. When asked directly 'Where does Gordon Lish enter into this?', Carver related an anecdote about the editor's eccentric habit of eating food from his author's plate, before offering warm but studiously bland praise that omitted any details of Lish's involvement in his work: 'He's remarkably smart and sensitive to the needs of a manuscript. He's a good editor. Maybe he's a great editor. All I know for sure is that he's my editor and my friend, and I'm glad on both counts' (Carver 1983, 215–43).

Upon the publication of the interview, both of these relationships came to an end. Shortly thereafter, Robert Gottlieb assumed responsibility for the collection and agreed to edit it lightly, and by the summer of 1983 the author had, in Stull and Carroll's words, 'declared his literary independence' (Gottlieb 2016, n.p.; Gallagher 2017; Stull and Carroll 2013, 45). Carver was quick to suggest to interviewers that the stories in *Cathedral* were more representative of his intentions than his previous ones, stating in 1983 that he felt 'closer to this book than to anything I've ever done' (Saltzman 1988, 155). He was also, however, keen to praise his former editor: in an interview conducted in May 1983, in the midst of the dissolution of their relationship, the interviewer noted that the author 'has a fierce sense of loyalty and he mentioned Lish's name at every opportunity, repeating that he was grateful to him from the bottom of his heart' (Carver 1990, 66). The mixed messages on display here indicate the difficulty of the position Carver had reached in moving on from a working relationship that had brought him unprecedented success and suggest a conflicted attitude that – as I will show in my final chapter – would surface in his work throughout the subsequent years.

Carver's success as a supposed 'Minimalist' auteur would leave an ambiguous legacy for both he and Lish. Sklenicka suggests that Lish's influence on Carver's work was 'a kind of Faustian secret for Carver', while Gallagher describes how 'at a certain point Ray began to accept what had become a fiction in his life, and that fiction became a kind of truth he had to live' (Sklenicka 2009a; Baker 2009, n.p.). Lish, for his part, was increasingly reluctant to accept this 'fiction', seeking counsel from friends on the advisability of revealing his involvement in Carver's stories. As Max has reported, however, DeLillo advised Lish against taking such steps, arguing that the reality was 'too complicated' for the reading public to absorb and that, in Max's words, 'this is a culture in which we want a single name on the front of the book' (Max 1998, n.p.). This cultural focus on single authorship is particularly powerful in the short story, a form understood by critics to depend for its success on the scrupulous refinement of an individual vision. The modern short story is distinguished precisely by the meticulous ordering of its narrative and stylistic elements, a generic trait traditionally figured as a solitary achievement: 'the great short story writers', as Suzanne Ferguson notes, 'have reputations as outstanding stylists, and much of the praise for their style, in terms of its "jewelling" or "polish", arises from a sense of the care lavished in the search for "le mot juste"' (Ferguson 2014, 226). The Minimalist story, in particular, ostentatiously performs its control over narrative expectation, ultimately drawing attention to the figure of the author. Ferguson notes how various experimental narrative techniques encourage 'attention to stylistic economy and the foregrounding of style' and argues that:

> The less we are occupied with verisimilitude, with physical action, with extended characterisation, the more obvious it is that the element which binds the whole *into* a whole is what readers perceive as a governing *theme* and often express as the 'author's intention': in old-fashioned stories, the 'moral'. (Ferguson 1994, 226–8)

The absence of anticipated textual signifiers does not, therefore, equate to a relinquishing of authorial control: rather than constructing the text's meaning for him or herself, the reader is liable to be led into a hermeneutical guessing game in which the notion of 'authorial intention' is a constant presence. Ultimately, while the author 'may disappear as a commentator on the action [. . .] he calls attention to himself through the special "signature" of his style' (Ferguson 1994, 226). In the case of Carver, lauded for the creation of overtly compressed and highly stylized 'super-short stories' (in Barth's words), the powerful author is, to borrow Foucault's terminology, a 'function' of the 'mode of discourse' in question (Barth 1986, n.p.; Foucault 2006, 290). In a genre in which so much emphasis is placed on craft, to be exposed as collaborator instead of craftsman – sketcher rather than sculptor – represents a significant drop in status.

If Carver was the clear beneficiary of this discourse, then Lish had done much to encourage it. The hardback edition of *WWTA*, for example, had come with a blurb from Frank Kermode that emphasized the author's mastery of his form:

> Carver's fiction is so spare in manner that it takes a time before one realizes how completely a whole culture and a whole moral condition is represented by even the most seemingly slight sketch. This second volume of stories is clearly the work of a full-grown master.

The praise here highlights the 'spare' nature of the artistic method and positions Carver as an artist who has fully realized the power of this method, 'a full-grown master' capable of encapsulating weighty social realities using only the most restricted means. These words, however, were apparently not Kermode's own. Lish has recalled that:

> Kermode had never made such a statement. I figured he would never see it, or that if he did, he would say, 'Oh, that's Gordon, that's OK', and he would forgive it. I knew Kermode through Denis Donoghue. I would do that with some regularity. (Lish 2018, 155)

The quote suggests the paradoxical impulses at play behind Carver's literary persona, with Lish carefully – and influentially – constructing an image of a powerful author figure while exercising an exceptional degree of editorial agency in doing so. Lish's work with Carver and others shows him in many ways to be that rare thing, an exhibitionist editor who did not restrict himself to the usual protocols in editing or promoting the authors for whom he was responsible. As we have seen, his intervention in *WWTA* cannot be satisfactorily understood in terms of harmonious collaboration, since he remained unwilling to compromise on elements of key stories that Carver still felt to be essential. His pedagogical methods display a similar tension, as the charismatic and influential teacher consistently inculcated in his students the need for their writing to establish authority, a quality which he told students was 'the most important element in doing prose fiction' (Winters 2016, 129). Lish's classes operated in a way that has been described – by himself and others – as competitive and hierarchical,[4] and his teaching modelled the relationship of author to work – and to reader – in a way that mitigates against notions of communal creativity. Lish's literary vision is not one in which authority is diffused among co-writers in a non-hierarchical collaborative endeavour, but rather of a contest in which the 'personal authority' of the author is imposed relentlessly upon the reader (Winters 2016, 129). To fold Lish's contribution into Carver's then, as Leypoldt and Rebein attempt to do,[5] or to designate Lish as co-author (or, as Hemmingson does, a 'silent co-writer') sits uneasily with the material history of these stories, since none of the protagonists involved in their production and publication have been willing to accept the blurred sense of creative agency this would demand (Hemmingson 2011b, 494). To experience collaboration as a disruptive act, as Wayne Koestenbaum has observed, requires the maintenance of a 'conservative allegiance to singular authority' (Koestenbaum 1989, 9). To each of the key players in this textual drama – Carver, who claimed not to be able to 'get any distance' from key stories whose events were drawn directly from his life and who experienced their editing as 'amputation' (Carver 1980k, 1982d); Lish, whose sense of grievance at his lack of recognition has clearly lasted across the decades (Max 1998, n.p.;

4 Lish has recalled that he 'fomented as much rivalry as I could' in his classes; Hempel noted that his 'confrontational methods' provoked 'obsession and animosity', while a journalist who attended his seminars described him assigning regular rankings to his students in order to encourage a competitive group dynamic (Lish 2018, 153; Hempel 1984, 91–92; Solwitz 1988, n.p.).

5 Leypoldt rejects the notion that there is a substantial difference between the different versions of Carver stories, describing Lish's interventions as one of the 'types of influences to which authors tend to be exposed'; Rebein claims that Lish 'simply pushed Carver further in the direction he had already chosen for himself' (Leypoldt 2002, 318–20; Rebein 2009, 26).

Lish 2015, 209); and Gallagher, who has spoken of *Beginners* as a 'restoration' of Carver's text and claimed that 'the core of him was in that book' (Wood 2009, n.p.; Gallagher 2017) – the authorship of these stories has manifestly been a matter of ongoing importance.

'Winner's history': Coming to terms with Carver's texts

Writing in 2006 in advance of the publication of *Beginners*, Stull and Carroll reflected on the work of scholarly editing and presentation that went into the volume. They noted that:

> It was challenging work, involving decipherment, transcription, and collation. It was also exciting work in that it quickly overturned erroneous assumptions that underlie nearly all past and present studies of Carver's writings. (Stull and Carroll 2006, 4)

They argued that the discovery of the extent of Lish's editing necessitated 'a fundamental reformulation of the research question' on the part of scholars, suggesting that the revelations of textual instability necessitated a reorientation of the focus of Carver studies towards an empirical project that would clarify the epistemological status of the stories attributed to him.

As I have suggested, though, this kind of concerted effort has been slow to materialize, and the volume of critical work on Lish's contribution to Carver's body of work has not grown substantially since 2009. To begin with, the work of generations of Carver scholars (as I suggested throughout my analysis of the different versions of his work) needs to be re-examined. Stull and Carroll's 2013 essay 'The Critical Reception of Raymond Carver' acknowledges this problem directly, providing background information on Lish's place in Carver's work and tracing the development of the 'Carver controversy'. They note that 'studies of Carver's work published before the year 2000 require varying degrees of reassessment', identifying several of these as being 'out of date in their coverage of the now expanded body of Carver's work and the genetic relationships among the multiple published versions of many of his stories' (Stull and Carroll 2013, 49).[6] The chapter on Carver in Hallett's study of three canonical Minimalist

[6] The specific monographs referred to are Saltzman's *Understanding Raymond Carver* (1988), Ewing Campbell's *Raymond Carver: A Study of Short Fiction* (1992) and Adam Meyer's *Raymond Carver* (1995).

writers, for example, does not mention Lish once, and the editor appears only briefly in her analysis of Hempel and Robison.[7]

Even in more recent monographs dealing with Carver's stories, the claims made about Carver's style are in immediate need of reassessment. Monographs by Bethea (2001) and Lainsbury (2004) acknowledge Lish's input but contain no information on the genetic development of Carver's stories; the analysis in McDermott's chapter on Carver in his 2006 examination of austere twentieth-century poetics leans heavily on the stories in Carver's early collections while making no reference to Lish. Indeed, claims such as 'Carver deploys an unadorned style that captures in language the minimalistic reality he intends to represent' would now appear to require, at the very least, an acknowledgement of the editor's hand in shaping this style (McDermott 2006, 90, 96). These kinds of claims, along with the critical consensus of Carver's 'development' (bolstered, as we have seen, by numerous misleading statements from Carver himself), reinforce a misleading narrative of Minimalist development that assumes the presence of a clear authorial intention. The identification of Carver with Minimalism has led to *WWTA* exerting a strong gravitational pull on critical discourse, as the numerous attempts to define the contours of the notoriously influential literary movement returned inevitably to the distinctive style features of that movement's most famous iteration.

Hannah Sullivan notes, in relation to *The Waste Land*, that Pound's interventions – regardless of aesthetic judgements – clearly made the poem more distinctively modernist in form (Sullivan 2013, 127). We might say something similar of *WWTA*, since critics – regardless of their opinions of the aesthetic worth of the volume or its place in the Carver canon – invariably agree on its status as his most Minimalist work. Even within his own lifetime, then, the identification of Carver with a Minimalist aesthetic had become a self-perpetuating critical trope, leading many critics to focus heavily on the Lish-edited collections in order to isolate the most distinctively 'Carveresque' examples of his stylistic practice. Hallett's self-reflective statement on her analysis of Carver's work exemplifies this trend: 'I have selected certain stories from the more representative of his minimalist crop because they seem best to exemplify

[7] The latter chapters contain no reference to the particulars of Lish's editing work, tending to attribute the textual features of Minimalism entirely to the authors: at one point, for example, Hallett quotes (without additional comment) a 1980 review of Robison's *Days* that praises 'Robison's fierce editing' (112).

the traits of minimalism as I have chosen to identify them and others because of their similarities to stories by Hempel and Robison' (Hallett 1999, 5). The critical problem here is clear, as Carver's most heavily edited stories are taken as his most 'representative', and his similarities to other writers who were edited by Lish are elucidated at length. As we have seen, this critical logic is no longer sound: Carver studies now need to reckon with a more complicated model of authorship, while accounts of Minimalist writing require a genetically informed perspective that pays close attention to Lish's own aesthetic.

An opposing critical consensus can also be detected, as critics keen to valorize Carver's literary achievement seek to detach him from what is perceived as a discredited, bygone genre. Leypoldt notes that 'during the turbulent debates of the eighties the term [Minimalism] appears to have been ruined for literary criticism', while May opens his preface to Hallett's study of Minimalism by acknowledging that the word is 'one of those disreputable literary terms that one dare not use without placing it within quotation marks or prefacing it with "so-called"' (Leypoldt 2002, 317; May and Hallett 1999, ix). Both critics note the effects on Carver studies, with Leypoldt suggesting that as a result of this development, 'critics intending to prove Carver's literariness often feel compelled to preface their arguments with disclaimers, emphasizing that he is first and foremost an original storyteller and only tenuously related to the minimalist trend' (Leypoldt 2002, 317). May also laments the effect of this critical act of distancing, claiming that he 'welcome[s] any critical effort that might readdress the reactionary response to so-called "minimalism" that has made critics prefer the conventional and "more generous" stories in Carver's last two collections to the powerfully hallucinatory, but alas, "minimalist", stories in his first two collections' (May and Hallett 1999, x). As we have seen, this is a critical move made repeatedly by Wallace, who appeared at pains, in any discussion of Minimalism or Carver, to place daylight between the two.

Stull and Carroll note that 'a new phase in the critical reception of the works of Raymond Carver has begun' (Stull and Carroll 2013, 48). The work of critical re-evaluation of previous assumptions can be seen in essays such as Enrico Monti's 'Minimalism, Dirty Realism, and Raymond Carver', an updated version of his 2007 examination (in the *Raymond Carver Review*) of the way in which Lish's edits determined the stylistic direction of Carver's early work. Likewise, Molly Fuller's comparative essay in the Summer 2014 edition of *The Raymond Carver Review* on the alternate versions of 'Why Don't You Dance?' engages in a close reading of the textual alterations, noting how Lish's interventions affected the 'narrative thrust' and 'intention' of the story (Fuller 2014, 2). However, this understanding is not in evidence throughout all of the contemporary criticism of the author's work. Indeed, within the same 2013 *Critical Insights* volume in which Stull and Carroll (and Monti) provide nuanced assessments of Lish's contribution to Carver's development, we find Françoise Samarcelli's 'What's Postmodern About Raymond Carver?' a close examination of textual features such as 'fragmentation' and 'gaps and silences' in his stories. Here, Samarcelli emphasizes the use of 'postmodern techniques' in Carver's stories, focusing on features such as the 'typography and textual layout' of the stories in *WWTA*, the terse and elliptical dialogue between the men in 'Tell The Women We're Going' and the abrupt, 'self-cancelling' final line of 'One More Thing', all of which were significantly altered by the editing process. Lish is not mentioned once, and a footnote explaining that 'where there are two versions of the same story, this essay usually quotes from the first, shorter version' demonstrates the critic's lack of interest in the textual background and attribution of the stories (Samarcelli 2013, 228–43). At the time of completion of the present study (almost nine years on from the publication of *Beginners*), it appears that only a handful of critics have undertaken sustained attempts to integrate the evidence of the Lish manuscripts into Carver studies. While it is now possible to conduct detailed close analyses of the differences between Carver's manuscripts and the edited stories, we still encounter arguments that assume a model of authorship untroubled by the textual evidence uncovered during the preceding decades.

The complicated history of Carver scholarship owes its many contradictions and confusions to the state of the archival evidence. The slow and sporadic nature of the uncovering of textual evidence has led to confusion and disparity between different assessments of Lish's influence; between 1998 and 2009, most Carver critics had only Max's reporting on which to base their assessments, and a genetic study would have required detailed archival research. Stull and Carroll refer to 'the near-unmaking' of Carver's critical reputation in the wake of 'The Carver Chronicles' and point to complicating factors such as the 'unresolved' issues raised by Max's essay and the continual appearance of posthumous work (in 2000's *Call If You Need Me*) as challenges to Carver studies during that period (Stull and Carroll 2013, 47–51). We might also speculate on the difficulty (both practical and psychological), for long-time Carver critics, of re-examining years and sometimes decades of previous work. Monti comments on the 'unexpected and upsetting' nature of the emerging story of Lish's influence, and the occasionally intense reactions evinced by the revelations of textual instability in Carver's work attest to the emotional investment of generations of readers in particular readings of canonical stories (Monti 2013, 60).

An apprehension of the complicated authorship of the most 'Carveresque' stories generates a degree of cognitive dissonance, since the importance of *WWTA* as an ur-Minimalist text – and the consequent valorization of its author as the originator of a movement – preceded the revelations of its textual genesis. Sullivan discusses, in relation to *The Waste Land*, the difficulty of perceiving the sense of possibility and change latent in a genetic study when the work in question is so deeply entrenched in the canon. Critics, she suggests, often analyse the poem's genesis in terms that suggest that its published version was 'predestined': this, she argues, constitutes an attitude of 'textual meliorism', an acceptance of a 'winner's history' that elides the complexities and confusions found in the draft materials (Sullivan 2013, 123, 142). It also inevitably elides the different agencies and intentions involved, as the work's most prominent attributes are taken to be preordained rather than the result of the selection by an editor of one possibility from among many. Critics have taken Pound's excisions as the inevitable fulfilment of Eliot's intentions, and the 'central themes and symbols' of the work to have been present from the beginning of the editing process. This perspective misrepresents the evidence of the manuscripts, since the development of the poem proceeded, in fact, from Pound's production of 'an elliptical, superposed version' of the poem 'from the many possibilities latent in the drafts', created 'at the moment when the two poets' sensibilities were beginning dramatically to diverge' (Sullivan 2013, 142). The resemblance between the process Sullivan describes here and the one I have outlined in relation to *WWTA* should be clear, and the difficulties for critical apprehension of the textual genesis are comparable ones. It is only when we appreciate the different agencies operating upon the text's development, the conflicting sensibilities of the contributors and the particularities of the historical moment of this development that we can gain an appreciation of the way in which the process informed the product.

To frame a work as 'co-authored' or 'collaborative' risks a merging of creative agency that effectively subsumes the editorial role within the authorial. *The Waste Land*, Sullivan argues, is often characterized as (in her phrase) 'efficiently self-purging' and is thus implicitly celebrated for the way in which Eliot's conservative poetic approach is successfully balanced against Pound's techniques of experimental revision. The success of the poem, she argues, lies in 'the aesthetically pleasing counterpoint between excision and accretion, economy and synthesis': the tension between these forces ultimately causes the work to achieve 'a maximal revision of aesthetic counterpoint' (Sullivan 2013, 122–45). This tension, however, is often attributed – despite critics' knowledge of Pound's contribution, sometimes effected in the face of the author's confusion and hesitancy – to Eliot's original set of intentions. *WWTA* also exemplified this dynamic of (in Sullivan's words) 'contrapuntal tension' for many critics, and the rush to acclaim Carver's willingness to apply merciless techniques of deletion to his own work credited him for the opposing forces of the dynamic (Sullivan 2013, 122–45). Reviewers understood both the subject and form of the stories to be the author's own, as he abbreviated his narrative methods in order to suit the foreshortened experience of the residents of his much-discussed 'Country'. Two influential contemporary reviews, for example, described the way the author had tailored form to content: LeClair wrote that the author 'obeys the linguistic limits of his subjects: no metaphor, no elegant variation, no allusions, nothing to learn or recognize or see through', while O'Brien claimed that 'like the best stories of Ernest Hemingway, Carver's fiction is reductive both in content and form, boiling down the lives of its characters until nothing remains but a pure, elemental residue – love, anger, desperation, loneliness, hopelessness' (LeClair 1982, 87; O'Brien 1981, 1). The sense of aesthetic counterpoint so central to the collection's success was for many years attributed to Carver alone, and critics often characterized the palpable tension between accretion and excision as a function of Carver's own internal artistic struggle: Howe's review of *Cathedral*, for example, suggested that the more expansive stories demonstrated that Carver had 'become aware of his temptations and perils', while Bloom's praise was hedged with a reference to the 'limits' that the author had imposed upon himself (Howe 1983, n.p.; Bloom 2002, 10).

An additional problem (as noted in Chapter 2) is that the stories in *Will You Please Be Quiet, Please*? have not been published in their unedited form, and critical discussions of these tend to take as their object of study a 'final' published version that does not take Lish's substantial contribution into account. Indeed, even in the post-*Beginners* era, it is possible to detect a degree of confusion about the attribution of these stories. In 2009, for example, Craig Raine contributed a lengthy polemical piece to *Arete* magazine in which he argued that Carver's unedited stories are 'manifestly inferior' to Lish's edited versions. Taking the text of *Beginners* as his evidence, Raine argued that stories such as 'So Much Water So Close to Home' and 'Popular Mechanics' were, in several cases, 'improved beyond recognition' (Raine 2009, n.p., italics in original). Some of his contentions, however, rest on less solid textual ground than others. He takes the early story 'Fat' as one point of comparison and the Cathedral story 'Feathers' as another, describing these as 'pre-Lish' and 'post-Lish', respectively. However, neither statement is quite accurate. In 1998 Max had already described 'Fat' as an example of an 'unusually extensive' edit, detailing several of Lish's technical changes and noting the 'resonance' resulting from these (Raine 2009, n.p.). 'Feathers', meanwhile, was in fact edited by Lish, albeit lightly. However, Lish does seem to have approved of the story – on the typescript, he described it to Carver as '*a beaut*' – and it is simplistic to characterize it as one over which he exercised no influence whatsoever (Carver 1982b). Even a close reading such as Raine's one, attending directly to the nature of Lish's interventions, contains inaccuracies and risks perpetuating overly simplistic assumptions about the textual status of several stories.

The importance of these stories to Carver's own development as a writer, and to any history of Minimalism, means that the manuscript versions retain their relevance for critics. The difficulty of assimilating the problems of textual instability into critical practice is still in evidence and Carver criticism is still, in several instances, guilty of betraying a lack of awareness of the material and institutional contexts embedded within his work.

A different kind of bleeding: Lish and Minimalism

By paying closer attention to these contexts, we can also better understand the development of Minimalism itself. Lish's role in the growth of Minimalism, as with his connection to Carver, has long been widely accepted: in 1986, for example, Sven Birkerts criticized the 'School of Lish and' its 'growing cult of small-stage pyrotechnics', and in 1989, Wallace could (as we have seen) make reference within his fiction to 'Field Marshal Lish' in the confidence that this reference would be understood by many of his readers (Birkerts 1987, 252–63; Wallace 1997a, 265). What this role entailed, though, has rarely been investigated at a textual level. Lish's importance in assembling and promoting the work of authors connected to a Minimalist aesthetic has been widely noted, but our understanding of his hands-on textual intervention in these authors' work remains, with some exceptions, largely in the realm of conjecture rather than evidence. Lish himself has made it clear on several occasions that Carver 'wasn't the only one' whose work he edited severely and has described how he would edit a piece 'three, four, five times in a day' (Lish 2015, 205; Sklenicka 2009b, 360). Lish's contribution to Hannah's work has, as I discussed in Chapter 2, been explored; Winters describes how Hempel's stories 'were often cut as much as Carver's', and his forthcoming biography of Lish promises to significantly advance our understanding of the editor's contributions to the works of a number of his former students (Winters 2016, 116). To reduce these contributions to his involvement with Minimalism would be a simplification of both Lish's considerable body of work – this body being understood to encompass his overlapping activities in editing, teaching and writing, each strand of which could be said to show its own distinct phases of development – and of the complex and divergent careers of the writers who have come into his orbit. Lish has argued, pointing to his involvement with the careers of Harold Brodkey and Cynthia Ozick, that Minimalism is 'a convenience for people who don't want to comprehend these matters. Minimalism has nothing to do with it' (Lish 2014).[8] Justin Taylor argues that 'similarity is a long way off from uniformity', citing the difference between Brodkey, Hempel, Lutz and Robison to illustrate that Lish's methods are not 'codified or rigid'; Winters, too, notes the reductive nature of the definition, pointing out that the Minimalist designation results partially from 'a misleadingly small sample size' and that the techniques of consecution and recursion communicated in Lish's teachings can lead to enormously varied results (Taylor 2015, n.p.; Winters 2016, 114–24).

We can acknowledge, nevertheless, that many of Lish's editorial methods and pedagogical tools lend themselves to the production of fiction that conforms in key respects to definitions of Minimalism such as the one offered by McDermott in the previous chapter. The most obvious of these is the 'elliptical' quality of a 'short-short' story defined by its radical resistance to quantity, a resistance encouraged by Lish in the development of writers like Hannah, who has testified that the editor 'taught me how to write short stories. He would cross out everything so there'd be like three lines left, and he would be right' (McDermott 2006, 13; Hannah 2004, n.p.). However, Lish's commitment to maintaining a particular form of 'discursive logic' in order to generate 'compositional unity' (to use Winters' terms) means that writing bearing his influence could, even when it exceeds the expected length of a Minimalist story, be said to be 'minimal' in

[8] I have discussed elsewhere Lish's extensive editing of Brodkey's story 'His Son, In His Arms, In Light, Aloft', which was published in *Esquire* in 1975 and won first prize in the 1976 O. Henry Short Story awards (Groenland 2015a).

key respects. Botha has defined minimalist works across a range of media as being 'comported towards minimum', with this minimum identified as 'the *least possible*, but also the *least necessary*' (Botha 2017, xiii, 1). Seen in this light, and keeping in mind Botha's notion of minimalism as a dynamic and transhistorical practice encompassing works that 'vary considerably in conception, medium, execution and commitment', Lish's methods have clear similarities to other writers and artists described as minimalists. The near-absence of plot and sense of 'entrapment' that McDermott identifies is a frequent outcome of the relentless 'formal recursion' and accompanying 'reduction of narrative exposition' that, as Winters describes, Lish developed with reference to theorists such as Bloom and Baudrillard (McDermott 2006, 13; Winters 2016, 122). Lish's own novel *Peru* is a prime example of these techniques, demonstrating how his idea of consecution tends towards a recursive, introverted narrative style that, at a sentence level, often uses the same word or phrase as a turning point or a spoke in a wheel. For many other writers, Minimalist or not, Lish's method was empowering to the extent that it encouraged them to build fictions from a deliberately restricted set of materials: Christine Schutt, for example, has recalled that Lish 'was the first to tell me all a writer had to have was one good sentence. His simply pointing that out made all the difference in the world'. Gary Lutz, in speaking of Lish's influence, encourages 'a fixation on the individual sentence', identifying this isolated unit of literary achievement as 'the one true theatre of endeavour' for a writer (Schutt 2012, n.p.; Lutz 2009, n.p.). The way in which these units combine might also be thought of as analogous to effects found in minimalist works in other media. Botha identifies, for example, the 'processual torsion' in the music of Steve Reich and La Monte Young as an essential aspect of minimal composition; elsewhere, he describes how minimalist writing frequently plays upon our understanding of the 'consecution' underlying the linguistic order (Botha 2017, 64, 129). There are resonances here with key concepts in Lish's pedagogical toolkit, such as his emphasis on the need to generate 'torque' through the provocative interaction of each sentence with its predecessor and his insistence upon writing 'with consecution, so that each sentence follows naturally from each preceding sentence [. . .] you want to swerve and torque, going forwards by looking backwards' (Callis n.d., 23 Oct. 1990).

Lish's poetics, then, are oriented towards what Botha describes as 'the parsimonious, or the *least necessary*' in crucial ways, setting out a thrifty yet adaptable compositional method designed to generate a 'total effect' from a single point of origin (Botha 2017, xiii; Lish 2018, 155). As a teacher, he urged students to 'be aware that *every morpheme*, *every phoneme* counts' and to ensure that the story would recur 'thematically, structurally, [and] acoustically' (Callis n.d., 9 Oct. 1990, italics in original). This emphasis on narrative and linguistic economy was continually reiterated and performed in Lish's classes, as he urged students to 'reduce your strategy to the most urgent sentence you can possibly find' (Callis n.d., Oct. 1991). Infamously, Lish's critiques of individual students' work delivered this 'reduction' in immediate and merciless terms: a student would read aloud from their work only until Lish found fault with it, with the story being judged on its ability to hold the sustained attention and approval of the workshop leader on a sentence-by-sentence basis. This pedagogical method punished students ruthlessly for perceived excess or slackness of formal rigour, making parsimoniousness a necessary demand for any student aspiring to read more than a single sentence of their work. Similarly, while the demand that apprentice writers establish 'personal authority' through the mastery of their own secrets and an obsessive focus on 'objects' around which the story might revolve does not prescribe a Minimalist composition, it clearly encouraged a 'diminutive scale of concern', a focus on the personal and local, that many of Lish's students took to heart (Winters 2016, 119, 129; McGurl 2009, 292).

It is in the combination of these different Minimalisms – the formal and linguistic restrictions of consecution and the thematic focus on the domestic – that we can more clearly apprehend the importance of Lish's editing of Carver in establishing Minimalism as the dominant narrative mode of the 1980s. Margaret Doherty has linked the National Endowment for the Arts (NEA) Literature Program to the development of Minimalism in these years, describing how the NEA – under fire for alleged elitism and in the face of Reaganite demands to respond to market pressure – began attempting 'to subsidize fiction that would be popular with a large audience without reneging on its promise to judge on artistic merit alone' (Doherty 2015, 86). State-funded fiction, in Doherty's telling, needed in these years to maintain a balancing act between innovation and accessibility that satisfied the demand to reach a larger audience than had been reached by some of the challenging works by previous recipients (such as Grace Paley, John Ashbery and Ishmael Reed) without sacrificing its claim to 'artistic merit'. The result was what Doherty terms 'populist minimalism' a mode of 'representational art' that was domestic both in the local sense (as Don DeLillo, with his description of 'around-the-house-and-in-the-yard' fiction, disdainfully noted) and in the political one, as writers represented recognizable American locales in colloquial and 'nonetheless formally innovative' prose to produce a new form of national literature (Harris 1982, n.p.; Doherty 2015, 87–9). Lish's work throughout the 1970s and 1980s reveals him to be a crucial player in this process, both in the way he helped to establish the short story as a site of homegrown literary experimentation in his magazine editing (Gerald Howard recalls that his taste was shaped in large part by the stories *Esquire* published during the 1970s) and in his licensing of writing that rendered, as Frederick Barthelme put it, 'ordinary things, ordinary places' in a way that was still 'as wholly constructed, as made up as any post-modernist's' (Howard 2017; Barthelme 1988, n.p.). Lish's teaching – and the fiction produced by his editees and students, who were frequently the same people – assured writers that they could write about the banal, about the everyday, about simple objects, while still producing highly stylized and (as Winters has shown) theoretically sophisticated prose.

Minimalism, then, as Doherty puts it, might be thought of as 'the very hinge in the transition from high postmodernism to the new literary realism in late twentieth-century American fiction' (Doherty 2015, 81). However, it is Lish's work with Carver – who received his second NEA award in 1980, having won an NEA Discovery award for poetry a decade earlier – that best illustrates the workings of this hinge, providing the touchstone for the particularly Minimalist fusion of form and content that became a 'much-needed alternate route' to the postmodernism of the 1960s and 1970s (Rebein 2009, 40). In a 1998 tribute to Carver, Richard Ford recalled a writer's conference in 1977 at which he saw his friend read 'Are These Actual Miles?' – a story that, like several of the stories from *WYPBQP* discussed in Chapter 2, owes much of its stylistic effect to Lish. Ford describes how the story created an effect 'of actual life being unscrolled in a form so distilled, so intense, so *chosen*, so affecting in its urgencies as to leave you breathless and limp when he was finished'. He recalls a sense

> that a consequence of the story was seemingly to intensify life, even dignify it, and to locate in it shadowed corners and niches that needed revealing so that we readers could practice life better ourselves. And yet the story itself, in its spare, self-conscious intensity, was such a *made* thing, not *like* life at all; it was a piece of nearly abstract artistic construction calculated to produce almost giddy pleasure. That night in Dallas, Ray put on a blatant display of what a story could do in terms of artifice, concision, strong feeling, shapeliness, high and surprising dramatics. The story was definitely *about* something, and you could follow it easily – it was about what two people did in adversity which changed their lives. But here was no ponderous naturalism. Nothing extra. There were barely the

> rudiments of realism. This was highly stylized, artistic writing with life, not art, as its subject. And to be exposed to it was to be bowled over. (Ford 1998, n.p.)

It was possible, in other words, to write about ordinary things in a way that maintained a hard, stylized surface; as Rebein (quoting the passage above) notes, Carver showed Ford and others 'how to be a serious artist without taking art as his subject matter, how to be the most literary of writers without becoming thereby a literary postmodernist' (Rebein 2009, 29). Rebein was writing before the publication of *Beginners*, and it should now be clear that this balance between style and substance should be understood less as Carver's own achievement than as an uneasy balance between the aesthetic aims of Carver and his editor. Doherty has described Minimalism as 'a compromise aesthetic', a narrative mode with 'just enough artistic edge to counterbalance its accessibility and popularity', and Lish's editing of Carver allows us to see this compromise in all of its tenuous and unstable clarity (Doherty 2015, 89).

McGurl has placed Carver's work – and the 'editorial sponsorship' of Lish – into the culture of the school as it developed in postwar US literary culture, showing how creative writing pedagogy facilitated the transfiguration of the lived experience of precarious social existence into a 'lower-middle-class modernism' bearing the visible marks of its own craft (2009, 273–97). Winters has shown how Lish appropriated the charismatic energy of theory in a way that echoed the logic of the school, devising a method whereby apprentice writers could establish personal authority through the rigorous application of a conceptually ambitious formal methodology (Winters 2016, 111–34). The genesis of Carver's texts shows Lish applying this logic in a strikingly hands-on manner, honing an ostentatiously stylized prose and exaggerating the sociocultural markers of its world of reference, all the while constructing a persona of austere avant-garde severity for its author. Lish's application of his developing aesthetic ideas to Carver's texts constitutes a materially substantial intervention operating at a more detailed and transformative level than that of 'sponsorship', and his role in constructing what McGurl calls a 'populist formalism' is as influential in its practical and textual dimension as in its symbolic one (McGurl 2009, 290). It would of course be too simple to say that Carver brought the content to Minimalism and Lish the form; we could more accurately say that Lish adapted the existing formal elements of Carver's stories in ways that sometimes radically altered the reader's perspective on their content. However, the division of qualities that Doherty proposes does map loosely onto the way in which Lish edited Carver. Carver's unedited work, as we have seen, tends to show a highly deliberate fidelity to realist conventions, while Lish's own fiction is more abstract and recursive, built around linguistic and sonic patterns rather than mimetic representation: reading his stories, in Max's resonant phrase, resembles 'looking at the gears of a clock that's missing a face'.[9] Lish recalls approaching Carver's work as raw material in need of being 'made new' by modernist acts of reshaping:

> I saw in Carver's pieces something I could fuck around with. There was a prospect there, certainly. The germ of the thing, in Ray's stuff, was revealed in the catalogue of his experience. It had that promise in it, something I could fool around with and make something new seeming. (Lish 2015, 205)

This retrospective description deliberately and dismissively reduces Carver's stories to a mere 'catalogue of his experience', but it does demonstrate the way in which he approached them – namely, as units of compelling narrative content which could be altered and remade in novel ways. In Lish's telling, Carver's hard-won storehouse of lower-middle-class experience presented a canvas on which the editor could 'fuck around' and exercise his own talents. In less partisan terms, we might say that Carver's gift for isolating telling dramatic moments from that experience – the abandoned husband selling his possessions to the teenage couple on his front lawn, the couples trading stories of emotional damage over drinks, the wife selling the car bought in better and more hopeful times – was adapted by Lish into a fiction that balanced the affective charge of art that represented contemporary experience (what Ford recognized as 'life') with a visible commitment to formal experimentation.

This balance (or 'compromise aesthetic') is also visible in the presentation of Carver's work. The cover designs for the books that Lish edited at Knopf tended to be simple and, in their tendency to present the title and author name with little in the way of accompanying illustration, visually minimal. Loren Glass has described how Barney Rosset used abstract expressionist paintings to create a distinct look for Grove Press's book covers throughout the 1950s and 1960s; taking the cover of Beckett's *Molloy* as an example, he shows how, 'as an aesthetic object in itself, it encourages [. . .] the sublimation of thematic meaning into formal abstraction and stylistic virtuosity' (41). This was, he argues, part of a larger strategy of 'siphon[ing] cultural capital from Paris to New York'

[9] Wallace, incidentally, noted in his drafts that this was a 'nice phrase', showing that he was aware of Lish's editing of Carver. There is no evidence to show whether or how this caused him to revise his earlier conceptions of Carver's 'genius' (Max 2016).

and invoking the aura of high art in order to create paratexts that would lay the groundwork for the marketing of Grove's books (Glass 2013, 10–11, 157). Lish presented his collections in a similar manner that, as Hemmingson notes, echoed the designs and practices of European publishers; Hannah's *Ray*, Robison's *Days* and Carver's *WYPBQP* all feature titles in large and stylized font, withholding any visual representation of the fictions therein and hinting at the aesthetic pleasures of formal abstraction rather than the realist satisfactions of plot (Hemmingson 2011a). The cover design for *WWTA*, in its abstraction and startling juxtaposition of colours (lime green, bright purple, neon yellow), marries this abstraction with a provocative chromatic effect that recalls the bold designs of the Op Art and Color Field painting movements of the preceding decades. The blurbs accompanying these designs also played a key role, and the discussions around the appropriate recommendations for these books further reveal the stylistic division between Carver's intentional fidelity to a realist tradition and Lish's self-conscious experimentation. In 1980, for example, when the time came to solicit blurbs for *WWTA*, the two men's suggestions were quite different and could be broken down into distinct types; while Carver wanted his book to bear the approval of American realists such as Updike, Oates and Cheever, Lish suggested Borges, Beckett and Handke, indicating a desire to position Carver's work in relation to an avant-garde European modernism with which the author himself was only in partial affinity (Carver 1980l).[10] In 1982, when he was preparing to send Lish the manuscript of *Cathedral*, Carver confronted the issue head-on, acknowledging the men's differences in taste and naming names in the process: while he noted that Lish did not think highly of Beattie, Updike, Oates and John Gardner, he insisted upon his own admiration for their work (Carver 1982d).

The story of the 'reinvigorated realism' of the 1980s, according to Doherty, begins with a 'tension between high and low, between elitism and populism', and this tension is exemplified in *WWTA*, a work, which, as we have seen, tends to be taken as the high point of Minimalism (Doherty 2015, 81–2). Much of the subsequent work bearing the minimalist designation was seen as a less successful imitation of Carver, 'assembly-line' fiction constituting a 'clonal fabrication' of the real thing (Aldridge 1992, 28). Wallace, as we have seen, bemoaned the 'crank-turners' who he saw as imitative of Carver's hard-won but deceptively

[10] The book eventually carried the aforementioned concocted blurb from Kermode along with praise from Denis Donohue, Stanley Elkin and James Dickey.

simple style, suggesting that younger writers had been deceived by the fact that 'it looks as if you can write a minimalist piece without much bleeding' (Wallace 2012d, 45–6). Wallace had a different kind of bleeding in mind than the one that had transpired, presumably referring to the wounds of experience and the lacerations of self-revision rather than the 'surgical amputation and transplant' that Lish had performed (Carver 1982d). As Hannah Sullivan and Toby Litt have noted, fiction produced through the counterpoint of creation and severe revision is likely to be markedly different than that written with the prior intention of being minimal, and many critics concluded that the writers who followed Carver's example had taken, in Rebein's words, 'a failed shortcut' (Sullivan 2013, 123; Litt 2009, n.p.; Rebein 2009, 40). The distinctive tension in the most celebrated of the Minimalist stories examined here – the temporary and uneasy balance between the lyrical depiction of lived experience on the one hand and the stylized formalism of recursive compositional play on the other – is one that neither Carver nor Lish could have accomplished alone and that would overshadow all subsequent attempts to surpass it.

'He took what he needed': Carver and Gallagher

Carver's interactions with the editors he worked with in the final years of his career – Gottlieb, Charles McGrath (the fiction editor at the *New Yorker*) and Gary Fisketjon (who assisted Carver in assembling *Where I'm Calling From* (1988)) – were structured by his increased confidence and status and show his determination to resist editing of the kind he had experienced with Lish. The editing process in each of these cases was relatively harmonious, with Carver maintaining a high degree of control over his texts. In these years, however, another significant change had become thoroughly integrated into Carver's writing processes, as he was collaborating frequently with Gallagher, who had published several books of poetry (and been awarded two NEA grants) by the early 1980s. Gallagher's editorial influence on Carver's work throughout the 1980s is significant, and it is beyond doubt that Carver sought her collaboration with his later stories. Drafts of 'Errand', for example, make it clear that she suggested the lines that close the story and that these suggestions occurred in several stages, with handwritten edits by both she and Carver filling in the margins of the same manuscript pages. A similar example, according to Gallagher, is the final paragraph of 'Blackbird Pie', which Carver incorporated into the story after she wrote it into one of his drafts. Gallagher is quick to downplay any suggestion of 'claiming' Carver's work here, framing it as a regularly collaborative endeavour in which Carver 'urged to me to write out any ideas of revision in full and then he took what he needed' (Gallagher 2017). Stull and Carroll's essay 'Two Darings', which served as the introduction to Gallagher's book *Soul Barnacles: Ten More Years with Ray* (a collection of essays, diary entries and poetry relating to the couple's time together, published in 2000), vividly illustrates aspects of this process, providing an overview of their 'creative collaboration' and presenting a reproduction of one of the relevant draft pages from 'Errand' that shows this collaboration in action (Stull and Carroll 2003, 1–11).

Carver and Gallagher's collaboration exists outside the scope of this book, in part because of the more complex and diffuse archival situation it has left behind. It is also the case, as Stull and Carroll have noted, that this collaboration is a large enough subject to merit an extended study of its own, bearing as it does upon everything Carver wrote from the late 1970s onwards. The two lived together for roughly a decade, and the terms of their partnership – namely, a collaboration between a writing couple – are of a fundamentally different order to the editing relationships at the heart of this book, in which the institutional affiliation of the editors and the power dynamics of the publication process were so clearly central to the work undertaken. The kind of layered, day-to-day creative interchange between a writing couple described here is, as Bette London observes, 'a partnership at once more intimate and pervasive but less easy to pinpoint' than the relatively structured interchanges between author and editor (London 1999, 211). Much of Carver and Gallagher's collaboration clearly took place at what we might call a pretextual stage – that is to say, in conversation or in notes that were unlikely to be preserved as drafts. As Max notes, their work together was frequently 'so intimate that no traces were likely to remain' and resists scholarly reconstruction (Max 1998, n.p.). No extended study yet exists of Gallagher's contribution to Carver's work, and if such a study is to be undertaken, it will need to focus on the substantial collection of Carver manuscripts and correspondence in Gallagher's archive of Carver papers in the William Charvat Collection of American Fiction in Ohio State; it will also need to account for Carver's substantial output of poetry in his late years, a development clearly influenced by the couple's time together. Such a study would add to our understanding of the different ways in which editorial assistance can manifest and would appear, at this point, as the most likely way in which our understanding of Carver's work might be further revised. It would, however, be limited by the intimacy to which Max alludes; by way of illustration, I was unable to confirm the situation surrounding 'Blackbird Pie' from an examination of the limited number of drafts of the story contained in the Ohio archive.

Thomas Augst has observed that archives frequently direct our attention away from 'the figure of the author we take for the usual protagonist of literary history', and in the case of Carver – who, as is now clear, worked most effectively in close concert with partners – this is clearly apposite (Augst 2017, 223). We might consider the protagonists of this slice of literary history, instead – the slice traditionally marked by the designations of 'Carver' and, for better or worse, 'Minimalism' – as a dynamic ensemble group, a small rotating cast of players variously acting as sounding boards, contributors and critics, alternately adding to (and, perhaps, subtracting from) the authorship of 'Raymond Carver'.

5

'Your devoted editee': David Foster Wallace and Michael Pietsch

In April 1994, shortly before delivering the full manuscript of *Infinite Jest*, Wallace wrote to Michael Pietsch to reassure him that the project was nearing completion. He told his editor to expect the manuscript within the coming months, claiming that it was, 'except for the last ten pages', finished; he complained about minor logistical setbacks ('losing computed stuff or finding stuff I thought I had done is not done'); and he updated Pietsch on the placement of excerpts from the novel in the *New Yorker* and the *Harvard Review* (Wallace 1994b). In the letter's longest passage, Wallace also informed Pietsch – who had, by this point, already read and responded to the first, incomplete, draft of the manuscript – that he had taken the decision to transfer 'a certain amount of harder stuff' (including 'medical lore' and 'math calculations') to 'an Endnote-format'. This narrative strategy, he wrote in his characteristic pre-emptively defensive manner, was one to which he had become 'intensely attached'. He presented several justifications for this decision (noting, for example, the way the endnotes enabled 'a discursive, authorial-intrusive style w/o Finneganizing the story' and their ability to 'mimic the information-flood and data-triage I expect'd be an even bigger part of US life 15 years hence'); however, he also argued that it would 'make the primary-text an easier read' and that it would allow him to 'feel emotionally like I'm satisfying your request for compression of text without sacrificing enormous amounts of stuff' (Wallace 1994b). The presence of endnotes in the novel, then – long understood to be one of its most distinctive features[1] – came early in the process of its production and arose, at least in part, from its editor's insistence on readability and accessibility as necessary values.

[1] David Letzler, for example, devotes an essay to examining the way in which the copious endnotes train the novel's readers to 'develop our abilities to filter information' (Letzler 2012, 321).

Throughout the renewed wave of scholarship on Wallace since the author's death, we can detect a recurring anxiety over the frequency with which he is discussed in ways that divorce him from his context. In 2011, for example, Burn lamented the paucity of readings that place Wallace within 'a larger literary and cultural matrix'; in 2012, Hayes-Brady identified a tendency to take the author as '*sui generis*', noting that the phrase appears in Eggers' foreword to the tenth anniversary edition of *Infinite Jest*; and, more recently, Lucas Thompson suggested that 'the persistent myth of the Romantic, impassioned author' whose works are 'unsullied by any form of mediation or compromise' is still prevalent in Wallace Studies (Burn 2011, 467; Hayes-Brady 2012, 481; L. Thompson 2016, 220). There have, of course, been numerous studies of Wallace's literary influences and of the way in which these operate.[2] The wave of monographs that present a 'synthetic reading' (in Severs' words) of the author's career by analysing his career-length output has seen important connections made between Wallace and his literary and philosophical influences, his geographical and intellectual environment, and his economic and cultural background, albeit in a manner that necessarily places the figure of the author himself at the centre of the survey (Hayes-Brady 2016; Hering 2016a; Severs 2017). However, there has been little focus on Wallace's practical working relationships with those in his literary networks – his agent, his one-time co-writer (in the form of Mark Costello), his editors and publishers, and others – whose involvement in his work was more direct. Bearing in mind the communicative, dialogic model that Wallace proposed as the goal of successful writing and his well-known conceptualization of fiction as 'a living transaction between humans', it is somewhat surprising that critics have not granted more attention to the work of the living humans involved in its production. Readings that historicize Wallace have tended to focus on contemporaneous political, economic and cultural frameworks (Boswell 2012c; Godden and Szalay 2014; McGurl 2014; Shapiro 2014), while a parallel trend has seen the author's reception become the subject of analysis, sometimes incorporating the work of cultural gatekeepers, reading communities and the 'Wallace Industry' in its purview (Coyle 2017; Finn 2012; Hungerford 2016; Kelly 2017, 2). The emergence of biographical and archival evidence in

[2] A. O. Scott was the first critic to offer an extended account of the influence upon Wallace of the 'postmodern old masters' (Barth, Gaddis, Pynchon et al.) and to articulate the terms of the author's engagement with these precursors; more recently, Lucas Thompson has presented several different models for understanding how Wallace engaged with intertexts. For a detailed list of studies of Wallace's literary influences, see Kelly's (2015) survey of the field of Wallace scholarship (Scott 2000, n.p.; L. Thompson 2016, 36–46; Kelly 2015, 46–62).

recent years, however, also enables us to reconstruct – if only partially – the relationships and social processes behind his works' journey to print. This chapter attempts such a reconstruction, tracking the development of the editing relationship between Wallace and his key collaborator in the mature phase of his career, Michael Pietsch. This relationship, I argue, represents perhaps the most vivid and lasting real-world model for the intensively collaborative dynamic that Wallace desired for his fiction's reception.

'Everything I've ever let go of has claw marks on it': Editing Wallace[3]

Editing Wallace, as even a cursory glance at the author's work will suggest, was not an easy job. Wallace was a grammarian as well as a writer of dense and allusive prose, and numerous reminiscences from editors and friends show him to have been an opinionated and occasionally combative editee. A letter (widely shared online since Wallace's death) to *Harper's* editor Joel Lovell in 1998 accompanying his piece 'Laughing with Kafka' effectively displays the writer's ability to argue for the integrity of his words in a manner both playful and passive-aggressive:

> What I'd ask is that you (or Ms. Rosenbush, whom I respect but fear) not copyedit this like a freshman essay. Idiosyncracies [*sic*] of ital, punctuation, and syntax ('stuff', 'lightbulb' as one word, 'i.e.'/'e.g.' without commas after, the colon 4 words after ellipses at the end, etc.) need to be stetted. (Wallace 2011e)

Wallace also enjoyed adopting the role of editor, a tendency clear from the beginning of his career: during his time in Arizona, collaborating with his friend JT Jackson on 'a parody issue of [the college's] writing programme newsletter' (Max 2012a, 72). In 1996, he guest-edited an issue of the *Review of Contemporary Fiction*, noting in his introduction that 'the job involved reading the essays as they came in and copyediting them – I'm a good copy editor, and this has been the only really comfortable part of the whole process as far as I'm concerned'

[3] The quote is taken from *Infinite Jest*:

> The 2-man seniorest males' bedroom has a bunch of old AA bumper-stickers on it and a calligraphic poster saying EVERYTHING I'VE EVER LET GO OF HAS CLAW MARKS ON IT, and the answer to Gately's knock is a moan, and Glynn's little naked-lady bedside lamp he brought in with him is on, he's in his rack curled on his side clutching his abdomen like a kicked man. (Wallace 2006, 606)

(Wallace 1996a, 7). Wallace took pride in his copy-editing abilities (he boasted to Steven Moore in 1990 that he was 'the best copyeditor I've ever seen'), and his correspondence with Don DeLillo suggests that when he received an advance copy of *Underworld*, he relished (along with his enjoyment of the book) the opportunity to act as one of its unofficial proofreaders (Wallace 1990). A note from DeLillo written to Gordon Lish in advance of the publication of the book, in fact, jokingly taunts Lish with the information that David Foster Wallace had found some typos that Lish has missed (DeLillo 1997). As Zac Farber observes, those who edited Wallace 'found themselves faced with the difficulty of correcting a man with a prodigious understanding of the byzantine syntactical and grammatical rules of the English language' (Farber 2009, 1).[4] *New Yorker* editor Deborah Triesman is one of the many editors to testify to this difficulty, recalling that she has 'worked with some people who were very precise about what they want in their work, but he was probably the most precise and the most obsessed with the tiniest details of the syntax' (Nadell 2012). This, however, does not tell the full story of Wallace's approach to editing. Archival documents show not only that Wallace's relations with editors varied depending on the circumstances of publication, but also that he came increasingly to accept and even invite editorial intervention, particularly into his fiction, as his career progressed. Wallace's dealings with a range of editors have been chronicled in several places, with Max's biography providing the most wide-ranging overview of these, and since my focus here is on his work with Pietsch I will not attempt to add to the list. I will begin, however, with some representative examples of how he interacted with other editors in order to provide context for the editing of his later works.

Wallace's first experience of the commercial editing process came during his work with Gerald Howard, the Viking Penguin editor who had acquired *The Broom of the System*. While Howard later claimed that Wallace 'was very polite in ignoring me' during the editing process, it is clear that the novelist was willing to accept a degree of revision (Neyfakh 2008). Wallace promised Howard in early correspondence that he would be 'neurotic and obsessive' but 'not too intransigent or defensive about my stuff', and Max writes that 'generally, he was true to his word' (Max 2012a, 68). Wallace was willing to make several minor cuts in response to Howard's suggestions, but when the editor proposed expanding the deliberately truncated ending and cutting sections dealing with

[4] Farber's short essay, written for the fan site *The Howling Fantods*, is based on publicly available comments from Wallace as well as several of his former editors.

the 'membrane theory' espoused by Dr Jay, he disagreed. Wallace wrote a letter in which he defended the membrane section in a paragraph (described by Max as 'hyperverbal') dense with philosophical and theoretical allusion – he invoked Hegel, Wittgenstein, Heidegger, De Man and Derrida in the space of a few lines – and this seems to have persuaded Howard to relent (Max 2012a, 68–9). Howard's criticisms of the manuscript focused primarily on the scenes featuring Dr Jay (which he described as 'long and loopy') and Rick Vigorous's stories ('in spots I got very tired of his overwriting') (Howard 1986). The editor took particular exception to the story told by Rick on the plane trip about the man whose 'emotional love-mechanism' is excessively strong and who eventually embarks on a doomed relationship with a woman with a tree toad living in the pit of her neck; Howard dismissed this as 'the first spot in the book where I felt genuine impatience', arguing that the story was 'too long, too disgusting in its details and it stops the novel's development dead in its tracks' (Wallace 2011a, 180–94; Howard 1986). Again, however, Wallace retained the story for publication. Both Howard and Bonnie Nadell – one of Wallace's first readers throughout his career – objected strongly to the lack of resolution, with the former urging the author not to 'deny yourself and your readers some basic satisfactions on an exceedingly abstract principle' and the latter insisting that 'you simply cannot end the book with an incomplete sentence' (Howard 1986; Nadell 1985; Max 2012a, 69–71). However, on this point, Wallace was indeed intransigent, and insisted on his original ending, as Howard recalls:

> And he wrote a five or six page, single spaced letter in which he told me that, yes, I was absolutely right in my suggestion and he knew that he really should do this, *but* here's why he can't. And won't. And the explanation was so convoluted but so heartfelt that at the end I just said, 'Oh, alright!' This wasn't something I was gonna win. (Neyfakh n.d., n.p., italics in original)

Wallace would later regret what he saw as youthful stubbornness here and came to regard the decision as an illustration of the need to be more receptive to editing suggestions; to David Lipsky in 1996, he said 'I was arrogant, and missed a chance to make that book better' (Lipsky 2010, 36).

The experience of editing *Girl with Curious Hair* appears to have been a gruelling one, due primarily to the legal issues that threatened to derail the collection. In addition, Howard moved from Viking to Norton in 1988, and Wallace's decision to follow his editor caused friction with his first publisher (Wallace 1988c). The book involved Wallace and Howard in a great deal of what we might call extra-literary editing, as Viking Penguin's legal department subjected the entire collection to intense scrutiny following the discovery that the story 'Late Night' contained dialogue from actual television footage (Max 2012a, 106–9).[5] The surviving editorial correspondence relates almost entirely to these legal difficulties and since many of the stories had already appeared in (and been edited for) magazines it appears that little 'literary' editing was deemed necessary. The legal struggles of this period clearly marked Wallace deeply since, as Boswell notes, he would later mine it for material in the 'Author Here' sections of *The Pale King* (Boswell 2014b, 37). Legal issues do not appear to have played an extensive role in his work with Pietsch, however, and I will not examine the issue in detail here.[6]

The editing of Wallace's non-fiction pieces represented a different proposition.[7] Despite regularly writing pieces that dramatically exceeded the commissioned length, Wallace seems to have approached the process of editing them as a distasteful yet unavoidable one, and this is surely due to practical reasons: the presence of fixed magazine publication deadlines meant that the editing often took place in short, finite bursts as opposed to the prolonged process involved in editing fiction for book publication, and the understanding that clear commercial reasons (such as standard magazine lengths and the need for advertising revenue) necessitated these cuts seems to have made Wallace's attitude more matter-of-fact. Wallace also clearly saw these changes as provisional, since he regularly took the opportunity to restore excised text to his essays in non-fiction collections (Moody and Pietsch 2012, 216).[8]

'Ticket to the Fair', published in *Harper's* in 1994, represents an early example of this process. According to editor Colin Harrison, the piece was commissioned to be 6,000 words, but Wallace sent in an extravagantly excessive 35,000/40,000: the resulting collaboration was akin to a 'tennis match' (Nadell 2012). Wallace's approach to the editing process here was, Max reports, 'strategic

[5] The title 'Late Night' is Playboy editor Alice Turner's according to her recollection; Wallace returned to his original title, 'My Appearance', when including it in *Girl with Curious Hair* (Wallace n.d.).

[6] An exception is the legal challenge posed by a real-life Kate Gompert to the use of her name in *Infinite Jest*; however, this took place some time after the novel's publication and was settled quickly, without necessitating textual alterations (Max 2012a, 161; Wallace 1998a).

[7] The editing of *Everything and More* (Wallace's book on mathematics and infinity) posed a highly specific set of challenges and was, according to Max, a tortuous experience for Wallace, as several mathematicians as well as a general editor weighed in with criticisms and suggested changes (Max 2012a, 274–6).

[8] The copyright page of *Consider the Lobster* alerts the reader to the higher authority of the longer, book-length versions, with a note announcing that 'The following pieces were published in edited, heavily edited, or (in at least one instance) bowdlerized form' (Farber 2009, 4).

and aggressive, but when he lost a point, he moved on', and ultimately the pair succeeded in shortening the piece 'by almost half' (Max 2012a, 186; Nadell 2012). Zac Farber refers to 'Wallace's tendency to write well-reasoned screeds to his editors arguing against even the most niggling alterations to his writing', and while this particular edit appears to have been conducted verbally, Wallace's famed attention to detail was very much in evidence (Farber 2009, 2). The work was 'a fairly technical magazine edit' as well as a textual one, and Harrison remembers 2 a.m. voicemails and 'insanely ornate conversations' by telephone regarding technical aspects of textual presentation such as lining footnotes up correctly with the text (Nadell 2012). This is typical of the way in which Wallace took an unusually intense interest in what McGann terms the 'bibliographical codes' of literary work (McGann 1991, 53–8). Marie Mundaca describes how, when she designed the layout and interior design of *Consider the Lobster* (with specific reference to how to adapt the essay 'Host' from its distinctive appearance in the *Atlantic Monthly*), Wallace would leave phone messages in the middle of the night as well as engaging in 'very intense discussions regarding the semiotics of the leaders (the lines going from the text to the boxes) and the tics and the line width of the boxes and ampersands' (Mundaca 2009, n.p.).

This transfer of visual elements from magazine presentation to book-length presentation was, in fact, an unusual process and suggests the difficulty of comparing magazine editing with the work behind book production. It also highlights the fact that Wallace's non-fiction work was often subject to pressures absent from the production of his fiction. The journalistic pieces, for example, were subject to fact-checking, a process which not only represented an additional layer of work during the editing process (Bill Tonelli of *Rolling Stone* recalls, of Wallace's piece on John McCain, that 'our fact-checker was with him on the phone [for] almost as much time as I was') but also arguably influenced the writing itself as Wallace tried to anticipate this stage of the process. Harrison took an equivocal attitude to possible authorial embellishments that 'could not be disproven' and Tonelli suggests that the author was 'smart enough to make up the stuff that you [were] not going to catch him on' (Max 2012a, 186; Nadell 2012).[9] Wallace could, it seems, be relied upon to anticipate many editorial demands to the extent that, in Farber's words, 'while different editors' experiences

[9] The question of Wallace's fidelity to fact in his non-fiction has received considerable attention since his death, with Franzen and others debating the ethics of his journalistic methods (Dean 2011, n.p.; Max 2012a, 184–7, 317–18n4,5,7; Roiland 2013, 148–61).

varied, there is a consensus that David Wallace's best editor was David Wallace' (Farber 2009, 4). Throughout Wallace's career, we see a pattern whereby he consistently incorporated an awareness of the formal and compositional quirks and limitations of each separate writing project into the works themselves, often in a deliberately provocative and challenging manner. Harrison notes the way in which several of his non-fiction pieces ('Consider the Lobster' and 'Democracy and Commerce at the U.S. Open', for example) seem to be aimed at 'subverting the DNA of certain magazines themselves' (Nadell 2012).[10]

'My gut tells me you can help me': Wallace's work with Pietsch

Michael Pietsch's contact with Wallace began in 1987 with an admiring letter in which he complimented the author's story 'Lyndon' (which had been published in *Arrival* in April of that year) and invited him to 'give me a call if you're ever in town with time on your hands'. Pietsch was at this point an editor at Harmony Books, where he had worked since 1985, having started his career at Scribner's (1979–85). In this letter (which he accompanied with two gifts, Martin Amis' *Success* and Stephen Wright's *Meditations in Green*), Pietsch coyly held out the prospect of future collaboration while presenting a varied list of the high-profile authors he had worked with to date: 'remember that you've got a fan here at the home of Martin Amis, Stephen Wright, Chuck Berry, and Little Richard' (Pietsch 1987a). Within a few days Wallace sent a friendly, chatty response in which he thanked Pietsch for the books (claiming not to have read Amis yet), stated his intentions of remaining with Howard, who he praised as 'that most precious of combinations – smart and laid-back', and suggested that as a writer he had 'gotten better at restricting verbal diarrhea and getting on with it – not a strength of last winter's novel' (Wallace 1987a). The pair met soon afterwards in New York, when Wallace visited the city to collect one of the ten Whiting Awards presented for that year, and they struck up a friendship. Correspondence from the subsequent years shows them exchanging book recommendations (and occasionally books)[11] as well as discussing samples of Wallace's work in a

[10] Mark O'Connell notes, of this aspect of Wallace's work, that 'to read his essays, reviews and articles is (for me at least) to feel a kind of retrospective anxiety on behalf of the unknown editors who commissioned them in the first place' (O'Connell 2012).

[11] Pietsch sent Wallace *Chuck Berry: The Autobiography* (which he had edited) and Brian Eno's *More Dark than Shark* and, later, the manuscript of Mark Leyner's *My Cousin, My Gastroenterologist*.

way that enabled a shared understanding of Wallace's developing aesthetic aims. Pietsch's supportive comments on 'Westward' and bemused response to *Broom*, for example, prompted Wallace to defend the former as 'the best thing I've done so far'[12] and to identify two recurring problems in his novel: namely, 'a constant need to entertain myself when writing' and 'an inability to render stuff I consider "deep" and "interesting" in a way that's both accessible and engaging to readers' (Wallace 1988a).

In 1992, when Wallace was seeking an advance for *Infinite Jest*, this friendship would form the basis for the acquisition of the manuscript by Little, Brown. Max writes that Howard was authorized by Viking's editorial board to offer an advance of $35,000, an offer insufficient to enable Wallace to write without teaching. Nadell then approached Pietsch with the manuscript and Little, Brown subsequently paid $85,000 (Max 2012a, 171). Pietsch told Nadell that he wanted to publish the novel 'more than I want to breathe', and his presentation at a sales conference was crucial to the publisher's acceptance: Lipsky quotes him as having declared 'this is why we publish books' (Max 2012a, 171; Lipsky 2010, 27). An internal memo from Pietsch to the Publication Board of Little, Brown demonstrates the editor's determined attempts to persuade his colleagues of Wallace's promise and shows that the final advance figure was close to his initial suggestion:

> I would like to offer $80,000 for world English language rights to the novel. It's a big commitment but he's one of the most talented young writers around, and it would make a good statement about Little, Brown, that in addition to publishing the established generation of literary grandmasters like Pynchon, Barth, and Fowles, we're developing the next generation. (Pietsch 1992)

Pietsch's description here, positioning Wallace as a future 'grandmaster' in the postmodern lineage, was an early indication of the way in which he would later be heavily branded with paratextual links to Pynchon, as Andersen and Finn have shown; it also demonstrates, more generally, the way in which an editor needs to operate (in Thompson's words) as 'a salesperson within his or her own

Pietsch introduced the latter by noting that Leyner was 'the first person I've ever met who's overjoyed by information overload'; Wallace not only provided a blurb for the book but repeatedly praised it in effusive terms, despite his later dismissal of the author as 'a kind of antichrist'.) Wallace recommended stories by Tim O'Brien and Lee K. Abbot as well as William Vollmann's *Rainbow Stories* (Pietsch 1987b, 1987c, 1989, Wallace 1988b, 1989a, 1989b, 198; Grimes 1992).

12 He also credited Pietsch for helping to convince Howard – in conversation – of the piece's merits and ensure its publication in *GWCH*.

organisation' (Andersen 2014b; Finn 2012, 164–5; J. Thompson 2012, 203). After signing the contract, Wallace wrote to Pietsch claiming that he had told Nadell throughout the negotiations that he wanted to work with the editor, whose reputation and prior relationship with the author evidently counted for a great deal (Wallace 1992). Pietsch had acted here as an acquisitions editor prior to his work as a textual editor, and his talent-scouting activities had clearly dovetailed with personal friendship.[13]

In the same letter, Wallace thanked Pietsch for agreeing to work with him and proceeded to address the editor in direct terms that combined a discussion of his own *modus operandi* with a manifesto of sorts. I quote here at length in order to illustrate the extent of Wallace's self-awareness with regard to his own need and desire for editing, as he both warns Pietsch of his working methods and openly solicits help:

> I do know that I function best when I have a core of readers whom I both trust and know – know where they're coming from, what their strengths and limitations are, when to heed them and when to go with my gut. For a long time, my triad was Bonnie, Gerry and Mark Costello, my best friend from Amherst. I would like to get to know you and be able to get help from you. I am going to need considerable help on IJ when the first draft's done. I may ask if I can come stay with you a couple days (assuming the paint's dry) during Editing and have you go over things with me for a few extended periods. I am a difficult editee – at once obsequious and arrogant, with both very little faith in myself and an incredible, Gila-Monsterish attachment to anything I've done; I am the world's worst cutter; rewriting for me always seem[s] to result in expansion. But I want to improve as a writer, and I want to author things that both restructure worlds and make living people feel stuff, and my gut tells me you can help me. (Wallace 1992)

Wallace's capitalization of the word 'editing' here suggests the importance of the concept to his approach to his work at this stage of his career and makes it evident that he was self-consciously attempting to challenge himself by working with Pietsch. As Farber notes, 'the capitulation, even in principle, to this type of extensive editing marked a change for Wallace' (Farber 2009, 6).

[13] A comparison could be made with Max Perkins' successful pursuit of Hemingway, which he carried out (with Fitzgerald's help) in a lengthy correspondence with the author (Berg 2013, 82–7).

'Playful combat': The editing of *Infinite Jest*

The editing of Wallace's second novel has been discussed in a number of venues, sometimes in close detail. While some contemporary reviewers took the book's length and stylistic approach as evidence of a lack of editorial oversight – with Dave Eggers sniping that 'the book seems like an exercise in what one gifted artist can produce without the hindrance of an editor'[14] and Michiko Kakutani lamenting that 'the book seems to have been written and edited (or not edited) on the principle that bigger is better' (Eggers 1996; Kakutani 1996, n.p.) – it has since come to be understood that the process of producing the book was a long and focused one.[15] The central facts of the editing process behind *Infinite Jest* have been established[16] and I will not attempt an exhaustive account of the process in this chapter: the volume of available manuscript material (comprising a full nine containers of drafts in the Ransom Center's Wallace Papers), along with the many interrelated complexities of the book's plot, would demand a treatment of significant length and a degree of detail difficult to accommodate here. We can, however, identify the key decisions made in the book's construction and hone in on the distinctive features of Wallace and Pietsch's working relationship. In the following section, I present an overview of the editing of *Infinite Jest* and isolate its key features to ascertain how this collaborative dynamic contributed to the book's form and presentation.

To begin with, we may note the size of the editing job involved and the ambiguity over the volume of material deleted from the enormous manuscript. Different figures have been given for the amount of material excised from the drafts, most of them by Wallace himself. In 1995, he told David Markson that the book had lost 600 pages on its route to print. In a 1996 radio interview, however, he described the novel as being 'about 400 or 500 pages shorter than it was before'; speaking to *Salon* in 1996, he stated that the manuscript had lost 'close to 500' pages; and, to Lipsky in the same year, he also claimed that 'about

14 Eggers would later amend this opinion, writing in his 2006 foreword that the novel was 'drum tight' with 'no discernible flaws' (Eggers 2006, xii–xiii).

15 The reviewer for *Entertainment Weekly*, in fact, threw up her hands in 'despair' at the book's length, claiming that its size and difficulty rendered the book an 'infinite burden' and left her 'longing for an unedited Joan Collins manuscript' (Schwarzbaum 1996).

16 Max provides a chronological account of the editorial negotiations, while Pietsch has discussed his experience of the process and reproduced selections from Wallace's correspondence on proposed changes (Max 2012a, 182–3, 193–6, 198–201, 205–7; Moody and Pietsch 2012, 208–17). Steven Moore also analyses one of Wallace's working drafts from 1993, providing a detailed discussion of excised material and commentary on aspects of the novel's evolution (Moore 2003).

five hundred pages' had been cut.[17] In 1999, though, speaking to Lorin Stein for *Publishers Weekly*, he pared the figure back dramatically, stating that Pietsch had cut 'two or three hundred pages' (Max 2012a, 212; Lydon 1996; Wallace 2012d, 64, 93; Lipsky 2010, 78). Pietsch places the figure in the latter range, stating that his calculation at the time put the figure at '250–300 pages' (Pietsch 2017c). The truth of these claims is difficult to determine since, as the manuscript materials show, many of these alterations were not straightforward cuts but often involved compression and rearrangement of material. The cuts were made in several stages, as I will go on to show, and Wallace frequently rewrote sections (often adding some new material) and moved material to footnotes rather than deleting it entirely.[18] The evidence in the Wallace papers suggests that the higher figures given by the author are unlikely to be accurate: based on the material currently in the archive, Hering puts the figure 'in the region of 150 pages', an estimate that accords with my impressions.[19] It seems likely that Wallace's early estimates were exaggerations, expressions either of his frustration at the laborious multistage processes involved in bringing the book to publication or of a desire to impress peers and interviewers with his absurdly maximalistic productivity. His comments to Markson, as Max observes, contain a note of ingratitude and represent a rare example of the author's criticism of his editor's work:

> About the holes and lacunae and etc., I bet you're right: the fucker's cut by 600 pages from the first version, and though many of the cuts (editor-inspired) made the thing better, it fucked up a certain water-tightness that the mastodon-size version had, I think. (Max 2012a, 212)

[17] Michael Silverblatt was one of the many readers enticed by the figures given by Wallace. In a letter written shortly after the publication of the novel, Pietsch wrote to Wallace that Silverblatt had contacted Little, Brown with the unusual request to see the unedited manuscript so he could 'read all the great parts that didn't make it into the book' (Pietsch 1996).

[18] Indeed, as has been documented, Wallace did not use the same formatting in each manuscript version, and his first draft featured a deliberately small font and narrow margins chosen in a forlorn attempt to deceive Pietsch as to its true length (Max 2012a, 182). Even a comprehensive study of the manuscripts, therefore, might encounter difficulties in ascertaining a definitive figure.

[19] Hering acknowledges that 'there may, of course, be more deleted material held outside the archive' although Pietsch has no knowledge of any, stating:

> There does not appear to be any surviving draft material from *Infinite Jest*. As part of our normal process, we returned all edited versions of the manuscript to David when publication was complete, and he doesn't appear to have kept them. I read interviews in which David said 500 pages had been cut, and I agree with your inference that he may have exaggerated. My own calculation at the time was that David had cut 250–300 pages. (Hering 2016a, 172; Pietsch 2017c)

This is a touch disingenuous, since many of the novel's 'lacunae' are ones that Wallace stubbornly defended in the face of Pietsch's requests for more narrative information. The comments also carry a hint of macho boastfulness ('mastodon size') that betrays the link between gender and genre in the tradition of the encyclopaedic mega-novel that he was adding to. The repeated references to excessive production in interviews and correspondence allow Wallace to simultaneously play up the size of his literary achievement and to take a perverse kind of credit for the effort needed to manage that production; in contrast to the writer of Minimalist fiction, the maximalist novelist can wear his editorial battle scars as a sign of authorial pride.

What follows is a brief description of the editing process, which can roughly be said to have taken place in three stages. The first of these occurred in the summer of 1993, when Pietsch delivered a quick response to the first, incomplete draft of the novel. Wallace continued writing after receiving this response, and in June 1994 he delivered the completed manuscript, which consisted of roughly 750,000 words (Max 2012a, 182–3, 196).[20] Pietsch then carried out his second reading (and his first close line edit) in the winter of 1994, during which time he sent two letters accompanied by detailed lists of possible cuts. Wallace in turn responded to these in February of 1995, thus concluding the second stage. In May of 1995, Pietsch set the book in sample type and wrote that further cuts were necessary, and he soon followed this with the news that, following another close line edit, it would be necessary to make another detailed series of revisions. In May and June of 1995, Wallace engaged in the final major round of cutting and rewriting, during which he agreed to more excisions and also acceded to Pietsch's requests for additional sections in order to clarify central plot strands (writing, for example, the scene in which Orin is interrogated and tortured by the Quebecois terrorists) (Max 2012a, 205–7).

The tone and overall dynamics of the editing process were determined by Pietsch's response to the initial unfinished manuscript. This manuscript was substantial: Steven Moore's description of his version of the same draft emphasizes the presence of different stages of revision, different fonts and

[20] This is to simplify matters a little, since the first manuscript (which corresponds to the version described in Moore's essay) consisted of only 'about two-thirds' of the novel, and the author continued writing after he had sent the initial manuscript to Pietsch, without waiting for the editor's response (Max 2012a, 183; Moody and Pietsch 2012, 212). Pietsch delivered his response rapidly, though (writing to Wallace with his impressions in June of 1993), and since Wallace was aware of Pietsch's thoughts for most of the time in which he completed the full-length manuscript, I take it to be the first significant stage of their collaborative editing process on the novel.

confusing pagination, observing that 'merely flipping through the 4-inch-high manuscript would give even a seasoned editor the howling fantods' (Moore 2003, n.p.). Pietsch's reply showed an understanding of Wallace's aesthetic, though, noting the importance of 'Hal's sadness' to the narrative and opining that the work was 'a novel made up out of shards'. Wallace would later note that the latter observation was 'the first time that anybody had ever conceptualized what was to me just a certain structural representation of the way the world operated on my nerve endings, which was as a bunch of discrete random bits, but which contained within them [. . .] very interesting connections' (Wallace 1996).[21] Pietsch also expressed his enjoyment of the reading experience, making his supportive attitude clear by referring to the 'huge pleasure' of reading the manuscript and enthusing that he was 'fascinated by these worlds and these characters and the mysteries of how the stories are starting to invade each other' (Pietsch 1993).[22] However, the second paragraph of the letter clearly warned the author of impending practical difficulties. After a rough calculation of the possible word count and length (which he projected as 600,000 words and 1,200 pages), Pietsch stated the logistical risks involved and his own attitude to them: 'this should not be a $30 novel so thick readers feel they have to clear their calendars for a month before they buy it' (Pietsch 1993).

Editors, states John Bryant, effectively serve 'as emissaries of social power', and Pietsch's words illustrate the numerous social pressures involved in publication (Bryant 2002, 59). The phrasing of his warning invokes possible reader response (the feelings of future readers), the material limitations of book technology (the thickness of the volume and the cost arising from a high page count) and concerns about the future marketing and cultural positioning of the literary product. Wallace would later remember this as 'a big mistake' on Pietsch's part, telling Lipsky that the letter had caused him considerable anxiety about his artistic integrity. Max writes that the letter 'left Wallace upset and unsatisfied'; he subsequently needed reassurance from friends and colleagues

21 See Hering for an analysis of this quote in relation to the novel's 'broken' and recursive form and for a development of this analysis with reference to images of broken glass (Wallace 1996b; Hering 2015, 2016a, 99–110).

22 Recalling this process in 2012, Pietsch highlighted the need for the editor to act as an encouraging presence:

> An editor's [. . .] primary job is always to express abundant, overwhelming delight and show that you appreciate what the writer has set out to do, because if they don't feel that you appreciate and understand what they've set out to do then why are they going to listen to you when you make suggestions for changes? (Pietsch and Nadell 2012)

that he would not be a 'whore' for cooperating in the editorial process (Lipsky 2010, 246; Max 2012a, 183).[23] However, Wallace clearly accepted Pietsch's criticisms to a significant degree. Pietsch forwarded his own letter to Nadell, noting the author's reluctant recognition of the validity of his objections: 'here's what I said to David. He seemed to agree with most of it, glumly' (Pietsch 1993). Despite being willing to stand his ground over many specific requests for cuts, Wallace never seems to have substantively disagreed with the need for cooperation with these publishing pressures – he never threatened to withdraw from the arrangement or questioned the need to market the book – and his response to Pietsch's letter signalled his early willingness to engage in a process of negotiation with them. Indeed, in a letter to DeLillo, he acknowledged the need for compromise: 'I am uncomfortable about making cuts for commercial reasons – it seems slutty – but on the other hand L,B is taking a big gamble publishing something this long and hard and I feel some obligation not to be a p.-donna and fuck them over' (Max 2012a, 205). His accommodation with the demands of commercial publishing seems to have been spurred by his editor's arguments, and his acquiescence to the repeated rounds of work involved in the editorial process clearly owes a great deal to Pietsch's presentation of the arguments for these demands.

Max describes the language of Wallace's editorial correspondence with Pietsch as that of 'playful combat', a phrase that aptly summarizes the tone of much of the process (Max 2012a, 206). The tone is that of a focused, occasionally tense but generally good-natured negotiation during which Wallace protected what he considered to be essential features of the project (most notably its inconclusive ending) while acceding to numerous micro-changes in order to forestall an excessive amount of what he described (paraphrasing Pietsch) as 'reader alienation' (Lipsky 247). Wallace had written to Pietsch before sending the full draft in order to express his conviction that the book would come to a conclusion that was 'aclimactic' rather than being 'any sort of conventionally linear ending' (Wallace 1994a). As I noted at the outset of this chapter, he also warned Pietsch that he had introduced endnotes (noting that he wanted to 'prepare [the editor] emotionally' for this fact), a narrative strategy to which he had become 'intensely attached' and that would allow him to preserve many of the detailed passages in his manuscript while presenting a more accessible main

23 Wallace alluded to helpful conversations with Richard Powers and Steve Moore (Lipsky 246) and also wrote to DeLillo for counsel on how to cope with editorial demands (Max 2012a, 205).

text to the reader (Wallace 1994b). Upon delivering the full manuscript, Wallace wrote that it was:

> Very long, but I have done my best to cut it. If further stuff needs to be cut I'm not apt to fight but to ask for an enormous amount of help, because everything in it is connected to everything else, at least in my head [. . .] at this point I have no idea [. . .] I just want it done. (Wallace 1994c)

From this point on, Pietsch's textual editing consisted of providing the requested help, and the bulk of his work with Wallace involved negotiating cuts in a process that might be characterized as the collaborative management of the textual excess they both acknowledged to be present. In his subsequent letters, the words 'condense' and 'cut' feature heavily, and his suggestions tend to emphasize narrative necessity and the dangers of fatigue on the part of readers who might be 'exhausted at having too much data crammed into their heads with very little story to keep them moving through it' (Pietsch 1994b). He focused heavily on the need to cut scenes from what he had earlier referred to as the 'superstructure' of the novel, with particular reference to the dialogues between Marathe and Steeply, and did not hesitate to describe these as 'vague', 'unfollowable' and 'dull' (Pietsch 1994b). Some of the documents from this phase have an intensely dialogic character, as Wallace returned to Pietsch's letters multiple times, writing annotations in different pens and sometimes changing his mind about particular scenes in different stages of revision.

Pietsch's method of negotiation was to continually urge upon Wallace the necessity of balancing his desire to challenge the reader against the demands of what Max describes as 'the physics of reading' (Max 2012a, 182), a line of argumentation that Wallace clearly found persuasive.[24] To Lipsky, he later recalled

> Michael being real smart about, 'All right, maybe you don't cut this scene, but you take five pages off this, and it's 30 percent easier to read. And save yourself 10 percent reader alienation, which you *need* thirty pages later for this part'. You know what I mean? Like *smart*. (Lipsky 2010, 247, italics in original)

[24] Severs emphasizes the career-long importance to Wallace of the notion of 'balance'; with this in mind, I note both that Pietsch's tactics here were well calculated to appeal to the author's sense of equilibrium and that Wallace clearly experienced the act of editing itself as a necessary balancing act between his own impulses and the needs of his imagined readership (Severs 2017).

The description suggests the size and complexity of the process, as both author and editor attempted to excise material with reference to detailed lists of possible changes and in relation to an imagined overall reading experience. Pietsch's letter of 22 December 1994, for example, which dealt with the second half of the novel, contained forty-five separate requests for alterations, each one accompanied by page numbers and comments requesting not only clarification and cuts but sometimes suggesting a change in the placement of a scene. He introduced these requests with the diplomatic suggestion that while his own confusion about certain plot points may have been a result of his tiredness while reading, he was 'going to ask you to err on the side of elaborating or stressing some points that are now made clearly but briefly'. A 16-page letter from February 1995 presents Wallace's responses in detail. In some cases, he refused the suggestions outright, insisting on keeping scenes depicting Mario's first romantic experience and video telephony, James Incandenza's filmography and on the heading 'Gaudeamus Igitur' for scenes of 'celebration/spectacle/entertainment'. In others, he consented either to cut or reduce material, shortening 'Joelle's walk to [the] party' and the Clipperton scene and removing a long list of footnotes; the latest draft had contained a number of references to Hal's suffering from a condition named 'jamais-vu', and Wallace accepted Pietsch's argument that these were unclear. Many of Wallace's responses were broken down into multiple sub-headings, with the defence of the Clipperton scene, for example, presented in three numbered points. His revisions often involved complex rearrangements, such as his edits to one of the Marathe/Steeply scenes, which was 'split into 4 littler bits' and 'moved way later': the 'Total bulk of [the] exchange', he informed Pietsch, was 'reduced by 20%' (Wallace 1995a). Pietsch also continually probed the intricacies of the plot, asking for confirmation and sometimes clarification on questions such as whether the words 'Happy Anniversary' on the killer cartridge received by the medical attaché was 'a suggestion that Himself somehow set all this in motion from the grave', a question to which Wallace responded in the affirmative (Pietsch 1995b).

These exchanges, it should be noted, form only part of the process and are, as Pietsch points out, 'what remains in the record'. Since much of the editing of *Infinite Jest* (and other works in the pre- and early-internet era) was completed by telephone, the 'line-by-line edits' are not captured in the correspondence. Pietsch recalls that:

> A lot of editing work was completed on the phone. I can reread letters between David and me and know that we had long phone conversations with the letters in front of us, going point by point, and there isn't a written record of what he decided. But any changes to the work were completely David's. (Pietsch 2017b, 2017c)

Our knowledge of Pietsch's work is limited, for the most part, to the kind of scene-by-scene commentary reproduced here rather than to the kind of detailed line editing that we saw in Lish's revisions of Carver. This is a significant loss – albeit a very common one – and prevents us from a detailed consideration of Pietsch's contribution to Wallace's style at a sentence level. As I have suggested, though, the contribution of an editor to the style of an author of maximalist fiction is necessarily less drastic than that of an editor of a minimalist story in which intense pressure is placed upon individual word choices and placement; all the available evidence, moreover, suggests that Pietsch's claim that all of these changes were approved by Wallace is indeed correct.

As the process developed, Pietsch began to accept the need to compromise significantly on the practicalities of length and price. In October 1994, he wrote that:

> My guiding principle is going to be that we should try to make the novel fit whatever length leaves it possible for us to price the book under $30. $30 is tough enough; I don't believe anyone will buy a book over that price no matter how great they hear it is. (Pietsch 1994a)

Two months later, he acquiesced to Wallace's preference for endnotes over footnotes and optimistically wrote that he was 'still hoping there are ways to make the novel much shorter [. . .] because the longer it is the more people will find excuses not to read it' (Pietsch 1994c). The evidence shows that Pietsch's work here accords with his conception of the editor's role as one which requires 'earn[ing] the writer's agreement that changes he or she suggests are worth making' (Pietsch 2009). He later recalled that the author frequently overruled his advice on the endnotes: 'he insisted that many of them stay that I thought could well have come out' (Moody and Pietsch 2012, 213). Pietsch also showed himself willing to be persuaded by Wallace's defence of certain scenes and to rethink his own assessment of them; in May of 1995, he wrote to accept that 'the Clipperton scene and puppet movie all seem pretty much as brief as they can be' and that he would 'like to see Jim on annular fusion back in the text' (Pietsch 1995b). The editor gradually accommodated himself to the demands of the work and while his focus initially fell on the management of the author's maximalist production, he began increasingly to consider the problem of how best to present that maximalism in the marketplace.[25]

Seen as a whole, the key feature of Pietsch's editing is surely the way in which he continually and successfully negotiated between commercial imperatives (the bottom-line necessity of producing a marketable book that would justify Little, Brown's investment) and the author's ambition and propensity for experimentation and textual abundance. To use Evan Brier's terms, this represents a skilful occupation of the editor's precarious territory of the 'border between middle-management employee and artist's advocate' (Brier 2017, 88). Despite Wallace's engagement with the demands for cuts, the final product did, in fact, turn out to be a $30 book[26] and was, in length, not far short of the figure of Pietsch's early fears (1,079 pages rather than 1,200). It is clear that both author and editor made numerous compromises, and the editor's chief concession was simply to accept the book's length as a necessary condition of production; in Steven Moore's words, 'it's to his editor's credit that, instead of insisting on further reductions, Pietsch decided to market the novel's gargantuan size as part of its appeal' (Moore 2003, n.p.). Indeed, this commercial presentation of the novel was successful enough for it to have later been described as a 'case study in how to sell' a lengthy and ambitious novel (Kachka 2015, n.p.). Max describes how Little, Brown adopted the strategy of sending out 'a campaign of postcards [. . .] to four thousand reviewers, producers, and bookstore owners', upon which were inscribed (as Tore Rye Andersen recounts) enigmatic, teasing phrases such as 'It's coming' (Max 2012a, 211; Andersen 2012, 276 n20). Each round of these postcards carried hyperbolic statements that served to reconceive the size and difficulty of the novel as essential selling points: one predicted it to be 'the biggest literary event of next year', while another quipped, 'just imagine what they'll say about his masterpiece' (Max 2012a, 211).

This approach was one that the author was reluctant to approve. When Wallace received the postcards, he replied to express his conflicted feelings, noting his concern that the use of superlatives (such as 'masterpiece') was

[25] Pietsch did, however, take the lead in determining the book's artwork. Wallace urged his editor to consider the cover of the 1985 edition of the Pam Cook-edited volume *The Cinema Book*, which he had torn from his own copy and which featured, in his description, 'Fritz Lang declaiming to the legions on the set of *Metropolis*'; Pietsch rejected the image on the basis that it was too familiar to use (Wallace 1995b; Pietsch 1995a). Elsewhere, Wallace explicitly accepted that 'graphics' were 'not my business' and pledged not to 'meddle much' in these (Wallace 1995a).

[26] Both Steven Moore and Michiko Kakutani's reviews listed its sale price at $29.95.

'icky' and asking for the size of his name to be reduced on the book's cover (Max 2012a, 211–12; Wallace 1995d). Indeed, Pietsch would later note that Wallace's unease here was characteristic, since 'the professional interface between [Wallace] and his readers' was 'a borderline he approached with vast apprehension' (Pietsch 2010, 11). However, the success of the strategy is undeniable, and the commercial apparatus employed in the service of this marketing campaign undoubtedly served to communicate the impression of a formidably accomplished, intellectually brilliant author. The blurbs on the back cover of the 'advance reading copy' of the book (of which, as Andersen notes, there were a remarkable eight) contained four iterations of the word 'brilliant' and one mention of 'genius'; Jeffrey Eugenides' blurb ended with the repetition of the phrase 'He's the man!'.[27] Pietsch noted his satisfaction in a letter to Nadell in January 1996, saying that 'all our drum beating seems to have been heard' (Max 2012a, 216), and the book would, of course, go on to be central in securing the reputation of its author as well as its editor.

The 'case study' of *Infinite Jest*'s marketing has, in fact, had a powerful afterlife. A 2001 profile of Pietsch on the occasion of his promotion to the role of publisher at Hachette noted that much of his reputation rested on the success of *Infinite Jest* and devoted some time to a narrative of the editor's role in this commercial triumph. The author described how, 'left with [. . .] a gargantuan manuscript and mindful of the fate of many other worthy but long-winded literary novels, Pietsch took the decisive step of his career'. The editor 'enlist[ed] the help of young writers like his author Rick Moody' in an effort 'to incite envy among Wallace's peers': 'the trick', Pietsch was quoted as saying, 'was getting other writers to recognize that this was the guy to beat'.[28] His approach to overcoming possible 'reluctance' on the part of general readers was, he remembered, based on a similarly confrontational gambit: '"I can show you the place", Pietsch recalls, "up on the hill by my house where I first thought of making this a challenge: Are you reader enough?"'. The author of the profile noted that an unnamed 'young novelist' had confided to her, 'with two parts

[27] Andersen analyses this ARC in detail to illustrate the way in which the paratextual elements functioned as a 'gateway' for readers (noting, e.g. the 'rebellious charisma' suggested by the unusual choice of author photo) and positioned Wallace within a 'constellation' of literary-historical reference points (Andersen 2012, 251–78); elsewhere, he examines how the novel's paratexts served to encourage an exaggerated focus on the author's continuities with Pynchon (Andersen 2014b).

[28] We might, in noting the success of this appeal to a spirit of writerly competition, recall Lorentzen's comment that other writers 'took to it [the novel] like Marines sprung from a sort of literary boot camp' (Lorentzen 2015, n.p.).

sarcastic envy and one part reverence', that Pietsch was '"the Maxwell Perkins of our generation"' (Maneker 2001, n.p.). In this narrative, Pietsch's editing of Wallace had itself become a canonical example of the editor's art, securing his reputation as one of the foremost editors of ambitious fiction and allowing him to ascend to the pantheon of American editing giants.

Like Perkins, whose early successes drew writers of ambition towards Scribner's from the 1920s onwards, Pietsch was able to deploy this status in future negotiations.[29] The effect can be seen most clearly in the narrative of his acquisition of Chad Harbach's *The Art of Fielding*, published in 2011. The book is one of the more celebrated case studies of recent publishing history due to the intensive bidding war that preceded its publication, a sequence of events detailed by Harbach's friend Keith Gessen in a *Vanity Fair* article published simultaneously with the novel.[30] Chris Parris-Lamb, at that point early in his career as an agent, sent Harbach's manuscript to Pietsch, who was 'the only editor I knew by name when I entered the business' (Parris-Lamb and Lee 2016, 177). Harbach himself was so eager to enter a working relationship with Pietsch and Little, Brown in order to develop his novel that he was prepared to accept a lower advance in exchange for the opportunity to work with the editor of *Infinite Jest* (Boroff 2010, n.p.; Gessen 2011, 538). Gessen details the negotiations as follows:

> Another difficult decision had to be made. The money difference was far from trivial; on the other hand, Michael Pietsch (the publisher of Little, Brown) said that he himself would edit the book. This clinched it. Chad and Chris (Parris-Lamb, his agent) would leave $85,000 on the table for the opportunity to work with the editor of David Foster Wallace. That editor had also, of course, put up $665,000. It was the biggest fiction auction in recent memory; it was especially eloquent after the darkness of 2009, when publishers had had to lay off staff. (Gessen 2011, 450)

This exchange illustrates the esteem in which young novelists held the editor and illustrates as vividly as we could hope for the operations of Pierre Bourdieu's notions of 'symbolic capital' – what John B. Thompson glosses as 'the accumulated prestige, recognition and respect accorded to certain individuals

[29] According to Berg, after Hemingway left his publisher Boni & Liveright in 1925, he approached the editor at Scribner's directly and ignored other publishers out of a combination of Perkin's prestige, Fitzgerald's recommendation and 'the impression he had formed of Perkins through his letters' (Berg 2013, 87).

[30] The piece was subsequently turned into a short e-book, *Vanity Fair's How a Book is Born: The Making of The Art of Fielding* (2011).

or institutions' – and 'field' – 'a structured space of social positions [. . .] in which agents and organizations are linked together in relations of cooperation, competition and interdependency'.[31] We see here a complicated transaction in which Pietsch, at this point further advanced in his career (due in no small measure to his editing of *Infinite Jest*), was able to offer far more for Harbach's novel than for Wallace's. He could offer less than his rivals, however, since Harbach was willing to forgo some of the actual capital offered by other publishers (an amount, indeed, exactly equal to the entire advance for *Infinite Jest*) in favour of the cultural and symbolic capital available from 'the editor of David Foster Wallace', offering an unintentionally ironic gloss on the art of 'fielding'.

The marketing of *Infinite Jest* and the operations of cultural prestige surrounding the novel have also had an important afterlife in criticism of Wallace. In her notorious explanation of her decision not to read Wallace (based on her reading of his biography alongside selected early stories, interviews and reviews), Amy Hungerford hones in on the system of production responsible for 'making Wallace into a literary celebrity' in order to suggest that the book's success (in Kelly's paraphrase) 'owes more to clever marketing than to genuine literary merit' (Hungerford 2016, 158–9, Kelly 2017, 3). Focusing on the 'dare' (as Max describes it) laid down to reviewers who were only too eager to respond to 'the aura of literary seriousness' projected by Little, Brown, she comments acerbically that 'the marketers knew their marks' (Hungerford 2016, 158). The insidious and ultimately successful calculations in play in this marketing endeavour, in which Pietsch and his associates played up the ambition and accomplishment of the book in order to ensnare critics and readers trained to value particular forms of cultural accomplishment, are cited by Hungerford as prime reasons for her decision 'to refuse the culture's rising call to attend to' the novel. Hungerford's account raises several unanswered questions: her description of the operations of 'the engine of canonization', for example, elides somewhat the distance between literary celebrity and canonicity, ignoring the countless marketing campaigns for ambitious books (and consequent commercial successes) that fail to generate lasting acceptance within the academy. The importance she grants to the particular marketing gambit in question is also problematically wide and undefined: the editor, here, is imagined as a powerful illusionist whose ability

[31] Both Thompson and English take the notions of 'capital' and 'field' to be the most useful contributions of Bourdieu's system of thought to the study of literary culture (English 2005, 9; J. Thompson 2012, 3–8).

to dupe future generations of readers and scholars stretches across multiple decades.[32] Her description of the role of gatekeepers and paratexts in positioning a work for reception, though – and her identification of the reciprocal 'cultural power' transferred between Wallace and Pietsch as a result of this reception – reminds us that the work of an editor extends far beyond the page. It also shows some of the ways in which a work of maximalist fiction foregrounds the work of its editor by virtue of its sheer size. To its author, and to many of its readers and critics, the successful editing and selling of a work of experimental and ostentatiously ambitious fiction within a major international publishing house constituted an achievement of almost heroic dimensions, making Pietsch into the closest modern-day analogue for the Perkins of editorial legend. To the book's time-pressed reviewers, on the other hand, as well as its later audience of overburdened and reluctant professors and deans, Pietsch could be held to be culpable on two fronts: first of having not edited the book stringently enough and then, perhaps, of having sold it too well.

'I feel like I know him, and I trust him, and that's priceless': After *Infinite Jest*

In November of 1995, Wallace wrote to tell Pietsch that he was, after reading through the galleys of *Infinite Jest*, 'feeling the gratitude afresh' for the editor's work. The book contained no list of thanks, but the author wrote that 'if there were such a list, your name would be first' (Wallace 1995c). Indeed, in the years after this unprecedentedly lengthy and extensive editing process, Wallace held a lasting respect for his editor. In 1996, speaking to Lipsky, he commended Pietsch's work in the strongest terms: 'I mean, I think he's a little bit of a hero, and it would be nice if he got some of the good attention' (Lipsky 2010, 103). Pietsch remained his editor for every book-length work for the rest of his career (with the exception *of Everything and More*), and Wallace's subsequent references to his editor's work on the novel were almost entirely positive. In a 1999 interview, Wallace praised Pietsch's textual editing as well as what the interviewer paraphrased as his 'diplomacy as he shuttled between [the author

32 Tom LeClair also identifies a degree of bad faith in Hungerford's failure to note the operation of analogous mechanisms – blurbs, excerpts, approval from literary gatekeepers – in the publication and marketing of her own book (LeClair 2016).

and] marketers, who worried over the novel's size' (Wallace 2012d, 93). In the same interview, Wallace suggested that Pietsch's role was deliberately distant and that their friendship was of a kind calibrated to enable improvement of his work: 'This wasn't a matter of liking my editor. We don't mix socially: I'm nervous around Michael; he's an authority figure for me. But I feel like I know him, and I trust him, and that's priceless' (Wallace 2012d, 93). Wallace's words here suggest that he required an awareness of external pressure in order to produce his best work, and Max speculates upon 'the usefulness [for Wallace] of imagining Pietsch as an unforgiving authority figure so he would get [*Infinite Jest*] written' (Max 2012a, 194).

Pietsch's work on Wallace's last two story collections, judging from the archival evidence as well as his own recollection, appears to have primarily involved selection and sequencing rather than any extensive changes to individual stories (Pietsch 2017c). The collections' relatively standard length meant that the spatial and physical constraints that had helped to shape *Infinite Jest* were no longer a factor; additionally, many of the stories had been previously edited and published in magazines. These processes of selection and sequencing were often complex ones in themselves, of course, particularly in the case of the presentation of the numbered title story sequence in *Brief Interviews with Hideous Men*. In his letter accompanying the manuscript of the collection, Wallace continued the playful and passive-aggressive dynamic of the previous collaboration, beginning by asserting his satisfaction with the work and self-deprecatingly describing his fear of 'all the various ways I imagine you trying to "hurt" it', before assuring Pietsch that he has 'extremely high credibility with me as a reader' and pledging to try to be 'a humble and lovable editee' (Wallace 1998c). Significant portions of the editing of the collection appear, however, to have been conducted by telephone, resulting in the same archival gaps we see with *Infinite Jest*. In a 1998 letter, Wallace alludes to a phone conversation and offers a list of changes, most of which he states are 'consequent to your input'. Most of these involve changes in sequencing: 'Datum Centurio', for example, was 'moved so that it doesn't immediately follow the abstract ending of "Octet" (Mark Costello suggestion)', and 'Crash of 62' (which would later be cut from the collection altogether, and remains uncollected)[33] was moved, on Pietsch's advice,

[33] 'Crash of '69' was published in 1989 in the journal *Between C & D*. However, as Severs observes, Wallace continued to refer to the story as 'Crash of '62' (which had been its original title) in correspondence after this point (Severs 2017, 66–70, 264).

to earlier in the collection. For the most part, however, the rationale for these changes is not presented in any detail. In the same letter, Wallace insisted upon the unorthodox pagination of the collection, saying only that 'starting at 0 is ordinally accurate, and I'm chronically annoyed at books starting at 1';[34] he also requested that 'whoever designed the migraine-yellow cover' of the *ASFTINDA* hardback not be involved in creating the cover for the new book (Wallace 1998d).

When submitting several pieces that would be included in *Oblivion*, Wallace requested advice not just on their individual merits but on their suitability for combination in a collection, praising his editor as being 'much better than I at seeing how things do or do not combine, and how, and what it's like to read pieces of mine serially'. Wallace reiterated his high opinion of his editor several times, and the same 2001 letter mentions that both works of fiction that Pietsch had assisted with by that point – *Infinite Jest* and *Brief Interviews with Hideous Men* – had been made 'better – in some cases substantially better – than they would have been otherwise' by the editorial process. He also signalled his own complex attitude towards his editor, alluding to 'the weird authority-figure-and-need-for-approval shit I constantly project onto you, Bonnie, magazine editors, etc' (Wallace 2001). This is an attitude I will return to in my final chapter, where I suggest that Wallace had, later in his career, internalized this 'authority figure' and begun to incorporate it as a presence in his own work. Wallace echoed the public praise (and direct thanks) for his editor in private correspondence, confiding to DeLillo that 'I need editing help and I really like and trust Pietsch and the L,B copyeditors' (Wallace 2000c).[35] The amount of editing involved in the collection itself appears to have been relatively minor, with Pietsch commenting that the stories are so accomplished that 'I don't feel like much of an editor here' (Pietsch 2003). He did, however, suggest a different running order, with 'Oblivion' to be followed by 'The Soul Is Not a Smithy'; while 'The Suffering Channel' would still have closed the collection in this format, it would have been preceded by the eventual opener, 'Mister Squishy'. Wallace demurred,

[34] The archive, then, does not provide any support for – while not necessarily invalidating – Dan Tysdal's analysis of 'A Radically Condensed History of Postindustrial Life', which argues that the pagination of the collection's opening story is intricately connected with its meaning (Tysdal 2003).

[35] Pietsch's copy-editing abilities also caused Wallace to revise his previous confidence in his own skills: in a letter from June 2000 written in response to Pietsch's edit of the electronic edition of *McCain's Promise*, Wallace wrote that he was 'appalled that you caught so many typos after the thing went through my filter [. . .] I don't think at 38 I get to call myself a near-great proofreader anymore' (Wallace 2000a). Correspondence from different editorial files also shows that the author repeatedly expressed his gratitude to copy-editors and designers in effusive terms (in particular, to Betsy Uhrig and Marie Mundaca, who worked on *Oblivion*).

based on his sense that 'Oblivion' would be an 'almost aggressively difficult piece to start with' and the fact that the story had failed to make it through the publication process at *Harper's* and the *New Yorker*.[36] Again, the written record is incomplete, and the final running order appears to have been decided in person shortly thereafter (Wallace 2003c).

Wallace's letters to Pietsch after this point continue to show a mixture of gratitude and deference for the editor's attention and judgement, and letters from 2003 and 2004, during the early stages of editing *Consider the Lobster*, show him signing off with the words 'Your Devoted Editee' (Wallace 2003b, 2004a). Pietsch expressed reservations about including 'Consider the Lobster', which he felt withheld too much of Wallace's own attitude towards meat eating, in the collection. In reply to Pietsch's comments on the proposed list of essays, Wallace professed respect and apologetic, belated deference to Pietsch's judgement on the sequencing of their previous collaboration:

> After overriding you about starting the fiction book with 'Mister S'. and then realizing what a serious mistake I'd made, I will not override you if you feel the Lobster thing is simply too slight and, well, fluffy to be even a breather-type piece in the collection. (Wallace 2004b)

Even at the late stage of March 2005 (*Lobster* was published in December of that year), Wallace agreed to cut two essays[37] if Pietsch requested it: 'But your track record on inclusion/arrangement issues is so good that I'll simply acquiesce if you're 100% sure' (Wallace 2005b).

It is clear, therefore, that Pietsch was, during the extended time of the composition of the work that would develop into *The Pale King*, a trusted and valued collaborator for Wallace. Wallace's abiding esteem for his editor is perhaps nowhere more clearly signalled than in a letter from 2003: during the process of writing and selecting the stories for *Oblivion*, Wallace heard rumours of Time

[36] Wallace's assumption that 'Mister Squishy' represented a more accessible entry point to the collection is a highly debatable one. Walter Kirn's review excerpted a sentence from the opening story to demonstrate the intimidating challenges of the author's prose style, while James Wood's review of the collection, which described 'Squishy' as 'fundamentally unreadable – deliberately, defiantly so' suggests that Wallace may have miscalculated (Kirn 2004, n.p.; Wood 2004, 27). However, Wood's misreading of 'Oblivion' in the same review suggests that the overall intricacy and verbal density of these pieces would have made any of them a challenging opener (Wood 2004, 28–9; Mason 2004, n.p.).

[37] These were 'Rhetoric and the Math Melodrama' and 'Form and Crapola', which were indeed cut on Pietsch's advice (on the basis that both were negative pieces, dealing with obscure works); both were subsequently published in the posthumous collection *Both Flesh and Not* (the latter was renamed as 'The Best of the Prose Poem').

Warner's impending sale of Little, Brown and let his editor know (in a paragraph he flagged as 'possibly inappropriate') that should the process end with Pietsch moving to a different publisher, he would be eager to follow (Wallace 2003a).[38] If Wallace's fiction continually bespeaks 'a fixation on the author's dialogic relationship with the reader', as Hering puts it, then his work with his editor – whose job is, as Pietsch phrases it, to be 'an ideal reader trusted to comment before a book goes out into the world' – is surely the clearest example of such a relationship to be found in his career (Hering 2016a, 17; Pietsch 2017b). Pietsch appears, moreover, to have become not only an accepted presence in Wallace's own work, but a necessary one. The assembly of the posthumous work, of course, would change the nature of this necessity and represent a very different challenge for the editor.

[38] This sale was finally completed in 2006, when Hachette UK (a subsidiary of Hachette Livre) took ownership of the company.

6

Consider the editor: Assembling *The Pale King*

When *The Pale King* was published in 2011 there was an immediate recognition of the work's quality and thematic richness as well as of the special interpretive problems it posed. Michael Cunningham, one of the jurors who nominated the book as one of the three contenders for the 2012 Pulitzer Prize, reflected – in the wake of the Pulitzer Prize Board's decision not to award a fiction prize that year – that the choice of an unfinished novel might have been seen as 'controversial' and that awarding it the prize 'would be, by implication, an acknowledgement not only of Wallace but also of Michael Pietsch, the editor' (Cunningham 2012). The scholarly response to the book also acknowledged the book's problematic status: Luc Herman and Toon Staes' introduction to a 2014 special issue of *English Studies* on the novel, which asked 'Can *The Pale King* (Please) be a Novel?' wryly implies a sense of vexation at the book's uncertain boundaries and articulates what Hering describes as 'a general desire, both readerly and scholarly, to be able to perceive the text as a coherent system' (Herman and Staes 2014; Hering 2016a, 124). One of the primary features of Wallace's fictions is the way in which they repay continued close reading and train readers to be attentive to textual detail; a reader coming to the author's final novel after encountering the artfully scattered clues and carefully encoded ambiguities of *Infinite Jest* is (to use a word that recurs repeatedly in *The Pale King*) 'primed' to embrace the role of critical detective and to scrutinize textual details with unusual care. In addition, *The Pale King* itself repeatedly dramatizes and valorizes close reading, depicting dedicated readers attentively turning pages as well as metafictionally urging its reader to be cognizant of the narrative and bibliographical codes at play in the text. Staes points to this latter feature of the book to emphasize the way in which it is 'overdetermined', sending 'mutually exclusive messages' in its presentation of an author who insists upon his presence and scrupulous 'veracity' on the one hand alongside the book's status as an 'unfinished novel' on the other (Staes 2014a, 38–9). Much as we might understand the work's provisional and contingent nature, then, it is difficult to resist the critical tendency to treat the text as a discrete, continuous interpretive object.

In his introduction to *The Pale King*, Pietsch directly confronts these difficulties, noting the fundamental questions posed by the work's form: 'How unfinished is this novel? How much more might there have been?' Any analysis of the book's content is obliged to acknowledge the work's unfinished nature and to at least gesture towards an acceptance that its conclusions, insofar as they touch upon authorial intention, are tentative. Boswell, for example, begins his examination of the 'David Wallace'-narrated sections of *The Pale King* by arguing that they are 'polished enough to provide fairly clear and decisive hints as to their larger purpose within the novel's thematic whole', while admitting that 'of course, just about anything one might say about [the novel] is, by necessity, provisional' (Boswell 2014b, 25–6). A common critical move has been to parse an aspect of textual presentation or arrangement before pulling back to acknowledge the impossibility of attributing this to the author.[1] Andersen praises the 'clever juxtaposition' of Fogle's monologue with 'David Wallace's' arrival in Peoria, but footnotes this by conceding that the juxtaposition may be Pietsch's rather than Wallace's and noting that 'since the structure of a book affects its meaning (and may in fact be hard to extricate from this meaning), Pietsch's editorial choices have a significant co-authoring function' (Andersen 2014a, 14).

The problems caused by the inherent instability of the text become clearer when we consider the fact that many critical readings take its unfinished nature as a focus for study. Several critics have, as Pietsch anticipated, argued that the novel's fragmentary nature is a deliberate authorial strategy. Burn, for example, argues that the novel displays a 'poetics of incompleteness' and suggests that 'to some extent we can think of the book's incompleteness as a feature rather than a bug' (Burn 2014, 91). The various drafts left by Wallace certainly provide a warrant for this kind of analysis. Pietsch includes (and quotes from) notes suggesting that the reader may never see the 'high end players' in the IRS and that 'something big *threatens* to happen but doesn't actually happen' (Wallace 2011b, 540, 544).[2] Several critics have also invoked the deliberately open endings

[1] See also Tom McCarthy (2011, n.p.) and McHale (2013, 192–3).

[2] A note from July 2005 (within an early version of §9) suggests that the narrative form might resist linearity:

of Wallace's previous novels in their analysis of the book (Boswell 2012b, 368–9; Staes 2014b, 74–5; Wouters 2012, 461–2). However, this illustrates the fact that a reading of a posthumous work necessarily comes up against an interpretive wall that can only be surmounted by conjecture or by inferring from previous works. This wall is one that is also encountered by the editor, as E. L. Doctorow noted in his review of Hemingway's *The Garden of Eden*: 'the truth about editing the work of a dead writer in such circumstances is that you can only cut to affirm his strengths, to reiterate the strategies of style for which he is known; whereas he himself may have been writing to transcend them' (Doctorow 1986).[3] Both editor and reader are obliged to make aesthetic judgements on the success of the existing material as well as guesses about intention based upon the author's prior work, and the impossibility of assuming that the author has granted 'passive authorization' to key textual decision makes the reader aware of editing processes usually hidden from view. John Jeremiah Sullivan describes a reading experience in which the author's intention is repeatedly reconstructed according to pre-existing norms: 'Every word you read and don't like, you think, "Well, he would have changed that". Whereas everything that does work, that's the real Wallace' (Sullivan 2011).

We can view some of these problems in greater detail by examining some specifics of the editing process. In the most extensive engagement with the manuscripts of *The Pale King* since its archive became available for study in 2012, Hering provides a detailed map of the novel's composition, illustrating its different phases of development and emphasizing the need to consider it in processual terms (Hering 2016a, 163–2). However, there has as yet been little focus on the novel's assembly, a lengthy and intensive process involving Pietsch's complex engagement with a chaotic set of materials. A focus on the editorial process allows us to better understand how Pietsch encountered the work as well as how the novel was mediated so as to make it accessible to readers. In the proceeding pages, I trace this process of mediation and highlight the interpretive difficulties it poses for critics.

> Towards end, as computers are implemented, someone is making record of various agents' lives, jobs, selves – as a kind of living archive. Hence the fragmented bits of narrative from different characters, which isn't explained for some time in the whole narrative. (Wallace n.d., 38.6)

However, this note is of course itself a fragment and does little to outline the extent to which the narrative fragmentation will be 'explained'.

3 This chimes with Max's discussion of Wallace's attempts at stylistic evolution, in which he claims that the author was, in his late work, 'trying to write differently' (Max 2009).

'No kind of order': Assembling *The Pale King*

The process of assembling and editing *The Pale King* took, in Pietsch's words, 'around two years from when I began reading until the manuscript was approved' (Pietsch 2017b). The drafts Wallace had left on his desk before his death contained no instructions for publication nor any guidelines for the editor, who had not seen any of the material save for some short magazine excerpts (Pietsch 2011a, vi). Subsequently, Pietsch collected the entire body of work relating to the novel (including notes, sketches and research material) from Wallace's home and proceeded to painstakingly edit the material into a publishable novel. He describes a laborious project of working through a complex mass of documentation in different formats:

> The material he'd left behind was massive, something like 3000 pages of drafts and finished manuscripts, but it was in no kind of order. It was a slow process of picking up sheaves of material in random order – some typed chapters, some handwritten, some notebooks of various kinds – and reading and logging them, to see what was there and identify different versions of the same chapters. (Pietsch 2017b)

The work was, as Pietsch's 'Editor's Note' to the novel explains, spread across various media: 'hard drives, file folders, three-ring binders, spiral-bound notebooks, and floppy disks contained printed chapters, sheaves of handwritten pages, and more'. It was also lacking in structural organization:

> Nowhere in all these pages was there an outline or any other indication of what order David intended for these chapters [. . .] there was no list of scenes, no designated closing point, nothing that could be called a set of directions or instructions for *The Pale King*. (Pietsch 2011a, vi–vii)

It was, the editor clearly states, 'not by any measure a finished work' but still 'an astonishingly full novel', implying that the work's thematic fullness is not matched by a similar structural accomplishment: 'I believe that David was still exploring the world he had made and had not yet given it a final form' (Pietsch 2011a, ix).

Pietsch, as we saw earlier, had one previous experience of posthumous editing, having worked on Hemingway's *The Dangerous Summer* (1985). Asked in a 2013 interview about these experiences and about the challenges involved in posthumous editing, he replied that both processes involved 'an estate that was very involved in the editing and presentation of the book. And both books gave me an opportunity to think through the publisher's obligation to make the editorial process transparent to readers' (Pietsch 2013, n.p.). While Pietsch edited the work alone, he liaised with Wallace's estate throughout in order to access, process and present the drafts in published form (with, e.g. the cover design being provided by Wallace's widow Karen Green). *The Dangerous Summer* had featured a commissioned introduction from James Michener that did not address the details of the editorial process, and (as mentioned in Chapter 1) the ambiguity in the book's presentation of its relationship to its source material was criticized (Mandel 2008, 75; Kennedy 1985). Pietsch describes learning from this experience the importance of 'an introduction that clarifies what the editor did and what licence has been taken' (Pietsch 2017c); the 'Editor's Note' can thus be seen, at least in part, as an attempt to render the process behind the book's construction 'transparent'. The introduction, while relatively brief, is forthright about the editor's role and about some of the specific challenges of bringing the novel to print. Pietsch admits the difficulty of the task, pointing to the problem of sequencing as his central challenge and quoting a note in which Wallace 'refers to the novel as being "full of shifting POVs, structural fragmentation, willed incongruities"'. He points to the existence of multiple chapters that are self-contained and lacking in chronological context, stating that 'arranging these freestanding sections has been the most difficult part of editing *The Pale King*'. He notes that he used the structure of *Infinite Jest* – in which 'large portions of apparently unconnected information [are] presented to the reader before a main story line begins to make sense' – as a reference for this sequencing work, citing notes from Wallace hinting at a 'tornadic' structure. Pietsch's method was to sequence apparently isolated chapters 'so that the information they contain arrives in time to support the chronological story line', with an awareness of 'pace and mood, as in siting short comic chapters between long serious ones'. In an interview elsewhere, he describes his job in more succinct terms: 'to find the last version of each bit of it and then find a sequence that made sense' (Pietsch 2011d).

Pietsch has noted that he 'edited mostly for consistency' (Pietsch 2011c) and his introduction expresses his aim in clear terms; 'my overall intent in sequencing and editing was to eliminate unintentional distractions and confusions so as to allow readers to focus on the enormous issues David intended to raise, and to make the story and characters as comprehensible as possible' (Pietsch 2011a, ix). The desire for a text that would attain a level of coherence and contain minimal 'distractions' makes it clear that narrative clarity took precedence over the need to reproduce the author's words with maximum accuracy. The goal here was clearly the production of a reader's edition, albeit with aspects of the transparency and accuracy of a scholarly one. John F. Callahan's stated aim of editing Ellison's *Juneteenth* into a 'single, coherent, continuous work' (Callahan 2000, 366) is apposite here, and his later co-editing of the much longer scholarly edition of the manuscript (published as *Three Days Before the Shooting* in 2010) illustrates some of the different possibilities for presenting an unfinished work; Boswell notes that *The Pale King* sits somewhere in between these two possibilities (Boswell 2014a, ix). Pietsch thus becomes (like Callahan) a literary as well as a critical editor, operating according to the demands of commercial publishing as well as to the dictates of textual fidelity; as with Dmitri Nabokov's presentation of *The Original of Laura*, we see an editor anticipating the demands of a wide readership that nevertheless included scholars and fans who could be expected to parse the published text with intense critical interest. The 'Notes and Asides' section following the main text of the novel demonstrates the tension between these demands. It reproduces material from Wallace's drafts in order to allow the reader 'a fuller understanding of the ideas David was exploring [. . .] and illuminate how much of a work in progress the novel still was' (Pietsch 2011e, 539). The origins of these notes are not documented in any detail, however; no chronological or material information is presented, and we are told only that they come 'from other parts of the manuscript' (Pietsch 2011e, 539). Textual variations throughout the text are not noted, and the individual chapters and notes are not accompanied by chronological or material information that would explain their place in the work's compositional history.

The majority of the material that Pietsch encountered was clearly unfinished and lacking a clear order. Wallace had assembled twelve chapters that appeared relatively complete including several 'finished and polished long chapters, in contemplation of sending them to Little, Brown to begin a conversation about a contract' (Pietsch 2017b).[4] However, the remainder of the drafts were not organized with anything like this degree of clarity. Of the latter, these files are drawn from multiple sources including a laptop, a desktop computer and several disks of varying formats with titles such as 'black unlabeled disk',

[4] These included, in order of length, §22 (Fogle's monologue), §24 (the second of the 'Author here' sections), §9 (the first of the David Wallace-narrated sections), §14 (the interviews with IRS examiners) and §8 (Toni Ware's childhood). In Pietsch's words, Wallace 'appears to have been almost ready to make the book's subject and main characters and plot elements known' (Pietsch 2017b).

'5' floppy disk #1' and 'WPF/PK '05 ZIP disk': some material is clearly in incomplete or damaged form, as indicated by the title 'Corrupted disk titled Little Brown Advance 103'. Pietsch collated all of this material and recalls that 'all the work was on paper, including the printouts from disc drives. I numbered each piece and kept a log in order to keep track of it all and identify different versions of the same chapter' (Pietsch 2017b). This 'log' opens the main series of manuscripts relating to *The Pale King*, which comprises six containers (36–41) in the Wallace Papers,[5] serving as the logical entry point for scholars. The length and scope of this document, titled 'Index of Documents for *The Pale King*', provide a vivid illustration of the difficulty of imposing coherence or completion on the extensive collection of drafts (Wallace n.d., 36.1). It takes the form of an extensive spreadsheet listing all of the material considered for inclusion, runs to 29 pages in its printed form and lists 474 items with sources ranging from handwritten drafts to printed typescripts to digital copies of word processing files.[6] The drafts are filed in the order in which they appear in the index. It is worth noting, then, that the editor's organization of the material structures the experience of visitors to the archive, highlighting the way in which the decisions of archivists, executors and editors will necessarily mediate subsequent encounters with manuscripts.[7]

These sources are tracked throughout the spreadsheet's columns according to a number of headings which I examine below. Firstly, each item is given a log number, making it identifiable as a discrete unit of textual material. This is followed by the 'Title', usually consisting either of the title given to the section by the author (e.g. 'WPF Electric Girl II Story Freewriting Feb 07' (Wallace n.d., 37.2)) or the first lines of the draft. The next column relates to the number of pages in the draft, with the subsequent one indicating the 'Format'. The next two columns, 'Word Count' and 'Date or Code', are blank in many instances. Following the latter column down through the list of entries provides an illustration of the

5 An additional container elsewhere in the collection (no. 26) consists mostly of research materials and correspondence related to the work.

6 Although it is possible to view descriptions in the index of all of the drafts used by Pietsch in his assembly of the novel, not all of the drafts themselves have been printed. The index lists 474 items but the printed materials in the boxes only runs to 328, meaning that 146 drafts from Wallace's desktop computer, laptop and some disks are, as confirmed by the Ransom Center's archivists, not currently accessible to scholars (Hansen and Adams 2017).

7 The withdrawal of a number of annotated books from Wallace's collection in 2011 on the request of his estate also supports the observations of archival scholars such as Lisa Stead who note that archives are 'necessarily fragmentary and changeable' entities whose 'physical and ideological boundaries are continually being reconstituted' (Gross 2011; Stead 2013, 2–3). For an analysis of this incident in terms of the relationship between Wallace's archive and his published fiction, see Roache (2017).

long gestation period of the work (which Hering has described in detail): much of the material is drawn from a floppy disk dated 1997, for example, and some items are dated as early as 1990 (Wallace n.d., 37.5). It appears that Wallace's last sustained burst of work took place in the summer of 2007, with the latest drafts listed in the index dating from August of that year (many of the drafts, though, are not accompanied by dates).

The subsequent column of the index, 'Related Drafts', lists the log numbers of drafts in which the same material appears in either complete or partial form and illustrates the extent of the dispersal of existing textual material.[8] Some scenes are present in solitary drafts, while others exist in up to 17 different versions (if we include backup versions stored digitally that may contain minimal or no textual variation). The published work includes pieces in various states of completion from stages of the novel's composition that were quite distinct in their character and aims, making Hering's 'processual analysis' of the work – and his analysis of these stages – necessary reading for any serious engagement with the novel (Hering 2016a, 125). The following column lists 'Characters' mentioned in the draft, and in several cases this field has also been left blank. Where characters are listed, though, they again illustrate the extent of the fragmentation in the work. Wallace appears to have constantly changed the names of his characters, a habit which presents a significant complication for interpretation, as I will show later in this chapter.[9] An additional difficulty in considering the work's composition is the difficulty of drawing a strict boundary around it. Hering describes the complex 'relational network' between Wallace's various writing projects, a network that seems to have been particularly strong at certain points in the compositional process (Hering 2016a, 128).[10] We can glimpse the complexity of this network in one of the drafts that Pietsch omitted from *The Pale King*.

[8] The 'Related Drafts' column accompanying log number 2, for example (a draft of §24 of the published novel in which David Wallace travels to 'intake processing'), lists eleven other numbers (Wallace n.d., 36.4).

[9] It is enough to note here, by way of example, that a draft from April 2007 (listed as log number 422 in the index and currently unavailable to scholars in its full length) refers to characters such as 'Wax, Blackwelder, Hornbaker, Wallace (3)' among others. Not only are the first three names among the many that refer to characters who appear to be entirely peripheral and are mentioned elsewhere only in passing, but the fourth also hints at an additional Wallace character whose presence could, of course, extend the metafictional manoeuvres in the novel and have implications for any reading that highlights its engagement with ideas of authorship.

[10] Log number 77, for example, is clearly a draft for the 'B.I. #14' interview from *Brief Interviews with Hideous Men*, and in the 'Related Drafts' column for this draft Pietsch has noted, simply, '*BIWHM*'.

'Fragmentco Unltd': 'Cede' and *The Pale King*

As Hering has shown, the origins of *The Pale King*'s §36, in which we encounter the child whose aim is to kiss every part of his own body (and who I will refer to throughout this section for clarity as the 'contortionist boy'), lie in a short narrative that was first drafted in 1997 and later reworked in two further iterations circa 2001 and 2006–2007 (Hering 2016a, 129). In its first iteration, the narrative – which takes the form of seventeen numbered paragraphs – alternates between the story of this contortionist boy and an elliptical series of vignettes set in Ancient Rome during the first and second century. My focus throughout this reading will be on the strand of the story that takes place in Ancient Rome, since this has not yet been addressed in Wallace criticism. *New Yorker* fiction editor Deborah Triesman reports that the author sent her a version of this in April 1999 for possible inclusion in the magazine's '20 Under 40' fiction issue but that it was rejected in favour of what she describes as a 'more polished piece' from the (then-forthcoming) *Brief Interviews with Hideous Men*.[11] Wallace presented the story in a way that self-consciously highlighted his awareness of its status as work in development: on the letter that accompanied the draft, he referred to the story as 'the Fragment' and listed his return address as 'Fragmentco Unltd', a seemingly self-deprecating move that highlighted what he saw, even at this early stage of his work on the follow-up to *Infinite Jest*, as his own failure to assemble these narrative pieces into a coherent whole (Triesman 2014). He subsequently read a version of the piece at a Lannan Foundation reading in December 2000. Drafts from 2001 show this narrative interspersed with the long monologue by Chris Fogle (who was, at that point, named Robbie Van Note): in the lengthy draft numbered as 124 in Michael Pietsch's 'Index of Documents for *The Pale King*', for example, Fogle's monologue is broken up repeatedly by shorter fragments of the stories of the contortionist boy as well as the Roman narrative. Wallace appears to have returned to each of these narratives intermittently, adding and occasionally subtracting material (apparently revising – or at least, judging by the 'last saved' dates on digital files, saving – the scene in 1997, 2000, 2001, 2005, 2006 and 2007). The Lannan Foundation reading omitted the portions of the narrative set in Ancient Rome;

[11] 'B.I. #40' was published in the magazine's '20 Under 40' issue in June 1999 as 'Asset'.

however, drafts make it clear that he continued to work on the chronologically earlier narrative after this point.[12]

The form of the 1997 'Cede', with its discrete fragments broken up by line breaks, lends the narrative a cryptic and detached feel. It begins with a short fragment describing the 'Pontic flights', a historical phenomenon invented by Wallace, detailing how mass starvation in AD 108–110 causes the 'neozoroastrian herdsmen of extreme eastern Pontus' to become so paper-thin – 'like dry dander, or sheets of fine Nile parchment' – that their bodies become capable of 'windborne flight'. The herdsmen attempt to fly to Antioch to appeal to Pliny the Younger (whose administration has caused starvation in Asia Minor) for aid, but when they pass over the 'lavish Plinian orchards of Antioch' they cannot resist pausing to eat the fruit from the trees.[13] The section ends by describing how the 'simple Pontic aeronauts' descend from the sky, 'hover[ing] above the bowed trees and gorg[ing] frantically upon the fruit', whereupon they are felled by gravity and 'set upon by the proconsul's Molossian hounds' and 'devoured' (Wallace n.d., 40.2).[14]

The next section of this timeline, numbered 4 in the 1997 draft and lasting half a page, takes place roughly 45 years earlier and is linked to the previous section by an opening that tells the story of the Molossian hounds, a historically real breed (related to today's mastiffs) used as war dogs in the ancient world (Coile 2005, 136). These hounds are ruthless creatures 'bred [. . .] for aggression' and used for several functions, most notably the persecution of Christians for the Emperor's pleasure. The Emperor is soon identified as Nero, and we are told that, 'attended always by Poppaea Sabina', he watches the slaughter in the passive and solipsistic manner characteristic of many of Wallace's spectators, peering through 'a Nubian emerald through which distant events appeared almost to be taking place in his cyan-coloured lap'. The final paragraph of the section suggests the political and moral stakes of the narrative, linking emperor, dogs and state

12 The sections concerning the contortionist boy and his father (with interpolations relating to the lives of mystics and religious martyrs) would develop substantially and be published posthumously by *The New Yorker*, in an excerpt which had developed since the reading (Esposito 2011; Wallace 2011c).

13 Pontus is the historical Greek designation for the region that roughly corresponds to the modern-day Black Sea Region of Turkey; Antioch is a major Roman city located in the south of modern-day Turkey (Lewis and Short 1966).

14 We are told no more about these aeronauts, whose fate combines allusions to Biblical temptation and Icarean tragedy. However, we may note the way in which their fate reflects the obsession with 'groundedness' that Jeffrey Severs finds throughout Wallace's work and observe that the metaphor of parchment so light it floats into the air represents something close to an image of unbalanced books (Severs 2017).

together in one political enterprise: 'It was under Nero that care and training of the Circi's Molossian Hounds came to be considered an art vital to the Imperial interests of Rome herself.'

The hounds' training is carried out by Corinthian trainers, who are handpicked by Poppaea: the narrator informs us that 'it was whispered that she consorted with the most impressive' of these in the Roman tunnels. The two subsequent sections in this draft focus on the family of one particular trainer: in the one-paragraph section numbered 14, we are introduced to 'Cedo, only child of the hounds' last and greatest *exercitor summum*' (which translates roughly as 'head trainer'). This section alludes to the Great Fire of Rome of AD 64, an event which led Nero to commence 'antiquity's first truly serious pogrom, the much-referenced Christian Persecutions' and hence to triple the quantity of hounds employed in the Circus. Poppaea favoured the trainer and had his family 'installed in sumptuous training facilities in the cuniculum of the Circus Maximus only months before the fire'; Cedo, it is tantalizingly mentioned, 'played a part' in these Persecutions. In the final part of the narrative written in 1997 (a one-page section numbered 16) we are given details of the trainer's brutal methods. The hounds are kept in a perpetual state of near-starvation and fury for use in the circus and are subjected to extreme confinement in 'tiny pens' (also described, in a phrase redolent of descriptions of solipsism in several other Wallace texts, as 'self-sized cages'). The boy, we are told, has been forbidden by the trainer's wife to take part in the training of the dogs, hinting at an impending familial conflict.

Returning to the narrative in 2001, Wallace developed this hint in several sections that were no longer numbered and now interleaved with what would become Fogle's monologue. In the first development, the narrator informs us that the boy – whose name Wallace amends (in handwritten corrections to a typescript draft) to 'Cedes' and, in one case, to 'Ceinus' – has 'betrayed both training and law' by 'developing attachments' to a handful of the dogs, and that he goes so far as to surreptitiously feed them leftover scraps. A separate fragment on the following page describes the mother's knowledge, withheld from her husband, that the boy's heart has been 'pierced and captured' by these hounds, as well as the detail that she is 'a *sub rosa* Christian, converted by the 13th/14th parts of an epistle delivered by the Tarsian Saul.' She weeps not only for the boy as well as the martyred Christians, but also for her husband, 'whose nightly consorts with Poppaea were known by all, it seemed, save the wacked-out Nero himself'.

In what appears to be the final piece of this narrative that Wallace wrote, the narrator continues to hint at the impending consequences of the fact that 'the child saw fit secretly to feed the circus' hounds in their pens'. The animals' carefully calibrated training regime, which requires them to be kept in 'a delicate state of starvation' that maintains their extreme hunger as well as the strength needed to attack, is being thrown disastrously off-kilter by the boy's actions, since a badly trained hound might 'attack slaves, sand, other hounds', or simply 'lope in crazed circles'. Nevertheless, the boy continues to enter the pens in the pre-dawn darkness, while the slaves who are guarding the animals still sleep, to dispense 'mercy'. The section ends by noting that 'Two of these slaves were in the employ of Poppaea Sabina, who by 64 AD was now Poppaea Augusta, Nero having murdered his wife – rather mother – and son. To the mobs' displeasure' (Wallace n.d., 38.6).

Boswell has noted that 'Wallace's longer work achieves its effect through accumulation and collage' (Boswell 2012b, 368), and the narrative method of Wallace's novels depends upon the interplay of scenes whose relation to each other is not always apparent on first reading. These sections certainly represent a significant part of the 'genetic dossier' for *The Pale King*, and a closer examination repays critical interest by uncovering several links with other strands of the unfinished novel.

To begin with, the piece adds a singular new perspective to the 'collage'. The narrative strand set in Ancient Rome was presumably excluded by Pietsch because of its temporal distance from the main action of the novel and its lack of clear relevance to what he describes as the 'central narrative', which follows 'a clear chronology' (Pietsch 2011a, vii).[15] It also seems possible that Wallace was ambivalent about this section: as previously noted, he excluded it from his reading at the Lannan foundation in 2000 and omitted most of it from later drafts. However, one draft (numbered 54 in Pietsch's index) shows that Wallace included the two-and-a-half-page section describing the 'Pontic Flights' in the longer 'contortionist boy' chapter as late as May 2007 (Wallace n.d., 37.2). It is clear that this strand of the narrative was worked on through multiple drafts and revised repeatedly, making it more polished at an individual level than

[15] While its omission from the published novel is understandable, however, it could have been included in the 'Previously Unpublished Scenes' with the paperback version. While there are at present no plans to publish the handful of relatively polished drafts that did not connect to what Pietsch describes as 'the central line and themes', he writes: 'I expect there will be a way of publishing those finished portions one day' (Pietsch 2017b).

other sections; §29, by contrast, exists in only a single handwritten draft. Hering argues for the significance of 'Cede' on the grounds that Wallace seems to have regarded it as 'essential to locking together several disparate sections' of the novel; the evident time and care expended on the narrative along with the failure to successfully accomplish this act of 'locking together', he suggests, make the piece 'perhaps the most characteristic piece of writing in the whole process of writing the third novel' (Hering 2016a, 129).

The inclusion of these sections in our conception of the novel would dramatically expand the work's temporal and geographical range and allow for an exploration of the further development of themes in ostensibly distant but parallel narratives. Burn argues that the book works by arranging 'rich metaphorical nodes' where meaning accumulates (Burn 2012a, 372) and one of these nodes may be the world of Ancient Rome itself. A comparative reading highlights the frequency with which Roman references recur in *The Pale King*. There are many examples of these, of which I will give just a few here: the Latin motto of the IRS, for example, '*alicui tamen faciendum est*' (Wallace 2011b, 102, 244); the 'Roman numerals' organizing the substitute lecturer's main points in §22 (Wallace 2011b, 224); the references to specific Roman figures such as Aurelius (Wallace 2011b, 16), which are sometimes more explicit in the draft material;[16] and Sylvanshine's reflection, upon reaching Peoria, that it has been some time since he last saw any 'Latin person' (Wallace 2011b, 47).[17] The frequent use of Latin words and phrases such as David Wallace's dry comment '*Hiatus valde deflandus*' (which translates roughly as 'a lack greatly to be deplored') on the absence of an illustrative photo from his narrative (Wallace 2011b, 283) is also striking.[18] Obscure or technical Latinate words such as the 'temblor' or foretaste of the conversion experience that Fogle receives in §22 and the 'peplum' that his jacket resembles when buttoned (Wallace 2011b, 220, 234) recur throughout.[19]

[16] In an earlier draft of Sylvanshine's plane journey, the character muses that 'According to Dr. Lehrl, Aurelius recommends always returning to first principles' (Wallace n.d., 39.7).

[17] Jorge Araya, it should be noted, interprets this last reference as an example of the monocultural racial environment of the novel, suggesting that the word 'Latin' rather than 'Latino' serves to indicate the character's cultural ignorance (Araya 2015, 238). As Thompson has shown, Wallace sometimes used the term to refer to Latin American literature as well as to Latin America's inhabitants (L. Thompson 2016, 51–88).

[18] Severs detects several such references, finding significance in the Latin word *pace* in Chris Acquistipace's name, observing that Sylvanshine's previous IRS posting was in 'Rome, New York' (an address that unsubtly links the two empires' capitals), and suggesting that the novel's title itself alludes to the Latin word *palus*, deriving from 'the staff or stave used for fighting in Ancient Rome' (Severs 2017, 202, 212, 223).

[19] Drafts show that Wallace deliberately worked to submerge these references; on one typewritten draft, he circled the word 'peplum' and wrote: '*No! Too often!*' (Wallace n.d., 38.6).

These sections also shed new light on the 'contortionist boy' section itself, which contains references to 'Roman legal texts' as well as dense passages filled with Latinate medical terminology (Wallace 2011b, 399, 401). Again, the links between the world of Ancient Rome and the world of the contortionist boy are sometimes more explicit in the first extant version of the piece: in the 1997 draft, for example, one of the inspirational maxims that the boy's father has taped to the mirror of his medicine cabinet is Virgil's 'Arma virumque cano' (Wallace n.d., 40.2). This draft opens with a heading in capital letters, spaced over three lines, that reads:

> AMERICANID REX
> ADVENTURES IN ACHIEVEMENT
> DOG, CREATUS, ACHIEVER

Below this appears the maxim '*Nam tue res agitur, paries proximus ardet*', a quote from Horace's *Epistles*: a note at the end of the same draft that appears to be from Wallace to himself rather than to the reader states 'Epigraph is Horace – "no time to sleep with a fire next door"'.[20] Taken together, these suggest the invocation of Roman history to explore a preoccupation with a particularly American striving for success and to frame an address to an urgent contemporary situation. The brief, capitalized phrases in the heading seem deliberately cryptic and the relationship between their individual words opaque. The heading's opening announcement of an 'American King' presumably refers to the contortionist boy (the primary American character in the draft), and its second line thereby immediately ironizes the word 'achievement', since a reader (certainly, any Wallace reader) is likely to be wary of the solipsistic nature of the boy's accomplishments. The phrase tantalizes, though, with its hint that the hypertrophied, self-contained child might be linked to the 'king' of the novel's eventual title.[21] The draft also invites the question of whether Nero might, in fact, fit the title as well as any other character we have seen. Severs suggests that the Cretan King Minos is one analogue for the pale king of the title, reflecting

[20] The relevant section of the Epistles urges the reader to be steadfast and to recognize danger when a trusted friend is being slandered; an alternative translation is 'You too are in danger when your neighbour's house is on fire' (Horace 1980, Book 1, xviii, line 84; Stone 2013, 65).

[21] Hayes-Brady convincingly identifies Keats' 'La Belle Dame Sans Merci' as the likeliest source for the novel's title, but it is unclear whether the appellation designates any of its characters. The only clue in the published novel comes in a reference in an early draft (which became the published novel's §18) to Glendenning's predecessor as REC Director (referred to simply as 'the Pale King'), but this does not seem to have been developed elsewhere; I was unable to find a definitive explanation in the draft material (Hayes-Brady 2016, 59–60; Wallace 2011b, 128).

the selfishness of the 'kingly solipsists' of modern-day America who refuse to submit a fair tax return (Severs 2017, 207); however, the diminished, degenerate and 'wacked-out' emperor we glimpse in these sections may be a likelier monarch for the role. The word CREATUS, meanwhile, derived from the Latin verb *creo* ('to create'), recalls Hal Incandenza, who helpfully glosses it in the opening pages of *Infinite Jest* as he protests that he is not a 'machine': 'I'm not just a creātus, manufactured, conditioned, bred for a function' (Wallace 2006, 12). Its appearance here surely refers to the dogs, who are literally bred for Rome's increasingly depraved purposes.

James Lasdun's (2011) review of *The Pale King* detected traces of W. H. Auden's poem 'The Fall of Rome', with its 'Agents of the Fisc' pursuing 'tax-defaulters' and its disgruntled 'unimportant clerk' (Lasdun 2011; Auden 2009, 188). 'Cede' supports the notion that Wallace was borrowing Auden's poem's method of juxtaposing the political problems and vices of ancient Rome with modern-day American professional life and also backs up Severs' assertion that the work 'portrays the decline of a decadent American empire for lack of social cohesion – and, potentially, the refounding (the regrounding) of a better nation' (Severs 2017, 212). The section adds significantly to our understanding of the scope of the novel's interrogation of the changing nature of civic values in contemporary US society. There is now a relative consensus around the notion that Wallace was concerned in his final work with tracking and interrogating the effects of neoliberal policies upon the civic sphere from the 1970s onwards.[22] Several of these readings have focused on the novel's most obvious engagement with political thought, the discussion on 'civics and selfishness' presented in §19, in which the civic achievements of the Founding Fathers are contrasted with the rise of corporations (a word which, as one of the men notes, comes from the Latin word for 'body') and the slow hollowing-out of the public sphere (Wallace 2011b, 140). This rise-and-fall narrative, paralleling the history of Rome with the story of the United States since its inception, is given added resonance by the extent to which the Founders's political ideas were informed by the legal

[22] Boswell provided the first extended political reading of *The Pale King*, identifying 'civics' as one the works' 'key words' and arguing that Wallace continually returns to the Reagan tax cuts of 1981 as 'Year Zero' of what he diagnoses as a contemporary democratic crisis (Boswell 2014a, 209–25); Adam Kelly has shown how Wallace uses dialogue in the novel to interrogate the roots of American citizenship in light of the 'rise of the corporation' since the 1960s (Kelly 2014a, 14–19); Ralph Clare focuses on the way in which Wallace uses the IRS to suggest a relationship between boredom and neoliberal politics (Clare 2012, 195–200); Severs argues that Wallace works in the novel to renovate value and support 'civic identification' (Severs 2017, 198–243); and Mark West examines Wallace's depiction of the transformation of civic ideals during the 1970s (West 2017).

and political structures of Ancient Rome: as Hannah Arendt has observed, the American revolutionaries drew heavily upon 'Roman history and Roman political institutions' and were 'conscious of emulating ancient virtue' (Arendt 2006, 188–97). A comparison of 'Cede' with §19 uncovers clear thematic and linguistic links. One of the men in the stalled elevator, most likely Glendenning, opens the discussion by stating what he believes to be the central problem facing the modern-day United States:

> As citizens we *cede* more and more of our autonomy, but if we the government take away the citizens' freedom to *cede* their autonomy we're now taking away their autonomy. It's a paradox. (My emphasis)

He goes on, a few lines later, to predict 'some sort of disaster' to be followed by a moment of crisis in which 'we'll either wake up and retake our freedom or we'll fall apart utterly. Like Rome – conqueror of its own people' (Wallace 2011b, 130–1). The recurrence of the word 'cede' here followed by an explicit reference to Ancient Rome indicates that these references can be read as part of a larger argument that Wallace is constructing about freedom, power and imperial decline.[23]

Rome under Nero conquers its own people in at least two senses: firstly, in the way that Nero (according to popular belief) deliberately set fire to Rome in order to gain the power to rebuild it to his own liking, sacrificing the city's inhabitants to his own will to power (Hurley 2013, 31; Shotter 2005, 60); and secondly in the brutal conquer and mass murder of the Christian portion of Rome's population, turning Roman military might against defenceless citizens. Both of these events are dramatized in the 1895 novel *Quo Vadis* by Nobel Prize-winning Polish author Henryk Sienkiewicz, a copy of which appears in Wallace's library and which he clearly used as a source text.[24] The novel is a somewhat didactic tale of Roman imperial decadence giving way to Christian spiritual renewal that nevertheless appears to have made an impression on Wallace, given his borrowing of the title for his introduction to the Spring 1996 *Review*

[23] Wallace uses an identical phrase in 'Big Red Son' when describing the venue for the Annual Adult Video News Awards ('In Caesars Palace is America conceived as a new kind of Rome: conqueror of its own people. An empire of Self'), demonstrating his recurring interest in linking his oft-discussed criticisms of the consumerist solipsism fostered by late capitalism with the decline of the Roman empire (Wallace 2012c, 9–10).

[24] Wallace's copy is a paperback edition of W. S. Kuniczak's translation, published in 2000. It is unclear when he read and annotated this; the date would allow us to conjecture that he used it as a source for his 2001 revision of the Rome material, although his use of the phrase in 1996 strongly suggests that he might also have read an earlier copy.

of Contemporary Fiction issue that he guest-edited.[25] It dramatizes this process through an ongoing contrast between an ageing courtier named Petronius, who describes himself as a 'merry-minded skeptic', and a young nobleman named Marcus Vinicius who is converted to Christianity through his love for a young princess held hostage by the Romans (who is herself, in secret, a committed Christian) and his growing realization of the 'inescapable and degrading horror of his times' (Sienkiewicz 2000, 277, 241). The novel also depicts a degenerate Nero, and Wallace underlined two separate passages describing the emperor's overweight and degraded appearance; beside one of these, he wrote the words 'Nero as grotesque'.[26] Sienkiewicz's Nero watches the bloody massacres of Christians, as does Wallace's, through a 'polished emerald' (Sienkiewicz 2000, 470). Poppaea also appears as a villainously cruel character in *Quo Vadis*, and Wallace underlined a sentence in Sienkiewicz's novel in which the Roman crowd disparagingly refers to her as a 'street-walker' (Sienkiewicz 2000, 316). Wallace seems to have used the work as a source from which to harvest vocabulary as well as details on historical setting, circling and underlining a number of Latin words and phrases throughout his copy. Many of these refer to details of the battles staged in the circus and most do not appear in 'Cede'; the word 'peplum' used by Chris Fogle, though, appears on one of the pages annotated by Wallace (Sienkiewicz 2000, 74).

Quo Vadis contains lengthy, vivid descriptions of battles in the circus arena in which Christians are thrown to the lions and one passage, beside which Wallace drew a vertical line, refers to animals who are 'tamed by expert trainers' (Sienkiewicz 2000, 315), a detail which may have provided inspiration for the

[25] The novel's title is an abridgement of the words '*Quo vadis, Domine*?' which translate as 'where are you going, Lord?'. The words are uttered by Peter, who is fleeing Rome and (in a retelling of the Acts of Peter) encounters Christ on the way; Christ responds by saying 'When you abandon my people [. . .] I must go to Rome to be crucified once more.' Peter's companion echoes the question, and Peter, shamed by the accusation, announces that he is returning to Rome (Sienkiewicz 2000, 554). The chapter ends with the narrator's explanation of Peter's revelation, and of the novel's thesis:

> He also understood why God turned him back on the road. This city of vanity, debauchery and power was ready to fall into his hands and to become that double capital of both God and man, that would rule the spirit and the flesh throughout the world. (Sienkiewicz 2000, 555)

[26] Wallace draw a vertical line next to the following passage, for example:

> His eyes seemed scrunched in suet. His image was corrupt, a whim-driven man overtaken by his own excesses; he was still young but was drowning in the rolls of his accumulated fat, was prone to quick illness, and was corroded by debauchery and slimy with spittle. (Sienkiewicz 2000, 65)

He underlined the first sentence in this passage and may have drawn upon it elsewhere for a description of the IRS's Compliance Training Officer, whose 'face was the color of suet' (Wallace 2011b, 317).

Roman narrative Wallace developed. A passage elsewhere is not marked by Wallace, but gives a description of the animals' training that is very close to the one we find in 'Cede': 'The keepers starved the animals for two days, teasing them by dragging slabs of bloody meat before their cages, goading them into a frenzy of hunger' (Sienkiewicz 2000, 452). Wallace also underlined sentences describing Vinicius, in which the word 'achieve' suggests the contradictory valence sensed in the heading 'ADVENTURES IN ACHIEVEMENT':

> Vinicius was a product of his civilization, born to command like every highborn Roman, and he would rather watch the world end and the city tumble into ruins than see himself fail to achieve what he set out to do. (Sienkiewicz 2000, 102)

Wallace clearly returned to *Quo Vadis* more than once: in a different coloured pen, he marked a passage in which Peter addresses the early Christians, speaking 'as a father admonishing his children and teaching them how to live' (Sienkiewicz 2000, 184). Despite the different narrative strategies we see in *Quo Vadis* and Wallace's work, the moral arc of the novel – which presents a movement from scepticism, decadent lethargy and spiritual exhaustion to renewed belief – is one that has resonance for both *Infinite Jest* and *The Pale King*.

The trope of fatherhood is integral to the presentation of this renewal of belief and to the continual tension between control and freedom. The work depicts several children – Cedo, the contortionist boy, and the 'fierce infant' of §35 – who are presented in symbiotic yet oppositional relationships with their fathers. The 'fierce infant' hanging in his papoose appears to be 'riding [his father] like a mahout does an elephant';[27] the contortionist boy's father appears to lack the self-possession and discipline of his son, but experiences a complementary problem of 'backbone' and is also driven by his desires to psychologically 'contort himself'; Cede, for his part, rebels against his father by extending 'kindness' and 'mercy' to the dogs under his care, an act for which, it is hinted, he will not be forgiven (Wallace 2011b, 387, 405, n.d., 39.6). The inclusion in *The Pale King* of an additional parallel narrative describing the complex relations between a father and son would render the theme more visible in the work and would highlight the way in which the notion of paternity (as in the discussion of the self-deceptive need for 1980s US citizens to believe that 'Daddy's in control') is repeatedly transposed onto the political sphere (Wallace 2011b, 148).

[27] Pietsch changed this word from 'maheeb' after the recording of the audio book of *The Pale King*, which was recorded before the final stage of editing, possibly due to the word's obscurity (the OED contains only a definition for 'mahout' (Wallace 2011d, 12.7)).

The Ancient Rome sections also strongly evoke the history of early Christianity, with the brutal persecutions of Christians in the circus forming the background for the story's narrative. Again it is clear that 'Cede', if included in *The Pale King*, would strengthen our apprehension of the theme in the work as a whole. Christianity (and, frequently, Catholicism in particular) is a recurring element in the textual world of the novel, and one which has only begun to attract critical attention in recent years.[28] Examples, once again, are multiple. Lane Dean's crises of faith, in which he repeatedly turns to the Bible and to prayer in response to his despairing thoughts, provides one obvious example (Wallace 2011b, 40–3, 387). Dean has a Christian bumper sticker depicting a fish (not to mention a girlfriend named 'Sheri Fisher'); the symbol of the fish appears repeatedly in *Quo Vadis* to connect persecuted Christians throughout Rome (Wallace 2011b, 273–4, 541–2). Fogle's monologue, as several critics have noted, abounds with religious references, and he repeatedly compares his conversion experience in the presence of the substitute Jesuit to the Christian conversion of his roommate's girlfriend (O'Connell 2015, 286–7; Wallace 2011b, 222, 230; West 2017, 5–10).[29] The historical breadth of the novel's interest in Christianity is hinted at when Garrity refers to the 'so-called *daemon meridianus*' that terrorized the early Catholic hermits of 'third-century Egypt'.[30] Indeed, the connection between the experiences of the early Christians and the struggles of the modern-day characters in *The Pale King* are limned in symbolic and linguistic terms. O'Connell notes that Drinion's supernatural ability to levitate 'connects him with the metaphysical abilities of the saints', and the reference to the 'Zoroastrian levitation' of the Pontic aeronauts makes this connection much more explicit (O'Connell 2015, 287; Wallace n.d., 37.2). Shortly after the

[28] Matt Bucher noted the emergence of religion and spirituality as a growing theme in Wallace scholarship from 2014 onwards (Bucher 2015, n.p.). While Max's biography is relatively dismissive of Wallace's interest in religion, several critics have demurred, pointing to specific religious (mostly Christian, and often specifically Catholic) references in the author's writing, the numerous annotated books on religion and spirituality in his collection and further biographical and archival evidence of his religious leanings (Brick 2014; Bustillos 2014; Miller n.d.; O'Connell 2015; L. Thompson 2016, 184–6). See O'Connell (2015) for the most extensive analysis of Wallace's response to Christian thought.

[29] Again, earlier drafts sometimes emphasize this element of the narrative: in one of these, Fogle is 'spinning the Christian's ball' on his finger while watching the TV show that prompts his epiphany (Wallace n.d., 38.6), a phrase that Wallace perhaps felt represented an overly obvious piece of symbolism.

[30] As Michael O'Connell observes, the problems faced by the examiners (boredom or 'acedia') as well as the appropriate response to these spiritual difficulties are both represented in ways that draw upon 'traditions of Christian mysticism (Wallace 2011b, 383; O'Connell 2015, 280–8). Severs also notes the monkish devotion of the tax examiners, whose work is figured as a 'holy office' (Severs 2017, 207–8).

narrator of §46 informs us that Drinion is hovering above his chair, he interrupts Meredith Rand to note that she was '"raised in the Catholic faith"', to which she responds '"That's not relevant"' (Wallace 2011b, 472). In the light of the presence of a narrative centring on key events in the development of Christianity, we can take this to be a clear piece of misdirection on Wallace's part, and the pun on the word 'raised' becomes more visible.

The ideas linking these sections are also explored in narratives that have an unmistakeably metafictional dimension. In the draft of 'Cede' in which these stories coexist, we are invited to draw a clear contrast between the psychologically weak father of the 'contortionist boy' and Cede's father, the head trainer who is utterly indifferent to the suffering undergone by the Molossian hounds as he shapes them into 'instruments of the will of Rome':

> His was the brutal, beautiful, technical detachment of the true artist. And in his own heart, the *exercitor summum* understood himself as a kind of god-like shaping creator, albeit one for whom there was in vulgar Greek no name. (Wallace n.d., 40.2)

There is a suggestion here of the austere sacrifice required of the artist – the reader may well surmise that the word missing from the Greek is 'author' – as well as a more complicated parallel between the power of the artist and that of the state. A contrapuntal relationship between the two stories is established, with a clear contrast between the two men as well as between both sets of fathers and sons. The grotesque, solipsistic dedication and 'queer heartcraft' of the contortionist boy could be related to the refined cruelty of the head trainer, whose confinement of the dogs involves keeping them in cramped conditions whose dimensions force their bodies into contorted positions (Wallace 2011b, 403). The contortionist boy's father, meanwhile, thinks of his son as being '*dutiful*' (italics in original) while suspecting himself of lacking 'backbone', and his dreams of 'contorted suffocation' seem to be caused by his deficiency in the discipline needed to reach his goals (Wallace 2011b, 403–6). Cede shows the dogs 'mercy', a word that alludes to the beliefs of the Christians who are to be the animals' victims and shows him to be oriented towards others.[31] We see here, perhaps, a concordance between Wallace's resistance to formal closure in his fiction and his exploration of authoritarian political systems. Hayes-Brady

[31] In one further intratextual link, we might note the echo this creates with Toni Ware's intense feeling of love for her dogs (which is described in two separate sections) and the anecdote of the dog tied to a chain that closes §14 (Wallace 2011b, 117, 151, 511).

observes that 'completion signifies [. . .] the failure of perfection' in Wallace's fiction, while Severs notes that 'final reconciliations' are invariably depicted as being 'potentially fascistic' (Hayes-Brady 2016, 8; Severs 2017, 8): the highly ambiguous representation of the drive to perfection incarnated in the 'brutal, beautiful' trainer (a 'true artist') imagines artistic success in terms of despotism.[32]

It is clear that Wallace used Ancient Rome as an imaginative space in which to bring together several recurring obsessions; the threats to American democracy posed by late-twentieth-century political and economic developments, the tension between reason and faith that manifests in his fascination with holy men and his own deeply self-reflexive search for new modes of expression. The material I have discussed here supports Hering's argument that the thematic and formal failures Wallace confronted in these drafts are key ones in our understanding of his late work. We see, here, that the excision of material from an unfinished work will have an effect on its interpretation, subtly altering its thematic focus, and that our perception of *The Pale King* is shaped by what is excluded as well as included by its editor.

Fragments and variants: *The Pale King*'s multiple editions

In his assembly of the novel, then, Pietsch was confronted with the need to make significant decisions at the 'macro' level of novelistic form and structure. I now turn to the 'micro' level of sentence structure and word choice, which also presented a significant degree of fragmentation and textual dissonance.

The study of textual variance in the transmission of literary works, along with the attempt to 'make the historical changes in [their] production and transmission visible to the general public', is a central concern of textual and genetic editors,[33] but this aspect of textuality tends to remain off the radar of criticism of contemporary fiction (Dedner 2006, 15–16). To take a notable recent example, Martin Eve compared the UK and US editions of David Mitchell's *Cloud Atlas* in order to analyse the considerable textual variance in one of its sections. Demonstrating that 'social, editorial and authorial processes' were responsible

32 The word 'fascia' or its plural 'fasciae' is used repeatedly in its biological sense throughout the narrative of the contortionist boy (Wallace 2011b, 395, 397, 398) and the word's political overtones – bearing in mind the boy's obsessive focus on a final goal and the existence of a parallel narrative portraying an authoritarian political system – are surely no coincidence.

33 See issue 5 of *Variants*, for example (2006), which is dedicated to the editing of texts that exist in multiple versions.

for this variation, he concludes that there is 'no singular "Cloud Atlas"' and shows how 'editorial and publishing labour' tends to be 'buried beneath the front-facing façade of author and text names' (Eve 2016, 1–34).[34] Textual variance, Eve shows, is a phenomenon that is not limited to texts from earlier eras of literary production (as is often thought), and the transmission history of contemporary texts can be equally tangled. In the case of *Cloud Atlas*, the author of the work was still living (and unaware of the variance); the book had been a huge commercial success, had been adapted for film and had been the subject of study for several years. In the case of *The Pale King*, much of which exists in a chaotically unfinished state and lacked an author to synchronize variants and approve a single version, this problem presents itself acutely. To begin with, the previously unpublished scenes included in a separate section following the main narrative in the 2012 paperback edition highlighted the contingent nature of the book's structure (Wallace 2012e, 550–73).[35]

There are a high number of variants in the audio version of *The Pale King*, which was published simultaneously with the hardcover edition in April 2011 and is available both as a CD and in downloadable audio formats. The majority of chapters in the audio book contain textual differences from the printed versions: of the audio book's 50 chapters, only 11 are identical to the hardback edition, and these unchanged sections are all less than 2 pages long. The audio version was in fact recorded from a version of the manuscript just prior to the final one, due to the demands of the production schedule (Pietsch 2017b; Tondorf-Dick 2014). Pietsch carried out one final round of editing before the book's publication in print, allowing us to treat the audio book itself as a genetic document: these edits are a visible thread allowing the reader to follow the stitches and reconstruct the final stages of the book's development. I note some of these variations here in order to more accurately ascertain what Wallace wrote, to emphasize the difficulties facing the editor and to highlight the buried 'editorial and publishing labour' to which Eve draws attention.[36]

[34] This variance is due to a series of editorial changes that were never incorporated back into the US edition of the text, causing the editions to fall out of sync.

[35] Many fans were surprised at the exclusion of 'All That' – a story which had been published as a standalone piece in *The New Yorker* in December 2009 – from the hardback edition of the published novel (see, e.g. a discussion on the Wallace-l listserv from April 2011 in which several contributors questioned its absence), and the piece was also absent from the paperback edition's section of additional scenes. The story, whose narrator's childhood memories of 'religious interests' and fascination with heroism are linked with his memories of his father, clearly occupies some of the same imaginative space as Fogle's monologue and could comfortably sit within the book's covers, if only as an additional scene ('All That' n.p.).

[36] A more detailed list of these changes can be found in Groenland (2015b).

The labour carried out in this final round of edits combines two types: firstly, an activity that Pietsch describes as 'second- or third-pass editing',[37] often minute line edits intended to remove stylistic errors that he surmised the author would not have allowed into print, and harmonizing changes aimed at ensuring that 'place names, job titles, and other factual matters match up throughout the book' (Pietsch 2017c, 2011a, ix). Of the former category, many changes appear as straightforward attempts to eliminate apparent stylistic redundancies and repetition. At one point, for example, Fogle ends a sentence by relating how he and his mother had 'read children's books together in childhood', a phrase from which Pietsch deleted the last two words[38] (Wallace 2011d, 5.9, 2011b, 162). In a description of Fogle's father, Wallace had used the word 'extreme' three times within two sentences, and two of these were changed to synonyms ('exaggerated' and 'prominent') (Wallace 2011d, 5.16, 2011b, 176). Several changes appear to have been made here as corrections of the author's own inaccuracies. While describing his experiences of drug use as a student, Fogle mentions listening to Brian Eno's *Another Green World*, an album '*whose cover has colourful cutout figures inside a white frame*' (Wallace 2011b, 182). In the audio book, however, the album cover is described as featuring '*a keyhole shape of green on a mostly white field*' (Wallace 2011d, 6.4). The former description conforms to the cover of the album in question, while Wallace's description does not.[39] This appears to be an exceptionally observant piece of editing by Pietsch: however, it also results in the silent substitution of the editor's phrase for the author's own. It also shows how individual edits may affect the reader's interpretation: a reader familiar with Wallace's story 'Good Old Neon', for example, may be tempted to connect the image described by Fogle with the use of the keyhole as a recurring metaphor in that story and to recall its climactic moment in which the 'David Wallace' character is seen attempting to imagine another person's existence 'through the tiny little keyhole of himself' (Wallace 2005a, 180).[40] In Chapter 7, I make such

[37] Robert Gottlieb refers to this as 'manicuring copyediting' (Gottlieb 2016).

[38] Most examples of these changes are apparent in *The Pale King*'s longest chapter, §22, in which Chris 'Irrelevant' Fogle tells the story of his conversion from aimless drifter to focused, attentive tax examiner. This section, as well as being the longest, contains the most differences between the audio and print versions: approximately sixty are present, with only the Happy Hour scene of §46 and the training presentation scene of §27 displaying a similar number.

[39] It may in fact refer to a detail on the back cover of the vinyl LP, on which the green Island Records logo could be seen as a keyhole shape.

[40] Boswell argues for a thematic connection between the stories, suggesting that Fogle's monologue, 'Good Old Neon' and 'The Depressed Person' can be read as 'a trilogy of pieces' ('Constant Monologue' 156–7).

a connection in my analysis of the 'keyhole' as a symbol of the reduced narrative aperture of Minimalism.

Pietsch liaised with Green and Nadell to ensure agreement on any changes to the text of the manuscripts: they 'read the final versions and approved all the changes that were made to enable readers to experience the book with as little confusion as possible' (2017c). Many of the changes made in this final round of editing were aimed at harmonizing character names. Pietsch explains that 'characters who appear to be the same person had different names in different draft chapters, and it was necessary sometimes to pick one of the names and make it consistent. This kind of change felt necessary if we didn't want the book to be impossibly confusing' (Pietsch 2017b). Again, Fogle provides a clear example. After Fogle's 98-page monologue (which Pietsch designated §22) Fogle essentially disappears from view: we see him directly only once more, in the penultimate chapter (§49) where he is 'pre-briefed' for a meeting with Lehrl by Reynolds and Sylvanshine. In early draft versions of the longer Fogle chapter, it is clear that Wallace considered alternate names for Fogle and that Shinn was one of these (Wallace n.d., 38.6). Wallace appears to have been a compulsive changer of character names, and this character is one of many whose name changed multiple times during the drafting process: in earlier drafts, as previously mentioned, he was referred to as Robbie Van Note (Wallace n.d., 38.6, 39.6). In the printed text, the character in §49 is also called Fogle, while in the audio book he is referred to as Andy Shinn throughout (Wallace 2011b, 527, 2011d, 16.10). This appears to follow drafts of the chapter in Wallace's papers named 'Shinn Prebriefing Aug 06 Rough' (Wallace n.d., 37.1, 40.3). The rationale for the editorial change here would seem to be obvious, then. However, Shinn is present earlier in the printed version of *The Pale King*, in the 2-page §31; in this case the character is named Shinn in the audio book and print versions and thus no changes appear to have been made (Wallace 2011d, 11.15). We are told little about Shinn in §31, a brief vignette detailing his journey with other examiners from the men's apartment complexes to their posts, and it is unclear why this character's name was also not changed to Fogle.[41] Indeed, potential links between the chapters are arguably obscured by the difference in character name. The section ends with Shinn listening to the songs of birds and imagining

[41] Shinn is described here as being 'long-bodied' and having 'very light baby-fine blond hair' (Wallace 2011b, 371), information which does not seem to be contradicted by any description of Fogle elsewhere.

these as brutal 'war cries' that make 'his spirits dip for some reason' (Wallace 2011b, 372). If this character were called Fogle, the reader might be drawn to make a link between this thought and the moment at the close of the earlier chapter when Fogle, describing the morning when he was about to submit his application forms to the IRS recruiter, notes in a brief aside that 'the bird-sounds at sunrise were incredible' (Wallace 2011b, 251). The recurrence of birdsong in a menacing context just as Fogle is seemingly beginning his Service posting in Peoria could then be seen as a moment of character development, as Fogle's zeal for the Service gives way to a darker and more competitive vision of society.[42]

The multiple versions of *The Pale King*, then, contain numerous differences that will subtly affect a reader's understanding of the novel and present unusual interpretive challenges.[43] In his analysis of the many post-publication changes to Beckett's texts, Van Hulle describes textual 'discordances' such as these as 'textual scars' that serve as reminders of the 'multi-versional' nature of the works.[44] Wallace's changing – and perhaps conflicting – intentions about central elements in the work result in the fact that discordant elements of plot and character have become embedded in the published text. The evidence here bears out McGann's contention that editorial decisions (and hence textual variations) will necessarily proliferate each time a text is reproduced as well as Eve's observation that 'while we seem adept at studying the inter-textuality of contemporary fiction, we are often poor at spotting the intra-textuality of single texts between published versions' (McGann 1991, 185; Eve 2016, 22). The radically unfinished nature of *The Pale King*'s plot is thrown into sharp relief when we consider the importance of small details to an understanding of the plot of *Infinite Jest*, a novel in which iterations of character and place names are sometimes separated by hundreds of pages and in which details such as the postal origin of a package (i.e. the

[42] The story of the Pontic aeronauts makes it clear that *The Pale King* depicts several ambiguous instances of failed or sabotaged attempts at flight. The narrative of Fogle (whose name, as Tom Tracey has pointed out to me, suggests the German word for 'bird', '*vogel*') suggests this trajectory at a more symbolic level; the references to birds here could be seen as key moments in this regard. The IRS recruiting station in which Fogle signs up to the Service shares its space with a US Air Force recruiting office, and the chapter ends with the recruiter offering him a smile that seems, as Severs notes, 'ominous' (Wallace 2011b, 252; Severs 2017, 200).

[43] It is worth noting, too, that *The Pale King*'s footnotes are absent from its audio version. This absence has clear implications for a reading of sections such as §24, in which important plot information is communicated by footnote (Wallace 2011b, 277–309).

[44] In Beckett's case, this is largely due to the processes of translation between his bilingual publications (Van Hulle 2014, 220). Bryant refers to these occasions as 'fluid-text moments' (Bryant 2002, 66); my preference is for Van Hulle's formulation, since it hints at the conflicts of the editing process and the desire for textual stability inherent in Pietsch's editorial labour and the implicit attempt to, so to speak, 'heal' these 'scars'.

one received by the medical attaché) or the date of a seemingly tangential event (such as the 'M.I.T Language Riots') have been identified by critics as being key to an understanding of chronology and plot (Wallace 2006, 37, 996n60; Burn 2012b, 35; Swartz 2009).[45] These details were, as we have seen, subject to an editorial process consisting of several stages of correspondence between author and editor, and were, in many cases, argued over at an individual level. While the manuscript papers for *The Pale King* contain several intricately realized individual chapters (and even some that could be said to be 'completed' in the sense of having been edited for magazine publication), it is clear that the plot as a whole never remotely approached the byzantine complexity or carefully calibrated interconnectivity of Wallace's previous novel.

Pietsch's work on *The Pale King* has been justly acclaimed, and his achievement in assembling a chaotic body of archival deposits into a novel that is sensitive to the author's own aesthetic – along with his editorial restraint in including the majority of the material developed during its composition, in contrast to other notable examples such as *The Garden of Eden* – is clear. The work is chronically unfinished in key respects, however, and some critics have objected to the way in which the editor and Little, Brown have brought it to the literary marketplace. Jeffrey Di Leo, for example, finds fault with the publication both at an ethical level – accusing the publisher of an eagerness to 'profit from the notion and prestige of authorship' with scant regard for the absent author's wishes – and in formal terms. The unfinished work, he writes, should be 'as close to a reproduction of the original materials left behind by the author as possible' in order to let readers 'engage it in its disorganized, textual glory' (Di Leo 2012, 132–4). Di Leo's suggestion is deliberately unpragmatic, ignoring the reality of a commercial publisher's imperative to bring their works to a wide readership (he admits that his ideal publication of the work would have 'effectively buried its sales') as well as the significant amount of scholarly and archival labour needed to bring it to fruition.[46] The evident amount of authorial labour expended upon the work is perhaps the strongest justification for its publication, since *The Pale King* is clearly far more than a hurried side project and represents a significant part of Wallace's late-career work. A genetic edition of the work that allowed

[45] Discussing the 'compositional paralysis' in *The Pale King*'s manuscripts, Hering notes that 'there is nothing approaching this level of incoherence in the manuscripts of *Infinite Jest*' (Hering 2016a, 135).

[46] His suggestion that 'we should use the legacy of writers like Wallace to drive readers back to libraries and archives to see the formative "stuff" of great writers' is also rather coercive and ignores the difficulties of access for those readers residing outside Austin, Texas (Di Leo 2012, 133).

scholars to engage with its compositional history in detail, though, would clearly be desirable. At an early stage, Pietsch considered the possibility of a digital edition which would allow readers to essentially remix the novel, but abandoned this idea due to technical constraints (Medley 2013). The closest model for such an edition is perhaps the *Samuel Beckett Digital Manuscript Project*, a collaboration between the Ransom Center and the University of Antwerp's Centre for Manuscript Genetics, which has developed online editions in which readers can view facsimiles and transcriptions of several of Beckett's works, access 'genetic maps' of each draft and use tools for comparison and a search engine.[47] The Ransom Center and the Wallace estate have already presented the work's Chapter 9 in a similar manner, allowing readers to view the different stages of its development and view Wallace's handwritten drafts (Wallace 2012b, 9). It is to be hoped that a future edition will build upon this, making it easier for readers to traverse the work in a way that preserves its textual multiplicity and clarifies the history of its long and complex development.

Dead ends and reroutings: Understanding Wallace's fluid text

The seductions of the supposedly stable text are considerable. Without ready access to documentary evidence, critics may be all too ready to proceed on the basis of assumptions of textual authority that ignore the complexities of literary production. This problem is particularly acute in the case of posthumous works, whose textual status is always at risk of being poorly understood: the critic, faced with what Bryant calls 'the smoothness of the clear reading text', may take this text to be the simple reproduction of (to borrow a phrase from Nabokov's Charles Kinbote) the 'marble finality of an immaculate typescript' (Bryant 2002, 27; Nabokov 1992, 15). In Chapter 1, I highlighted the way in which the editor's involvement in such works can result in enduring contributions to their transmission. With a work as complex and chronologically extensive as *The Pale King*, some understanding of its history is, as Hering notes, essential if we are to avoid inaccuracies and assumptions (Hering 2016a, 12).

A notable feature of recent Wallace criticism has been the turn towards an examination of the political and economic contexts surrounding his work,

[47] The *BDMP*, along with information on its history and aims, can be found at http://www.beckettarchive.org/.

manifested primarily in a focus on *The Pale King*. Three essays by Richard Godden and Michael Szalay, Mark McGurl and Stephen Shapiro, all published towards the end of 2014, present readings of the novel that track, respectively, its dramatization of the rise of 'financial derivatives' in contemporary capitalism, its author's engagement with 'the emergent conditions of institutionalization' during the Program Era and its narration of the 'competing temporalities' of classical capitalism and contemporary neoliberalism (Godden and Szalay 2014, 1275; McGurl 2014, 31; Shapiro 2014, 1249). Each of these readings contains acute insights into the work's central tensions and argues persuasively for Wallace's growing awareness of the political structures governing contemporary Western democracy. However, these analyses are less detailed in their apprehension of the complex processes governing the production and genesis of the work itself.

Godden and Szalay's analysis serves to illustrate some of the difficulties inherent in reading posthumously edited work. One section of their lengthy essay, which traces the depiction of abstraction in the novel by arguing that its characters are continually shown to 'possess two bodies, one abstract and one concrete, in ways that vividly recall Marx's account of money' (Godden and Szalay 2014, 1280), consists of a meticulous reading of its §29. This chapter corresponds to number 293 in Michael Pietsch's index of documents for the novel and portrays a dialogue between a number of IRS agents on a surveillance shift who regale each other with stories 'about shit', culminating in a description of an ill-fated series of school pranks involving a character called 'Fat Marcus the Moneylender' (Wallace 2011b, 347–55, n.d., 36.1). The authors devote over 4 pages of analysis to this scene in order to demonstrate the way in which, 'for Wallace, shit and blood both figure circulatory monetary flows' and to trace the way in which the dialogue's recurring 'faecal images' signify 'money emptied of value' within finance capitalism (Godden and Szalay 2014, 1289–93). They trace detailed, subtle intratextual links between §29 and earlier chapters in order to bolster their claim that the section performs a 'critique of "flow and output"' (1289). The reading continues for several pages of close textual analysis that relies heavily on linguistic associations.[48] They go on to argue that the story of Fat Marcus, which closes the chapter, 'refines the link between money and human waste' (1290).

[48] The authors admit, for example, that in their associative reading, 'much [. . .] depend[s] on Wallace's choice of faecal colour' (a reference to the character's 'yellow' excrement is taken as a symbolic allusion to the 'flexible gold' of the financial derivative) (Wallace 2011b, 347; Godden and Szalay 2014, 1290).

An examination of the drafts, though, suggests that Wallace himself accomplished very little refining on this chapter. The published text of the chapter was transcribed from the only existing draft of the scene, a draft which, as the words 'Glitterer freewriting' in the corner of the first page suggests, was an early one that had not yet been subject to any revision at all by the author (Wallace n.d., 40.5).[49] On some pages, cryptic notes suggest undeveloped ideas, and we can see snatches of additional dialogue that were not incorporated into the story: some lines from the manuscript have been cut, most likely because of their oblique relationship to plot. The final page contains notes that suggest that the story may have continued further in subsequent drafts.[50] These notes, along with the fact that none of the characters in the scene – Bondurant, Hurd, Gaines and Lumm – play a significant role in the more fully developed chapters of the novel, suggest that this draft came from a relatively early stage of the work, probably from 2001 or earlier. The year of the draft's composition is not given, but the fact that it came (according to the index) from a binder labelled 'Glitter/SJF' is a strong indicator of its chronological status.[51]

It seems difficult to argue that this draft has the same status – and that it deserves the same hermeneutical attention – as the chapters drawn from more advanced drafts. If this argument were to be made, it would surely need to be made explicitly. Instead, the analysis presented seems predicated on the assumption of a relatively stable text, and the attribution of key textual features is rarely examined in detail. We are told that the reference to Fat Marcus' Jewish ethnicity 'fits Wallace's scheme' (Godden and Szalay 2014, 1291). However, it is unclear to the reader of their analysis that much of Wallace's 'scheme' is being inferred here from handwritten drafts that were never intended for direct publication and certainly earmarked for extensive revision. As in many other chapters, minor editorial changes, when detected, may subtly alter the terms of critical analysis: the reference to faeces in the final sentence of the chapter

49 'Freewriting' was Wallace's term for the method used in his early-stage attempts to draft scenes: Max describes this as 'the characteristic tiny, forward-charging handwriting with which he attempted new fiction' and notes that this is often difficult to decipher (Max 2012c, n.p.). In a 1999 interview, Wallace described himself as a 'Five Draft Man', stating that the first two of these were always on pen and paper (Wallace 1999, n.p.).

50 On another page, a text box marked '*Ins- note to Dave*' contains short notes and quotes from the story. These may have been intended as chapter headings: in earlier iterations of the novel, Wallace explored the idea of introducing each chapter with archaic, synoptic headings like those in McCarthy's *Blood Meridian* (Wallace n.d., 39.3, 39.5).

51 As Max and Hering note, 'Glitterer' and 'Sir John Feelgood' were two earlier working titles for the book (Wallace n.d., 36.1; Max 2012a, 321; Hering 2016a, 127–35).

was, in fact, added by Pietsch (possibly from another draft as yet unavailable to scholars), which adds to the problematic nature of the interpretive jumps being made here (Wallace 2011b, 355; 2011d, 11.8).[52]

This is indicative of a general problem in the analysis. Godden and Szalay refer, in the conclusion to their argument, to 'the typescript' (1315), a word that suggests a unified piece of work corresponding roughly to the published novel. As I discussed in my description of Pietsch's encounter with the material, though, no linear, self-contained 'typescript' of the work can be said to exist.[53] The authors also state that Wallace 'printed out the manuscript of his novel just before he hanged himself, and left it in another room, a light shining upon it' (1315). They cite Max at this point, but there is some ambiguity in the source of this information: it is not clear at all from Max's account that Wallace printed the drafts at this point, just that he 'tidied up the manuscript' (Max 2012a, 301).[54] The authors refer to 'the text' and 'the pro forma entity' and later add the apparent clarification that they are referring to 'the published manuscript, in conjunction with the typescript' (1315), descriptions which cumulatively suggest an inadequate apprehension of the multiplicity and complexity of material involved. The approach taken throughout the piece, then, suggests an insufficiently close consideration of the extensive process bridging the author's draft page with the published text. The final pages of their analysis cast the editor's role in metaphorical terms, suggesting that Pietsch acted 'in the manner of a derivative trader' (1315) and notes the 'daunting' nature of the task facing him, but the consideration given to the practicalities of the textual editing involved in the book is minimal.

Stephen Shapiro's analysis of *The Pale King* approaches the novel through a similar conceptual framework, invoking a Marxist theoretical tradition in its limning of the work's attention to the power structures of the modern neoliberal state and its awareness of the effects of the late-capitalist abstraction of credit into a 'derivative commodity' (1264). The explanation of the way in which the

[52] The phrase 'and ~~Marcus' scream bringing~~ everybody in pyjamas' was changed to 'and **Fat Marcus took a shit in fear and pain and his screams brought** everybody in pyjamas'.

[53] As Lawrence Rainey notes of the prepublication manuscripts of *The Waste Land*, the critical tendency to append the definite article to a plurality of disordered draft papers ('the manuscript', 'the typescript') suggests a 'monolithic entity' that is at odds with the complexity of the textual situation (Rainey 2005, 2).

[54] In any case, it is very clear from Pietsch's introduction that this 'neat stack of manuscript' comprised only twelve chapters of the work and that the published version draws from other, less orderly sources such as 'drafts in David's miniscule handwriting', 'notes' and drafts that 'contained abandoned or superseded plotlines' (Pietsch 2011a, viii–ix).

work engages with the problem of narrating 'different capitalist temporalities' by enacting a 'turn against individual singularity' (1250, 1267) is patient and cogent, and its argument that the 'anti-aesthetic' and 'non-narrative' text aligns Wallace with 'a left aesthetic' (1268) is convincing. However, little attention is paid to the material processes of the book's production; aside from passing acknowledgements of the fact that the work is 'incomplete' and 'edited', the complicated genesis of the work is ignored (1250, 1268). Pietsch's name does not appear in the essay, and the analysis appears to proceed on the assumption that its textual object is a stable one. A sentence stating that the work 'documents the life passage of its characters according to both the general derangement of capitalism and the more period-specific one involving the neoliberal liquidation of the State', for example, surely requires some qualification: as I demonstrated earlier in this chapter, the manuscripts display an occasionally startling lack of clarity in establishing who exactly these characters are and what their 'life passages' consist of (1258). The argument depends upon the assumption that the 'new novelistic form' presented in the published work is an intentional structural feature and implies that the 'anti-style' on display within this 'non-narrative text' represents an active political intervention on the part of its author (Shapiro 2014, 1249, 1268). The argument implies a teleological assumption about the form and content of the text, and the call at the close of the essay for 'an observant textual practice' does not sit entirely comfortably with its own lack of attention to the material and social genesis of the text under discussion (Shapiro 2014, 1268).

McGurl's analysis is, on occasion, similarly guilty of a lack of attention to the process encoded within the product. While he acknowledges the work's unfinished nature, his description of the editorial process involved in its creation is perfunctory and not entirely accurate: he reports that Pietsch assembled the work 'from a pile of fragments the author left neatly stacked on his desk before hanging himself a few feet away', an account that simplifies the range of materials drawn upon by the editor (McGurl 2014, 29). The essay could also be said to be guilty of presenting the kind of 'winner's history' that Sullivan critiques, where features of a complexly authored text are assumed to be inevitable extensions of the author's intention. The thrust of the analysis, which moves towards a critique of the 'limits' of Wallace's 'seductively fine mind' and of the political 'terms' within which the 'project' operates, surely gives insufficient weight to the fact of the editor's partial and selective presentation of material. McGurl confidently asserts that the novel has 'no protagonist', quoting a note included by Pietsch as evidence that the notion of an authorial 'crypto-protagonist' was rejected by the author: this note, we are told, 'makes it clear that this was not the plan' (McGurl 2014, 47–9). It could of course be objected, here, that the reading relies upon the editor's selection for presentation of this note rather than others and that inferences about the author's 'plan' are based on the editor's decisions as well as the critic's own assumptions.

There is a risk, therefore, judging by current work on *The Pale King*, of inaccurate textual assumptions becoming entrenched in Wallace scholarship. In his discussion of developments in editorial perspectives in the past half century, Eggert describes the hostile attitude of several critics to the presentation of texts that bring textual variation to the surface, characterizing the critical position as one of 'innocence' and suggesting that 'the reviewers' desire [. . .] is for the unambiguous transcendence of product – the "single work" out of process' (Eggert 2009, 179).[55] The same criticism could be made in the cases I quote here; certainly, these readings evince little interest in exploring the 'dysteleological sidepaths, dead ends and reroutings' that tend to feature in the genesis of any text (Van Hulle 2014, 15). In the case of *The Pale King*, these sidesteps and second thoughts are an inescapable part of the work, and its editor's role in bridging process and product cannot easily be discounted.

[55] Eggert focuses on the critical reaction to Hans Walter Gabler's 1984 edition of *Ulysses*, as well as the response during the same years to new editions of Proust's *A la recherche du temps perdu* (Eggert 2009, 162–80).

7

'Magical compression': Wallace's return to Minimalism

We have seen, in the previous chapter, how *The Pale King* reached – and, ultimately, never escaped from – a kind of structural deadlock as key characters and plot developments failed to cohere. We have also seen how after Wallace's death Pietsch proceeded, in a one-sided continuation of the men's working relationship, to arrange and prepare the material contained in the manuscripts of the work into the published version of *The Pale King* and how the decisions he made served to frame the material in particular ways. In this chapter, we return to this structural deadlock and to the period in which Wallace was attempting, in isolation, to overcome it. During these years, Pietsch was – as we have seen – working with the author to bring *Consider the Lobster* and *Oblivion* into print; however, Wallace never showed his editor any of the novel in progress.[1] As he forged deeper into the project, Wallace increasingly became his own editor, struggling to manage an increasingly (and, for him, unprecedentedly) fractured and fragmented mass of material. In this chapter, I examine the drafts of the novel in order to trace Wallace's continuing struggles with the demands of producing and reducing, writing and editing, as he negotiates the contradictory problem – one that he himself recognized and that David Hering isolates as a key one – of having both 'too much and too little' material (Hering 2016b, n.p.). Here we see the author as his own editor, and the tensions between these functions, I suggest, are incorporated into the work in the form of an oblique argument about literary style.

Wallace's work, as I discussed in my introduction, displays a long-standing fascination with – and ambivalence towards – models of narrative compression. His antipathy to the dominant model of 1980s Minimalist fiction is (as Hoberek

[1] In his 'Editor's Note' to *The Pale King*, Pietsch writes that 'at the time of David's death [. . .] I had not seen a word of this novel except for a couple stories he had published in magazines' (Pietsch 2011a, vi).

argues) essential to an understanding of his own turn to Pynchonesque excess, and the diegetic and stylistic overload of *Infinite Jest* could be seen as his definitive statement against abridgement, concealment and condensation. Critics have noted the degree of ambiguity in this turn within Wallace's narratives, however. Simon de Bourcier, for example, has demonstrated how Wallace's 'long, complex sentences' are often associated with addiction, whereas his simpler sentences often connote 'authentic emotion associated with recovery' (de Bourcier 2017, 4, 22). The ostentatiously complex syntax of Wallace's maximalist sentences is, as De Bourcier shows, frequently linked with 'unhealthy mode[s] of thought': in opposition to the sophistic, loquacious arguments of Geoffrey Day or the manic, uncontrolled excess of the 'Methamphetamine-Dependent' headline writer, we are presented with the hard-won, terse sincerity of Gately, who instructs Joelle to 'Use less words' (Wallace 2006, 271, 391, 535). In *Infinite Jest*, Wallace hints that verbal overload is indicative of part of the prevailing cultural problem and counterpoints verbal excess (often associated with the avoidance and insincerity of characters like Day and Erdedy) with the pithy, minimalistic AA maxims that function as practical mechanisms for its characters' release from addiction. If AA is the antidote, it is a problematic one, as others have pointed out (Holland 2006, 218–42); nevertheless, the dialectical relationship between the novel's own narrative strategies and the direct and sometimes simplistic modes of communication favoured by some of its most morally commendable characters suggests a continued interest on the part of the author in the possibility that less could, in fact, be more.

In Wallace's late work, this fascination enters a new phase. In *The Pale King*, his focus repeatedly returns to Minimalism again, long after it has ceased to be necessary as an antagonistic model. I am not making, here, the counter-intuitive suggestion that Wallace returns to an upper-cased 1980s Minimalism; nor that his interest in modes of compression represents the entirety of his focus during his work on the novel; nor that the focus of this interest represented an abandonment of his earlier methods. However, there is evidence to show Wallace continuing to look towards models of narrative compression in order to focus his own exploration of the ethics of storytelling. Wallace retains an interest in narrative austerity as both a strategy and an ideal and invokes a longer tradition of minimalist practice – what McDermott refers to as a wider movement of 'lower-cased "literary minimalism"' and Botha calls a recurring and 'transhistorical phenomenon' – in order to explore questions of ethical and aesthetic value (McDermott 2006, 2; Botha 2017, xiv). Strategies of narrative excess are often used here alongside characters and situations that pointedly refer back to narrative modes based on reduction and compression.

The Pale King, after all, is a collection of fragments that never became more than the sum of its disparate parts before its author's death. Several sections work as stand-alone stories: four were published during Wallace's lifetime,[2] while several other pieces were, as I have mentioned (and as David Hering has shown), diverted into *Oblivion* (Hering 2016a, 128–9). It must be acknowledged, of course, that Wallace clearly conceived of this material as part of a larger project, even if many of the individual pieces grew into self-contained entities: the synchronic drafts were evidently written in relation to the notion, however distant, of a diachronic product, and we cannot ignore what Van Hulle refers to as 'the complex interplay between completion and incompletion' (Van Hulle 2014, 246). At the level of bibliographical categorization, though, it is accurate to describe the work as an aggregation of brief narratives and meditations, almost none of which would seem too lengthy for a volume of short fiction.[3] The longer pieces often take their own length as a thematic focus, being self-reflexive in their use of detailed, exhaustive narrative techniques as well as pointing the reader towards images of compression and clarity. In order to frame the textual analysis that follows, we will briefly reconsider some of Wallace's public statements about minimalist techniques.

'Clarity, precision, plainness, lucidity': The value of compression

In an interview with *Bookworm*'s Michael Silverblatt upon the publication of *A Supposedly Fun Thing* in 1997, Wallace discussed the narrative strategies used in his essays. While ostensibly focusing on his non-fiction, the interview slides repeatedly into discussion of his fiction, and a close reading reveals aspects of Wallace's thinking on literary style after *Infinite Jest*. At one point, Silverblatt observes the obsession with 'information gathering' in Wallace's essays, to which Wallace replies by explaining the challenge of reporting factual experience and

2 These are: 'Peoria (4)' and 'Peoria (9) "Whispering Pines"' published in *TriQuarterly* #112, June 2002 (these would become the novel's §1 and the beginning of §8, respectively); 'Good People' in *The New Yorker* 5 Feb. 2007; and 'The Compliance Branch' in *Harper's* February 2008.

3 §22 (Fogle's monologue) lasts for 99 pages, while §46 (the 'Happy Hour' section) is 66 pages long; §24 (the second of the 'David Wallace'-narrated chapters) is 54 pages long.

notes that his emerging 'rhetorical strategy' in the essays became 'simply to be really candid about it and invite the reader to kind of empathize both with my anxiety and with the overload'. Silverblatt turns the conversation to the question of Wallace's footnotes, and the author mentions the editing process involved in this technique, noting Pietsch's help.[4] At this point, the host addresses the question of literary style, mentioning their shared admiration for David Markson's *Wittgenstein's Mistress* and praising the way 'the intelligence in [the book] is really swallowed by a narrative situation that wants to compress it and make it nearly impossible to express'. He presents the book's achievement – namely, the tension in modes of affect provoked by the urge towards narrative compression – as a counterpoint to Wallace's work in fiction, in an exchange I will reproduce at length here:

> MS: And we talked about that kind of book – I say that Rilke and Kafka do it – that manages to be extremely self-conscious and yet to attain some kind of sanctity or purity or holiness or humanness or all at the same time – that I sense is the alternative to the massive book of *Infinite Jest* and the massive self-consciousnesses and paralyses this kind of book involves. I wanted to talk about that.
>
> DFW: I think – I mean, I agree with you, and I think *Wittgenstein's Mistress* is a magical book. Not because it alternates between incredible intellectual stunt-pilotry and pathos, but because it manages to marry the two in a way that – I mean, that's what my dream is: to someday be able to do something like that.

Wallace appears to agree, here, with the interviewer's suggestion that the 'sanctity or purity or holiness or humanness' displayed in the books he mentions is an alternative to the 'massive' example of his recent novel and suggests that it is his ambition one day to write a book encompassing the kind of 'deeper, wiser' self-consciousness found in '*Wittgenstein's Mistress* or *The Notebook of Malte Laurids Brigge* or "The Hunger Artist" or *The Metamorphosis*'. Wallace continues to explain the way in which his stylistic approach is 'mimetic of a very kind of late twentieth-century American experience', but Silverblatt's subsequent comments return the discussion to the possibility of narrative compression. He announces himself to be 'very curious about that ability to heroically throw away

[4] Wallace claims to have been lucky to have the assistance of Pietsch, who 'gets it, and he sees [. . .] some of the virtues of the footnotes, but he was very good at figuring out where I had just kind of lost it with ceasing to identify with the reader in any way'.

what might be brilliant stand-up stuff [...] and have the essence', prompting an exchange that is worth quoting at almost its full length for the way it reveals Wallace's ambivalent attitude towards compression in literary form:

> DFW: I agree with 90% of what you're saying in principle. The problem is in practice. What you're talking about is a very condensed, aphoristic – you're talking about *Thus Spake Zarathustra* or *The Philosophical Investigations* or *The I Ching* or really really good, really really good poetry. And the problem with doing something like that kind of thing in non-fiction is that I think then you're setting yourself up as a . . . teacher, rather than as a companion . . . I agree with a lot of what you're saying, and in fact even though *Infinite Jest* is really long, the thing I'm most proud of is that for once I did not reptilianly fight and hang on to every single page that I did. And I let – I allowed myself to have faith in a really smart editor and cut some of it – and . . . that, that for me was what was valuable about that process. But I am not yet good and smart enough to be able to do what you're talking about. I agree . . . about what would be magical about that, and I think one of the most toxic things about the movement called Minimalism in the 1980s was that it aped the form of that without any of its spirit, or any of what would truly be magical – it's moments in Carver, maybe the end of 'So Much Water So Close to Home',[5] but for the most part it got Americanized: it got reduced to a set of formal schticks, an appearance, a persona. For now, given my limitations – at least like in the non-fiction book – I wanted much more to set myself up as . . . a kind of companion or tour-guide who was very observant but was also every bit as bound up and Americanized and self-conscious and insecure as the reader. Now, I realize that what I'm giving you is a literary defence for a kind of literature that is inferior to the kind you're talking about. But I don't think, I don't think it's without value.
>
> MS: No, you're very present. And I guess what I'm talking about is a literature that implicitly takes to heart the Zen maxim, 'Live as if you were already dead'.
>
> DFW: Oh yeah. Well, you're talking about an effaced narrator where it's not a literary choice, but it's in fact a truth. And, except for very rare, transcendent pieces of fiction, I haven't seen that done anywhere

[5] It is difficult to ascertain which version of the story Wallace is referring to here; I have refrained from any extended analysis of the story for this reason.

> except spiritual and religious literature. Or, you know, at the end of Wittgenstein's *Tractatus*. I mean, you're talking about the sort of thing that an absolute genius – I mean, a Mozart of living – comes up with after decades of effort. And I'm comfortable, I'm comfortable saying I'm not there yet. (Wallace 1997b)

Wallace reprises the critical stance he has taken earlier in his career, disparaging the Minimalist movement for what he sees as its empty formal gestures and its facile adoption of pre-existing structures without reference to a larger aesthetic vision. He also goes out of his way, as he had previously, to exempt Carver – or, at least, 'moments in Carver' – from criticism.[6] The implication, however, is that the 'spirit' of the attempt to, as Silverblatt puts it, 'have the essence' can lead to work that is 'magical' (a word Wallace returns to several times); we might argue that what is being dismissed here is not an artistic stance or set of methods, but a specific movement within a particular historical situation. The kinds of 'magical' moments Wallace finds only in certain works of Carver are, he suggests, present to a greater degree in philosophical and religious texts; 'spiritual and religious literature' is held up here as the ideal of literary compression and self-effacement. Wallace's final comment – 'I'm not there yet' – highlights the suggestion, repeated several times in this discussion, that this mode of 'magical' compression, rather than being antithetical to his own fictional project, is in fact his long-term aesthetic. Wallace's admiration for literature that successfully achieves stylistic reduction is clear, and he ends the interview by wryly alluding to his frustration at his current inability to achieve this: as Silverblatt signs off, he announces: 'I'm now going to beat my head against the wall for 30 seconds.'

I take this exchange to be an example not just of Silverblatt's characteristic perceptiveness with regard to the structures and tensions in Wallace's work (his observation, during his 1996 interview with the author, on the way *Infinite Jest* operates upon fractal structures is perhaps the most impressive example of this), but of the author's ongoing struggle with the notion that less can be more. Indeed, some brief comments by the author at a symposium on Kafka the following year show Wallace's continuing interest in textual reduction. Discussing Kafka's technique, Wallace noted that both great jokes and great short stories 'depend on what communication-theorists sometimes call "exformation", which is a certain quantity of vital information *removed from* but *evoked by* a communication in

[6] It is worth noting, too, that Wallace himself introduces 1980s Minimalism – and Carver – into the discussion.

such a way as to cause a kind of explosion of associative connections within the recipient' (Wallace 1998b, 23, emphasis in original). The term and its explanation (both clearly taken from Tor Nørretranders' book *The User Illusion*, published in English in the same year; an annotated copy resides in Wallace's library)[7] evoke the way in which literary minimalism achieves its effects by the deliberate redaction of expected content, in a manner perhaps not dissimilar to the way Hemingway's famous 'iceberg' looms invisibly but indispensably beneath a text.[8] Wallace goes on to note: 'Nor is it an accident that the technical achievement of great short stories is often called "compression" – for both the pressure and the release are already inside the reader' (23). The particular humour found in Kafka's work, according to Wallace, is essentially a form of 'harrowing spirituality' that is 'a religious humor, but religious in the manner of Kierkegaard and Rilke and the Psalms' (26).

Indeed, if we move forward to a piece published ten years later – at the opposite end of the decade-long stretch during which Wallace wrote the majority of *The Pale King* – we see the writer meditating, in print, on many of the same concerns. In 'Deciderization 2007', Wallace's introduction to *The Best American Essays 2007*, we see him not only returning to some of the same ideas, but also using similar language in the process. I agree with Severs's contention that the essay bears an important relationship to Wallace's later work, and I read it here as an extended meditation on the related issues of editing and style, as Wallace – in the context of his own function as 'guest editor' – contemplates the qualities of compression in prose (Severs 2017, 171–3; Wallace 2012a, 299). The introduction is alive to its own context in a particularly Wallacean way, gesturing towards the reader in its acknowledgement of the conditions and limitations inherent in its production. Wallace opens by self-deprecatingly speculating that the reader is likely to read his introduction 'last, if at all' (Wallace 2012a, 299), placing his own struggles to the forefront by presenting the image of the guest editor seated helplessly at his desk, 'sitting there reading a dozen Xeroxed pieces in a row', attempting to process the 'Total Noise that's also the sound of our U.S. culture right now' into some 'kind of triage of saliency or value' (Wallace 2012a, 301). Considering the different challenges of writing fiction and non-fiction – 'nonfiction's based

7 Staes traces some of the ways in which Wallace engaged with *The User Illusion* as a research source for *The Pale King*, suggesting that the activities of the IRS rote examiners serve to illustrate Nørretranders' arguments about the way in which information functions (Staes 2014b, 72–7).

8 *Death in the Afternoon* contains Hemingway's famous analogy in which he espoused a fiction of omission and ellipsis: 'The dignity of movement of an ice-berg is due to only one-eighth of it being above water' (Hemingway 1932, 154).

in reality [...] Whereas fiction comes out of nothing' (Wallace 2012a, 302) – he appears to downplay that difference in favour of the insight that both are performed 'on tightropes, over abysses':

> Fiction's abyss is silence, *nada*. Whereas non-fiction's abyss is Total Noise, the seething static of every particular thing and experience, and one's total freedom of infinite choice about what to choose to attend to and represent and connect, and how, and why, & c. (Wallace 2012a, 302–3, italics in original)

The distinction drawn here between formal categories is arguably less important than the commonality evoked by the fear of the 'abyss' and by his identification of the necessity of the writer's selectivity in negotiating a terrifying expanse of potential. We might also note that the *nada* here surely alludes to Hemingway by way of an example of a writer who has displayed such selectivity.[9]

Wallace's own editing, he suggests, is – since it involves neither line editing nor copy-editing – unworthy of the name, with his position more accurately described as 'an evaluative filter, winnowing a very large field of possibilities down to a manageable, absorbable Best for your delectation' (Wallace 2012a, 303; capitalization in original). A footnote here considers the fact that the editor's job consists primarily of excluding entries, 'since the really expensive, energy-intensive part of such processing is always deleting/discarding/resetting'; the final words here also suggest word-processing functions that evoke the writer's drafting process (Wallace 2012a, 304). Our attention is then drawn to the 'series editor' Robert Atwan, noting 'the amount of quiet behind-the-scenes power he wields over these prize collections' in order to further emphasize the contextual horizons of publishing (Wallace 2012a, 306).

At this point, the links between the themes of the essay and those of Wallace's parallel fiction project begin to grow noticeably stronger. Wallace uses a term borrowed from information theory to consider his function as editor – 'my Decidering function is anentropic and therefore mostly exclusionary'[10] – and

9 The allusion, of course, being to the waiter's 'conversation with himself' at the close of 'A Clean, Well-Lighted Place': 'he knew it all was nada y pues nada y nada y pues nada. Our nada who art in nada, nada be thy name thy kingdom nada thy will be nada in nada as it is in nada . . .' (Hemingway 2004, 424). Mary Holland notes that Wallace also alludes to this moment in 'A Supposedly Fun Thing I'll Never Do Again' when he refers to the ocean as a 'primordial *nada*' (Holland 2006, 221; Wallace 2010, 262, italics in original).

10 The term 'entropy' was coined in 1948 by Claude Shannon, who – as Andrew Warren and Conley Wouters have noted – appears to be referenced in *The Pale King* (Warren 2012, 399; Wouters 2012, 458). Wallace's interest in the notion of entropy likely came via Pynchon; Boswell traces the way in which *Broom* makes use of the ideas of thermodynamic and informational entropy in a manner reminiscent of *The Crying of Lot 49* (Boswell 2003, 51–9).

points out that he has been consistent in his exclusion of 'Memoirs', which he tends not to 'trust' (Wallace 2012a, 308). He highlights the 'agenda' behind the form and suggests that contemporary memoirs often conceal 'an unconscious and unacknowledged project, which is to make the memoirists seem as endlessly fascinating and important to the reader as they are to themselves' (Wallace 2012a, 309). There is a clear link between Wallace's criticism here of the impulses driving memoir writing and the 'David Wallace' narrator's revelation of his own mercenary motives for writing *The Pale King* in the form of a memoir (Wallace 2011b, 79–81). This link is also genetically verifiable: Pietsch's index of draft material shows that Wallace worked on the 'Author here' section between November 2006 and May 2007 and thus wrote the material more or less contemporaneously with 'Deciderization' (Wallace n.p., 36.1).

From here, Wallace begins to consider the values of a writing that displays the marks of successful deletion and discarding. He confesses his admiration for work that exhibits 'clarity, precision, plainness, lucidity, and the sort of magical compression that enriches instead of vitiates', using the same word as he had in the *Bookworm* interview – 'magical' – to describe an act of successful literary condensation (Wallace 2012a, 310). From this admission, he asks the reader to consider the possibility that 'it is possible for something to be both a quantum of information and a vector of meaning', with an essay capable of being both factually informative and structurally instructive: the essays, he claims, act as 'models and guides for how large or complex sets of facts can be sifted, culled and arranged in meaningful ways' (Wallace 2012a, 312). The following pages explore the political implications of Wallace's accusation that the 'polity and culture' have failed, during the Bush years, at the task of 'paying attention and handling information in a competent grown-up way' (Wallace 2012a, 313). Wallace identifies one essay as being representative of 'a special subgenre I've come to think of as the service essay, with "service" here referring to both professionalism and virtue';[11] ultimately, what Wallace appears to value most in these pieces is 'a special kind of integrity in their handling of fact' (Wallace 2012a, 315).

This 'special kind of integrity' (which manifests itself in the responsible culling and arranging of detail) leads Wallace to offer a warning, in the essay's final pages, which provides a clear hint as to the concerns behind his final novel's

[11] The essay in question is Mark Danner's 'Iraq: the War of the Imagination', first published in *The New York Review of Books* in December 2006.

Keatsian title.[12] Wallace praises the essays he has selected for being 'utterly different from the party-line pundits and propagandists [...] for whom writing is not thinking or service but more like the silky courtier's manipulation of an *enfeebled king*' (Wallace 2012a, 316, my emphasis). Wallace then begins a new paragraph, but his ellipsis pulls the reader forward and the repetition of the royal simile serves to drive home the point:

> ... In which scenario we, like *diminished kings* or rigidly insecure presidents, are reduced to being overwhelmed by info and interpretation, or else paralyzed by cynicism and anomie, or else – worst – seduced by some particular set of dogmatic talking-points. (Wallace 2012a, 316, opening ellipsis in original, italics added)

Wallace ends by suggesting that the work of the ethical writer represents a kind of mindful selectivity that is alive to the danger of 'reflexive dogma' and 'rigid filters', akin to a morally wielded form of editorial power (Wallace 2012a, 316). He acknowledges his own failings – 'I'm aware that some of the collection's writers could spell all this out better and in much less space', before ending by stating that the pieces he has selected are 'models – not templates, but models – of ways I wish I could think and live in what seems to me this world' (Wallace 2012a, 317). The state of affairs in which we find ourselves akin to pale, diminished kings, then, requires the construction of 'models' not just for writing, but for thinking and living. This activity, carried on in the midst of the present-day swirl of information, suggestion and analysis – what DeLillo described in Wallace's memorial service as 'the vast, babbling, spin-out sweep of contemporary culture' (DeLillo 2012, 24) – is (as *The Pale King*'s Sylvanshine realizes) as difficult as 'trying to build a model in a high wind' (Wallace 2011b, 9), but it is a necessary act, combining creation as well as compression, development as well as reduction, authoring as well as editing.

'Not another word': Reticence and reserve

Wallace's stated interest in the possibility of expressing oneself 'better and in much less space' is not – or, at least, not entirely – a self-deprecating strategy

[12] As noted in Chapter 6, Hayes-Brady suggests Keats' 'La Belle Dame Sans Merci' as the source for the novel's final title (Hayes-Brady 2016, 59–60). The function of this title, however, remains opaque, as Wallace's drafts do not appear to contain any clear comments on its relationship to the form and thematic preoccupations of the text.

and is explored in an increasingly self-conscious thematic way within his late fiction. 'A Radically Condensed History of Postindustrial Life', for example, was published in *Ploughshares* in Spring 1998, less than a year after the aforementioned *Bookworm* interview. Dan Tysdal's complex reading of the story takes it to be a careful rewriting of Carver's early stories (with its characters afflicted by 'muteness' and 'inarticulation'); in this reading, Wallace takes Minimalism as the 'discursive field' of the story, working through the problems and limits of the model in order to achieve a new application of the form and 'reveal the communication still possible' within its boundaries (Tysdal 2003, 66–83). In writing *The Pale King*, Wallace frequently returns to these boundaries, creating images of narrative compression that are often keyed to literary references. Several critics have already identified within *The Pale King* references to authors associated with a minimal or compressed style: §8, for example, which details the childhood of Toni Ware, has prompted a number of comparisons. While the style of the chapter has been compared to Cormac McCarthy (Bucher 2012, n.p.; Kirsch 2011, n.p.), its narrative content also points towards writers with whom Wallace is rarely associated. Stephen Burn suggests that the character of Toni Ware 'seems to represent Bret Easton Ellis' shock-based aesthetic, an approach that Wallace felt was antithetical to his own, which might explain why Toni has a first name that yields the anagram of NOT I' (Burn 2012a, 382). This is suggestive, but leads one to wonder why Wallace was still, many years after his criticisms of Ellis in his interview with McCaffery, concerned with dissociating himself from the writer (Wallace 2012d, 25–6); if we accept this suggestion, it would support my contention that Wallace was still engaged in an aesthetic dialogue with Minimalism long after the evolution of his own style. The anagram suggested by Burn could also, as Clare Hayes-Brady has suggested, be read as a direct reference to the Beckett play of the same title (Hayes-Brady 2016, 135); further references to Beckett, as I will discuss shortly, can be seen elsewhere.

We might also observe, though, that the story takes place in what has been described as 'Carver Country', a place of trailer parks, truck stops and helpless poverty, described by Carver as 'the dark side of Reagan's America' (Carver 1990, 201). In her introduction to *Carver Country: The World of Raymond Carver*, Gallagher notes that among the features of this semi-imaginary landscape (a place, as McGurl notes, whose borders are shifting, 'stretching to encompass almost any overtly ordinary, obscurely hurtful place') are: bad luck, poverty, 'the tyranny of family' and 'unexpected malice' (Carver, Adelman and Gallagher

1990, 8–19; McGurl 2009, 179).[13] Toni, we are told, 'read stories about horses, bios, science, psychiatry, and *Popular Mechanics* when obtainable [. . .] she read halves of many torn and castoff things' (Wallace 2011b, 58), a line that suggests a synecdoche for the fragmentary form that Wallace considered for the novel itself and also provides a possible intertextual link to Carver's *WWTA*. Carver's story 'Popular Mechanics' (which portrays a couple arguing violently over custody of a baby) is, at less than 2 pages, the shortest in the collection. The title was, in fact, given to the story by Gordon Lish, although this fact did not emerge until *Beginners*, with its accompanying bibliographical apparatus, was published in 2009.[14] Elsewhere, critics have noted in *The Pale King*'s §6 – in which Lane Dean and his girlfriend talk around the question of her pregnancy – a close thematic echo of Hemingway's 'Hills Like White Elephants', in which a couple indirectly discuss the possibility of an abortion (Deresiewicz 2011, n.p.; Max 2012a, 292–3; Meatto 2011, n.p.; Wouters 2012, 453).[15]

These intertextual links are often submerged, however, and a closer examination of Wallace's drafts shows a recurring engagement with some of the canonical writers of what could be termed the twentieth-century lineage of minimalist fiction. To begin with, we may observe that several of the characters who serve as focal points for questions of moral value in the novel are associated with a minimal, compressed style of communication. I will begin by looking at §22, the lengthiest section and certainly one of its least 'minimal' in terms of narrative style. While Chris Fogle's own narrative method is one of verbal excess – it is characterized by 'David Wallace' as being hamstrung by its habit of 'foundering in extraneous detail' (Wallace 2011b, 271) – it is notable that the two father figures who influence his commitment to the Service are characterized by their verbal reserve. Fogle's biological father is reticent – 'he and I never talked about it directly' – as well as pithy, as he demonstrates in his

[13] Gordon Burn introduced his 1985 interview with Carver with a description of his view from the train from New York to Syracuse, encompassing 'the non-deluxe tract homes and trailer parks that for a growing number of devotees are coming to mean Carver country'. He opined that 'Underclass America is a territory which [. . .] Carver has made so distinctively his own that you feel you can almost hear the baby wails, vacuum-cleaner squeals and recriminatory, ketchup-hurling brawls emanating from the trackside dwellings as the train flies past' (Carver 1990, 117).

[14] The story had previously been published in journals as 'Mine' and 'Little Things', respectively (Carver 2009, 1009).

[15] McGurl's lengthy 2014 essay on Wallace's relationship to institutions is structured around a comparison of the author to Hemingway: he detects – in spite of the obvious contrast between the 'terseness' of Hemingway and the 'incessant talkiness' of Wallace – a shared 'conservatism' in the way their works display 'a conception of therapeutic community' and suggests that the 'bounded infinity' Wallace creates in *Infinite Jest* represents 'the maximalist version of the clean, well-lighted place' (McGurl 2014, 35–9).

one-sentence, Shelley-quoting summation when his early return home catches his son stoned with friends (Wallace 2011b, 170). His clothing – 'understated and conservative' – and appearance – the texture of his hair is 'stiffer than my own' (Wallace 2011b, 173–4) – are characterized by compression and reserve. His bodily movements, meanwhile, display a discipline and self-denial that manifest themselves as controlled, deliberate behaviour: 'He was both high-strung and tightly controlled, a type A personality but with a dominant superego, his inhibitions so extreme that it came out mainly as exaggerated dignity and precision in his movements' (Wallace 2011b, 174). If we were to take this description as an analogy for prose style, we might think of the fiction of early Hemingway (who liked to be known, of course, as 'Papa'), with its clipped, terse sentences hinting at underlying trauma.[16]

If this association seems an interpretive stretch, it is at least partly supported by the references to Hemingway in Wallace's archive. Indeed, drafts for the Fogle chapter contain one direct reference to the writer. At one point, Fogle notes in an aside that 'the Service material made those textbooks look like Hemingway's *In Our Time* by comparison' (Wallace n.p., 39.6). A handwritten note, with an arrow pointing to this, simply says '*Hemmway Michener?*'.[17] Wallace also owned a copy of Hemingway's first collection of stories (the edition is a 1986 *Scribner Classic* one; there are no indications as to when Wallace read it), and his annotations within the volume show a close study of the author's style. Most of these consist of observations on the technique of the stories, as Wallace observes, for example, the use of understatement in 'My Old Man' – '*Echoes of spare style of other stories*' – and ellipsis in 'Big Two-Hearted River Part 1': '*doesn't tell the reader who Hopkins is*' (Hemingway 1986, 129, 141). On one page of the latter story, he twice wrote the word 'discipline' beside descriptions of Nick making camp. In the final paragraphs of the narrative, he underlined the following lines of Hemingway's: 'His mind was starting to work. He knew he could choke it because he was tired enough.' (Hemingway 1986, 140, 142). With reference to

[16] Hallett observes that 'repressed or compressed emotion is a key function of minimalism – emotion resounding below a fragile, deceptively mute surface' (Hallett 1999, 16).

[17] This reference is opaque and does not appear to have been followed up. The obvious allusion here would appear to be James Michener's introduction to Hemingway's *The Dangerous Summer* (1985), later reprinted in his collection *Literary Reflections* (1993). This suggests an intriguing interpersonal link, since (as previously discussed) this posthumous work was edited by Pietsch; however, the editor is not mentioned by name in the piece, though, as Michener simply provides a general approbation of the double editing job necessitated by the enormous size (120,000 words when only 10,000 were needed) of Hemingway's manuscript (Michener 1994, 182–4). We may note that Wallace was (as detailed earlier) often similarly guilty of 'overwriting' for magazine publication.

this, Wallace wrote in the margin the words '*Wants to shut his head off*. This phrase recalls the many struggles between characters and their 'heads' in *Infinite Jest*[18] and is directly echoed in one of that novel's passages: 'Gately gets to the shelter at 0459.9h. and just shuts his head off as if his head has a kind of control switch. He screens input with a fucking vengeance the whole time' (Wallace 2006, 435). The annotations, then, suggest a thus-far-unexplored intertextual link between Hemingway's alter-ego and one of the principal protagonists of Wallace's most celebrated novel.

Returning to Fogle, it is notable that his other father figure – the 'substitute father' (Wallace 2011b, 176) – is also presented in terms that suggest narrative compression. His choice of clothing is reminiscent of Fogle's father's – he wears 'an archaically conservative dark-gray suit' – and his physical presence is compact and concentrated: 'He seemed lithe and precise; his movements had the brisk economy of a man who knows time is a valuable asset' (Wallace 2011b, 215). The visual impact of this presence, for Fogle, is striking, recalling archaic images of selfhood: '[He] had a steel-colored crew cut and a sort of pronounced facial bone structure. Overall, he looked to me like someone in an archaic photo or daguerreotype' (Wallace 2011b, 217). His appearance creates associations of masculinity and military control (the substitute has his hands behind his back, as in the 'military position' (Wallace 2011b, 227)), and in attempting to explain the man's visual appeal, Fogle turns to an analogy that again hints at the scorched intensity of Hemingway's post-war stories:

> One way to explain it is that there was just something about him – the substitute. His expression had the same burnt, hollow concentration of photos of military veterans who'd been in some kind of real war, meaning combat. His eyes held us whole, as a group. (Wallace 2011b, 218)

In one draft of this chapter, in fact, the substitute's appearance creates associations of a more specifically literary nature: the Jesuit, here, 'also looked like Samuel Beckett', and Wallace's handwritten note in the margin amends this to '*a little like photos of Samuel Beckett, or a Dust Bowl farmer in Walker*

[18] The word 'head', or variations thereof, appears abundantly in *Infinite Jest* to designate a site of suffering: examples include the narrator's observation that 'The Disease makes its command headquarters in the head'; Otis P. Lord's misfortune in emerging from the Eschaton debacle with a 'Hitachi monitor […] over his head'; James Incandenza's chosen method of suicide, executed by 'putting his head in the microwave'; Gately's understanding that 'What's unendurable is what is own head could make of it all' and his sensation of being 'trapped inside his huge chattering head' (Wallace 2006, 272, 527, 693, 860, 922).

Evans' Let Us Now Praise Famous Men' (39.6, underlining in original). The double association here links Beckett's minimalist austerity with the economic austerity embodied in Evans's photographs of impoverished sharecroppers. The allusion to Beckett's appearance can surely be placed alongside what appears to be a reference to *Waiting for Godot* elsewhere in the novel. One examiner's description of his or her idea for a play without any action – 'He sits there longer and longer until the audience gets more and more bored and restless, and finally they start leaving' – contains (in its provocative refusal of expected narrative development) strong echoes of Beckett's major theatrical work; it is notable that the word 'minimal' – 'the setting is very bare and minimalistic' – appears here in one of two instances in the published version of the novel.[19] The examiner's description of his compositional process here pointedly refers to his reflexive wielding of the editorial function: 'At first there was a clock behind him, but I cut the clock' (Wallace 2011b, 106). The invocation of Beckett and Hemingway within the same draft suggests a focus on the ideas and methods common to the minimalist approach: Hallett suggests, in a chapter entitled 'Tracing the Roots of Minimalism', that 'if Beckett's aesthetic psyche can be seen as the philosophical matrix for minimalism, so too Hemingway's artistic formula can be identified as the stylistic genitor of contemporary minimalist prose' (Hallett 1999, 37).

Indeed, Fogle soon begins to comment upon the substitute's technique as well as his appearance, noting that he uses 'transparencies' (a word suggesting a clear, modest style) and discusses different methods of effecting 'deductions' (a word suggesting cutting and compressing) (Wallace 2011b, 218). In one striking moment, the man's technique and his appearance appear almost as one: 'when he put the first transparency on the overhead projector and the room's lights dimmed, his face was lit from below like a cabaret performer's, which made its hollow intensity and facial structure even more pronounced' (Wallace 2011b, 218). The substitute's economical and transparent methods of communication lead Fogle to something of a double revelation about both his late father and methods of presentation more generally:

> This was partly due to the substitute's presentation, which was rapid, organized, undramatic, and dry in the way of people who know that what they are saying is too valuable in its own right to cheapen with concern about delivery or

[19] The second occurs in relation to Drinion's bodily movements (Wallace 2011b, 448).

> 'connecting' with students. In other words, the presentation had a kind of zealous integrity that manifested not as style but as the lack of it. I felt that I suddenly, for the first time, understood the meaning of my father's term 'no-nonsense', and why it was a term of approval. (Wallace 2011b, 219)

In a draft of this section, the description quoted here reads: 'not as ~~affect~~ **style** but as the lack of it'; the change of word here strengthens the analogy with literary style (Wallace n.p., 39.6). Fogle realizes, for the first time, the power of a mode of communication that allows for minimal interference and eschews digression. Indeed, the substitute's delivery uses silence and absence as a structuring feature: 'It might be fair to say that I remembered the substitute Jesuit as using pauses and bits of silence rather the way a more conventional inspirational speaker use physical gestures and expressions' (Wallace 2011b, 231).[20] The substitute goes on to extol the values of 'Effacement. Sacrifice. Service' before declaring: 'To put it another way, the pie has been made – the contest is now in the slicing. Gentlemen, you aspire to hold the knife. Wield it. To admeasure. To shape each given slice, the knife's angle and depth of cut' (Wallace 2011b, 231–2). The imagery here is that of cutting and selecting, and if we are to pursue the literary analogy, we might note that what the substitute is describing comes closer to revision, or to editing, than to writing.

Wallace's interest here is not only in the auto-editorial techniques of literary compression themselves, but also in the ethics of a writing that attempts to distil experience to its essence. His engagement here with what I loosely term 'minimalism' is not tied to a particular writer or school and is decidedly ambiguous. However, as I have shown, clusters of references link several of the characters depicted as conveying qualities of authority, focus and integrity to some of the key figures in the lineage (a primarily male lineage, insofar as Wallace alludes to it) of twentieth-century minimal style. Intertextual allusions show a recurring fascination with the way in which minimalist techniques – Beckettian brevity, Hemingwayesque reticence, Carverian silence – display the power of withholding. In 2001, James Wood had accused Wallace and others of displaying, in their conspicuously generative maximal fictions, a 'fear of silence'

[20] Silence tends to feature in any analysis of minimalist technique: Ihab Hassan's (1971) study of postmodern literature, for example, focused on 'certain authors [namely, Hemingway, Kafka, Genet, and Beckett] (who give themselves to silence)' (Hassan 1971, ix). The term was often used in relation to Carver's technique, as in Michael Wood's (1981) review of *WWTA*, 'Stories Full of Edges and Silences'; we might recall Wallace's own description of Carver's world as one 'full of mute, beaten people' (Wallace 2012d, 45–6).

(Wood 2001, n.p.); the evidence suggests that in his late work, the author was consciously taking a different approach.[21]

It is surely not coincidental that Wallace, during this time, refused to involve his editor in the processes of textual compression and distillation. During the years of composition, Pietsch received none of this work in progress, and the author appears instead to have reserved and appropriated the editorial function for himself. In 1996, Wallace had described the editor to Lipsky as a 'hero',[22] and it is notable that the word recurs multiple times in *The Pale King*, often in ways that suggest an editorial function. The narrator of §17 praises 'institutional heroes, bureaucratic, small-h heroes [...] the kind that seemed even more heroic because nobody applauded or even thought about them', and the substitute Jesuit's announcement that 'the heroic frontier' now lies in 'ordering and deployment' of material specifically valorizes the act of conscientious mediation as the highest good (Wallace 2011b, 127, 232). Indeed, Even Brier argues that the editor becomes a kind of 'hero' in the era of 'the conglomerate takeover of the US publishing industry'; in an industry being rapidly subsumed within corporate structures, the literary editor becomes 'the protagonist in the struggle to defend literature from the forces of capital, commercialism, and homogenization, assuming the role occupied by suffering artists in so many earlier accounts' (Brier 2017, 85, 101). In Chapter 1, I noted Mark McGurl's claim that 'postwar American fiction has been driven by a strong polarity of minimalist and maximalist compositional impulses' (McGurl 2009, 377); in *The Pale King*, Wallace appears deliberately to incorporate this polarity into the developing text, with the heroic editor moving to the forefront of the ideologically freighted struggle between them. The continual tension – manifested in multiple sections of the work – between narrative expansion and restraint creates a dialectical relationship between minimal and maximal modes of literary expression and constitutes an ongoing dialogue within the text over its own methods (a dialogue that, as I will show in the final chapter, manifests itself repeatedly in Wallace's drafting process).[23]

21 Severs points out that Wallace often paid close attention to his reviews, arguing – with particular focus on Wood's use of the phrase 'irrelevant intensity' to characterize *Oblivion*'s prose, and Wallace's subsequent invention of 'irrelevant' Chris Fogle – that he was influenced by criticisms of his work and responded to them within his fiction (Severs 2015, 129–32).

22 Wallace encouraged Lipsky to acknowledge Pietsch's contribution to *Infinite Jest*: 'I mean, I think he's a little bit of a hero, and it would be nice if he got some of the good attention' (Lipsky 2010, 103).

23 McGurl proposes a particular meeting of competing artistic impulses in late twentieth-century US fiction, arguing that maximalist and minimalist energies come together in a 'collision of opposites' he refers to as 'miniaturism'. This mode, exemplified in *The Program Era* by Bharati Mukherjee, Robert Olen Butler and Donald Barthelme, endeavours to condense 'a maximalist relation to language into

While my analysis here focuses on *The Pale King*, I wish to briefly consider Wallace's final story collection, which demonstrates some of the same concerns. Boswell has argued that the intense experience of reading *Oblivion*, which he describes as Wallace's 'bleakest' book (Boswell 2013, 151), is intimately related to the spectre of claustrophobic narrative excess it presents: the maximalism of the narrative method (incorporating the formatting of the text and the grammatical constructions) works to create an experience of suffocating solipsism, rendering 'a visual analog for the state of consciousness Wallace depicts in the stories themselves' (Boswell 2013, 151–2).[24] Noting the 'lack of mental control' afflicting many of the collection's 'key figures', Boswell argues that *Oblivion* is 'unique' in Wallace's oeuvre in its 'unrelenting pessimism', with the ensuing novel intended as 'a corrective, or at least a dialectical partner' (Boswell 2013, 160, 168). This 'corrective', I suggest, works to portray a positive counterexample to the unrelenting maximalist nightmare of solipsistic interiority experienced by the characters in *Oblivion* whom Boswell (paraphrasing a line from Wallace's *This Is Water*) claims are 'hypnotized by the constant monologue inside their own heads' (Boswell 2013, 163).

Indeed, if we take as an example the celebrated story 'Good Old Neon' (which Boswell, as I mentioned earlier, reads as part of a 'trilogy' including the Fogle chapter (156)), we can see how this 'corrective' or tension between opposing narrative impulses is incorporated into the narrative in a similarly complex form.[25] As in Fogle's monologue, we are presented with a narrative style that is digressive and, at times, self-confessedly 'clumsy and laborious' (Wallace 2005a, 153). Neal acknowledges the irony of the fact that the monologue – intended, he says, as 'an abstract or sort of intro' – is, in its maximalist method, 'exhausting and

small forms' and presents a performance of linguistic mastery and 'total vision' within carefully established boundaries (McGurl 2009, 375–80). Wallace's late fiction draws much of its energy from this 'collision of opposites', but does not sit comfortably within this mode; the coexistence of maximalist ambition and minimalist silence in *The Pale King* is, I argue, far less comfortable than in the examples McGurl gives, and the tension between them is highlighted rather than elided. It would be more accurate to say, in this case, that Wallace attempts to import an intractable minimalist resistance into the encyclopaedic novel, generating an ostentatiously self-critical maximalism that frequently appears to be animated by an urge towards reduction.

24 The 'entire volume', Boswell argues, 'appears on the page as a vast, unbroken wall of text', and the narratives, at an individual level, use textual plenitude as a mimetic (and perhaps antagonistic) strategy: 'each story locates the reader in the protagonist's word-drunk interior and traps her there for the story's gruelling duration' (Boswell 2013, 152).

25 One draft of this story, in fact, is introduced with a quote from Beckett's *The Unnamable* ('It is well to establish the position of the body from the outset, before passing on to more important matters' (Wallace n.d., 24.3)).

solipsistic' for the listener (148–53).[26] Like Fogle, he repeatedly gestures towards the excessive nature of his comprehensive explanatory narrative, pointing out 'all the English that's been expended on just my head's partial contents' (note, again, the distancing word 'head') and suggesting, in the way he ends a particularly long explanation with the word 'etc', that he himself is exhausted by his narrative methods (153, 162, 177). Neal's ostentatiously comprehensive discourse is illustrative of nothing so much, here, as his 'mind's ceaseless conniving about how to impress people' (160), and the textual overload serves as a mimetic device for his depression and narcissism. We are presented with several images of this fraudulent and self-defeating verbiage: he continues his relentless verbal baiting of Dr Gustafson, for example, partly in order 'to see how much he'd put up with' (156). The episode in which Neal attempts to impress his religious acquaintances by 'speaking in tongues', meanwhile, is notable for the way in which he manages to convince himself 'that the tongues' babble was real language', as he abandons 'plain English' in his quest to impress (157). Towards the end of the story, Neal drives past a 'cement overpass so covered with graffiti that most of it you can't even read' (176–7), a sight that reflects the way in which his relentless mental and verbal activity cancels itself out.

As the story progresses, we are given occasional glimpses of alternative discourses, approaches that would counteract this relentless and paralysing accumulation of language. The first of these comes when Neal notes, almost as an aside, that Gustafson occasionally provides 'helpful models or angles for looking at the basic problem' (164); the doctor's focus on the simple division between fear and love is, he admits (repeating the word Wallace focuses on in 'Deciderization'), 'a different *model* or lens' (166, my emphasis) through which to consider his despair. Shortly after this, Neal suggests that language loses its 'temporal ordering' after death, with the words reaching (in his mathematical metaphor) towards 'some limit toward which the series converges' (166–7). This limit is described as 'epiphany or insight' (the traditional goals of the short story, we may note) and is figured in terms of linguistic compression: 'imagine everything anybody on earth ever said or even thought to themselves all getting collapsed and exploding into one large, combined, instantaneous sound' (167). Neal coins the description 'word-sum' to describe this moment of insight, a

26 The monologue is, we are told, designed to mimic 'the internal head-speed' of the 'ideas, memories, realisations, emotions and so on' taking place within the narrator's consciousness (Wallace 2005a, 148–53).

compound word which emphasizes the way in which this limit of language is imagined in terms of compression and distillation.

This anticipates the image of the 'keyhole', which will recur several times in the story's final pages (172, 178, 180) – a word which, as I noted in Chapter 6, Pietsch removed from one of the drafts of the Fogle chapter. The word suggests the compression of perspective necessary for communication ('As though inside you is this enormous room [...] and yet the only parts that get out have to squeeze out through one of those tiny keyholes' (178)) and can be read as a meta-commentary on the story's narrative method, a movement from exhaustive maximalist discourse towards an acceptance of the need for a refining, filtering 'model' that may be necessary to combat the disabling plenitude of the lines of thought that go 'into the sort of inbent spiral that keeps you from ever getting anywhere' (181).[27] Driving through the fog, Neal notes the 'minor paradox' of the fact that 'sometimes you can actually see farther with low beams than high', an observation that takes little interpretive pressure to be understood as a suggestion that a deliberately restricted focus may prove more illuminating or that less might, in some circumstances, be more (177). Indeed, the final lines of 'Good Old Neon' suggest that the relentless chatter of consciousness can only be stilled by the author-figure's 'commandment' to himself to utter '"Not another word"', an injunction that echoes the minimalist rebuke of language made explicit in several canonical minimalist short stories (181). The reader, may, at this point, be reminded of Jig's outburst in Hemingway's 'Hills Like White Elephants' – 'would you please please please please please please please stop talking?' (Hemingway 2004, 406) – or, indeed, the title of Carver's 'Will You Please Be Quiet, Please?'.[28]

'The monk's cell and the hermit's cave': Wallace's 'Via Negativa'

In one section of John Barth's (1986) essay on Minimalism, he chose to frame the opposite poles of narrative technique by invoking contrasting impulses embedded deep within the Western religious tradition:

[27] Hallett claims that Minimalist stories offer 'a key-hole perspective through which the reader can infer a vista of knowledge, experience, or meaning' (Hallett 1999, 19).

[28] Indeed, Hallett refers to both of these examples in her analysis of the final lines of Mary Robison's story 'May Queen', in which the protagonist demands of her father: 'Will you shut up?' (Hallett 1999, 109).

> The medieval Roman Catholic Church recognized two opposite roads to grace: the *via negativa* of the monk's cell and the hermit's cave, and the *via affirmativa* of immersion in human affairs, of being in the world whether or not one is of it. Critics have aptly borrowed those terms to characterize the difference between Mr. Beckett, for example, and his erstwhile master James Joyce, himself a maximalist except in his early works. (Barth 1986, n.p., emphasis in original)

The connections between these differences, and their historical links to contrasting spiritual approaches, are visible in a work in which, in Severs's words, figures 'tax examining as holy office' (Severs 2017, 207). In his study of the maximalist novel, Stefano Ercolino considers the relationship of his chosen genre to literary Minimalism and takes issue with Barth's suggestion that these compositional impulses can be considered to alternate in a cyclical manner. As well as arguing for the necessity of 'a *longue durée* perspective', he suggests that Minimalism and maximalism can be seen as concurrent, related phenomena that are '*dialectically coexistent*':

> Two elementary possibilities of human expression which have always existed side by side (as in the 1980s and 1990s for example) or alternated [. . .] in determining the aesthetic horizon of a given literary system. A dialectical coexistence in which both tendencies have undergone *phases of dormancy* and *acute phases*, without one or the other, however, ever disappearing completely. (Ercolino 2014, 70)

Ercolino's conception of the relationship between Minimalism and maximalism is persuasive in the way it allows for the complexity of their interrelationship and guards against simplistic understandings of literary periodicity. Indeed, its emphasis on a long historical perspective is a useful lens through which to view Wallace's late interest in compression, fragmentation and reduction. We can, I suggest, consider *The Pale King*'s interest in narrative compression alongside McDermott's related attempt to, as he puts it, 'expand the valences of "literary minimalism"' and further explore Barth's suggestion that 'minimalist practices' can be found 'everywhere in the history of world literature' (McDermott 2006, 2).

The Pale King, after all, as we saw in the previous chapter, contains explicit references to Catholicism and religious asceticism, and the drafts of the 'Cede' section set in Ancient Rome seem to demand the kind of deep-focus historical lens Ercolino advocates. Botha, indeed, argues that asceticism – 'the systematic pursuit of existential austerity by various processes of discipline, abstinence, renunciation, privation and denegation' – is one of the 'most pervasive and curious transhistorical minimalist phenomena' (Botha 2017, 137). Certainly, the novel displays a recurring impulse to retreat to the 'hermit's cave', in Barth's words, even as it valorizes the civic engagement of the IRS immersives who show their attention to human affairs in the way they 'attend fully to the interests of the client' (in the substitute Jesuit's words) and 'give [themselves] to the care of others' money' (Wallace 2011b, 231). Keeping Barth's formulation in mind, we could say that the novel explores both of these 'roads to grace', while depicting an asceticism that requires intense personal struggle and, perhaps, an internalization of the disciplinary mechanisms of the editorial function.

The drafts of the 'Cede' narrative, as I have noted, are interspersed in one draft (the same draft in which we find the references to Hemingway and Beckett), with Fogle's story and that of the 'kissing boy'. The former section contains clear references to early religious practices and describes a scene of spiritual and physical austerity caused by food shortages in 109 AD:

> Only the Neozoroastrian goat-herders of eastern Pontus – nomadic and apolitical, whose dietary reliance on the hardy goat and long-standing custom of drinking their own urine insulated them somewhat from the ravages of drought – only the herders of eastern Pontus survived in any numbers; and of these a certain percentage found themselves so denuded and refined by inanition that they became, like dander or sheets of fine Nile parchment, capable of airborne flight. (Wallace n.d., 39.6)

The goat-herders, here, are presented as physical emblems of reduction. Their bodies are so 'denuded and refined', indeed, that they find themselves to be capable not just of 'the passive, static Zoroastrian levitation touted in the *Zend Avesta* but [. . .] actual flight' (italics in original). The reference to the collection of sacred Zoroastrian texts as well as to the 'sheets of fine Nile parchment' creates a clear analogy between religious asceticism and literary minimalism, as the men's bodies themselves become so reduced as to be comparable to the pages of a holy text. If we are to read this sentence as another oblique image of literary minimalism, then the author's meta-commentary provides another layer of interest: beside the passage quoted above, Wallace wrote on the draft page (seemingly as a direction to himself) the words '*shorten sentence*'.

The subsequent paragraph frames the fictional phenomenon as a spiritual and physical occurrence:

> The resemblance of the airborne Neozoroastrians to 'seraphic visitations' – a resemblance compounded by the sheaths of sparks that reportedly encased and

> illumined any activity in the dry night air of second-century Asia Minor – is believed by some scholars to render the Pontic Flights the probable source of the 'Martyred Angels of Bythnia' motif so favored by fourth-century Byzantine mosaicists.

The flights, we are told (in the final paragraph of the section), are curtailed by a temptation that recalls Christianity's Edenic myth; the men glimpse the orchards of Antioch and cannot resist gorging themselves on the fruit, 'losing altitude and motility with each mouthful' until they are devoured by enormous hounds. This short section has the gnomic intensity of a parable – we are told no more about the goat-herders in the subsequent pages – and it may, in Wallace's hypothetical 'final' version of the novel, have been developed further or discarded. It evokes ascetic practices, however – to borrow some terms from the *Bookworm* interview discussed earlier, the men 'condense' themselves almost to the point of self-'effacement' – and it strengthens the impression that Wallace was looking beyond the twentieth century and, indeed, beyond fiction in his search for models of textual austerity. Recall that Wallace's literary references, in his conversation with Silverblatt, moved quickly from works of fiction – Markson, Rilke, Kafka – to a set of texts whose compressed styles work in the service of philosophical and spiritual enlightenment: 'What you're talking about is a very condensed, aphoristic – you're talking about *Thus Spake Zarathustra* or *The Philosophical Investigations* or *The I Ching* or really really good, really really good poetry.' *The Pale King* contains several allusions to works which, like the ones mentioned here, express philosophical ideas in an elliptical, fragmented and distilled manner. In the previous chapter I noted allusions to Marcus Aurelius' *Meditations*, a text that proceeds through a series of non-chronological fragments (Wallace 2011b, 18; Wallace n.d., 39.7). In §19, Nichols refers (during the discussion on civics) to Pascal, while in §33, Garrity's ghost alludes to the writer's *Pensées* as well as to figures of religious asceticism, the 'monks under Benedict' and 'the hermits of third-century Egypt' (Wallace 2011b, 143, 383). The narrator of §36 refers to mystics from various religious traditions as well as to E. M. Cioran's aphoristic (1937) study of the ascetic practices of the saints, *Lacrimi Si Sfinti* (Wallace 2011b, 396–402). The 'idiosyncratic rites' of the 'unorthodox priests' that Severs finds in *The Pale King* might be seen as a particular form of ascetic practice, gesturing towards what Botha terms a 'holy minimalism' that works towards 'a transfigurative encounter with the divine' (Botha 2017, 142).

In his analysis of the *Philosophical Investigations*, McDermott takes Wittgenstein's final work as an example of what he refers to as 'the episodic remark text', arguing that 'we should understand [the book] to be collection not of structures built up through painstaking addition but of lesser fragments that remain after a negative regime of subtraction and paring down'. He focuses on the style of Wittgenstein's argument in the *Investigations*, arguing that the author's 'minimal style – his exclusion of unifying style features so consistently that their absence becomes a dominant feature of his writing –' is essential to the argument expressed (McDermott 2006, 18–19). I do not attempt, here, to pursue a substantial analysis of the influence of the *Investigations* on *The Pale King* (not least because of the ample body of existing criticism that traces Wittgenstein's influence on Wallace's thought).[29] Nor do I intend to present a thorough consideration of Wallace's engagement with any of the individual religious and philosophical texts mentioned here: such an examination is beyond the scope of this book. I do, however, suggest that the minimal 'episodic remark text' is frequently present in Wallace's final novel as an intertextual genre or, indeed, a 'model', to use Wallace's words, and that its morally responsible use of silence and absence functions in part as an implicit critique of the surrounding cultural noise.

Literary minimalism, McDermott has argued, is inherently oppositional in nature, with methods of textual compression implicitly functioning to 'rebuke the inauthenticity of a set of contemporary discursive practices' (McDermott 2006, 3). A conspicuously reduced narrative mode serves immediately to evoke a 'comparison' with a discursive mode or linguistic field that is implicitly critiqued, placing the writer in the role of 'discursive reformer' who adopts 'a critical, adversarial role' in relation to predominant modes of discourse (McDermott 2006, 4–6, 12, 40).[30] In this manner, he suggests an understanding of a lower-cased literary minimalism as a reactive strategy used by writers who, while working in very different historical circumstances, share a suspicion of master narratives and discourses of certainty. McDermott's analysis of the political implications

[29] In his recent survey of Wallace scholarship to date, Kelly notes that the references to Wittgenstein are too numerous to list (Kelly 2015, 56); Boswell's early reading of Wallace's engagement with the philosopher's thought in *Broom* has been particularly influential (Boswell 2003, 21–64).

[30] Wittgenstein's style, for example, implicitly challenges 'metaphysical philosophy and its claims to logocentric Truth' (McDermott 2006, 12). The austere style of the early Carver stories, meanwhile, challenges its historical context in the way it calls into question 'Reaganite propaganda and its claims to essentialist community'. McDermott here follows the way in which critics have often seen Minimalism as, to quote McGurl, 'a form of resistance to the self-assertive blare of modern American gigantism' (McDermott 2006, 12; McGurl 2009, 295).

of Carver's aesthetic – and, indeed, of the minimalist aesthetic more generally – overlaps significantly with Andrew Hoberek's re-evaluation of the aesthetic strategies of DeLillo's fiction. Hoberek argues provocatively that DeLillo's writing can be said, under close scrutiny, to be 'engaged in a shared project with the minimalist school that came to prominence during the same period in which his career took off', in the way that he 'transposes a typical minimalist strategy onto the nonminimalist terrain of the big novel concerned with history' (Hoberek 2010, 102–3). Against the distinctions made in received narratives of US literary history (between Minimalism's private, domestic focus and the 'maximalist novel about history whose standard DeLillo takes up'), Hoberek argues that DeLillo's attention to objects acts 'as a kind of counterweight to abstract theory' and the universalizing abstractions of the post-war school of 'Modernization theory' that found their expression in the ambitious US foreign policy strategies that ran aground in Vietnam and Iran in the 1970s. The word 'counterweight' here emphasizes the reactive, socially aware practice contained in the writer's aesthetic response to a flawed and broken public discourse and recurs in the claim that *White Noise*'s 'investment in fragments' can be seen as 'a deliberate formal counterweight to the abstractions of U.S. foreign policy' in the same period (102–17). We might be reminded, here, of Wallace's letter to *New Yorker* editor Deborah Triesman in which he not only referred to the accompanying story as a 'fragment' but also listed his return address as 'Fragmentco Unltd', figuring his post-*Infinite Jest* artistic practice as the unending production of partial narrative elements rather than coherent wholes (Triesman 2014).

These analyses, which presents the literary minimalist as a 'discursive reformer' who reduces and curtails narrative methods in order to enter into an implicitly antagonistic relationship with a particular field of discourse, are, I suggest, relevant to an understanding of Wallace's late work. In 'Deciderization 2007', the 'model' of the successfully compressed, ethically aware non-fiction piece functions as a response to the 'Total Noise' of the cultural environment and as an implicit rebuke to the 'silky courtier[s]' whose irresponsible discourse pervades the body politic (Wallace 2012a, 316). In that piece, Wallace presents the writers of the selected essays as discursive reformers of a kind, offering up edifying texts that 'yield and illuminate truth instead of just adding more noise to the overall roar' and counteract the disabling plenitude of contemporary communication: such texts can be seen as socially responsible, civic-minded contributions to discourse ('service essay[s]' (312–15)). In this case, responsible minimalist practice is presented as a 'counterweight' (Hoberek 2010, 114) to the dogma, propaganda and cant of a debased contemporary discourse. The interpretive leap from Wallace's critique of essayistic style towards his own fiction is, I argue, not a great one. After all, in the conversation with Silverblatt quoted previously, Wallace himself appears to think about non-fictional and fictional forms together, moving from *ASFTINDA* to *Infinite Jest* to Carver to the *Philosophical Investigations* within the same answer. We might also note, as Severs does, the 'massive archives' of factual information Wallace accumulated in researching his final novel (the Ransom Center holds material relating to his attendance at accounting classes as well as numerous documents on the IRS and contemporary tax law) and conclude that the 'abyss' Wallace was attempting to traverse in his writing of *The Pale King* was, in part, one of informational abundance: Max quotes a note from Wallace to a former colleague in which he writes, 'You can drown in research. I've done it. I'm arguably doing it now' (Severs 2017, 283; Wallace n.d., 26.2–7, 41.8; Max 2012a, 322). The fact that the language of 'Deciderization' contains such clear echoes of the concerns addressed in *The Pale King*, moreover, would appear to licence a critical pathway similar to that followed by the many critics who have taken Wallace's 'essay-interview nexus' of 1993 as an interpretive key to understanding *Infinite Jest* (Kelly 2010, n.p.).

I do not suggest that this analysis maps neatly onto Wallace's own late literary style (which is, of course, frequently 'maximal' in its verbal density); rather, I argue that Wallace writes the dynamic explored here into the world of *The Pale King*, presenting certain of its characters as figures of discursive reform and returning repeatedly to a suggestion of the 'overall value' possible as a result of successful literary compression (Wallace 2012a, 311). In *The Pale King*, canonical high-modernist minimalism, along with a 'holy minimalism' (in Botha's words) exemplified by the compressed austerity of 'spiritual and religious literature' (to use Wallace's formulation from the *Bookworm* interview) is repeatedly pointed to as a model for the kind of service that the writer can provide. These models are frequently invoked in oblique allusions (e.g. descriptions of clothing and bodily movements) as well as more explicit intertextual ones such as those noted above. Moments such as Fogle's 'conversion' scene, meanwhile, model the way in which a recuperated, morally serious minimalist practice can be not only effective, but also necessary. The figure of the edifying, authoritative minimalist is presented in *The Pale King* as a 'counterweight' to a decadent cultural present in which, as the men in §19 put it, citizens have abdicated personal responsibility in favour of consumerist excess ('we all go about our individual self-interested business and struggle to gratify our appetites') and public discourse serves as 'surface rhetoric' acting only to enable social degeneration (Wallace 2012e, 138). The substitute Jesuit's focused, 'no-nonsense' presentation functions as an implicit rebuke to this rhetoric and to the cultural discourses that have left Fogle (to borrow Wallace's words from 'Deciderization') 'paralyzed by cynicism and anomie' (Wallace 2012a, 316).

In this way, Wallace's late writing carries on an oblique and unresolved argument about literary style that had preoccupied the author for a number of years. We have seen that the kinds of virtues he extolled in his public comments on writing during this time (as, e.g. when he praised the essays he had selected in 2007 for their 'limpidity, compactness' and 'absence of verbal methane' and hence their sense of 'overall value' (Wallace 2012a, 311)) were in many ways editorial ones, while the writers he praised and alluded to were often those he valued for their abilities to make less out of more. These abilities, as Severs argues, are intimately tied to the author's moral and philosophical concerns about the role of the writer in the information age, since the 'technocratic authority' established through the judicious application of professional skills had, in Wallace's understanding, become a prerequisite for serious political engagement. The 'technicians, technocrats and bureaucrats' Severs sees in Wallace's late fiction – *The Pale King*'s 'institutional heroes, bureaucratic, small-h heroes' humbly going about their work – are heroes to the extent that their technical expertise and information management skills enable them to become 'worthy, democratic moral authorities' (Severs 2017, 247–9; Wallace 2011b, 127). In 'Deciderization', Wallace made the ostentatiously self-aware admission that he was 'aware that some of the collection's writers could spell all this out better and in much less space' than he himself could (Wallace 2012a, 317); similarly, 'David Wallace's' own narrative techniques in *The Pale King* are comically loquacious and exhaustive and provide an ambiguous counterpoint to figures such as the substitute Jesuit and Drinion. In the final chapter, I will pursue this argument further, tracing this anxious self-critique through Wallace's manuscripts as the author begins more and more explicitly to grapple with the problem of editing his own work.

8

The anxiety of editorial influence

The editor's art, as we have seen, is one that can profoundly affect a work's development. By examining the degree of editorial involvement in particular texts (or sets of texts), we strengthen the empirical foundations of our criticism and gain a clearer view of the different and often complex forms of agency involved in their development. However, we can also gain new insights by reading the story of the work's development back into the writing itself. Fordham quotes Tzvetan Todorov's contention that 'every work, every novel tells across the fabric of its events, the story of its own creation, its own story' (Fordham 2010, 29), and a genetic awareness can allow us a clearer view of such stories. Manuscripts can display the complex, dynamic relationship between process and form and help us better understand how, in Van Hulle's words, 'the composition process is an integral part of what [. . .] authors' works convey' (Van Hulle 2008, 2). The close editorial relationships described in the previous chapters are often implicitly characterized as discrete episodes divorceable from authorial intention – impersonal, ephemeral outsourcing arrangements that can be neatly bracketed off from the rest of the writers' oeuvres. However, the sustained editorial processes that were so essential to Carver and Wallace in their development can be apprehended not just in the work that resulted directly from these encounters but also in the work produced over subsequent years as the authors, in their different ways, integrated the demands and dynamics of editing into their compositional processes.

Writing is inherently social, after all, and the act of producing a written document involves entering into a complex series of social transactions.[1] This chapter will focus on the writer's continual negotiation with these concerns and

[1] Bryant writes, for example, of how the editors of the 1968 Northwestern-Newberry edition of *Typee* worked to uncover a unitary 'private Melville' unencumbered by political and commercial considerations. In response to this, he argues for a perspective that accounts for the multiple and sometimes contradictory intentions involved: 'aesthetic and social concerns', Bryant writes, 'impinged upon [Melville's] intentions throughout all periods of composition' (Bryant 2002, 23–40).

the editor's central role in representing them. Editing is necessarily dialectical rather than harmonious, a process that (as we have seen) involves continual arbitration between sensibilities and agendas that may be quite distinct. The editor's role is, to a significant extent, that of a necessary antagonist, an ambassador of cultural and practical forces whose responsibility it is to effect some degree of alteration to the existing textual situation. This necessary antagonism is perhaps the primary reason for the critical importance of understanding the editor's role. I follow Bryant here in seeking to preserve some distinction between the role of author and editor: the designation of 'co-author' or (in Bryant's phrase) 'authorial collaborator' seems an imprecise label for the functions performed by Lish, Pietsch and editors in general (Bryant 2002, 7). An editor always works with an existing set of documents, and the movement towards a published text is unlikely to take place without a degree of friction and dissent: 'most collaboration', as Bryant observes, 'derives from conflict'. To collapse the distinction between author and editor into a vague notion of 'collaboration', therefore, or to fold the entirety of the editor's activity into an expansively defined set of authorial intentions inevitably obscures the 'conflicting sensibilities' upon which the editing process depends (Bryant 2002, 7–8).

In an address to a creative writing class in 2009, author Toby Litt discussed the Carver controversy, warning of the dangers of imitating the distinctively austere style in the light of the emerging understanding of the stories' complex textual genesis. These stories, he noted, describing Carver and Lish's stylistic and thematic struggle, were 'the painful achievement of not one but two men'. He warned students that if they tried to imitate these stories, they would 'be internalising what was (to begin with) a two-way process' (Litt 2009, n.p.). I wish here to highlight this notion of struggle and to examine the way an awareness of the tensions involved in textual negotiation might result in a kind of 'internalising' process on the part of the author. An author will, after all – over a period of years and a variety of publications – come inevitably to anticipate particular forms of critical presence and to more readily apprehend the inevitable mediating influence of the publishing apparatus, as represented most directly and forcefully by the editor. This anticipation of editorial opposition, I suggest, feeds back into the work as the writer internalizes the dynamics of the editorial process and manifests itself as an oblique sense of anxiety. I frame this anxiety, drawing on Harold Bloom's celebrated theory of poetic transmission, as one of editorial influence.

Adapting Bloom's formulation allows us to focus on the tension and anxiety inherent to the textual encounter. To accept the notion that conflict is essential to successful collaboration is to understand the editing process as inevitably, to some degree, antagonistic – or, to use a term favoured by Bloom, agonistic. Bloom's notion of the 'agon', of course, refers to the struggle carried on by 'strong poets' against their precursors by way of deliberate misreading; conflict, in his theory, is essential to the creative process, and literary development proceeds through a dialectical process of 'both contraction and expansion' as the 'ratios of revision' alternate with the processes of creation (Bloom 1973, 95). This conflict is understood within a paradigm of solitary creation, however, as the singular artist wrestles with a chosen 'prior poet': the social dynamics of textual production are narrowed to relationships between individual artists, and the possibility of editorial agency is not considered.[2] Bloom's notion of poetic struggle, then, has little to say about the social processes of composition – and, specifically, the dynamics of editorial intervention – which this book has taken as its subject, or about the way in which this 'dialectical process' might involve editorial agency: the 'revisionary ratios' upon which he outlines do not incorporate the evidence of literal textual revision.[3] My borrowing of Bloom's terminology, therefore, does not imply an acceptance of all of the assumptions upholding his theoretical apparatus, but is grounded in the belief that Bloom's diagnosis of anxious self-definition as an essential dynamic of creation and his view of literary development as a contest for aesthetic supremacy (a 'battle between strong equals' (Bloom 1973, 11)) can be productively brought into contact with theories that emphasize the social nature of writing.

One of these points of contact can be found in Bloom's emphasis on the future-oriented nature of the condition he diagnoses: 'the anxiety of influence', he writes, 'is an anxiety in expectation of *being flooded*' (Bloom 1973, 57, italics in original). While the writer is concerned with overcoming the force of the precursor or 'prior poet', therefore, the fear is of future influence. Bloom is drawing on Freud here in order to advance a notion of 'separation anxiety' in

[2] In a line that summarizes the thesis of *The Anxiety of Influence*, the qualifying clause explicitly limits the theory to the psychological struggles between individual artists: '*Poetic Influence – when it involves two strong, authentic poets, – always proceeds by a misreading of the prior poet, an act of creative correction that is actually and necessarily a misinterpretation*' (Bloom 1973, 30, italics in original).

[3] To take one example, Bloom invokes *The Waste Land* as an example of how Eliot 'became a master at reversing the *apophrades*' and succeeded in overcoming the influence of Tennyson: Pound's involvement in the poem is not mentioned (Bloom 1973, 142, italics in original).

a parallel between poetic and biological birth: however, his emphasis on the forward-looking nature of this tension – the way it implicitly operates in relation to an impending textual event – is useful in considering the editorial transaction. McGann, after all, also emphasizes the future-oriented nature of literary work when he argues that being in 'the textual condition' is to be 'constrained and determined by a future which at all points impinges upon [the] present text' (McGann 1991, 95). This sense of the approaching future – whether manifested as excitement or apprehension – is an inevitable aspect of the editing process, as Eggert's definition stresses: 'an editor', in his words, 'mediates [. . .] between the text or texts [. . .] and the audience of *the anticipated publication*' (Eggert 2009, 156, italics added). We might consider the anxiety of editorial influence as a sense of unease informed by past textual mediation and an awareness of the inevitability of the way in which synchronic writing processes will lead, via this mediation, to a diachronic publication.

In the following section, I trace this sense of anxiety through Carver and Wallace's late work as they reckon with the role of the editor in their fiction. In Carver's late stories we see him obliquely representing the difficulties involved in social authorship in narratives that dramatize the struggle of co-authorship and the resulting separation of author from work. In Wallace, we see an increasingly auto-editorial presence in his drafting process, a critical dialogue with the writing self that contributes towards the structural deadlock of his final novel.

'The handwriting business': Carver's editorial anxiety

In Chapter 2 we saw how, in the final stages of Carver and Lish's collaboration, their struggle over textual control was often carried on obliquely and in public, with paratextual materials showing barely concealed efforts to assert control over the production and interpretation of the texts they produced together. Critical accounts of the end of their relationship have tended to describe it as ending in a clean break. Monti, for example, writes that 'after *Cathedral*, the writer and editor finally parted ways: Carver to become the praised master of the short story and Lish to continue his work as fiction editor, talent scout, and writer with discontinuous success and a slow descent in popularity on the literary scene' (Monti 2013, 62–3). Stull has declared that with *Cathedral*, Carver 'declared his independence as a master. In the five years that remained to him, the only "outside" influences on his work were Gallagher and Chekhov' (Stull 1989, n.p.), while in his assessment of the Lish papers, Max suggested that the editor's influence could be viewed as an 'apprenticeship' that the author ultimately 'transcended' (Max 1998, n.p.). Upon closer inspection, however, these narratives come to seem altogether too neat. While these statements perhaps hold true as factual descriptions of the men's working relationship, they simplify and underplay the extent to which Lish's extensive and continuous involvement in Carver's career continued to inform the author's writing life.

The most obvious evidence for this lies in Carver's interviews and the way in which they show – as I discussed in Chapter 4 – that the author was continually obliged to respond to questions about his early style. Throughout his final years, interviewers repeatedly probed Carver on the question of Minimalism and his supposed stylistic 'evolution'. In 1986, he denied the stylistic tag in conversation with John Alton, later crediting the shift to a more 'hopeful' and 'positive' style to 'the circumstances of my life' such as sobriety and remarriage; in the same year, he claimed (to Stull) that the different versions of 'So Much Water So Close to Home' derive from 'a period when I rewrote everything'; and in 1987, he told David Applefield that the stories in *Cathedral* 'weren't pared down as much as the earlier stories' and were 'fuller, more generous' as a result (Carver 1990, 153–67, 187, 209–10). At times, interviewers asked him directly about his former editor, as Michael Schumacher did in 1987. Carver responded with praise both effusive and evasive, praising Lish for being 'a great advocate for my stories' and 'very important to me at a time when I needed to hear what he had to offer' while ignoring the question of textual editing: elsewhere in the same interview, he repeated the claim that stories republished in *Fires* and *Cathedral* were his own 'revisions' (Carver 1990, 229–35). Even in the spring of 1988, during one of the final interviews of his life, Carver was describing his later stories, without elaboration, as 'more companionable' and 'more affirmative' than his early ones (Carver 1990, 245). Even if we disregard the personal toll of the men's acrimonious falling out, we can see that the success of Carver's work with Lish, and its importance in defining the parameters within which his subsequent work would be judged, ensured that their relationship remained a continuous presence in the author's public life. The after-effects of these editorial experiences echo within Carver's post-*WWTA* writing, much of which reflects upon processes of mediation and textual negotiation.

The title story of *Cathedral*, for example, has been tentatively considered in these terms by a handful of Carver critics. The narrative, which depicts a churlish, unlikeable narrator achieving a moment of unexpected transcendence when his wife's blind friend offers to help him draw a cathedral, could be read as depicting a process of co-authorship. Runyon, for example, argues that the story 'invites us to reflect on artistic collaboration' and notes that 'the blind man [. . .] learned from the television program that a cathedral is a collaborative effort among generations' (Runyon 2013, 170). He explores a connection, first made at the close of Max's (1998) piece, between the story and comments that Carver made during a question-and-answer session at Akron University in the spring of 1982, after the story had been first published:[4]

> So take advice, if it's someone you trust, take any advice you can get. Make use of it. This is a farfetched analogy, but it's in a way like building a fantastic cathedral. The main thing is to get the work of art together. You don't know who built those cathedrals, but they're there.
>
> Ezra Pound said, 'It's immensely important that great poems be written, but makes not a jot of difference who writes them'.
>
> That's it. That's it exactly. (Carver 1990, 23)

Runyon notes the loss of 'control' so necessary to collaboration, claiming that at the story's close, 'their joint effort becomes something more like a true collaboration, the kind of collaboration that made cathedrals possible' (Runyon 2013, 171). He notes the way that the controlling image of the blind man's fingers at the close of 'Cathedral' – 'his fingers rode my fingers and my hand went over the paper. It was like nothing else in my life up to now' – echoes the moment at the close of the previous story, 'The Bridle', in which the narrator (upon finding an abandoned horse's bridle left in her motel by a guest) muses that 'Reins go up over the head and up to where they're held on the neck between the fingers' (Runyon 2013, 171; Carver 2009, 513, 528).[5] Craig Raine reads the story's conclusion in a less positive light, arguing that the narrative is a self-revelatory one displaying exactly 'what Carver thought of Gordon Lish':

> It is a story about writing, a story about the editorial process – in which someone without talent is used by someone else to write. The major contributor is the blind man [. . .] It was brave of Carver to write the story. And it is odd that no one, I think, has seen what it is about – mainly because it tells us something we'd

4 Sklenicka dates the composition of the story to the summer of 1981, noting that it was bought for publication by *Atlantic Monthly* in July of that year (Sklenicka 2009b, 371–2). It was published there in September 1981 and republished in *Cathedral* in 1983.

5 Saltzman also notes that 'the bridle is a clear symbol of restraint, of being controlled from without' (Saltzman 1988, 142).

> rather not know – that Carver had courage to disclose the raw material, this kind of self-exposure, but Lish had the literary talent. (Raine 2009, n.p.)

The narrative, he suggests, is an oblique confession that implicitly credits the editor with the skills of literary artifice that enabled the achievement of Carver's stories. We do not need to share Raine's harsh value judgement on Carver's technique (or accept the neatness of the analogy) to note the striking correspondence between an editorial collaboration and the narrative presentation of two agents jointly holding the pen. Indeed, read at this remove, it is difficult not to read 'Cathedral' as a meditation (oblique at the time, but rather less so in the light of the biographical evidence) upon the uncomfortable dynamics of multiple authorship.

The presence of Lish's 'fingers' (to pick up on Runyon's metaphor) in 'Cathedral' is less pervasive – and, as the correspondence and drafts show, more consensual – but nevertheless present in the version of this story published in the eponymous collection (and later republished in *Where I'm Calling From*). Moreover, the story itself allegorizes writing as a social act and also gestures towards the institutional structures – the 'cathedrals' – that surround these acts: a recognition that 'literary production [. . .] is a social and institutional event' (McGann 1983, 100). While the scene of the men's collaboration is private and domestic, it does not require a great interpretive stretch to link their shared efforts to the social processes of the writer–editor relationship or, as McGurl does with Carver's oeuvre as a whole, to the institutionalization of literature as a university-based activity in the years spanning the author's career. The analogy between the act of creation accomplished by the men in 'Cathedral' and the works of fiction jointly produced by Carver and Lish is, though, incomplete. The story itself ends in transcendence, depicting only the moment of joyful artistic achievement, without the contentious aftermath. The stakes for the men's fictional act of creation are low indeed: we assume that the image of the cathedral resulting from their collaboration will not enter the artistic marketplace, that no cultural and financial capital will accrue from its sale and that the attribution of the work will not be contested. The disjunction between the processes of social literary production – the acquisition of 'craft' through shared knowledge and practice, the communal energies of the editorial office and the university classroom – and the singular attribution of a work of fiction on the literary marketplace is not dramatized. This division, I suggest, shows itself later in Carver's work, to a degree largely unexamined in criticism thus far.

Speaking on the occasion of the publication of Carver's *Collected Stories* in 2009, Gallagher suggested that the author's long letter to his editor on 8 July 1980 shows an awareness of a textual shift that will be both shameful and irrevocable:

> His torn state of mind is clearly evident in that letter to Gordon Lish. Ray understands that he owes a great deal to his editor. He also knows that his vision and accomplishment in the stories have been altered so radically that the result will separate him from his work in a painful, compromising way. (Kelley 2009, 2–3)

The editorial incursion into his stories was, she suggests, a discomfiting and traumatic one: 'I do think he felt the story had been violated' (Kelley 2009, 4). Sklenicka's framing of the arrangement as 'a kind of Faustian secret for Carver' points to a similar dynamic of complicity and shame (Sklenicka 2009a, n.p.). Lish himself has described Carver's work as having been 'deformed, reformed, tampered with in every respect' by his editorial intervention (Lish 2015, 209). McGurl's identification of a 'dialectic of shame and pride' structuring the pedagogical environment that produced Minimalism is given a different, more individual cast here, with the 'shame' of editorial intervention lingering beyond the point of 'pride' marked by publication (McGurl 2009, 281–94). We might recall that in the letter to which Gallagher refers, the author suggested that some of the stories were, autobiographically and emotionally, 'too close' for an extensive edit to be acceptable to him, raising the prospect of psychological breakdown: 'my very sanity is on the line here.' He described the prospect of accepting the editorial intervention as a kind of transgression, suggesting that the result would be a sense of separation affecting his relationship to the very act of writing:

> If the book comes out and I can't feel the kind of pride and pleasure in it that I want, if I feel I've somehow too far stepped out of bounds, crossed that line a little too far, why then I can't feel good about myself, or maybe even write again; right now I feel it's that serious, and if I can't feel absolutely good about it, I feel I'd be done for. I do. (Carver 2007, 8 July 1980)

We might also recall Carver's fear, as he expressed to Lish two years later, that if he expected the editor to 'rewrite' his subsequent stories 'from top to bottom', he would be fatally 'inhibited': 'the pen will fall right out of my fingers, and I may not be able to pick it up' (Carver 2007, 11 Aug. 1982).

Some of the dynamics on display here reveal themselves at key moments in Carver's later stories. Several of these contain a more ostentatiously metatextual dimension than the bulk of Carver's early work: the narrator of 'Intimacy', for example, visits his ex-wife in order to gather materials for his fiction, while the late story 'Errand' dramatizes the final hours of Chekhov.[6] However, my focus here will be on 'Blackbird Pie', first published in the *New Yorker* on 7 July 1986 (Sklenicka suggests that it was written earlier the same year (Sklenicka 2009b, 442–3)). The narrator of the story begins by describing a night in his study when, upon hearing a noise in the corridor, he looked up to see 'an envelope slide under the door' (Carver 2009, 598). The envelope, the narrator tells us, was addressed to him, and the nature of the letter inside (and of the story's plot) immediately becomes apparent to the reader:

> I say 'purported' because even though the grievances could only have come from someone who'd spent twenty-three years observing me on an intimate, day-to-day basis, the charges were outrageous and completely out of keeping with my wife's character. Most important, however, the handwriting was not my wife's handwriting. But if it wasn't her handwriting, then whose was it? (Carver 2009, 598)

This problem will structure the remainder of the story, even as the reader comes to realize its illusory and absurd nature. The narrator proceeds to quote from the letter, which announces his wife's desire for an amicable separation, but breaks off repeatedly to address what Sklenicka calls the 'impossible textual puzzle' facing him (Sklenicka 2009b, 443): even while he acknowledges the unlikeliness of any third-party interference and the implausible nature of his disbelief – 'How much more can I say and still retain credibility?' – he insists that he remains, even after many years, 'convinced' of the fact that 'it was not her handwriting that covered the pages of the letter' (Carver 2009, 601). He cites his familiarity with his wife's handwriting as well as his conviction that she would never underline words for emphasis (as the writer of the letter has done), finally stating his case clearly:

[6] Claire Fabre-Clark notes the increased prevalence of 'writer-characters' in Carver's late work (Fabre-Clark 2008, 173–4). A metatextual awareness, it should be noted, is not entirely absent from the author's early work: indeed, McGurl shows how 'the theme of the writing life as an occupation' underlies early stories such as 'Night School' and 'Put Yourself in My Shoes' (McGurl 2009, 273–81). However, the presence of self-referential literary tropes within the stories is, for the most part, far more prominent in those written after 1980. Recall that Ford and others were drawn to Carver's early work precisely because of the absence of overt metafictional play and the way in which it took 'life, not art, as its subject' (Ford 1998, n.p.).

> What I want to say, all I want to say, is that while the sentiments expressed in the letter may be my wife's, may even hold *some* truth – be legitimate, so to speak – the force of the accusations levelled against me is diminished, if not entirely undermined, even discredited, because she *did not* in fact write the letter. Or, if she *did* write it, then discredited by the fact that she didn't write it in her own handwriting! Such evasion is what makes men hunger for facts. (Carver 2009, 601–2, italics in original)

The narrator presently leaves the house, finding his wife – who is holding her suitcase – in the yard, and the remaining pages of the story provide ample evidence of his delusion as she refers repeatedly to her 'letter' and proceeds to leave their home (and, presumably, marriage). A dream-like atmosphere prevails as several horses graze in the couple's yard and the local sheriff and deputy arrive to convey the wife elsewhere: watching her leave, the narrator still finds 'the handwriting business' a 'bewilderment' (607–13).

In 'Blackbird Pie', the authorial status of the written document is central to the plot, and the protagonist's inability to accept its attribution is a structural feature. Our narrator reads the text with the uncanny, unshakeable conviction that it has been inexplicably separated from its author, and this estrangement of the writer from the work becomes a 'bewilderment' that the narrator is unable to surmount. Sklenicka reads the story biographically, noting its place in a 'run of stories' drawing on family material and dealing with marital separation and suggesting that the husband's inability to recognize his wife's handwriting indicates his emotional paralysis: the story, she writes, demonstrates the 'well-worn truth' that 'people change and are no longer recognizable to their own spouses' (442–3). It is, however, also possible to read it as a metafictional meditation on writing in which the threat of textual interference hovers as an unresolved and inexplicable difficulty. The textual integrity of the letter has, in the mind of the narrator, been violated, and the written word is suspected of being uncannily unstable. The reactions of his wife suggest a similar discomfort on her part with the reliability of the document. When he demands explanations, she exclaims '"You didn't read my letter, did you? You might have skimmed it, but you didn't read it. Admit it!"' (607). She refers to the document several times, stating '"it's all in the letter you read"' and anxiously repeats: '"It's all in the letter – everything's spelled out in the letter. The rest in is the area of – I don't know. Mystery or speculation, I guess. In any case, there's nothing in the letter you don't already know"' (Carver 2009, 608, 611).

The story dramatizes the persistent failure of language and the instability of textual communication. Recalling the couple's silent dinner on the night in question, the narrator suggests that 'something – a few words maybe – was needed to round things off and put the situation right again', and the departure of his wife results in an unprecedented linguistic failure: 'for the first time in my life I felt at a loss for words' (Carver 2009, 603, 611). This failure of language is most evident, however, in its written transmission. The narrator performs his own act of mediation throughout the story, presenting three excerpts from his wife's letter (which, he tells us, he can reproduce because 'things stick in my head' (599)). His selectivity is clear, as he reproduces her words only 'in part' (599), and, by the time he presents her third extract, he has decided to deliberately perform an act of editorial fragmentation:

> But now here's the curious thing. Instead of beginning to read the letter through, from start to finish, or even starting at the point where I'd stopped earlier, I took pages at random and held them under the table lamp, picking out a line here and a line there. This allowed me to juxtapose the charges made against me until the entire indictment (for that's what it was) took on quite another character – one more acceptable, since it had lost its chronology and, with it, a little bit of its punch. (Carver 2009, 605)

The text that follows is a fragmented one, a kind of hallucinatory poetic collage of domestic destruction (or, perhaps, deconstruction):

> . . . withdrawing further into . . . a small enough thing, but . . . talcum powder sprayed over the bathroom, including walls and baseboards . . . a shell . . . not to mention the insane asylum . . . until finally . . . a balanced view . . . the grave. Your 'work' . . . Please! Give me a break . . . No one, not even . . . Not another word on the subject! . . . The children . . . but the real issue . . . not to mention the loneliness. . . Jesus H. Christ! Really! I mean . . . (Carver 2009, 605–6, ellipses in original)

The narrator enacts a textual interference of his own as he deliberately rearranges and excises the words on the page; the domestic trauma depicted in so many of Carver's stories is conveyed here in unprecedentedly linguistic terms.

The text is studded with clichés which are conspicuously italicized and is pervaded by a metafictional impulse that continually draws attention to its own language: 'But there was *something else afoot* tonight'; 'I was, I think, *in a rage*'; 'It was at that moment I heard *the muted sound of a doorknob being turned*'; I found it *worth noting* that both men were wearing hats'; 'then *I took heart* and said to my wife . . .' (Carver 2009, 604–11, italics in original). During an interview conducted soon after the story appeared, Carver was asked about 'the deconstructionists', and his answer was unequivocal: he professed no affinity with their approach to literature ('we don't share any common assumptions') and described their 'way of thinking' as 'downright creepy' (Carver 1990, 159–60).[7] In 'Blackbird Pie', though, we see some of the most celebrated tenets of poststructuralist thought figured as literary motifs: the text seemingly divorced from its author, words ostentatiously estranged from their referents and a continual sense of language evading the subject's grasp. This textual instability is presented as an uncanny (even, perhaps, 'creepy') event that causes the narrator 'to feel *uneasy*' and soon to experience anger and 'panic' (Carver 2009, 604, italics in original). The sense of textual mediation – called forth by a letter, a document exemplifying a text on the point of being socialized[8] – hovers throughout the narrative as an opaque and inexplicable threat. The story portrays the painful dissolution of a relationship by displacing the emotional trauma of separation onto the contested authorship of a letter. Carver – who, in Gallagher's words, had been separated from his own work 'in a painful, compromising way' – places the anxiety of attribution centre stage here, echoing the textual struggles through which his relationship with Lish had ended (Kelley 2009, 2–3). Read alongside 'Cathedral' and the other more ostentatiously metafictional stories from the post-Lish years, the story indicates the degree to which Carver had internalized a sense of the instability and contingency of authorship. Central to my argument here is the assumption that editing leaves a mark; that when an author has seen their text 'deformed, reformed' and 'tampered with' (in Lish's words) the process haunts their subsequent work, leaving a reflexive anxiety that registers a lack of control and certainty over the stability of the words on the page (Lish 2015, 209). Carver had, in Gallagher's words, felt himself to be in danger of being

7 In answer to John Alton's question (posed during an interview conducted in October 1986), 'Do you know much about the deconstructionists?', Carver replied: 'A little. Enough to know that they're crazy. They're a very strange bunch. They really don't have that much to do with literature, do they? They don't even *like* literature very much. I don't think they do, anyway. They see it as a series of texts and textual problems and writers as signifiers and such like.' He went on to assert that while the deconstructionist critics with which he was familiar were 'very cordial, very smart, immaculate dressers, and all that [. . .] we're not even talking about the same thing when we talk about literature' (Carver 1990, 160).

8 Churchwell notes, in her analysis of Ted Hughes' *Birthday Letters*, the way in which letters 'ambivalently bridge the public and the private': 'letters', she suggests, 'could be said to literalize the move from the private to the public, as they move from the sender "out" into the world' (Churchwell 2006, 279).

'subsumed by Lish's imagination', an anxiety of influence in which the authorial fear of being 'flooded' (in Bloom's words) by his editor's vision remained as a powerful presence (Gallagher 2017). In this context, the fear that a text might be, as 'Blackbird Pie's' narrator puts it, 'discredited' by the presence of someone else's handwriting takes on a distinctly metafictional resonance.

In Carver's late work, then, we see a repeated turn towards tropes of authorship: the complex yet triumphant portrayal of collaboration in 'Cathedral' gives way to the melancholy unease of disputed textuality in 'Blackbird Pie', which gestures towards the role of the reader in interpreting the 'scraps' left from the writing process. Even as the wife of the narrator of 'Blackbird Pie' leaves him, the couple seek stability in language, as the wife promises to 'write after I'm settled' and the narrator compulsively reflects upon his choice of words in his description of the scene (612). At the story's conclusion, he concedes that 'the letter is not paramount at all – there's far more to this than somebody's handwriting' and yet his closing remarks return the focus towards the written word. This final paragraph – written or at least suggested in part by Gallagher, it appears, albeit that this may be impossible to verify (Gallagher 2017) – gestures towards the textual remnants of a separation:

> It could be said, for instance, that to take a wife is to take a history. And if that's so, then I understand that I'm outside history now – like horses and fog. Or you could say that my history has left me. Or that I'm having to go on without history. Or that history will now have to do without me – unless my wife writes more letters, or tells a friend who keeps a diary, say. Then, years later, someone can look back on this time, interpret it according to the record, its scraps and tirades, its silences and innuendos. That's when it dawns on me that autobiography is the poor man's history. And that I am saying goodbye to history. Good-bye, my darling. (Carver 2009, 613)

The focus here returns to the material documents of a life and the narrator seems, while claiming to be 'outside history', to hold out hope for the persistence of written communication. The writings that make up an archive (or a genetic dossier), he hints, will remain – 'more letters', 'a diary' – and the textual evidence – 'the handwriting business' – will be 'interpreted' in his absence.

The textual 'record' imagined here, with its 'silences and innuendos', is itself not free of ambiguity, and these lines could be read as a gesture towards the future adjudications that will necessarily follow upon a separation. Following the publication of *WWTA*, Carver apparently promised Gallagher to 'get those stories back', a phrase that echoes the sense of dispossession in his earlier complaint to his editor that some of the stories had 'lost too much'; Lish, for his part, was counselled by DeLillo to keep his anger private and to 'take good care of your archives' (Kelley 2009, 4; Max 1998, n.p.). Lish continued to assert his sense of authorship of Carver's stories in private while doing as DeLillo had suggested and 'saving everything that came to me'. His sale of the Carver papers, which he hoped would prove 'combustible' and bring him the 'recognition' he felt his due, figures archival preservation as a form of editorial revenge (Lish 2015, 207). Both author and editor, while continuing their paratextual struggles over a canon that was already being significantly problematized even within Carver's lifetime, were obliged to displace their disagreements onto the evolving archival record, leaving the handwriting business, along with its 'scraps and tirades', to be parsed and interpreted by others.

'What if this book just isn't supposed to be all that long?': Editing and anxiety in *The Pale King*

Anxiety has long been understood as a generative force within Wallace's work. Several critics have invoked Bloom's framework of influence as a model for understanding Wallace's vexed relationship to his literary forebears (primarily, but not exclusively, taken to be the postmodernists of the 1960s and 1970s). A. O. Scott's influential essay from 2000 adapted Bloom's formulation to suggest that Wallace was afflicted by a 'panic of influence' with regard to these precursors, highlighting the way in which the author's fiction portrays 'the self-dramatizing frustrations of the creative process' (Scott 2000, n.p.). Charles B. Harris has argued that Wallace's relationship to John Barth should be understood as 'agonistic', drawing (as do each of these readings) on the author's evident familiarity with Bloom's theories to support the notion that 'Westward' is a '*self-aware* misprision' of 'Lost in the Funhouse' (Harris 2014, emphasis in original). More recently, Lucas Thompson has argued for the importance of Bloom's notion of the *tessera* (or 'antithetical completion') in understanding Wallace's fiction, while suggesting that Bloom's combative notion of influence cannot properly account for the presence of 'multiple and overlapping influences' in Wallace's work (L. Thompson 2016, 40–6, 194–6). Indeed, when we survey Wallace's later work, it becomes clear that the author was beginning to 'include himself' in his pantheon of 'strong precursors' (Harris 2014, 120). Boswell argues that Wallace's anxiety of influence became more individuated in *The Pale King* as the author began to reckon in a sustained way with 'his own aggravating influence', making 'himself the object of his own resentment' (Boswell 2014b, 28). Mike Miley, too, suggests that Wallace was in his later years reckoning with the complex legacy of his own persona, emphasizing how Wallace's anxious self-awareness manifested at every stage of his writing process (even, as Miley shows, in the ostensibly 'private space of reading') (Miley 2016, 193). Hering pursues the appearance of metafictional traces through Wallace's drafts, showing how much of the later fiction – in particular, the dramatic appearance of 'David Wallace' as a central narrator in the drafts of *The Pale King* from 2005 onwards – can be read as evidence of the 'steadily increased presence of an implied author figure' in his work (Hering 2016a, 18).

The anxiety detectable in Wallace's final novel, as these latter analyses show, is of a different order to that visible in his earlier works, resulting from both a practical confrontation with an unprecedentedly intractable structural deadlock and a self-conscious attempt to reckon with the maximalism with which he had become synonymous. Hering describes how the entrance of the 'David Wallace' narrator into the novel represents a 'new and extraordinarily convoluted mode of collative composition, in which Wallace's staging of anxiety over his style is framed within a real-world attempt to make *The Pale King* coherent and publishable' (Hering 2016a, 145). The theme of mediation dramatized in several of the most substantial sections of Wallace's final novel – the need, in the words of the 'substitute Jesuit', to approach the 'heroic frontier' of 'classification, organization, presentation' – coincides with and is exacerbated by the author's own struggle to manage the increasing disorder of his drafts (Wallace 2011b, 232). This 'collative' mode of composition incorporates an 'oppositional motif' into the work, as the stylistically discordant and chaotic mass of drafts are juxtaposed with the controlling energies of the 'master narrator' in a way that foregrounds the tensions of informational abundance (Hering 2016a, 136–7). This 'master narrator', I argue, is also a kind of master editor, since the 'textual presence' represented by the metafictional narrator is, as Hering notes, an 'explicitly curatorial' one primarily concerned with the processes of mediating prior textual information (Hering 2016a, 18). The problem of *The Pale King* becomes in large part the problem of editing, with its author internalizing the editorial function in a sustained attempt to incorporate this heroic capacity to 'hold the knife' and cut responsibly (Wallace 2011b, 232). Gottlieb describes editing as, in essence, a 'service job', a description that resonates strongly with Wallace's valorization of the moral authority of the responsible knowledge work involved in editorial selection and omission in his later years (Gottlieb 2016). Wallace's description of his own editor as a 'hero', his praise of the combination of both 'professionalism and virtue' in the 'service essay' and his dramatization of the heroic effort of discipline required to enter the 'Service' and commit to a life of austerely disciplined desk work allow us to see *The Pale King* as a deliberate and sustained attempt to treat the notion of a 'service job' with the utmost seriousness (Wallace 2012a, 315; Lipsky 2010, 103).

This growing need for the author to select, compress and synthesize his own pre-existing work causes the novel-in-progress, and the authorial persona, to fracture in distinctive ways. In considering the work's complex and self-reflexive genesis, Ferrer's description of a draft as 'a protocol for making a text' hints at the internal conflict attendant upon the accumulation of drafts material. The word 'protocol' appears repeatedly in *The Pale King* (Reynolds and Sylvanshine negotiate a protocol for the following week in their conversation, for example, while David Wallace tells us that he is 'making it a point to violate protocol' and address the reader directly (Wallace 2011b, 369–70, 67)). The word's primary meaning refers to 'the accepted code of procedure or behaviour in a particular situation', clearly a relevant concern in Wallace's continual interrogation of the fraught balance between writer and reader.[9] However, the second meaning given by the *OED* – 'the original draft of a diplomatic document, especially of the terms of a treaty agreed to in conference and signed by the parties' – is highly suggestive here. A protocol in this sense suggests an ongoing process subject to negotiation between competing interests, which may take the form not only of external pressures (such as commercial and editorial demands) but also of internal ones, such as the different intentions put into play by the varying creative impulses of the writer as well as the demands of the different chronological stages of composition. If a writer can be said to be his or her own 'first reader', he or she will inevitably (and repeatedly) return to the work with an auto-editorial perspective (Van Hulle 2014, 11). As the writer becomes an editor, therefore, the fracturing of writerly selves means that the draft page becomes a diplomatic document taking on a dialogic character: this is what Ferrer refers to when he

[9] The word's resonance to the world of computing, too (*OED*: 'a set of rules governing the exchange or transmission of data between devices') resonates powerfully in a novel that dramatizes the onset of the computer age and questions the way in which data is exchanged and processed.

claims that 'the draft page is the locus of a dialogue between the writer and his later self or selves' (Ferrer 1998). The writing process thus makes a work – particularly one with a long and complex gestation period – auto-dialogic.

This reflexive dialogic tension is clearly evident in the 'crisis point' that Hering identifies in Wallace's compositional process. In the note-to-self from May 2005 that Hering quotes, we see Wallace sifting through several years of draft material, searching for a 'key or clue in these old documents', lamenting the fact that several of the 'promising nuggets' in his accumulated manuscripts 'just stop' and reassuring himself that this material does not all have to be 'preserved and used' (Hering 2016a, 123–4). Editorial intelligence is precisely what is needed here in order to bridge the micro and macro levels of narrative unity and conscript the 'discrete achievements' of individual sections into the 'apparently insurmountable large-scale goal' of the novel as a whole (Hering 2016a, 138–9). Rather than turning to his editor at this point of structural crisis, Wallace instead adopts an increasingly editorial posture towards his own writing, consciously trying (in the words of the substitute Jesuit, spoken as he takes hold of his 'dark-gray business fedora') to 'wear the hat' of the responsible, self-effacing Decider (Wallace 2011b, 233). Seen in this moment, Wallace appears almost to become his own Max Perkins, wearing the editor's iconic hat,[10] hunched over boxes of drafts attempting to piece together a coherent narrative from the chaos of incoherent authorial overproduction. Wallace's editorial struggles rapidly come to be enacted in the book's form, as the metafictional narrator who enters the drafts after this point of crisis relates his struggles with the 'abstruse dullness' of archival material, highlights the 'myriad little changes and rearrangements' necessary to present a coherent narrative and apologizes for the lengthy soliloquies of his co-workers (which he claims to have 'heavily edited and excerpted') (Wallace 2011b, 67, 81, 255). The Wallace-narrator justifies the discordant set of narrative strategies (what Hering refers to as the 'convoluted and amalgamated accretion of narrative registers') and acts as the structural backbone of the work, albeit at the risk – as Hering notes – of dominating the text and thereby closing off its communicative possibilities. Wallace's defence against the risk of monologism is to admit and dramatize his mediating activity in order to mitigate this risk and encourage the reader to share the burden of editorial pressure, to insist that the heroic work of sorting and filtering and discarding is our common

[10] Perkins was famous for his eccentric habit of wearing his 'soft gray-felt fedora' hat constantly, both indoors and out (Berg 2013, 52).

responsibility – to join him, as Severs puts it, on 'the cutting-room floor' (Hering 2016a, 145–6; Severs 2017, 243).

The auto-editorial dialogue that results from this strategy is, as I suggested in the previous chapter, a fraught one, as the tensions between narrative expansion and restraint cause Wallace to become his own antagonist. Nick Levey takes *The Pale King*'s enactment of boredom, its 'long and information-filled sentences that describe beyond the needs of mimesis or desire', as evidence of its 'maximalist poetics' and a continued 'promotion of the value of the maximalist literary object' (Levey 2016, 78). This analysis, however, ignores both the extent to which its editor is responsible for the book's textual abundance (indeed, Levey nowhere mentions Pietsch's role in the novel's construction) and the substantial evidence of Wallace's very real reservations about maximalist methods. These reservations are encoded within the work in multiple ways, enacting the conflict between stylistic expansion and contraction: John Jeremiah Sullivan, indeed, noted the degree of conflict in the work by characterizing the clash of styles as a writer's internal argument, suggesting that 'it's as if [Wallace] had inside his head a fully formed hostile critic who despised his own work' (Sullivan 2011). This antagonism to narrative techniques associated with the author's own writing is incarnated in moments where the novel's characters sharply criticize each other's diegetic strategies: 'David Wallace' refers dismissively to Fogle's habit of 'foundering in extraneous detail' while Reynolds loses patience with Sylvanshine's habit of making him listen to 'incidentals' rather than supplying 'useful data' (Wallace 2011b, 271, 360). The 'anticipatory anxiety' that Kelly detects in Wallace's characters' attempts to communicate with one another is keyed here to a fear of suffocating verbosity: Fogle displays an awareness of his own digressive storytelling technique ('Does this make any sense?') while the Happy Hour scene includes Rand's observation that her conversational partner is 'tiring', Drinion's admission that he is 'confused' by her narrative and her own worry that her story is 'boring' (Kelly 2012, 270; Wallace 2011b, 214, 461, 495, 501). The narrator of this scene, in fact, interjects to note the frustration of Rand's co-workers with her communicative abilities (their judgement is that she 'just won't shut up if you get her started' (Wallace 2011b, 489)). Fogle and Drinion both cause their conversational partners to rotate their hands in frustration (Wallace 2011b, 271, 493). To these examples could be added Hering's sharp observation on the self-conscious allusion to compositional techniques in Meredith Rand's difficulties with 'cutting', a problem 'addressed by her husband, the pointedly named "Ed"' (Hering 2016a, 137).

The self-mocking exaggeration of authorial style in the 'David Wallace' chapters also incorporates a comical hint of self-disgust in the repeated references to 'Wallace's horrible skin problems and inability to realise his mistaken assignation' (Wallace 2011b, 286, 309, 335, 337). A hostile critical commentary – indeed, a quasi-editorial one – is embedded within the narrative at several points, and this is sometimes clearly directed at the author-figure himself in what Konstantinou suggests is a parody of 'what Wallace came to dislike most about his own literary style' (Konstantinou 2011, n.p.). The struggle to complete the text becomes the struggle between writer and editor, voluble maximalist and austere minimalist, and is modelled in dialogues that reflect upon the 'attempt to corral and control data' (Hering 2016a, 181). Even without Pietsch's posthumous intervention, therefore, it seems likely that any iteration of *The Pale King* would have encoded the process within the product, like ostentatious sketch lines left in a painting. Indeed, a comparison with the self-editing techniques of the high modernists is instructive here. Hannah Sullivan writes of modernist writers' propensity for 'leaving traces of the revision in the final product' and discusses the 'thematized self-critique' in Jake's narrative in Hemingway's manuscript of *The Sun Also Rises* (Sullivan 2013, 22). Hemingway, she reports, also wrote anxious notes to himself about narrative technique within his drafts, and the novel's genetic development reveals that the writer eventually removed Jake's 'hesitant and self-reflective monologue'; this, by contrast, is exactly what Wallace amplified in *The Pale King* (Sullivan 2013, 115–16).

Drafts can allow us not only to see the inherent 'fluidity' of literary texts (which, as John Bryant notes, is usually hidden from readers) but also, as Bradley puts it in his discussion of the drafts of Ellison's final novel, to see 'writerly conflicts' as a force within the 'living text' opened up by draft material (Bryant 2002, 64–6; Bradley 2010, 4–15). Fordham's analysis of Joyce's 'process of layered revision' in the writing of the 'Circe' chapter of *Ulysses*, for example, argues for a correlation between Joyce's compositional techniques and his textual interest in multiple identity, showing how Joyce's 'process of layered revision' in the 'Circe' chapter of *Ulysses* causes identities to 'multiply like rabbits' (Fordham 2010, 213–26).[11] Wallace's work could be said to show the same continual fracturing of selves: as

[11] An intertextual allusion suggests the extent to which the author was aware of this development: in drafts of the section on Cusk's childhood (§13 of *The Pale King*), the book the protagonist is reading changes from '*Bleak House*' to '[The Picture of] *Dorian Gray*', a work far more explicitly structured around the notion of split personality. This change occurs between log#23 and the apparently later draft designated log#6 (both drafts appear to have been composed from May 2006 onwards) (Wallace n.d., 36.2, 36.4).

I have demonstrated, the identities of several of *The Pale King*'s characters seem to shift and mutate throughout its drafts, generating a 'Tornado of characters' that creates a problematic dissonance in the character of Fogle/Shinn, for example (Hering 2016a, 123). The novel also explicitly dramatizes a problem of mistaken identity in its plot, and a draft note suggesting that there will be '3 David Wallaces' in the novel suggests the dizzying metafictional heights to which this strategy may have led (Wallace n.d., 38.4). Wallace's writing is described by Michael North as 'fissiparous', and his drafts allow us to identify moments when this process of fission was at its most acute and how it was incorporated into the text's development (North 2009, 178).

The dialogic nature of composition thus sometimes renders the experience of reading Wallace's drafts like looking at minutes of a protracted board meeting, the agenda of which concerns the dangers of maximalist overproduction. While this sense of internal division may be a source of dramatic tension in the aforementioned scenes, it is indicative of the 'compositional paralysis' that would threaten to overwhelm the project as a whole (Hering 2016a, 135). Indeed, if we treat *The Pale King* as the result of a dialogue between the writer's many selves, then Wallace's conversation with himself became, primarily, a conversation about the difficulty of completing the work. The work is, after all, studded with images of incomplete or damaged structures. Examples include the 'slapdash and unsound tree house' that Sylvanshine and 'the Roman Catholic boy' had attempted to construct as children; the 'abortive SSP [Self-Storage Parkway] construction' caused by a 'horrific mess of litigation and engineering mishaps'; the 'easily correctable institutional idiocy' that causes a 'snafu' resulting in the complicated floor layout in the REC; the complicated carts of the 'turdnagels', whose 'jerry-rigged' nature causes them to clatter distractingly; and the 'big structural crisis' that Fogle gets 'stuck dealing with' during the Chicago blizzard of '79, as he is attempting to 'make a meaningful, real-world choice' (Wallace 2011b, 12, 235, 296, 305, 237). The language in other instances seems to hint less obliquely at the difficulties of novelistic practice as, for example, Sylvanshine's struggle to organize a study structure is identified as primarily a narrative difficulty: 'what killed him were the story problems' (Wallace 2011b, 9). Fogle notices, in the IRS recruiting station he visits, an 'overfull wastebasket, around which a litter of balled-up papers suggested idle hours of trying to throw balled-up papers into it – a pastime I knew well from "studying" at the UIC library' (Wallace 2011b, 243). Lane Dean's despair as he toils at his desk is accompanied by the sound of tearing paper, summoning an archetypal image of writerly frustration (Wallace 2011b, 378–9).

Max quotes several letters from Wallace to Franzen, dating from November 2005 to June 2007, in which the author discusses the difficulties of structuring and revising his novel. In one, Wallace writes of his difficulty in confronting 'the idea that I'll have to write a 5,000 page manuscript and then winnow it by 90%' (presenting a stark outline of the literal 'revisionary ratios' required to bring his work to completion) and uses the image of torn paper as the physical embodiment of the failures involved in this attempt: 'stuff literally goes right into the wastebasket after being torn from the top of the legal pad' (Max 2012a, 289). The aforementioned chapter featuring Lane Dean's workplace struggles (§33) appears to have been written primarily during this period and while it may not be possible to date the first handwritten draft of the scene, Pietsch's index indicates that several revisions took place in April 2007.[12] According to Pietsch, Wallace described working on the novel as akin to 'wrestling sheets of balsa wood in a high wind', a description echoed within the novel in Sylvanshine's failure to study effectively: 'It was like trying to build a model in a high wind' (Pietsch 2011a, v; Wallace 2011b, 9).[13] Wallace used various narrative techniques to deliberately inscribe his working difficulties within the work, and *The Pale King* illustrates the operations of what Bryant refers to as the 'self-collaborative feedback' implicit in the creative process (Bryant 2002, 99). The manuscripts for Wallace's final novel show a hesitant, painstaking process as the author repeatedly inscribes his frustration and self-doubt within an auto-editorial commentary: in 2006, he wondered, 'what if this book just isn't supposed to be all that long?' (Wallace n.d., 36.1).

§9, of course, consists of David Wallace's lengthy semi-explanation of the 'tortuous backstory' behind his struggles to publish the book we hold in our hands, a struggle involving a 'microscopically cautious [legal] vetting process'

12 The fact that these drafts were almost all composed in a digital medium, of course, highlights the artifice of the ripped-paper image and lends an ironic awareness of compositional medium to the metafictional trope.

13 The drafts of the Sylvanshine chapter appear to have been written in 2005 and 2006. The author's notes in drafts dated between 1999 and 2001 contain an earlier version of this image: 'TRYING TO REVAMP IRS SYSTEM/PERSONNEL SYSTEM/COMPUTER SYSTEM IS LIKE TRYING TO BUILD A CHICKENCOOP IN A HURRICANE' (Wallace n.d., 40.3, capitals in original). Wallace adapted the formulation from Faulkner, as he acknowledged in a letter to DeLillo written while he was struggling to write the essay that would become 'Authority and American Usage': 'Different people have quoted to me something Faulkner apparently said about writing being like trying to build a chicken coop in a hurricane, and it's never quite resonated with me until now' (Wallace 1998e).

instigated at the behest of the publisher and its 'corporate counsel' (Wallace 2011b, 68–70). It is not difficult to see the counterfactual 'Author here' chapters as a lengthy meditation on the difficulties of telling a story (the 'trials and tribulations of process', in Fordham's words (Fordham 2010, 2)); the various institutional tensions and publication difficulties could be seen to stand in for the writer's own working problems here, as the legal delays lamented in the pseudo-autobiographical sections of the narrative echo the discarded pages from Wallace's 'legal pad'. Metafiction fundamentally depends on the fracturing of selves implied in the act of self-reference, and a chronological, genetic view of the manuscripts of *The Pale King* allows us to view this deliberate multiplication of authorial selves as a process that intensified in response to the increasing difficulties involved in writing the novel. Drafts of §9 show Wallace making explicit links to the metafictional legacy of his postmodern predecessors and suggest that the author was drawing on this legacy as a result of the problems (here figured as legal necessities) involved in telling his story: in the second draft, the words 'the last thing in the world this text is is some kind of precious metafictional titty-pincher' are accompanied by a footnote, crossed out by Wallace in the same draft, reading:

> In fact [the] last Barth or Coover I ever read all the way through was 1985, which was also the year I worked at the IRS's Regional Examinations Center in Peoria, Il, where the job was so incredibly tedious and dry that even avant-garde metafiction seemed like a treat in comparison. (Wallace 2012b)

Indeed, the drafts allow us to see Wallace's own response to this deliberate imbrication of his authorial persona within the story and to trace the auto-dialogic nature of even this response: in the first draft of §9, a note-to-self at the bottom of the final page asks 'Dumb? The real-or-fiction theme is cool. But it could get annoying, especially if it keeps interrupting the narrative' (Wallace 2012b). This multiplication of selves is intricately linked with the awareness of the pressures and processes involved in eventual publication. The first draft names his (fictional) literary agent – 'Janet Lear of Turner and Lear' – and also mentions that the manuscript is making its way around 'the big New York publishing houses'; a note in the margin suggests that part of the way through the chapter will come the news that the manuscript has been accepted and that it is 'to be co-edited by Little, Brown's legal dept. along with Mr. Michael Pietsch, to whom I am deeply indebted' (Wallace 2012b).

The drafts of David Wallace's lengthy meditation on the difficulties involved in telling his story not only begin by imagining the material circumstances in which *The Pale King* (called, at the time of this draft, *Net of Gems*) will appear, but also include a named reference to its editor. Wallace's attempt to write his editor into his final novel as a character suggests the degree to which he internalized the struggles of editorial processes and attempted to subsume these within a metafictional, auto-editorial performance. In the previous chapters, we saw evidence of Wallace's powerful awareness of Pietsch's editorial accomplishments: he repeatedly expressed his appreciation for the way in which his editor had managed to pare back the extreme maximalism of *Infinite Jest* to one that maintained the ability to 'identify with the reader' and to maintain a consistent 'track record of inclusion/arrangement issues' (Wallace 1997b, 2005b). These skills are precisely the ones that became essential throughout the long gestation period of *The Pale King*, a period during which Wallace was not yet ready to hand over his work. The mention of Pietsch takes place within a section that encompasses the whole field of contemporary literary production, alluding to the way in which the production of fiction is now taking place in the service of large, conglomeratized publishing houses. It is notable that the scenario presented in this draft implies that Wallace would join Pietsch in 'co-editing' the novel, a move that aligns the author's role entirely with that of the editor.

We know from numerous biographical sources, of course, that the account of the specific publishing difficulties related by the narrator in these chapters is entirely untrue – Pietsch claims that 'at the time of David's death […] I had not seen a word of this novel except for a couple stories he had published in magazines' (Pietsch 2011a, vi) – and it is perhaps not too speculative to suggest that Wallace here is using the entire systemic apparatus behind the production of literary fiction as an expression of his own difficulties in finding a way to bring his work to a conclusion, with the publisher and the 'corporate counsel' being together invoked as a kind of authorial superego regulating the limits of production. The knowledge of future socialization, as McGann suggests, clearly constrains and 'impinges' upon the textual condition (McGann 1991, 95), and inevitable publication seems, in this novel, to be anticipated to a suffocating degree: notes in the drafts of §9 read 'Some parts blacked out by publisher's lawyers', and 'Cross-outs & black-outs in actual book', suggestions which would have encoded the visible marks of the impending editorial process onto the pages of the final product (Wallace 2012b, underlinings in original). The work here becomes a contested document publishable only under conditions of farcical compromise, and its editor occupies the role not only of necessary mediator but also of executive 'Decider'. If we can view *The Pale King* as a diplomatic document, then, a protocol subject to negotiation between multiple competing and even hostile authorial selves, it remains unsigned: its editor's role, ultimately, was to force a compromise between absent and perhaps unwilling parties.

Conclusion

This book is based upon the assumption that an editorial relationship, if it spans a significant period of an author's career, is likely to be, as one editor puts it, 'the author's primary relationship in his or her working life' (Witte 2017, 97). My project has been to redescribe these influential texts in a way that accounts for the strength of this 'primary relationship', emphasizing the social dimension it brings to the creation and reception of the works produced through it.

In both of the cases I have studied, the importance of the editor's contribution is clear. Many of Lish's and Pietsch's activities – the former's aggressive and at times coercive textual changes, the latter's assumption of an executive function in the absence of the author – clearly go beyond an auxiliary role. However, we can also detect a subtler process whereby editorial activity feeds back into the dynamics of writing. In Carver's case, the work produced late in his career bears submerged traces of the lengthy editorial relationship so essential to his early success. The stories written after his break from Lish display this editorial anxiety in displaced allegories of co-creation and textual change in which the process of textual mediation haunts the compositional process. Wallace, meanwhile, appears in *The Pale King* to subsume the editorial function into his authorial performance: figures who might be described as editorial proxies (not to mention the editor himself) become characters in the work, and the problem of managing textual, informational and structural excess arguably becomes its central theme. The bulk of the would-be novel appears to have remained in what De Biasi refers to as the 'compositional phase' of writing, and its author approached the prospect of the text's socialization with extreme hesitancy (De Biasi and Wassenaar 1996, 34–5).[1] Wallace worked for over a decade on his final novel without inviting editorial comment, and the resulting internalization of editorial pressures and anxieties is so visible in the extant work that it could be said to define it.

[1] Apart from those excerpts published in magazine form, little of the work appears even to have entered the 'prepublishing phase' characterized by the presence of 'definitive manuscript'[s] (De Biasi and Wassenaar 1996, 34–5).

In surveying studies of literary collaboration, Stone and Thompson criticize the tendency to construct 'an overarching historical theory from a small number of examples limited by genre, gender, race, and historical context' and suggest that 'historical and empirical research' can be more fruitful than theoretical approaches in challenging assumptions about the way working relationships function (Stone and Thompson 2006, 310–20). This study has proceeded on the assumption that the workings of the editorial processes in questions can best be illuminated by close attention to material evidence and that detailed genetic analysis can be the most effective complement to theoretical abstraction in clarifying the various tensions and conflicts involved. By maintaining a focus on this evidence, we can maintain a productive tension between large-scale literary histories and the singularity and specificity of literary texts and their creators (Foley 2016, 441–2). Lish, for example, is a deeply singular figure: even McGurl's analysis of the way in which he exemplifies a kind of 'programmed' creativity acknowledges the idiosyncratic nature of his own production (Lish's stories, he writes, are 'inconceivable except as the product of Gordon Lish' (McGurl 2009, 292)). Pietsch is not as obviously idiosyncratic in his aesthetic or working methods but is described by Gessen, nevertheless (due to his simultaneous dedication to commercial imperatives and author satisfaction), as 'not a typical editor' (Gessen 2011, 846). A similar desire for precision lies behind my inclination to preserve a distinction between authorial and editorial roles. While the two undoubtedly overlap at crucial moments – we have seen, for example, Lish's 'authoring' of the endings of certain Carver stories, as well as Wallace's increasingly fierce channelling of auto-editorial energy – I argue that this overlap contributes a highly particular dynamic to the writing as well as serving to highlight the problematically liminal position of the editorial role. By preserving the designation 'editor' and resisting the urge to dissolve this work into a vaguely defined 'co-authorship', we maintain a sense of the conflict and struggle that clearly informs the processes of textual development.

We can, however, note some clear differences in how the editorial role operates within different generic modes: the role of the editor in the production of the Minimalist short story, after all, clearly differs from its involvement in the maximalist novel. In the case of Carver's stories, Lish's work was a palpable force, and the severity of textual excision was essential to their stylistic effect: McGurl notes that the discernible 'excess of negative narrative space' in Carver's most heavily edited stories paradoxically signals the editor's 'overbearing presence' (McGurl 2009, 292). Here, we could say that Lish was, in the case of several of the stories, acting at times as something like an equal partner in the dialectic of creation and destruction, composition and decomposition, that structures the development of writing. Lish's place as an outlier on the spectrum of editorial mediation – as an editor, that is, disposed not only to impose his own vision upon an author's work to an unusual degree but also to expect public recognition for doing so – served both to drive the influence of the Minimalist mode and also to make the position of the author in that mode more fraught. Despite the accusations of the mode's reliance upon the systematized methods of the workshop, the figure of the solitary author is central to the successful Minimalist narrative production, as the ostentatiously stylized and compressed piece of short fiction implies a single creator linked to a history of individualized creation.

In the case of maximalist fiction, though, the editor's role appears closer to the traditional self-effacing presence that Perkins imagined himself to be: this is the editor as silent partner, as midwife, as (to recall Perkins's own words) 'a little dwarf on the shoulder of a great general advising him what to do and what not to do, without anyone's noticing' (Berg 2013, 155). The editor becomes a co-manager of excess rather than a merciless surgeon: indeed, Pietsch was so successful in this role that Wallace considered writing him into his final novel as a character. The fact that the work of the editor of maximalist fiction is not palpable at the level of style makes the role less problematic for reader and author. While Carver clearly struggled all his life with the fact of Lish's influence, Wallace was able to make, in the spirit of a boast, the (probably exaggerated) claim that his editor had cut 500 pages. Every word counts in a short story (indeed, in 'On Writing', Carver approvingly cited a line by one of Babel's narrators hailing the power of 'a period put just at the right place' (Carver 2009, 730)): on the other hand, if a page – or even several hundred pages – is cut from a 1000-page-plus novel, it is less clear that the reading experience is altered in such a fundamental fashion. The editor appears here more in the role of a studious curator of the author's words rather than an intimidatingly powerful impresario. Pietsch's influence on Wallace's work – and, by extension, the revival of maximalist fiction – is clear, though, even within Wallace's lifetime. His eagerness to publish, as he put it to his superiors, the next wave of literary 'grandmasters' (Pietsch 1992), his decision to make length and difficulty a commercial selling point and his implicit willingness to publish a book whose size would test the limits of the commercial book production and marketing machine: all were essential factors in the immediate success and subsequent impact of *Infinite Jest*. Since 2008, his importance to Wallace's reception is difficult to overstate. He has worked as the custodian of the author's reputation and of his aesthetic, producing a Pulitzer-nominated novel for which he personally performed publicity duties and curates the author's legacy from the position of CEO of one of the major publishing houses of English-language fiction.[2]

The processes described here have taken place in a rapidly changing publishing environment: Ginna, indeed, claims that 'the publishing marketplace, and the business of serving it, has changed more drastically in the past fifteen years than in the half-century before' (Ginna 2017b, 269). One of these changes has seen agents assume an increasing central position in the network of production of literary fiction, and a study of authors of the generations following Wallace might find itself focused on editorial changes made within the context of a relationship traditionally thought of as a secondary one. John Thompson, for example, devotes a chapter to this phenomenon, arguing that editors at major publishing houses have in effect not only 'outsourced the initial selection process to agents' but have come to expect agents to provide a degree of textual guidance and consultation before the submission of manuscripts (J. Thompson 2012, 59–100). Agent Chris Parris-Lamb has, according to Jonathan Lee, 'been known to work with an author through six entire drafts before deeming their manuscript ready for submission to editors', and this consequence of what the agent refers to as 'the blockbusterization of the book industry' makes it clear that the archival basis for comparative textual studies of this kind may, in future, lie elsewhere (Parris-Lamb and Lee 2016, 175, 183). If, as Gerald Howard puts it, there is a degree to which the increased stakes of publishing and greater managerial pressures upon editors has meant that 'the editing function has shifted to agents', then scholars need to account for this expanded role (Howard 2017). It seems clear that, as Laura B. McGrath claims, agents are 'shaping the field of contemporary literary production' in ways that are not yet fully visible; it may even be the case that the rise of the agent is, in Dan Sinykin's words, 'a great unwritten story of contemporary literary history' (McGrath 2017, n.p., Sinykin 2018, 471).

Pietsch's introduction to *The Pale King* offers readers the chance to 'see what [Wallace] created [. . .] to look once more inside that ~~beautiful~~ **extraordinary** mind' (Pietsch 2011a, vii, 2011b, 1.2). I return to this quotation here (illustrating the replacement of one of Pietsch's words with another in the interval between the

[2] The most notable example of this is perhaps *The David Foster Wallace Reader*, a 2014 sampler aimed at future students.

audiobook and hardback version) as it serves to exemplify several of the themes of this book: the layers of textual mediation hidden beneath the smooth surface of the reading text, the continuing reliance among literary producers and readers on a conceptual model of solitary authorship, the editorial tendency towards self-elision and the critical importance of examining the genesis of writing in order to make this mediation visible. The emergence of a corpus of archival materials around Carver's and Wallace's canonical works – what Gontarski refers to as an author's 'grey canon' (Gontarski 2006, 143) – will undoubtedly inflect future criticism in complicated ways. The status of this canon is uncertain (in Wallace's case, it is only beginning to be negotiated), and it is necessary to read these materials with the same degree of critical engagement as published texts rather than using manuscripts as a way of (as Daniela Caselli, also discussing the 'issue of marginality' in Beckett's oeuvre, puts it) 'bringing interpretation to a close' (Caselli 2010, 13–14). However, manuscripts can, as this study has shown, shed necessary light on what Eggert refers to as 'the central roles of agency and time' in the textual development of works whose complicated provenance is easily ignored, allowing us to see editorial interventions as vivid, decisive events rather than abstract concepts (Eggert 2009, 237). Understanding the temporal and material dimension of texts allows us to see the competing forces operating upon the text in process and to appreciate the fact that even extraordinary minds never work alone.

Bibliography

Adams, Tim. 2009. 'Beginners by Raymond Carver'. *Guardian*, 1 November 2009, sec. Books. http://www.theguardian.com/books/2009/nov/01/beginners-raymond-carver-tim-adams.

Addington, Wells. 2016. 'Will You Please Be Edited, Please?: Gordon Lish and the Development of Literary Minimalism'. *CEA Critic* 78(1): 1–23.

Aldridge, John W. 1992. *Talents and Technicians: Literary Chic and the New Assembly-Line Fiction*. New York: Scribner.

Amir, Ayala. 2010. *The Visual Poetics of Raymond Carver*. Lanham, MD: Lexington Books.

Amir, Ayala. 2012. 'Harsh and Hopeful World'. *American Book Review* 33(4): 5.

Andersen, Tore Rye. 2012. 'Judging by the Cover'. *Critique* 53(3): 251–78.

Andersen, Tore Rye. 2014a. 'Pay Attention! David Foster Wallace and His Real Enemies'. *English Studies* 95(1): 7–24.

Andersen, Tore Rye. 2014b. 'Covered in P: David Foster Wallace's Paratextual Curse'. Presented at the 'Infinite Wallace' conference, Sorbonne Nouvelle, Paris, September 12.

Araya, Jorge. 2015. 'Why the Whiteness?: Race in *The Pale King*'. In *Critical Insights: David Foster Wallace*, edited by Philp Coleman, 238–51. Ipswich, MA: Salem Press.

Arendt, Hannah. 2006. *On Revolution*. Edited by Jonathan Schell. New York; London: Penguin Books.

Athill, Diana. 2011. *Stet: An Editor's Life*. London: Granta.

Atlas, James. 1981. 'Less Is Less'. *Atlantic* June: 96–98.

Auden, W. H. 2009. *Selected Poems*. Expanded Edition. London: Faber and Faber.

Augst, Thomas. 2017. 'Archives: An Introduction'. *American Literary History* 29(2): 219–27.

Baker, Jeff. 2009. 'Northwest Writers at Work: Tess Gallager in Raymond Carver Country | OregonLive.com'. *The Oregonian: Oregon Live*, 19 September 2009. http://www.oregonlive.com/O/index.ssf/2009/09/northwest_writers_at_work_tess.html.

Barekat, Houman, Robert Barry, and David Winters. 2017. *The Digital Critic: Literary Culture Online*. New York: OR Books. Ebook file.

Barrodale, Amie. 2007. 'Gary Fisketjon Edits Your Heroes'. Vice. 1 December 2007. https://www.vice.com/en_us/article/bndnxv/gary-fisk-v14n12.

Barth, John. 1986. 'A Few Words About Minimalism'. *New York Times*, 28 December 1986.

Barthelme, Frederick. 1988. 'On Being Wrong: Convicted Minimalist Spills Beans'. *New York Times*, 3 April 1988. http://www.nytimes.com/1988/04/03/books/on-being-wrong-convicted-minimalist-spills-beans.html.

Beattie, Ann. 1978. 'Carver's Furious Seasons'. *Canto* 2: 177–80.

Bellamy, Joe David. 1985. 'A Downpour of Literary Republicanism'. *Mississippi Review* 14(1/2): 31–9.

Berg, A. Scott. 2013. *Max Perkins: Editor of Genius*. London: Simon & Schuster.

Bethea, Arthur F. 2001. *Technique and Sensibility in the Fiction and Poetry of Raymond Carver*. Studies in Major Literary Authors. New York; London: Routledge.

Bethea, Arthur F. 2007. 'Raymond Carver's Inheritance from Ernest Hemingway's Literary Technique'. *The Hemingway Review* 26(2): 89–104.

Biguenet, John. 1985. 'Notes of a Disaffected Reader: The Origins of Minimalism'. *Mississippi Review* 14(1/2): 40–5.

Birkerts, Sven. 1987. *An Artificial Wilderness: Essays on 20th-Century Literature*. New York: Morrow.

Bloom, Harold. 1973. *The Anxiety of Influence: A Theory of Poetry*. New York: Oxford University Press.

Bloom, Harold. 2002. *Raymond Carver: Comprehensive Research and Study Guide*. Broomall, PA: Chelsea House.

Boddy, Kasia. 2010. *The American Short Story since 1950*. BAAS Paperbacks. Edinburgh: Edinburgh University Press.

Boroff, Philip. 2010. 'Unemployed Harvard Man Auctions Baseball Novel for $650,000'. *Bloomberg.com*, 31 March 2010. http://www.bloomberg.com/news/articles/2010-03-31/harvard-man-unemployed-living-cheap-sells-baseball-novel-for-650-000.

Boswell. 2014a. 'Preface: David Foster Wallace and "The Long Thing"'. In *David Foster Wallace and 'The Long Thing': Essays on the Novels*, edited by Marshall Boswell, vi–xii. New York; London: Bloomsbury.

Boswell, Marshall. 2003. *Understanding David Foster Wallace*. Columbia: University Press of South Carolina.

Boswell, Marshall. 2012a. 'Introduction: David Foster Wallace and "The Long Thing"'. *Studies in the Novel* 44(3): 263–6.

Boswell, Marshall. 2012b. 'Introduction: David Foster Wallace's *The Pale King*'. *Studies in the Novel* 44(4): 367–70.

Boswell, Marshall. 2012c. 'Trickle-Down Citizenship: Taxes and Civic Responsibility in David Foster Wallace's *The Pale King*'. *Studies in the Novel* 44(4): 464–79.

Boswell, Marshall. 2013. '"The Constant Monologue Inside Your Head": Oblivion and the Nightmare of Consciousness'. In *A Companion to David Foster Wallace Studies*, edited by Marshall Boswell and Stephen J. Burn, 151–70. New York: Palgrave Macmillan.

Boswell, Marshall. 2014b. 'Author Here: The Legal Fiction of David Foster Wallace's *The Pale King*'. *English Studies* 95(1): 25–39.

Botha, Marc. 2017. *A Theory of Minimalism*. London; New York: Bloomsbury.

Boyle, T. C. 1988. 'A Symposium on Contemporary American Fiction'. *Michigan Quarterly Review* XXVII(1): 707–9.

Bradley, Adam. 2010. *Ralph Ellison in Progress: From Invisible Man to Three Days Before the Shooting*. New Haven, CT; London: Yale University Press.

Brick, Martin. 2014. 'A Postmodernist's Progress: Thoughts on Spirituality Across the David Foster Wallace Canon'. *Christianity and Literature* 64(1): 65–81.

Brier, Evan. 2009. *A Novel Marketplace: Mass Culture, the Book Trade, and Postwar American Fiction*. Philadelphia: University of Pennsylvania Press.

Brier, Evan. 2017. 'The Editor as Hero: The Novel, the Media Conglomerate, and the Editorial Critique.' *American Literary History* 30(1): 85–107.

Broyard, Anatole. 1981. 'Books of the Times.' *New York Times*, 15 April 1981.

Bryant, John. 2002. *The Fluid Text: A Theory of Revision and Editing for Book and Screen*. Ann Arbor: University of Michigan Press.

Bucci, Richard. 2003. 'Tanselle's "Editing without a Copy-Text": Genesis, Issues, Prospects'. *Studies in Bibliography* 56(January): 1–44.

Bucher, Matt. 2012. 'Pale Winter'. *Simple Ranger* (blog). 13 April 2012. http://www.simpleranger.net/category/paleking/.

Bucher, Matt. 2015. 'A Few Trends in DFW Studies'. *Simple Ranger* (blog). 8 June 2015. http://www.simpleranger.net/a-few-trends-in-dfw-studies/.

Buford, Bill, ed. 1983. *Granta 8: Dirty Realism: New Writing from America*. Cambridge: Granta Publications.

Burk Carver, Maryann. 2006. *What It Used to Be Like: A Portrait of My Marriage to Raymond Carver*, 1st edn. New York: St. Martin's Press.

Burke, Seán. 2008. *The Death and Return of the Author: Criticism and Subjectivity in Barthes, Foucault and Derrida*, 3rd edn. Edinburgh: Edinburgh University Press.

Burn, Stephen J. 2011. 'Consider David Foster Wallace (Review)'. *Modernism/Modernity* 18(2): 465.

Burn, Stephen J. 2012a. '"A Paradigm for the Life of Consciousness": Closing Time in *The Pale King*'. *Studies in the Novel* 44(4): 371–88.

Burn, Stephen J. 2012b. *David Foster Wallace's Infinite Jest: A Reader's Guide*. London; New York: Continuum.

Burn, Stephen J. 2014. 'Toward a General Theory of Vision in Wallace's Fiction'. *English Studies* 95(1): 85–93.

Bustillos, Maria. 2014. 'Philosophy, Self-Help, and the Death of David Wallace'. In *Gesturing toward Reality: David Foster Wallace and Philosophy*, edited by Robert K. Bolger (ed.) and Scott Korb (ed. and introd.), 121–39. New York: Bloomsbury.

Callahan, John F. 2000. 'Afterword: A Note to Scholars'. In *Juneteenth*, 368. Penguin Classics. London: Penguin.

Callis, Tetman. n.d. 'The Gordon Lish Notes'. *The Art of Tetman Callis* (blog). Accessed 30 June 2014. http://www.tetmancallis.com/the-gordon-lish-notes/.

Carver, Raymond. n.d.(a). '"Neighbors", Version 1'. Box 43. Lish Mss., 1951–2012. Lilly Library, Indiana University.

Carver, Raymond. n.d.(b). '"Neighbors", Version 2'. Box 43. Lish Mss., 1951–2012. Lilly Library, Indiana University.

Carver, Raymond. n.d.(c). '"Jerry and Molly and Sam", Version 1'. Box 43. Lish Mss., 1951–2012. Lilly Library, Indiana University.

Carver, Raymond. n.d.(d). '"Jerry and Molly and Sam", Version 2'. Box 43, WYPBQP Draft ms 3. Lish Mss., 1951–2012. Lilly Library, Indiana University.

Carver, Raymond. n.d.(e). '"Jerry and Molly and Sam", WYPBQP, Draft Ms 3'. Box 43. Lish Mss., 1951–2012. Lilly Library, Indiana University.

Carver, Raymond. n.d.(f). '"Sixty Acres", Version 1'. Box 43. Lish Mss., 1951–2012. Lilly Library, Indiana University.

Carver, Raymond. n.d.(g). '"Will You Please Be Quiet, Please?", Version 1'. Box 43. Lish Mss., 1951–2012. Lilly Library, Indiana University.

Carver, Raymond. n.d.(h). '"Will You Please Be Quiet, Please?", Version 2'. Box 43, Printer's Ms. Lish Mss., 1951–2012. Lilly Library, Indiana University.

Carver, Raymond. n.d.(i) ' "The Student's Wife", Version 1'. Box 43. Lish Mss., 1951–2012. Lilly Library, Indiana University.

Carver, Raymond. 1969a. 'Letter to Gordon Lish, 12 November 1969'. Box 2, 1970. Lish Mss., 1951–2012. Lilly Library, Indiana University.

Carver, Raymond. 1969b. 'Letter to Gordon Lish, N.d. December 1969'. Box 2, 1970. Lish Mss., 1951–2012. Lilly Library, Indiana University.

Carver, Raymond. 1969c. 'Letter to Gordon Lish, 4 December 1969'. Box 2, 1970. Lish Mss., 1951–2012. Lilly Library, Indiana University.

Carver, Raymond. 1970a. 'Letter to Gordon Lish, N.d. 1970'. Box 2, 1970. Lish Mss., 1951–2012. Lilly Library, Indiana University.

Carver, Raymond. 1970b. 'Letter to Gordon Lish, 20 August 1970'. Box 2, 1970. Lish Mss., 1951–2012. Lilly Library, Indiana University.

Carver, Raymond. 1975. 'Letter to Gordon Lish, 28 Sep 1975'. Box 2, 1975. Lish Mss., 1951–2012. Lilly Library, Indiana University.

Carver, Raymond. 1977. 'Letter to Gordon Lish, 27 Sep 1977'. Box 3, 1976–1977. Lish Mss., 1951–2012. Lilly Library, Indiana University.

Carver, Raymond. 1980a. '"After the Denim", 2nd Rewrite'. Box 44, What We Talk About When We Talk About Love, 'After the Denim', 2nd Rewrite. Lish Mss., 1951–2012. Lilly Library, Indiana University.

Carver, Raymond. 1980b. '"Tell the Women We're Going", 2nd Rewrite'. Box 44: What We Talk About When We Talk About Love, 2nd Rewrite. Lish Mss., 1951–2012. Lilly Library, Indiana University.

Carver, Raymond. 1980c. '"The Bath", 2nd Rewrite'. Box 44, What We Talk About When We Talk About Love, 2nd Rewrite. Lish Mss., 1951–2012. Lilly Library, Indiana University.

Carver, Raymond. 1980d. 'What We Talk About When We Talk About Love, 2nd Rewrite'. Box 44. Lish Mss., 1951–2012. Lilly Library, Indiana University.

Carver, Raymond. 1980e. 'What We Talk About When We Talk About Love, Master Proofs'. Box 44. Lish Mss., 1951–2012. Lilly Library, Indiana University.

Carver, Raymond. 1980f. 'What We Talk About When We Talk About Love, Printer's Mss.' Box 44. Lish Mss., 1951–2012. Lilly Library, Indiana University.

Carver, Raymond. 1980g. 'Letter to Gordon Lish, 10 May 1980'. Box 3, 1980. Lish Mss., 1951–2012. Lilly Library, Indiana University.

Carver, Raymond. 1980h. 'Letter to Gordon Lish, 10 May 1980 (B)'. Box 3, 1980. Lish Mss., 1951–2012. Lilly Library, Indiana University.

Carver, Raymond. 1980i. 'Letter to Gordon Lish, 18 May 1980'. Box 3, 1980. Lish Mss., 1951–2012. Lilly Library, Indiana University.

Carver, Raymond. 1980j. 'Letter to Gordon Lish, 13 June 1980'. Box 3, 1980. Lish Mss., 1951–2012. Lilly Library, Indiana University.

Carver, Raymond. 1980k. 'Letter to Gordon Lish, 10 July 1980'. Box 3, 1980. Lish Mss., 1951–2012. Lilly Library, Indiana University.

Carver, Raymond. 1980l. 'Letter to Gordon Lish, 17 August 1980'. Box 3, 1980. Lish Mss., 1951–2012. Lilly Library, Indiana University.

Carver, Raymond. 1980m. 'Letter to Gordon Lish, 6 October 1980'. Box 3, 1980. Lish Mss., 1951–2012. Lilly Library, Indiana University.

Carver, Raymond. 1980n. 'Letter to Gordon Lish, 22 November 1980'. Box 3, 1980. Lish Mss., 1951–2012. Lilly Library, Indiana University.

Carver, Raymond. 1981a. 'Letter to Gordon Lish, 19 January 1981'. Box 3, 1981. Lish Mss., 1951–2012. Lilly Library, Indiana University.

Carver, Raymond. 1981b. 'Letter to Gordon Lish, 30 January 1981'. Box 3, 1981. Lish Mss., 1951–2012. Lilly Library, Indiana University.

Carver, Raymond. 1982a. '"Cathedral" typescript'. Box 43. Lish Mss., 1951–2012. Lilly Library, Indiana University.

Carver, Raymond. 1982b. '"Feathers" typescript'. Box 43. Lish Mss., 1951–2012. Lilly Library, Indiana University.

Carver, Raymond. 1982c. '"Fever" typescript'. Box 43. Lish Mss., 1951–2012. Lilly Library, Indiana University.

Carver, Raymond. 1982d. 'Letter to Gordon Lish, 11 August 1982'. Box 3, 1982. Lish Mss., 1951–2012. Lilly Library, Indiana University.

Carver, Raymond. 1982e. 'Letter to Gordon Lish, 13 November 1982'. Box 3, 1982. Lish Mss., 1951–2012. Lilly Library, Indiana University.

Carver, Raymond. 1983. The Art of Fiction: Raymond Carver Interview by Mona Simpson and Lewis Buzbee. *Paris Review* 88.

Carver, Raymond. 1988. 'A Symposium on Contemporary American Fiction'. *Michigan Quarterly Review* XXVII(1): 710–11.

Carver, Raymond. 1989. *What We Talk About When We Talk About Love*. David Foster Wallace, former owner. New York: Vintage Contemporaries. David Foster Wallace Library, Harry Ransom Center.

Carver, Raymond. 1990. *Conversations with Raymond Carver*. Edited by Marshall Bruce Gentry and William L Stull. Jackson: University Press of Mississippi.

Carver, Raymond. 2000. *Call If You Need Me: The Uncollected Fiction and Prose*. London: Harvill.

Carver, Raymond. 2007. 'Letters to an Editor'. *New Yorker*. 24 December 2007. http://www.newyorker.com/magazine/2007/12/24/letters-to-an-editor.

Carver, Raymond. 2009. *Collected Stories*. Edited by William Stull and Maureen Carroll. New York: Library of America.

Carver, Raymond, Bob Adelman and Tess Gallagher. 1990. *Carver Country: The World of Raymond Carver*. New York: Arcade Publishing.

Caselli, Daniela, ed. 2010. *Beckett and Nothing: Trying to Understand Beckett*. Manchester: Manchester University Press.

Chekhov, Anton Pavlovich. 1975. *The Oxford Chekhov, Vol IX: Stories 1898–1904*. Edited and translated by Ronald Hingley. London: Oxford University Press.

Chekhov, Anton Pavlovich. 2011. *Short Stories: About Truth, Freedom, Happiness, and Love*. Translated by Constance Garnett. London: Sovereign.

Chen, Jimmy. 2012. 'Raymond Carver's OKCupid Profile, Edited by Gordon Lish.' 16 November 2012. *McSweeney's Internet Tendency*. Accessed 1 July 2014. http://www.mcsweeneys.net/articles/raymond-carvers-okcupid-profile-edited-by-gordon-lish.

Chettle, Judith. 1981. 'Books in Brief.' *National Review* 33(24): 1501.

Churchwell, Sarah. 2006. 'Your Sentence Was Mine Too: Reading Sylvia Plath in Ted Hughes' Birthday Letters'. In *Literary Couplings: Writing Couples, Collaborators, and the Construction of Authorship*, edited by Marjorie Stone and Judith Thompson, 260–87. Madison: University of Wisconsin Press.

Churchwell, Clare. 2009. 'The Final Cut'. *Guardian*. 24 October 2009.

Clare, Ralph. 2012. 'The Politics of Boredom and the Boredom of Politics in David Foster Wallace's *The Pale King*'. *Studies in the Novel* 44(4): 428–46.

Cliffe, Nicole. 2013. 'What We Talk About: The Authoritative Cut'. *Toast*. 6 November 2013. http://the-toast.net/2013/11/06/what-we-talk-about-the-authoritative-cut/.

Cohen, Samuel and Lee Konstantinou. 2012. 'Introduction: Zoologists, Elephants, and Editors'. In *The Legacy of David Foster Wallace*, edited by Samuel Cohen and Lee Konstantinou, xi–xxv. Iowa City: University Press of Iowa.

Coile, D. Caroline. 2005. *Encyclopedia of Dog Breeds*, 2nd edn. Hauppauge, NY; London: Barron's.

Collins, Joan. 1997. *Second Act*. London: Boxtree.

Contat, Michel, Denis Hollier, Jacques Neefs and Alyson Waters. 1996. 'Editors' Preface'. *Yale French Studies* no. 89(January): 1–5.

Coughlan, David. 2015. '"Sappy or No, It's True": Affect and Expression in Brief Interviews with Hideous Men'. In *Critical Insights: David Foster Wallace*, edited by Philip Coleman, 160–75. Ipswich, MA: Salem Press.

Coyle, Deirdre. 2017. 'Men Recommend David Foster Wallace to Me'. *Electric Literature*. 17 April 2017. https://electricliterature.com/men-recommend-david-foster-wallace-to-me-7889a9dc6f03.

Crispi, Luca and Sam Slote, eds. 2007. *How Joyce Wrote Finnegans Wake: A Chapter-by-Chapter Genetic Guide*. Madison: University Press of Wisconsin.

Cunningham, Michael. 2012. 'Letter from the Pulitzer Fiction Jury: What Really Happened This Year'. *New Yorker*, 9 July 2012. https://www.newyorker.com/books/page-turner/letter-from-the-pulitzer-fiction-jury-what-really-happened-this-year.

De Biasi, Pierre-Marc and Ingrid Wassenaar. 1996. 'What Is a Literary Draft? Toward a Functional Typology of Genetic Documentation'. *Yale French Studies* no. 89(January): 26–58.

de Bourcier, Simon. 2017. '"They All Sound Like David Foster *Wallace*": Syntax and Narrative in *Infinite Jest, Brief Interviews with Hideous Men, Oblivion* and *The Pale King*'. *Orbit: A Journal of American Literature* 5(1).

Dean, Michelle. 2011. 'A Supposedly True Thing Jonathan Franzen Said About David Foster Wallace'. *The Awl*, 11 October 2011. http://www.theawl.com/2011/10/a-supposedly-true-thing-jonathan-franzen-said-about-david-foster-wallace.

Dedner, Burghard. 2006. 'Highlighting Variants in Literary Editions'. *Variants: The Journal of the European Society for Textual Scholarship* 5(January): 15.

DeLillo, Don. 1972. 'Letter to Gordon Lish, 14 Sep 1972'. Box 3, 1972–1978. Lish Mss., 1951–2012. Lilly Library, Indiana University.

DeLillo, Don. 1997. 'Letter to Gordon Lish, 27 January 1997'. 99.4. Don DeLillo Papers. Harry Ransom Center, University of Texas.

DeLillo, Don. 2012. 'Informal Remarks from the David Foster Wallace Memorial Service in New York on October 23, 2008'. In *The Legacy of David Foster Wallace*, edited by Samuel Cohen and Lee Konstantinou, 23–4. Iowa City: University Press of Iowa.

Deresiewicz, William. 2011. 'The Children's Hospital: On David Foster Wallace'. *The Nation*, 15 June 2011. http://www.thenation.com/article/161456/childrens-hospital-david-foster-wallace.

Di Leo, Jeffrey R. 2012. 'Sovereignty of the Dead: Authors, Editors, and the Aesthetic Text'. *The Comparatist* 36: 123–36.

Dickstein, Morris. 1991. 'The Pursuit for the Ordinary'. *Partisan Review* 58: 506–13.

Doctorow, E. L. 1986. 'Braver Than We Thought'. *New York Times*, 18 May 1986.

Doherty, Margaret. 2015. 'State-Funded Fiction: Minimalism, National Memory, and the Return to Realism in the Post-Postmodern Age'. *American Literary History* 27(1): 79–101.

Doloughan, Fiona J. 2016. *English as a Literature in Translation.* New York: Bloomsbury Academic.

Eaglestone, Robert and Jonathan Beecher Field. 2015. *Studying English: A Guide for Literature Students.* Ebook. London: Routledge.

Echevarría, Ignacio, ed. 2009. 'Note to the First Edition'. In *2666*, by Roberto Bolaño, 895–98. London: Picador.

Ede, Lisa S. and Andrea Lunsford. 1992. *Singular Texts/Plural Authors: Perspectives on Collaborative Writing.* Carbondale: Southern Illinois University Press.

Eggers, Dave. 1996. 'America in 2010: Everyone's Hooked on Something.' *The San Francisco Chronicle*, 11 February 1996.

Eggers, Dave. 2006. 'Foreword'. In *Infinite Jest*, by David Foster Wallace, xi–xvi. New York: Back Bay Books.

Eggert, Paul. 2007. 'The Bushranger's Voice: Peter Carey's True History of the Kelly Gang (2000) and Ned Kelly's Jerilderie Letter (1879)'. *College Literature* 34(3): 120.

Eggert, Paul. 2009. *Securing the Past: Conservation in Art, Architecture and Literature.* Cambridge: Cambridge University Press.

English, James F. 2005. *The Economy of Prestige: Prizes, Awards, and the Circulation of Cultural Value.* Cambridge, MA; London: Harvard University Press.

English, James F. and Ted Underwood. 2016. 'Shifting Scales: Between Literature and Social Science'. *Modern Language Quarterly* 77(3): 277–95.

Epstein, Jason. 2002. *Book Business: Publishing Past, Present and Future.* New York; London: W. W. Norton.

Ercolino, Stefano. 2014. *The Maximalist Novel: From Thomas Pynchon's Gravity's Rainbow to Roberto Bolaño's 2666.* New York: Bloomsbury.

Esposito, Scott. 2011. 'Is This What *The Pale King* Should Have Looked Like?' *Conversational Reading*, 4 March 2011. http://conversationalreading.com/is-this-what-the-pale-king-should-have-looked-like/.

Eve. 2016. '"You Have to Keep Track of Your Changes": The Version Variants and Publishing History of David Mitchell's Cloud Atlas'. *Open Library of Humanities* 2(2).

Fabre-Clark, Claire. 2008. 'The Presence of the Banal in Elephant and Other Stories'. In *New Paths to Raymond Carver*, edited by Robert Miltner and Sandra Lee Kleppe, 173–86. Columbia: University Press of South Carolina.

Farber, Zach. 2009. '"Neurotic and Obsessive" but "Not Too Intransigent or Defensive"; Editing David Foster Wallace'. *The Howling Fantods*, 2009.

Ferguson, Priscilla Parkhurst. 2014. *Word of Mouth: What We Talk About When We Talk About Food.* Berkeley: University of California Press.

Ferguson, Susanne C. 1994. 'Defining the Short Story: Impressionism and Form'. In *The New Short Story Theories*, edited by Charles E. May, 218–30. Athens: Ohio University Press

Ferrer, Daniel. 1998. 'The Open Space of the Draft Page: James Joyce and Modern Manuscripts'. In *The Iconic Page in Manuscript, Print and Digital Culture*, edited by George Bornstein and Theresa Lynn Tinkle, 249–68. Ann Arbor: University Press of Michigan.

Finn. 2012. 'Becoming Yourself: The Afterlife of Reception'. In *The Legacy of David Foster Wallace*, edited by Samuel Cohen and Lee Konstantinou, 151. Iowa City: University of Iowa Press.

Foley, Abram. 2016. 'Ghosts from Limbo Patrum: Dalkey Archive Press and Institutional Literary History'. *ASAP/Journal* 1(3): 439–59.

Ford, Richard. 1998. 'Good Raymond'. *New Yorker*, 28 September 1998. https://www.newyorker.com/magazine/1998/10/05/good-raymond.

Fordham, Finn. 2010. *I Do I Undo I Redo: The Textual Genesis of Modernist Selves in Hopkins, Yeats, Conrad, Forster, Joyce, and Woolf*. Oxford: Oxford University Press.

Foucault, Michel. 2006. 'What Is an Author?' In *The Book History Reader*, 2nd edn, edited by David Finkelstein and Alistair McCleery, 281–91. Milton Park, Abingdon, Oxon; New York: Routledge.

Franzen, Jonathan. 2015. Interview by Emma Brockes. *Guardian* 21 August 2015. http://www.theguardian.com/global/2015/aug/21/jonathan-franzen-purity-interview.

Friedman, Alan W. 2010. 'Manuscript Genetics, Joyce's Know-How, Beckett's Nohow (Review)'. *Textual Cultures: Texts, Contexts, Interpretation* 5(2): 92–4.

Fuller, Molly. 2014. 'Intentionality and Narrative Thrust in the Beginners Version of "Why Don't You Dance?"' *The Raymond Carver Review* 4. http://dept.kent.edu/english/rcr/issues/04/.

Gabler, Hans Walter. 2018. *Text Genetics in Literary Modernism and Other Essays*. Cambridge: Open Book Publishers.

Gallagher, Tess. 2017. Interview by Tim Groenland. Personal interview. Dublin. August 2017.

Gallop, Jane. 2011. *The Deaths of the Author: Reading and Writing in Time*. Durham; London: Duke University Press.

Gates, David. 2009. 'Nabokov's Last Puzzle'. *New York Times*, 15 November 2009, sec. Books/Sunday Book Review. http://www.nytimes.com/2009/11/15/books/review/Gates-t.html.

Genette, Gérard. 1997. *Paratexts: Thresholds of Interpretation*. Translated by Jane E. Lewin, foreword by Richard Macksey. Cambridge: Cambridge University Press.

Genette, Raymonde Debray. 2004. 'Flaubert's "A Simple Heart," or How to Make an Ending: A Study of the Manuscripts'. In *Genetic Criticism: Texts and Avant-Textes*, edited and intro. by Jed Deppman, Daniel Ferrer and Michael Groden, 69–95. Material Texts. Philadelphia: University of Pennsylvania Press.

Gessen, Keith. 2011. *Vanity Fair's How a Book Is Born: The Making of The Art of Fielding*. Kindle file. Vanity Fair.

Ginna, Peter. 2017a. 'Introduction: The Three Phases of Editing'. In *What Editors Do: The Art, Craft, and Business of Book Editing*, edited by Peter Ginna, 17–29. Chicago: University of Chicago Press.

Ginna, Peter. 2017b. 'Conclusion: As Time Goes By: The Past and Future of Editing'. In *What Editors Do: The Art, Craft, and Business of Book Editing*, edited by Peter Ginna, 269–72. Chicago: University of Chicago Press.

Glass, Loren. 2013. *Counterculture Colophon: Grove Press, the Evergreen Review, and the Incorporation of the Avant-Garde*. Post 45. Stanford, CA: Stanford University Press.

Godden, Richard and Michael Szalay. 2014. 'The Bodies in the Bubble: David Foster Wallace's *The Pale King*'. *Textual Practice* 28(7): 1273–322.

Gontarski, S. E. 2006. 'Greying the Canon: Beckett in Performance'. In *Beckett After Beckett*, edited by S. E. Gontarski and Anthony Uhlmann, 141–57. Gainesville: University Press of Florida.

Goodman, Walter. 1996. 'She Just Promised to Write, Not Make Sense'. *New York Times*, 20 August 1996, sec. Books.

Gornick, Vivian. 2015. 'Feminist icon Vivian Gornick, still in the fight: A conversation with Jonathan Lethem'. *Salon*. 21 May 2015.

Gottlieb, Robert. 1994. Robert Gottlieb, The Art of Editing No. 1. Interview by Larissa MacFarquhar. *Paris Review* 132.

Gottlieb, Robert. 2016. *Avid Reader: A Life*. New York: Farrar, Straus and Giroux.

Greenberg, Susan. 2010. 'When the Editor Disappears, Does Editing Disappear?' *Convergence: The International Journal of Research into New Media Technologies* 16(1): 7–21.

Grimes, William. 1992. 'The Ridiculous Vision of Mark Leyner'. *New York Times*, 13 September 1992. http://www.nytimes.com/1992/09/13/magazine/the-ridiculous-vision-of-mark-leyner.html.

Groden, Michael. 2007. 'Preface'. In *How Joyce Wrote 'Finnegans Wake': A Chapter-by-Chapter Genetic Guide*, edited by Sam Slote and Luca Crispi, vi–xi. Madison; London: University Press of Wisconsin.

Groenland, Tim. 2015a. 'The Poetics of the Sentence: Examining Gordon Lish's Literary Legacy'. *Irish Journal of American Studies* no. 4(Summer). http://ijas.iaas.ie/index.php/the-poetics-of-the-sentence-examining-gordon-lishs-literary-legacy/.

Groenland, Tim. 2015b. 'A King of Shreds and Patches: Assembling Wallace's Final Novel'. *Critical Insights: David Foster Wallace*, May, 221.

Gross, Joe. 2011. 'Ransom Center Restricts Part of Wallace Archive'. *Statesman*, 8 September 2011.

'Guidelines for Editors of Scholarly Editions'. 2011. Modern Language Association. 29 June 2011. http://www.mla.org/cse_guidelines.

Hallberg, Garth Risk. 2010. 'Is Big Back?' *The Millions*, 8 September 2010.

Hallett, Cynthia. 1999. *Minimalism and the Short Story : Raymond Carver, Amy Hempel, and Mary Robison*. Lewiston, NY: Edwin Mellen Press.

Hannah, Barry. 2004. The Art of Fiction No. 184. Interview by Lacey Galbraith. *Paris Review*.

Hansen, Grace and Abigail Adams. 2017. 'Pale King Materials', 5 October 2017.

Harris, Aisha. 2015. The 'How Does a Book Editor Work?' Slate 'Working' podcast. Audio. http://www.slate.com/articles/podcasts/working/2015/08/jordan_pavlin_of_knopf_how_does_a_book_editor_work.html.

Harris, Charles B. 2014. 'The Anxiety of Influence: The John Barth/David Foster Wallace Connection'. *Critique: Studies in Contemporary Fiction* 55(2): 103–26.

Harris, Robert R. 1982. 'A Talk with Don DeLillo'. *New York Times*, 10 October 1982. http://www.nytimes.com/books/97/03/16/lifetimes/del-v-talk1982.html.

Harvey, Giles. 2010. 'The Two Raymond Carvers'. *New York Review of Books*, 27 May 2010. http://www.nybooks.com/articles/archives/2010/may/27/two-raymond-carvers/.

Hassan, Ihab. 1971. *The Dismemberment of Orpheus: Toward a Postmodern Literature*. New York: Oxford University Press.

Hawlin, Theodora. 2017. 'The Re-Birth of the Author'. In *The Digital Critic: Literary Culture Online*, edited by Houman Barekat, Robert Barry and David Winters. New York: OR Books.

Hay, Louis. 2004. 'Genetic Criticism: Origins and Perspectives'. In *Genetic Criticism: Texts and Avant-Textes*, edited by Jed Deppman, Daniel Ferrer and Michael Groden, 17–27. Philadelphia: University of Pennsylvania Press.

Hayes-Brady, Clare. 2012. 'Rev. of The Legacy of David Foster Wallace, Eds. Samuel Cohen and Lee Konstantinou'. *Studies in the Novel* 44(4): 481.

Hayes-Brady, Clare. 2016. *The Unspeakable Failures of David Foster Wallace*. New York: Bloomsbury.

Hemingway, Ernest. 1932. *Death in the Afternoon*. Charlottesville: Scribner.

Hemingway, Ernest. 1985. *The Dangerous Summer*. London: Hamish Hamilton Ltd.

Hemingway, Ernest. 1986. *In Our Time: Stories*. David Foster Wallace, Former Owner. 1st Scribner Classic/Collier edn. New York : Collier Books/Macmillan Pub. Co. David Foster Wallace Library, Harry Ransom Center.

Hemingway, Ernest. 2004. *The Essential Hemingway*. London: Vintage.

Hemmingson, Michael. 2011a. 'Will You Please Be Quiet, Please?—R. Carver'. *Gordon Lish Edited This* (blog). 15 May 2011. https://gordonlisheditedthis.wordpress.com/2011/05/15/will-you-please-be-quiet-please-r-carver/.

Hemmingson, Michael. 2011b. 'Saying More without Trying to Say More: On Gordon Lish Reshaping the Body of Raymond Carver and Saving Barry Hannah'. *Critique: Studies in Contemporary Fiction* 52(4): 479–98.

Hempel, Amy. 1984. 'Captain Fiction'. *Vanity Fair*, December 1984.

Hering, David. 2015. 'Form as Strategy in Infinite Jest'. In *Consider David Foster Wallace: Critical Essays*, edited by Philip Coleman, 128–43. Ipswich, MA: Salem Press.

Hering, David. 2016a. *David Foster Wallace: Fiction and Form*. New York; London: Bloomsbury.

Hering, David. 2016b. 'Too Much and Too Little: A History of David Foster Wallace's "*The Pale King*"'. *Los Angeles Review of Books*. 14 September 2016. https://lareviewofbooks.org/article/much-little-history-david-foster-wallaces-pale-king/.

Herman, Luc and John M. Krafft. 2007. 'Fast Learner: The Typescript of Pynchon's V. at the Harry Ransom Center in Austin'. *Texas Studies in Literature and Language* 49(1).

Herman, Luc and Toon Staes. 2014. 'Introduction: Can *The Pale King* (Please) Be a Novel?' *English Studies* 95(1): 1–6.

Herman, Victor. n.d. 'Coming Out of the Ice'. Box 81. Lish Mss., 1951–2012. Lilly Library, Indiana University.

Herzinger, Kim A. 1985. 'Introduction: On the New Fiction'. *Mississippi Review* 14(1/2): 7–22.

Hills, Rust. 1987. 'Esquire's Guide to the Literary Universe'. *Esquire* 108(August): 51.

Hoberek, Andrew. 2010. 'Foreign Objects, Or, DeLillo Minimalist'. *Studies in American Fiction* 37(1): 101–25.

Hoberek, Andrew. 2013. 'The Novel after David Foster Wallace'. In *A Companion to David Foster Wallace Studies*, edited by Marshall Boswell and Stephen J. Burn, 211–28. American Literature Readings in the 21st Century. New York: Palgrave Macmillan.

Hodson, Sara S. 2013. 'To Reveal or Conceal: Privacy and Confidentiality in the Papers of Contemporary Authors'. In *The Boundaries of the Literary Archive: Reclamation and Representation*, edited by Carrie Smith and Lisa Stead, 157–69. Farnham: Ashgate.

Hoffman, Jan. 1996. 'Reporter's Notebook; Editor to Joan Collins: Don't Quit the Day Job'. *New York Times*, 13 February 1996, sec. N.Y./Region. https://www.nytimes.com/1996/02/13/nyregion/reporter-s-notebook-editor-to-joan-collins-don-t-quit-the-day-job.html.

Holland, Mary K. 2006. '"The Art"s Heart's Purpose': Braving the Narcissistic Loop of David Foster Wallace's "Infinite Jest"'. *Critique* 47(3): 218–42.

Horace. 1980. *Horace, Epistles, Book 1*, 3rd (revised) edn. Edited by O. A. W. Dilke. Letchworth: Bradda Books.

Hornby, Nick. 1992. *Contemporary American Fiction*. New York: St. Martin's Press.

Hotchner, A. E. 2009. 'Don't Touch "A Moveable Feast"'. *New York Times*, 20 July 2009, sec. Opinion. http://www.nytimes.com/2009/07/20/opinion/20hotchner.html.

Houston, Robert. 1981. 'A Stunning Inarticulateness'. *Nation* 233(1): 23.

Howard, Gerald. 1986. 'Letter to David Foster Wallace, 10 January 1986'. Box 1, Folder 5. Bonnie Nadell: David Foster Wallace Collection. Harry Ransom Center Archive, University of Texas at Austin.

Howard, Gerald. 2007. 'I Was Gordon Lish's Editor'. *Slate*, 31 October 2007. http://www.slate.com/articles/news_and_politics/book_blitz/2007/10/i_was_gordon_lishs_editor.html.

Howard, Gerald. 2016. 'The Open Refrigerator'. In *Literary Publishing in the Twenty-First Century*, edited by Travis Kurowski, Wayne Miller, and Kevin Prufer, 190–201. Minneapolis: Milkweed Editions.

Howard, Gerald. 2017. Interview by Tim Groenland. Phone conversation. August 2017.

Howe, Irving. 1983. 'Stories of Our Loneliness'. *New York Times. Web*, 11 September 1983. http://www.nytimes.com/books/01/01/21/specials/carver-cathedral.html.

Hungerford, Amy. 2016. *Making Literature Now*. Stanford, CA: Stanford University Press.

Hurley, Donna. 2013. 'Biographies of Nero'. In *A Companion to the Neronian Age*, edited by Emma Buckley and Martin Dinter, 29–44. Chichester: Wiley-Blackwell.

Jacobs, John Timothy. 2003. 'The Eschatological Imagination: Mediating David Foster Wallace's *Infinite Jest*'. *Open Access Dissertations and Theses*, July. http://digitalcommons.mcmaster.ca/opendissertations/827.

Jenny, Laurent and Richard Watts. 1996. 'Genetic Criticism and Its Myths'. *Yale French Studies* no. 89(January): 9–25.

Kachka, Boris. 2015. 'When Did Books Get So Freaking Enormous? The Year of the Very Long Novel'. *Vulture*, 19 May 2015. http://www.vulture.com/2015/05/year-of-the-very-long-novel.html.

Kakutani, Michiko. 1996. 'A Country Dying of Laughter. In 1,079 Pages'. *New York Times*, 13 February 1996, sec. Books. http://www.nytimes.com/1996/02/13/books/books-of-the-times-a-country-dying-of-laughter-in-1079-pages.html.

Kelley, Rich. 2009. 'The Library of America Interviews Tess Gallagher, William L. Stull, and Maureen P. Carroll about Raymond Carver'. Library of America. 2009. http://www.loa.org/images/pdf/LOA_interview_Gallagher_Stull_Carroll_on_Carver.pdf.

Kelly, Adam. 2010. 'David Foster Wallace: The Death of the Author and the Birth of a Discipline'. *Irish Journal of American Studies* no. 2(June). http://ijas.iaas.ie/index.php/article-david-foster-wallace-the-death-of-the-author-and-the-birth-of-a-discipline/.

Kelly, Adam. 2012. 'Development Through Dialogue: David Foster Wallace and the Novel of Ideas'. *Studies in the Novel* 44(3): 267–83.

Kelly, Adam. 2014a. 'David Foster Wallace and the Novel of Ideas'. In *David Foster Wallace and 'The Long Thing': New Essays on the Novels*, edited by Marshall Boswell, 3–22. New York: Bloomsbury.

Kelly, Adam. 2014b. 'Dialectic of Sincerity: Lionel Trilling and David Foster Wallace'. *Post45*, October. http://post45.research.yale.edu/2014/10/dialectic-of-sincerity-lionel-trilling-and-david-foster-wallace/.

Kelly, Adam. 2015. 'David Foster Wallace: The Critical Reception'. In *Critical Insights: David Foster Wallace*, edited by Philip Coleman, 46–62. Ipswich, MA: Salem Press.

Kelly, Adam. 2017. 'David Foster Wallace and New Sincerity Aesthetics: A Reply to Edward Jackson and Joel Nicholson-Roberts'. *Orbit: A Journal of American Literature* 5(2).

Kemp, Peter. 1988. 'The American Chekhov: Elephant and Other Stories by Raymond Carver'. *Sunday Times*, 8 August 1988.

Kennedy, William. 1985. 'The Last Ole.' *New York Times*, 9 June 1985. https://www.nytimes.com/books/99/07/04/specials/hemingway-summer.html.

Kennedy, X. J., ed. 1991. *Literature : An Introduction to Fiction, Poetry, and Drama,* 5th edn. David Foster Wallace, former owner. New York: Harper Collins. David Foster Wallace Library, Harry Ransom Center.

King, Daniel Robert. 2016. *Cormac McCarthy's Literary Evolution: Editors, Agents, and the Crafting of a Prolific American Author*. Knoxville: The University of Tennessee Press.

King, Stephen. 2009. 'Raymond Carver's Life and Stories'. *New York Times*, 22 November 2009, sec. Books/Sunday Book Review. http://www.nytimes.com/2009/11/22/books/review/King-t.html.

Kirn, Walter. 2004. 'Staring Either Absently or Intently'. *New York Times*, 27 June 2004, sec. Books. https://www.nytimes.com/2004/06/27/books/staring-either-absently-or-intently.html.

Kirsch, Adam. 2011. 'The Importance of Being Earnest'. *New Republic*, 28 July 2011. http://www.newrepublic.com/article/books/magazine/92794/david-lipsky-foster-wallace-pale-king.

Kirschenbaum, Matthew G. 2016. *Track Changes: A Literary History of Word Processing*. Cambridge, MA: Belknap/Harvard University Press.

Knox, Bernard. 2007. 'Introduction'. In *The Aeneid, by Virgil, translated by Robert Fagles, 1–41*. London: Penguin.

Koestenbaum, Wayne. 1989. *Double Talk: The Erotics of Male Literary Collaboration*. New York; London: Routledge.

Konstantinou, Lee. 2011. 'Unfinished Form.' *Los Angeles Review of Books*, 6 July 2011.

Konstantinou, Lee. 2016. *Cool Characters: Irony and American Fiction*. Cambridge, MA: Harvard University Press.

Kurowski, Travis, Wayne Miller and Kevin Prufer. 2016. 'Introduction'. In *Literary Publishing in the Twenty-First Century*, edited by Travis Kurowski, Wayne Miller, and Kevin Prufer, vii–xii. Minneapolis: Milkweed Editions.

Laming, Donald. 2003. *Human Judgment: The Eye of the Beholder*. Devon: Thomson Learning.

Lanchester, John. 2013. *What We Talk About When We Talk About The Tube: The District Line*. London: Particular Books.

Lasdun, James. 2011. '*The Pale King* by David Foster Wallace – Review'. *Guardian*, 16 April 2011, sec. Books. http://www.theguardian.com/books/2011/apr/16/pale-king-david-foster-wallace-review.

Latimer, Andrew. 2017. 'Editing Gordon Lish'. *Foyles* (blog). 8 June 2017. http://www.foyles.co.uk/Blog-Andrew-Latimer.

LeClair, Tom. 1982. 'Fiction Chronicle: January to June, 1981'. *Contemporary Literature* 23(1): 83–91.

LeClair, Tom. 1996. 'The Prodigious Fiction of Richard Powers, William Vollmann, and David Foster Wallace'. *Critique* 38: 12–37.

LeClair, Tom. 2016. 'Review of Making Literature Now by Amy Hungerford'. *Full Stop*, 20 October 2016. http://www.full-stop.net/2016/10/20/reviews/tomleclair/making-literature-now-amy-hungerford/.

Lerner, Betsy. 2017. 'What Love's Got to Do With It: The Author-Editor Relationship'. In *What Editors Do: The Art, Craft, and Business of Book Editing*, edited by Peter Ginna, 69–76. Chicago: University of Chicago Press.

Letzler, David. 2012. 'Encyclopedic Novels and the Cruft of Fiction: Infinite Jest's Endnotes'. *Studies in the Novel* 44(3): 304–24.

Levey, Nick. 2016. *Maximalism in Contemporary American Literature: The Uses of Detail*. New York: Routledge.

Lewis, Charlton T. and Charles Short, eds. 1966. *A Latin Dictionary: Founded on Andrews' Edition of Freund's Latin Dictionary*. Oxford: Clarendon Press.

Leypoldt, Günter. 2001. 'Raymond Carver's "Epiphanic Moments"'. *Style* 35(3): 531.

Leypoldt, Günter. 2002. 'Reconsidering Raymond Carver's "Development": The Revisions of "So Much Water so Close to Home"'. *Contemporary Literature* 43(2): 317–41.

Lipsky, David. 2010. *Although of Course You End Up Becoming Yourself: A Road Trip with David Foster Wallace*, 1st edn. New York: Broadway Books.

Lish, Gordon. 1971. 'Letter to James Hall', 8 July 1971. Box 2, 1970. Lish Mss., 1951–2012. Lilly Library, Indiana University.

Lish, Gordon. 1976. 'List of writing workshop questions entitled 'LISH/FICTION WRITING November 76'. Box 110. Lish Mss., 1951–2012. Lilly Library, Indiana University.

Lish, Gordon. 1987. 'Letter to Bonnie Nadell, 25 September 1987'. Box 1. Bonnie Nadell Collection of David Foster Wallace. Harry Ransom Center, University of Texas.

Lish, Gordon. 1998. Gordon Lish Interview. Interview by Alexander Laurence. Alexander Laurence's Blog. http://portable-infinite.blogspot.com/2018/09/gordon-lish-interview-1998.html.

Lish, Gordon. 2015. Gordon Lish, The Art of Editing No. 2. Interview by Christian Lorentzen. *Paris Review* 215.

Lish, Gordon. 2018. 'An Interview with Gordon Lish'. Interview by David Winters. In *Conversations with Gordon Lish*, edited by David Winters and Jason Lucarelli, 153–66. Jackson: University of Mississippi Press.

Litt, Toby. 2009. '"Keep It Simple, Stupid": Minimalism in Prose'. University of London, Birkbeck, April 28. https://www.academia.edu/7541579/Minimalism_in_Prose.

London, Bette Lynn. 1999. *Writing Double: Women's Literary Partnerships*. Ithaca and London: Cornell University Press.

Lorentzen, Christian. 2015. 'The Rewriting of David Foster Wallace'. *New York Magazine*, 29 June 2015. http://www.vulture.com/2015/06/rewriting-of-david-foster-wallace.html

Lucarelli, Jason. 2013. 'The Consecution of Gordon Lish: An Essay on Form and Influence'. *Numéro Cinq*, February 2013. http://numerocinqmagazine.com/2013/02/04/the-consecution-of-gordon-lish-an-essay-on-form-and-influence-jason-lucarelli/.

Lutz, Gary. 2009. 'The Sentence Is a Lonely Place'. *Believer*. January 2009. http://www.believermag.com/issues/200901/?read=article_lutz.

Lydon, Christopher. 1996. 'A Lost 1996 Interview with David Foster Wallace'. *Medium*. February 1996. https://medium.com/@kunaljasty/a-lost-1996-interview-with-david-foster-wallace-63987d93c2c.

MacDonald, Claire and William H. Sherman, eds. 2002. *On Editing*. Performance Research, 7: 1. London: Routledge.

Mahler, Jonathan. 'James Patterson Inc.' *New York Times Magazine*, 20 January 2010. https://www.nytimes.com/2010/01/24/magazine/24patterson-t.html.

Mandel, Miriam B. 2008. *Hemingway's The Dangerous Summer: The Complete Annotations*. Lanham, MD; Plymouth: Scarecrow Press.

Maneker, Marion. 2001. 'House Cleaning'. *New York Magazine*, 19 February 2001. http://nymag.com/nymetro/arts/columns/culturebusiness/4378/.

Marek, Richard. 1994. 'Foreword'. In *Editing Fact and Fiction: A Concise Guide to Book Editing*, edited by Leslie T. Sharpe, vii–ix. Cambridge: Cambridge University Press.

Marling, William. 2016. *Gatekeepers: The Emergence of World Literature and the 1960s*. New York: Oxford University Press.

Martin, Tim. 2009. 'Beginners by Raymond Carver: Review', 30 October 2009, sec. Culture. http://www.telegraph.co.uk/culture/books/bookreviews/6460630/Beginners-by-Raymond-Carver-review.html.

Mason, Wyatt. 2004. 'Don't Like It? You Don't Have to Play'. *London Review of Books*, 18 November 2004.

Max, D. T. 1998. 'The Carver Chronicles'. *New York Times*, 9 August 1998.

Max, D. T. 2009. 'The Unfinished'. *New Yorker*, 9 March 2009. http://www.newyorker.com/reporting/2009/03/09/090309fa_fact_max?currentPage=all.

Max, D. T. 2012a. *Every Love Story Is a Ghost Story: A Life of David Foster Wallace*. London: Granta.

Max, D. T. 2012b. 'Rereading David Foster Wallace'. Presented at The New Yorker Festival, 6 October 2012. https://www.youtube.com/watch?v=JqN52yKI4pg.

Max, D. T. 2012c. 'In the D.F.W. Archives: An Unfinished Story About the Internet'. *New Yorker*, 11 October 2012. http://www.newyorker.com/books/page-turner/in-the-d-f-w-archives-an-unfinished-story-about-the-internet.

Max, D. T. 2016. Episode 8: Discussing David Foster Wallace with D T Max. Interview by Matt Bucher and David Laird. The Great Concavity. Podcast.

http://greatconcavity.podbean.com/e/episode-8-discussing-david-foster-wallace-with-dt-max/.

Maxwell, William. 1982. William Maxwell, The Art of Fiction No. 71. Interview by John Seabrook. *Paris Review* 85.

Maxwell, William and Frank O'Connor. 1996. *The Happiness of Getting It Down Right: Letters of Frank O'Connor and William Maxwell, 1945–1966*, 1st edn. Edited by Michael Steinman. New York: Knopf.

May, Charles E. 1994. '"Chekhov and the Modern Short Story"'. In *The New Short Story Theories*, edited by Charles E. May, 218–30. Athens: Ohio University Press.

May, Charles E. 1995. *The Short Story: The Reality of Artifice*. Studies in Literary Themes and Genres, no. 4. New York; Oxford: Twayne/Toronto: Maxwell Macmillan International.

May, Charles E. 1999. 'Preface'. In *Minimalism and the Short Story: Raymond Carver, Amy Hempel, and Mary Robison*, by Cynthia Hallett, ix–x. Lewiston, NY: Edwin Mellen Press.

McCarthy, Tom. 2011. 'David Foster Wallace: The Last Audit'. *New York Times*, 14 April 2011, sec. Books/Sunday Book Review. http://www.nytimes.com/2011/04/17/books/review/book-review-the-pale-king-by-david-foster-wallace.html.

McCormack, Thomas. 2006. *The Fiction Editor, the Novel, and the Novelist*, 2nd edn. Philadelphia: Paul Dry Books.

McDermott, James Dishon. 2006. *Austere Style in Twentieth-Century Literature: Literary Minimalism*. Lewiston, NY: Edwin Mellen Press.

McGann, Jerome. 1983. *A Critique of Modern Textual Criticism*. Chicago; London: University of Chicago Press.

McGann, Jerome. 1991. *The Textual Condition*. Princeton, NJ: Princeton University Press.

McGann, Jerome. 2006. 'The Socialization of Texts'. In *The Book History Reader*, 2nd edn, edited by David Finkelstein and Alistair McCleery, 66–73. Milton Park, Abingdon, Oxon; New York: Routledge.

McGrath, Laura B. 2017. 'Agented Fiction'. Blog Post. http://laurabmcgrath.com/research/middlemen/asap9/.

McGurl, Mark. 2009. *The Program Era: Postwar Fiction and the Rise of Creative Writing*. Cambridge: Harvard University Press.

McGurl, Mark. 2014. 'The Institution of Nothing: David Foster Wallace in the Program'. *Boundary 2* 41(3): 27–54.

McHale, Brian. 2013. '*The Pale King*, or, The White Visitation'. In *A Companion to David Foster Wallace Studies*, edited by Marshall Boswell and Stephen J. Burn, 192–210. New York: Palgrave Macmillan.

Meatto, Keith. 2011. 'Bored to Death – A Review of *The Pale King*'. *Frontier Psychiatrist* (blog). 11 May 2011. http://frontpsych.com/bored-to-death-a-review-of-the-pale-king/.

Medley, Michael. 2013. 'How *The Pale King*'s Man Put David Foster Wallace Together Again'. *National Post*, 15 April 2013. http://arts.nationalpost.com/2011/04/15/how-the-pale-king%e2%80%99s-man-put-david-foster-wallace-together-again/.

Meyer, Adam. 1989. 'Now You See Him, Now You Don't, Now You Do Again: The Evolution of Raymond Carver's Minimalism'. *Critique* no. 30: 239–51.

Michener, James A. 1994. *Literary Reflections*. New York: Forge Books.

Miley, Mike. 2016. '. . . And Starring David Foster Wallace as Himself: Performance and Persona in *The Pale King*'. *Critique: Studies in Contemporary Fiction* 57(2): 191–207.

Miller, Adam S. 2016. *The Gospel According to David Foster Wallace*. New York: Bloomsbury.

Monti, Enrico. 2013. 'Minimalism, Dirty Realism, and Raymond Carver'. In *Critical Insights: Raymond Carver*, edited by James Plath, 56–69. Ipswich, MA: Salem Press.

Moody, Rick and Michael Pietsch. 2012. 'Editing Wallace: An Interview with Michael Pietsch'. In *The Legacy of David Foster Wallace*, 208–17. Iowa City: University Press of Iowa.

Moore, Steven. 2003. 'The First Draft Version of Infinite Jest'. *The Howling Fantods*, 10 May 2003. http://www.thehowlingfantods.com/ij_first.htm.

Morrison, Blake. 2009. 'Rev. of Beginners by Raymond Carver'. *Guardian*, 17 October 2009. http://www.theguardian.com/books/2009/oct/17/raymond-carver-beginners-blake-morrison.

Mundaca, Marie. 2009. 'The Influence of Anxiety: Wading In'. Internet Archive Wayback Machine. *Hipster Bookclub*. 5 June 2009. http://web.archive.org/web/20090605155500/http://www.hipsterbookclub.com/features/influenceofanxiety/June09/index.html.

Murakami, Haruki. 2006. *Birthday Stories*. New edition. London: Vintage Books.

Nabokov, Vladimir. n.d. 'Myself Incomplete: A True Autobiography'. Box 67. Lish Mss., 1951–2012. Lilly Library, Indiana University.

Nabokov, Vladimir. 1992. *Pale Fire*. New edition/with introduction by Richard Rorty. London: D. Campbell.

Nadell, Bonnie. 1985. 'Letter to David Foster Wallace, 28 October 1985'. Bonnie Nadell Collection of David Foster Wallace. Harry Ransom Center Archive, University of Texas at Austin.

Nadell, Bonnie. 2012. 'Editors on Wallace'. Discussion with Colin Harrison, Bill Tonelli, and Deborah Triesman. Harry Ransom Center, University of Texas, Austin, 14 May. YouTube. http://www.youtube.com/watch?v=IAfuZRryjHk&feature=youtube_gdata_player.

Nesset, Kirk. 1995. *The Stories of Raymond Carver: A Critical Study*. Athens: Ohio University Press.

Neyfakh, Leon. 2008. 'Gerry Howard on Discovering, Editing, and Hatching David Foster Wallace: "He Was the First Person Who Ever Called Me 'Mister'"'. *New York Observer* 17 September 2008. Accessed 23 April 2018. http://observer.com/2008/09/gerry-howard-on-discovering-editing-and-hatching-david-foster-wallace-he-was-the-first-person-who-ever-called-me-mister/.

North, Michael. 2009. *Machine-Age Comedy*. Oxford and New York: Oxford University Press.

O'Brien, Tim. 1981. 'Review of What We Talk About When We Talk About Love'. *Chicago Tribune*, 5 April 1981, sec. 7.

O'Connell, Mark. 2012. 'Rev. of Both Flesh and Not'. *Observer*, 30 December 2012, sec. Books. http://www.theguardian.com/books/2012/dec/30/foster-wallace-both-flesh-review.

O'Connell, Michael J. 2015. '"Your Temple Is Self and Sentiment": David Foster Wallace's Diagnostic Novels'. *Christianity & Literature* 64(3): 266–92.

Parris-Lamb, Chris and Jonathan Lee. 2016. 'The Art of Agenting: An Interview with Chris Parris-Lamb', 174–89. Minneapolis: Milkweed Editions.

Perkins, Maxwell E. 1991. *Editor to Author: The Letters of Maxwell E. Perkins*. Edited by John Hall Wheelock. Atlanta, GA: Charles Scribners Sons.

Peters, K. J. 1991. 'The Thematic Integrity of The Garden of Eden'. *Hemingway Review* 10: 17–29.

Philpotts, Matthew. 2012. 'The Role of the Periodical Editor: Literary Journals and Editorial Habitus.' *The Modern Language Review* 107(1), 39–64.

Pietsch, Michael. 1987a. 'Letter to David Foster Wallace, 17 September 1987'. Box 1, Folder 1. Little, Brown and Company Collection of David Foster Wallace. Box 1–5. Harry Ransom Center Archive, University of Texas at Austin.

Pietsch, Michael. 1987b. 'Letter to David Foster Wallace, 18 November 1987'. Box 1, Folder 1. Little, Brown and Company Collection of David Foster Wallace. Box 1–5. Harry Ransom Center Archive, University of Texas at Austin.

Pietsch, Michael. 1987c. 'Letter to David Foster Wallace, 9 December 1987'. Box 1, Folder 1. Little, Brown and Company Collection of David Foster Wallace. Box 1–5. Harry Ransom Center Archive, University of Texas at Austin.

Pietsch, Michael. 1989. 'Letter to David Foster Wallace, 14 April 1989'. Box 1, Folder 1. Little, Brown and Company Collection of David Foster Wallace. Box 1–5. Harry Ransom Center Archive, University of Texas at Austin.

Pietsch, Michael. 1992. 'Letter to Publication Board, 5 June 1992'. Box 3, Folder 2. Little, Brown and Company Collection of David Foster Wallace. Box 1–5. Harry Ransom Center Archive, University of Texas at Austin.

Pietsch, Michael. 1993. 'Letter to David Foster Wallace, 10 June 1993'. Box 3, Folder 2. Little, Brown and Company Collection of David Foster Wallace. Box 1–5. Harry Ransom Center Archive, University of Texas at Austin.

Pietsch, Michael. 1994a. 'Letter to David Foster Wallace, 21 October 1994'. Box 3, Folder 2. Little, Brown and Company Collection of David Foster Wallace. Box 1–5. Harry Ransom Center Archive, University of Texas at Austin.

Pietsch, Michael. 1994b. 'Letter to David Foster Wallace, 30 November 1994'. Box 3, Folder 2. Little, Brown and Company Collection of David Foster Wallace. Box 1–5. Harry Ransom Center Archive, University of Texas at Austin.

Pietsch, Michael. 1994c. 'Letter to David Foster Wallace, 22 December 1994'. Box 3, Folder 2. Little, Brown and Company Collection of David Foster Wallace. Box 1–5. Harry Ransom Center Archive, University of Texas at Austin.

Pietsch, Michael. 1995a. 'Letter to David Foster Wallace, 27 April 1995'. Box 3, Folder 3. Little, Brown and Company Collection of David Foster Wallace. Box 1–5. Harry Ransom Center Archive, University of Texas at Austin.

Pietsch, Michael. 1995b. 'Letter to David Foster Wallace, 22 May 1995'. Box 3, Folder 3. Little, Brown and Company Collection of David Foster Wallace. Box 1–5. Harry Ransom Center Archive, University of Texas at Austin.

Pietsch, Michael. 1996. 'Letter to David Foster Wallace, 18 April 1996'. Box 2, Folder 7. Little, Brown and Company Collection of David Foster Wallace. Box 1–5. Harry Ransom Center Archive, University of Texas at Austin.

Pietsch, Michael. 2003. 'Letter to David Foster Wallace, 3 October 2003'. Box 3, Folder 5. Little, Brown and Company Collection of David Foster Wallace. Box 1–5. Harry Ransom Center Archive, University of Texas at Austin.

Pietsch, Michael. 2009. 'Michael Pietsch: Editing Infinite Jest'. *Infinite Summer* (blog). 3 July 2009. http://infinitesummer.org/archives/569.

Pietsch, Michael. 2010. 'On David Foster Wallace'. *Five Dials*, January 2010.

Pietsch, Michael. 2011a. 'Editor's Note'. In *The Pale King: An Unfinished Novel*, by David Foster Wallace, v–x. New York: Little, Brown.

Pietsch, Michael. 2011b. 'Editor's Note'. In *The Pale King*, by David Foster Wallace. Read by Robert Petkoff. CD. New York: Little, Brown.

Pietsch, Michael. 2011c. Interview by Joe Fassler. *The Pale King*: David Foster Wallace's Editor on the Book's Path to Print. *Atlantic*. Web. ttp://www.theatlantic.com/entertainment/archive/2011/04/the-pale-king-david-foster-wallaces-editor-on-the-books-path-to-print/236925/?single_page=true.

Pietsch, Michael. 2011d. Interview by Michael Feldman on *Whad'ya Know*, Wisconsin Public Radio Interview by Michael Feldman. Web. http://www.publicbroadcasting.net/wyk/arts.artsmain?action=viewArticle&id=1817748&pid=1149&sid=10.

Pietsch, Michael. 2011e. 'Notes and Asides'. In *The Pale King: An Unfinished Novel*, by David Foster Wallace, 541. London: Penguin.

Pietsch, Michael. 2013. 'Corner Office: Editor Ascendant: Michael Pietsch. Interview by Lynn Rosen'. *Book Business*. January 2013. http://www.bookbusinessmag.com/article/michael-pietsch-ceo-hachette-interview/1.

Pietsch, Michael. 2017a. 'The Flip Side of the Pizza: The Editor as Manager'. In *What Editors Do*, edited by Peter Ginna, 119–30. Chicago: Chicago University Press.

Pietsch, Michael. 2017b. Interview with Michael Pietsch (1). Interview by Tim Groenland. Email.

Pietsch, Michael. 2017c. Interview with Michael Pietsch (2). Interview by Tim Groenland. Phone conversation. August 2017.

Pietsch, Michael and Bonnie Nadell. 2012. 'Everything and More: A Conversation about David Foster Wallace'. Discussion with Bonnie Nadell and Michael Pietsch. Interview by David Ulin. Harry Ransom Center, University of Texas at Austin. 5 April 2012. YouTube. https://www.youtube.com/watch?v=DCbshd_CRrI

Pitchel, Samantha. 2011. 'This Is Water: The Ransom Center Welcomes Waves of Researchers and Biographers – 2011-Jul-28'. CultureMap Austin. 28 July 2011. http://austin.culturemap.com/news/arts/07-28-11-12-00-this-is-water-the-ransom-center-welcomes-waves-of-researchers/.

Polsgrove, Carol. 2001. *It Wasn't Pretty, Folks, But Didn't We Have Fun?: Esquire in the Sixties*. Oakland: RDR Books.

Purdum, Todd. 2015. 'The Henry Ford of Books'. *Vanity Fair*, 2015. http://www.vanityfair.com/culture/2015/01/james-patterson-best-selling-author.

Rabb, Margo. 2009. 'Steal These Books'. *New York Times*, 20 December 2009, sec. Books/Sunday Book Review. http://www.nytimes.com/2009/12/20/books/review/Rabb-t.html.

Raine, Craig. 2009. 'Raymond Carver'. *Arete Magazine* no. 29(August). http://www.aretemagazine.co.uk/29-autumn-2009/raymond-carver/.

Rainey, Lawrence S. 2005. *Revisiting 'The Waste Land'*. New Haven, CT; London: Yale University Press.

Rebein, Robert. 2009. *Hicks, Tribes, and Dirty Realists: American Fiction after Postmodernism*. Reprint edition. Lexington: University Press of Kentucky.

Roache, John. 2017. '"The Realer, More Enduring and Sentimental Part of Him": David Foster Wallace's Personal Library and Marginalia'. *Orbit: A Journal of American Literature* 5(1).

Roiland, Josh. 2013. 'David Foster Wallace and the Nature of Fact'. *Literary Journalism Studies* 5(2): 148–61.

Runyon, Randolph. 2013. 'Cycling Fiction: On the Structure of Raymond Carver's Three Major Story Collections'. In *Critical Insights: Raymond Carver*, edited by James Plath, 159–71. Ipswich, MA: Salem Press.

Ryan, Judith. 2014. *The Novel after Theory*. New York: Columbia University Press.

Saltzman, Arthur M. 1988. *Understanding Raymond Carver*. Understanding Contemporary American Literature (UCAL), xi, 190 pp. Columbia: University of South Carolina Press.

Samarcelli, Francoise. 2013. 'What's Postmodern About Raymond Carver?' In *Critical Insights: Raymond Carver*, edited by James Plath, 226–46. Ipswich, MA: Salem Press.

Schiffrin, Andre. 2000. *The Business of Books: How International Conglomerates Took over Publishing and Changed the Way We Read*. London: Verso.

Schiffrin, Andre. 2010. *Words and Money*. London: Verso.

Schutt, Christine. 2012. An Interview with Christine Schutt. Interview by Michelle Y. Burke. http://htmlgiant.com/random/an-interview-with-christine-schutt/.

Schwartzburg, Molly. 2012. 'Conclusion: Observations on the Archive at the Harry Ransom Center'. In *The Legacy of David Foster Wallace*, edited by Samuel Cohen and Lee Konstantinou, 241–59. Iowa City: University of Iowa Press.

Schwarzbaum, Lisa. 1996. 'Read It and Weep: Plowing through Infinite Jest'. *Entertainment Weekly*, 15 March 1996. http://www.smallbytes.net/~bobkat/jest5.html.

Scott, A. O. 1999. 'Looking for Raymond Carver'. *New York Review of Books*, 12 August 1999. http://www.nybooks.com/articles/archives/1999/aug/12/looking-for-raymond-carver/.

Scott, A. O. 2000. 'The Panic of Influence'. *New York Review of Books*, 10 February 2000. http://www.nybooks.com/articles/archives/2000/feb/10/the-panic-of-influence/.

Severs, Jeffrey. 2015. 'David Foster Wallace, James Wood, and a Source for "Irrelevant" Chris Fogle'. *The Explicator* 73(2): 129–32.

Severs, Jeffrey. 2017. *David Foster Wallace's Balancing Books: Fictions of Value*. Columbia University Press.

Shapiro, Stephen. 2014. 'From Capitalist to Communist Abstraction: *The Pale King*'s Cultural Fix'. *Textual Practice* 28(7): 1249–71.

Sharpe, Leslie T. 1994. *Editing Fact and Fiction: A Concise Guide to Book Editing*. Cambridge: Cambridge University Press.

Sheridan, Mark. 2015. 'Interpret You, INTERPRET-ME? Or, Fictional Pasts and Fictional Futures: The Predecessors and Contemporaries of David Foster Wallace'. In *Critical Insights: David Foster Wallace*, edited by Philip Coleman, 78–93. Ipswich, MA: Salem Press.

Shotter, D. C. A. 2005. *Nero*, 2nd edn. Lancaster Pamphlets in Ancient History. London: Routledge.

Sienkiewicz, Henryk. 2000. *Quo Vadis*. Translated by W. S. Kuniczak. David Foster Wallace, former owner. New York: Hippocrene Books David Foster Wallace Library, Harry Ransom Center.

Silverblatt, Michael. 2011. 'Everything and More: A Tribute to David Foster Wallace, Conversation, 16 March 2011 – Video'. Lannan Foundation, Lensic Theater in Santa Fe, New Mexico, 16 March. http://podcast.lannan.org/2011/03/26/everything-and-more-a-tribute-to-david-foster-wallace-conversation-16-march-2011-video/.

Sinykin, Dan. 2018. 'The Conglomerate Era: Publishing, Authorship, and Literary Form, 1965–2007'. *Contemporary Literature* 58(4).

Simpson, Craig S. 2017. 'Lish/Carver Mss', 4 September 2017. Email to the author.

Sjoerdsma, Ann G. 1996. 'Collins' Win Airs Publishing Secrets'. Tribunedigital-Orlandosentinel. 10 March 1996. http://articles.orlandosentinel.com/1996-03-10/entertainment/9603070546_1_collins-random-house-editors.

Sklenicka, Carol. 2009a. 'A Conversation on Raymond Carver'. Interview with Carol Sklenicka. Interview by Carol Polsgrove. Carol Polsgrove on Writers' Lives. http://carolpolsgrove.com/interview/.

Sklenicka, Carol. 2009b. *Raymond Carver: A Writer's Life*. New York: Scribner.

Slote, Sam. 2007. 'Blanks for When Words Gone: Chapter II.I'. In *How Joyce Wrote 'Finnegans Wake': A Chapter-by-Chapter Genetic Guide*, edited by Luca Crispi and Sam Slote, 181–213. Madison; London: University Press of Wisconsin.

Smith, Helen. 2017. *An Uncommon Reader: A Life of Edward Garnett, Mentor and Editor of Literary Genius*. London: Farrar, Straus and Giroux.

Solwitz, Sharon. 1988. 'The Gospel According to Gordon Lish'. *Chicago Reader*, 9 June 1988. http://www.chicagoreader.com/chicago/the-gospel-according-to-gordon-lish/Content?oid=872324.

Staes, Toon. 2014a. 'Wallace and Empathy: A Narrative Approach'. In *David Foster Wallace and 'The Long Thing': New Essays on the Novels*, edited by Marshall Boswell, 23–42. New York; London: Bloomsbury.

Staes, Toon. 2014b. 'Work in Process: A Genesis for *The Pale King*'. *English Studies* 95(1): 70–84.

Stanford, Peter. 2018. *What We Talk About When We Talk About Faith*. S.l.: Hodder & Stoughton.

Stead, Lisa. 2013. 'Introduction'. In *The Boundaries of the Literary Archive: Reclamation and Representation*, edited by Carrie Smith and Lisa Stead, 1–12. Farnham: Ashgate.

Stillinger, Jack. 1991. *Multiple Authorship and the Myth of Solitary Genius*. New York; Oxford: Oxford University Press.

Stone, Jon R. 2013. *The Routledge Dictionary of Latin Quotations: The Illiterati's Guide to Latin Maxims, Mottoes, Proverbs, and Sayings*. New York and London: Routledge.

Stone, Marjorie and Judith Thompson. 2006. *Literary Couplings: Writing Couples, Collaborators, and the Construction of Authorship. ACLS Humanities E-Book*. Madison: University Press of Wisconsin.

Stull, William L. 1989. 'Raymond Carver: Biographical Essay'. In *Dictionary of Literary Biography Yearbook: 1988*, edited by J. M. Brook. Detroit: Gale Research. https://web.archive.org/web/20110612022100/http://www.whitman.edu/english/carver/biography1.html.

Stull, William L. and Maureen P. Carroll. 2003. 'Two Darings'. In *Soul Barnacles: Ten More Years with Ray*, edited by Greg Simon, 1–11. Ann Arbor: University Press of Michigan.

Stull, William L. and Maureen P. Carroll. 2006. 'Prolegomena to Any Future Carver Studies'. *Journal of the Short Story in English. Les Cahiers de La Nouvelle* no. 46(March): 13–17.

Stull, William L. and Maureen P. Carroll. 2013. 'The Critical Reception of the Works of Raymond Carver'. In *Critical Insights: Raymond Carver*, edited by James Plath, 39–55. Ipswich, MA: Salem Press.

Sullivan, Hannah. 2013. *The Work of Revision*. Cambridge, MA: Harvard University Press.

Sullivan, John Jeremiah. 2011. "Too Much Information'. *GQ*. 31 March 2011. http://www.gq.com/entertainment/books/201105/david-foster-wallace-the-pale-king-john-jeremiah-sullivan.

Swartz, Aaron. 2009. 'What Happens at the End of *Infinite Jest?* (Or, the *Infinite Jest* Ending Explained)'. *Raw Thought* (blog). 16 September 2009. http://www.aaronsw.com/weblog/ijend.

Syme, Holger S. 2016a. 'The Text Is Foolish: Brian Vickers's "The One King Lear"'. *Los Angeles Review of Books*, 6 September 2016. https://lareviewofbooks.org/article/text-foolish-brian-vickerss-one-king-lear/.

Syme, Holger S. 2016b. '"King Lear" at the Stationers, Again: A Response to Brian Vickers'. *Los Angeles Review of Books*, 18 December 2016. https://lareviewofbooks.org/article/king-lear-stationers-response-brian-vickers/.

Taylor, Justin. 2015. 'Craft Talk Nobody Asked For'. *BOMB Magazine*, 11 September 2015. http://bombmagazine.org/article/922899/craft-talk-nobody-asked-for.

Theroux, Alexander. 2009. 'In the Cards, A Last Hand'. *Wall Street Journal*, 20 November 2009. http://online.wsj.com/news/articles/SB10001424052748704576204574530052854454092.

Thompson, John B. 2012. *Merchants of Culture: The Publishing Business in the Twenty-First Century*, 2nd edn. Cambridge: Polity.

Thompson, Lucas. 2016. *Global Wallace: David Foster Wallace and World Literature.* David Foster Wallace Studies, vol. 1. New York: Bloomsbury.

Tondorf-Dick, Mary. 2014. '*The Pale King*', Email to the author. 6 March 2014.

Towers, Robert. 1981. 'Low-Rent Tragedies'. *New York Review of Books*, 14 May 1981. http://www.nybooks.com/articles/archives/1981/may/14/low-rent-tragedies/.

Tracey, Janey. 2017. 'Raymond Carver, Gordon Lish, and the Editor as Enabler'. *Ploughshares Blog* (blog). 25 October 2017. http://blog.pshares.org/index.php/raymond-carver-gordon-lish-and-the-editor-as-enabler/.

Triesman, Deborah. 2014. 'Afterword to Chapter 36, *The Pale King*'. In *The David Foster Wallace Reader*, edited by David Foster Wallace, Ebook file. London: Hamish Hamilton.

Tysdal, Dan. 2003. 'Inarticulation and the Figure of Enjoyment: Raymond Carver's Minimalism Meets David Foster Wallace's 'A Radically Condensed History of Postindustrial Life'. *Wascana Review of Contemporary Poetry and Short Fiction* 38(1): 66–83.

Van Hulle, Dirk. 2008. *Manuscript Genetics, Joyce's Know-How, Beckett's Nohow*. Florida James Joyce Series. Gainesville: University Press of Florida.

Van Hulle, Dirk. 2014. *Modern Manuscripts: The Extended Mind and Creative Undoing from Darwin to Beckett and Beyond*. Historicizing Modernism. London: Bloomsbury.

Van Mierlo, Wim. 2013. 'The Archaeology of the Manuscript: Towards Modern Paleography'. In *The Boundaries of the Literary Archive: Reclamation and Representation*, edited by Carrie Smith and Lisa Stead, 15–29. Farnham: Ashgate.

Vickers, Brian. 2016. 'A Response to Holger Syme'. *Los Angeles Review of Books*, 6 November 2016.

Viollet, Catherine. 2004. 'Proust's "Confession of a Young Girl": Truth or Fiction?' In *Genetic Criticism: Texts and Avant-Textes*, edited and introd. by Jed Deppman, Daniel Ferrer and Michael Groden, 171–92. Material Texts (Material Texts). Philadelphia: University of Pennsylvania Press.

Walkowitz, L. Rebecca. 2017. *Born Translated: The Contemporary Novel in an Age of World Literature.* New York: Columbia University Press.

Wallace, David Foster. 1987. 'Letter to Gordon Lish, 29 August 1987'. Box 19. Lish Mss., 1951–2012. Lilly Library, Indiana University.

Wallace, David Foster. 1987a. 'Letter to Michael Pietsch, 22 September 1987'. Box 1, Folder 1. Little, Brown and Company Collection of David Foster Wallace. Box 1–5. Harry Ransom Center Archive, University of Texas at Austin.

Wallace, David Foster. 1988a. 'Letter to Michael Pietsch, 17 January 1988'. Box 1, Folder 1. Little, Brown and Company Collection of David Foster Wallace. Box 1–5. Harry Ransom Center Archive, University of Texas at Austin.

Wallace, David Foster. 1988b. 'Letter to Michael Pietsch, 24 July 1988'. Box 1, Folder 1. Little, Brown and Company Collection of David Foster Wallace. Box 1–5. Harry Ransom Center Archive, University of Texas at Austin.

Wallace, David Foster. 1989a. 'Letter to Michael Pietsch 7 March 1989'. Box 1, Folder 1. Little, Brown and Company Collection of David Foster Wallace. Box 1–5. Harry Ransom Center Archive, University of Texas at Austin.

Wallace, David Foster. 1989b. 'Letter to Michael Pietsch 23 May 1989'. Box 1, Folder 1. Little, Brown and Company Collection of David Foster Wallace. Box 1–5. Harry Ransom Center Archive, University of Texas at Austin.

Wallace, David Foster. 1992. 'Letter to Michael Pietsch, 22 June 1992'. Box 3, Folder 2. Little, Brown and Company Collection of David Foster Wallace. Box 1–5. Harry Ransom Center Archive, University of Texas at Austin.

Wallace, David Foster. 1993. 'E Unibus Pluram: Television and U.S. Fiction'. *Review of Contemporary Fiction* 13: 151–94.

Wallace, David Foster. 1994a. 'Letter to Michael Pietsch, 16 January 1994'. Box 3, Folder 2. Little, Brown and Company Collection of David Foster Wallace. Box 1–5. Harry Ransom Center Archive, University of Texas at Austin.

Wallace, David Foster. 1994b. 'Letter to Michael Pietsch, 29 April 1994'. Box 3, Folder 2. Little, Brown and Company Collection of David Foster Wallace. Box 1–5. Harry Ransom Center Archive, University of Texas at Austin.

Wallace, David Foster. 1994c. 'Letter to Michael Pietsch, 27 May 1994'. Box 3, Folder 2. Little, Brown and Company Collection of David Foster Wallace. Box 1–5. Harry Ransom Center Archive, University of Texas at Austin.

Wallace, David Foster. 1995a. 'Letter to Michael Pietsch, 2 February 1995'. Box 3, Folder 2. Little, Brown and Company Collection of David Foster Wallace. Box 1–5. Harry Ransom Center Archive, University of Texas at Austin.

Wallace, David Foster. 1995b. 'Letter to Michael Pietsch, 3 April 1995'. Box 3, Folder 3. Little, Brown and Company Collection of David Foster Wallace. Box 1–5. Harry Ransom Center Archive, University of Texas at Austin.
Wallace, David Foster. 1995c. 'Letter to Michael Pietsch, November 1995'. Box 3, Folder 3. Little, Brown and Company Collection of David Foster Wallace. Box 1–5. Harry Ransom Center Archive, University of Texas at Austin.
Wallace, David Foster. 1995d. 'Letter to Michael Pietsch, 20 September 1995'. Box 3, Folder 3. Little, Brown and Company Collection of David Foster Wallace. Box 1–5. Harry Ransom Center Archive, University of Texas at Austin.
Wallace, David Foster. 1996a. 'Quo Vadis – Introduction'. *Review of Contemporary Fiction* 16(1): 7–8.
Wallace, David Foster. 1996b. Interview for KCRW's Bookworm. *Infinite Jest.* Interview by Michael Silverblatt. https://www.kcrw.com/news-culture/shows/bookworm/david-foster-wallace-infinite-jest.
Wallace, David Foster. 1997a. *Girl with Curious Hair*. London: Abacus.
Wallace, David Foster. 1997b. Interview for KCRW's Bookworm. *A Supposedly Fun Thing I'll Never Do Again.* Interview by Michael Silverblatt. https://www.kcrw.com/news-culture/shows/bookworm/david-foster-wallace-a-supposedly-fun-thing-ill-never-do-again.
Wallace, David Foster. 1998a. 'Letter to Michael Pietsch, 28 January 1998'. Box 3, Folder 3. Little, Brown and Company Collection of David Foster Wallace. Box 1–5. Harry Ransom Center Archive, University of Texas at Austin.
Wallace, David Foster. 1998b. 'Laughing with Kafka'. *Harper's*, July 1998.
Wallace, David Foster. 1998c. 'Letter to Michael Pietsch, 17 August 1998'. Box 1, Folder 6. Little, Brown and Company Collection of David Foster Wallace. Box 1–6. Harry Ransom Center Archive, University of Texas at Austin.
Wallace, David Foster. 1998d. 'Letter to Michael Pietsch, 10 October 1998'. Box 1, Folder 6. Little, Brown and Company Collection of David Foster Wallace. Box 1–6. Harry Ransom Center Archive, University of Texas at Austin.
Wallace, David Foster. 1999. Brief Interview with a Five Draft Man Interview by Stacey Schmeidel. *Amherst Magazine*. https://www.amherst.edu/aboutamherst/magazine/extra/node/66410.
Wallace, David Foster. 2000a. 'Letter to Michael Pietsch, 30 June 2000'. Box 3, Folder 5. Little, Brown and Company Collection of David Foster Wallace. Box 1–5. Harry Ransom Center Archive, University of Texas at Austin.
Wallace, David Foster. 2000b. Interview for KCRW's Bookworm. *Brief Interviews II.* Interview by Michael Silverblatt. https://www.kcrw.com/news-culture/shows/bookworm/david-foster-wallace-5.
Wallace, David Foster. 2001. 'Letter to Michael Pietsch, 13 October 2001'. Box 3, Folder 5. Little, Brown and Company Collection of David Foster Wallace. Box 1–5. Harry Ransom Center Archive, University of Texas at Austin.

Wallace, David Foster. 2005a. *Oblivion: Stories*. New York: Back Bay.
Wallace, David Foster. 2005b. 'Fax to Michael Pietsch, 29 March 2005'. Box 3, Folder 3. Little, Brown Papers. Harry Ransom Center, University of Texas.
Wallace, David Foster. 2006. *Infinite Jest*. New York: Back Bay Books.
Wallace, David Foster. 2010. *A Supposedly Fun Thing I'll Never Do Again*. London: Abacus.
Wallace, David Foster. 2011a. *The Broom of the System*. London: Abacus.
Wallace, David Foster. 2011b. *The Pale King: An Unfinished Novel*. New York: Little, Brown.
Wallace, David Foster. 2011c. 'Backbone'. *New Yorker*, 7 March 2011.
Wallace, David Foster. 2011d. *The Pale King. Read By Robert Petkoff*. CD. New York: Hachette Audio.
Wallace, David Foster. 2011e. 'Attempted Fax Cover Sheet (1998)'. *Letters of Note* (blog). 20 October 2011. http://www.lettersofnote.com/2011/10/attempted-fax-cover-sheet.html.
Wallace, David Foster. 2012a. *Both Flesh and Not: Essays*. New York: Little, Brown.
Wallace, David Foster. 2012b. 'Chapter 9, "Author's Foreword"'. Harry Ransom Center: Digital Collections. 2012. http://www.hrc.utexas.edu/collections/digital/dfw.
Wallace, David Foster. 2012c. *Consider the Lobster and Other Essays*. London: Abacus.
Wallace, David Foster. 2012d. *Conversations with David Foster Wallace*. Edited by Stephen J. Burn. Literary Conversations. Jackson: University Press of Mississippi.
Wallace, David Foster. 2012e. *The Pale King: An Unfinished Novel*. London: Penguin.
Wallace, David Foster. 2013. 'Late Night: David Foster Wallace's First Published Fiction for a Major National Magazine'. Playboy. Accessed 23 April 2014. http://playboysfw.kinja.com/late-night-david-foster-wallaces-first-published-fict-1304018034.
Wallace, David Foster. n.d. 'Wallace Papers, Series IV, *The Pale King*, Containers 36 to 41. Harry Ransom Center Archive, University of Texas at Austin.'
Wallace, David Foster. 1987b. 'Letter to Bonnie Nadell, 2 September 1987'. Box 1. Bonnie Nadell Collection of David Foster Wallace. Harry Ransom Center, University of Texas.
Wallace, David Foster. 1988c. 'Letter to Steven Moore, 18 January 1988'. Box 1, Folder 1. Steven Moore: David Foster Wallace Collection. Harry Ransom Center, University of Texas.
Wallace, David Foster. 1990. 'Letter to Steven Moore, 20 November 1990'. Box 1, Folder 1. Steven Moore: David Foster Wallace Collection. Harry Ransom Center, University of Texas.
Wallace, David Foster. 1998e. 'Letter to Don DeLillo, 25 November 1998'. Box 101, Folder 10, Don DeLillo Papers. Harry Ransom Center, University of Texas.
Wallace, David Foster. 2000c. 'Letter to Don DeLillo, April 28 2000'. Box 101, Folder 10. Don DeLillo Papers. Harry Ransom Center, University of Texas.

Wallace, David Foster. 2003a. 'Letter to Michael Pietsch, 2 April 2003'. Box 3, Folder 5. Little, Brown and Company Collection of David Foster Wallace. Box 1–5. Harry Ransom Center Archive, University of Texas at Austin.

Wallace, David Foster. 2003b. 'Letter to Michael Pietsch, 21 June 2003'. Box 3, Folder 5. Little, Brown and Company Collection of David Foster Wallace. Box 1–5. Harry Ransom Center Archive, University of Texas at Austin.

Wallace, David Foster. 2003c. 'Letter to Michael Pietsch, 7 October 2003'. Box 3, Folder 5. Little, Brown and Company Collection of David Foster Wallace. Box 1–5. Harry Ransom Center Archive, University of Texas at Austin.

Wallace, David Foster. 2004a. 'Letter to Michael Pietsch, April 19 2004'. Box 2, Folder 2. Little, Brown Papers. Harry Ransom Center, University of Texas.

Wallace, David Foster. 2004b. 'Letter to Michael Pietsch, 26 October 2004'. Box 2, Folder 3. Little, Brown and Company Collection of David Foster Wallace. Box 1–5. Harry Ransom Center Archive, University of Texas at Austin.

Walsh, John. 2009. 'Hit & Run: Would We Care If He Were Alive?' *The Independent*, 17 November 2009. http://www.independent.co.uk/news/people/hit-and-run/hit--run-would-we-care-if-he-were-alive-1821712.html.

Warren, Andrew. 2012. 'Narrative Modeling and Community Organizing in *The Pale King* and Infinite Jest'. *Studies in the Novel* 44(4): 389–408.

West, Mark. 2017. '"Observacion of These Articles": Surveillance and the 1970s in David Foster Wallace's *The Pale King*'. *Critique: Studies in Contemporary Fiction* 0(0): 1–12

Whitehead, Colson. 2012. 'Colson Whitehead's Rules for Writing'. *New York Times*, 26 July 2012, sec. Books/Sunday Book Review. http://www.nytimes.com/2012/07/29/books/review/colson-whiteheads-rules-for-writing.html.

Widiss, Benjamin. 2011. *Obscure Invitations: The Persistence of the Author in Twentieth-Century American Literature*. Stanford: Stanford University Press.

Wilde, Alan. 1985. 'Shooting for Smallness: Limits and Values in Some Recent American Fiction'. *Boundary 2* 13(2/3): 343–69.

Williams, Alan D. 1993. 'What Is an Editor?' In *Editors on Editing: What Writers Need to Know About What Editors Do*, 3rd edn, edited by Gerald C. Gross, 3–9. New York: Grove Press.

Winters, David. 2016. 'Theory and the Creative Writing Classroom: Conceptual Revision in the School of Gordon Lish'. *Contemporary Literature* 57(1): 111–34.

Winters, David and Jason Lucarelli, eds. 2018. *Conversations with Gordon Lish*. Jackson: University of Mississippi Press.

Witte, George. 2017. 'This Just Needs a Little Work: On Line Editing'. In *What Editors Do: The Art, Craft, and Business of Book Editing*, edited by Peter Ginna, 96–105. Chicago: University of Chicago Press.

Wood, Gaby. 2009. 'Raymond Carver: The Kindest Cut'. *Guardian*, 27 September 2009.

Wood, James. 2001. 'Tell Me How Does It Feel?' *Guardian*. 6 October 2001. http://www.theguardian.com/books/2001/oct/06/fiction.

Wood, James. 2004. 'The Digressionist'. *New Republic* 231(6): 26–31.

Wood, Michael. 1981. 'Stories Full of Edges and Silences'. *New York Times*, 26 April 1981, sec. Books. http://www.nytimes.com/1981/04/26/books/stories-full-of-edges-and-silences.html.

Worden, Suzanne. 1996. 'Random House versus Joan Collins'. www.youtube.com/watch?v=JEyP-uJ6YN0'. TV documentary. *Court TV*. US.

Wouters, Conley. 2012. '"What Am I, a Machine?": Humans, Information, and Matters of Record in David Foster Wallace's *The Pale King*'. *Studies in the Novel* 44(4): 447–63.

Index

Lightning Source UK Ltd.
Milton Keynes UK
UKHW021840250221
379363UK00011B/335

9 781501 367601